CREOLIZING POLITICAL THEORY

just ideas

transformative ideals of justice in ethical and political thought

series editors

Drucilla Cornell

Roger Berkowitz

CREOLIZING POLITICAL THEORY

READING ROUSSEAU THROUGH FANON

Jane Anna Gordon

FORDHAM UNIVERSITY PRESS

NEW YORK 2014

Copyright © 2014 Fordham University Press

All rights reserved. No part of this publication may be reproduced, stored in a retrieval system, or transmitted in any form or by any means—electronic, mechanical, photocopy, recording, or any other—except for brief quotations in printed reviews, without the prior permission of the publisher.

Fordham University Press has no responsibility for the persistence or accuracy of URLs for external or third-party Internet websites referred to in this publication and does not guarantee that any content on such websites is, or will remain, accurate or appropriate.

Fordham University Press also publishes its books in a variety of electronic formats. Some content that appears in print may not be available in electronic books.

Library of Congress Cataloging-in-Publication Data

Gordon, Jane Anna, 1976–
 Creolizing political theory : reading Rousseau through Fanon / Jane Anna Gordon. — First edition.
     pages cm. — (Just ideas)
 Includes bibliographical references and index.
 ISBN 978-0-8232-5481-1 (hardback) — ISBN 978-0-8232-5482-8 (paper)
  1. Rousseau, Jean-Jacques, 1712–1778—Political and social views. 2. Fanon, Frantz, 1925–1961—Political and social views. 3. General will. 4. Legitimacy of governments. 5. Political science—Philosophy. I. Title.
  JC179.R9G67 2014
  320.01—dc23

                                                                2013019537

Printed in the United States of America

16 15 14 5 4 3 2 1

First edition

In loving memory of Yvonne Patricia Solomon Garel (or Grandma Pat), Jack Garel, Thelma Young, David Levy, Don Belton, Gary Tobin, and William R. Jones
  and
to kerido *Lewis, in whom so many worlds converge and are made new*

Contents

	Acknowledgments	xi
	Introduction	1
1	Delegitimating Decadent Inquiry	18
2	Decolonizing Disciplinary Methods	63
3	Rousseau's General Will	95
4	Fanonian National Consciousness	129
5	Thinking Through Creolization	162
	Conclusion	203
	Notes	221
	References	265
	Index	287

Acknowledgments

I had the unique good fortune of undergoing two periods of concentrated intellectual apprenticeship. In a fundamental way, this book is my effort to synthesize them in ways that pay due service to the greatest strengths of both, creatively making them speak to each other where they otherwise might not with losses that would be both scholarly and political.

The first of these periods of education involved my graduate studies at the University of Pennsylvania during a moment of its transition. I was drawn to the institution by Nancy Hirschmann, Ellen Kennedy, Andrew Norris, Anne Norton, Rogers Smith, and Bob Vitalis. I deliberately sought and found through their mentorship a thoroughly unconventional training in political theory for which each year makes me more grateful. From Ellen, I particularly appreciated her conveying of the *gravitas* that informs German social theory. This seemed to demand a reflexive repugnance toward much of the overly sanguine and self-congratulatory work that goes on within the discipline of political science. From Anne, there was first the challenge and inspiration as a political theorist to aim also to be a writer and second to refuse the parochialism that would suggest that one could undertake an adequate study of politics while ignoring urgent and exciting developments in other fields. Countless conversations with Bob about unlikely connections stimulated some of the more creative ideas that I have had and a better sense of both the pleasures and frustrations of maintaining commitments that are considered marginal to the academic domain in which one primarily resides. Rogers offered a remarkable model of what is required of committed graduate teaching and of what can and cannot be achieved by tirelessly involving oneself in a critical way in hegemonic debates about race and racism in US life. My education at Penn was also enriched immeasurably by the life-affirming, funny, and insightful Kahlil Williams, Amel Ahmed, Cheng Chen, Lia Howard, and Justin Wert.

The founding and early meetings of the Caribbean Philosophical Association were for me, and many others, a second, simultaneous training. Those who undertook the magnificent tasks under the not-so-humble motto of "shifting the geography of reason," first George Belle, B. Anthony Bogues, Patrick Goodin, Lewis Gordon, Clevis Headley, Paget Henry, Nelson Maldonado-Torres, Charles Mills, and Supriya Nair, soon joined by Marilyn Nissim-Sabat, Marina Banchetti-Robino, Brinda Mehta, Michael Monahan, and Kristin Waters are exemplary in their combination of intellectual vision and collegiality. They have cultivated a movement of thought that breaks with so much of the inevitable decadence of thinking within the world's reigning power. Their efforts have oriented the substance and form of all of my writing. Among them, requiring separate mention, is Paget, not only for his friendship and ongoing conversation from which I always learn but also for the opportunity to guest-edit with Neil Roberts the issue of the *C. L. R. James Journal* through which so many ideas explored here developed their greater precision.

My colleagues at Temple University heard the core ideas of this book four years ago—in Joe Schwartz and Heath Fogg Davis's case, twice. I am grateful to have had the chance to work together with faculty specializing in political theory in the Department of Political Science to build a vibrant and growing graduate student community that included the talented, engaging, and integrity-filled Matthew Smetona, Greg Graham, John Hykel, Jim Delise, Ashish Vaidya, Danielle Scherer, Nick Catsis, Erin Meagher, Justin Murphy, Brett Miller, Alex Melonas, Francis Boyle, Arnold Kim, Nathan Schrader, and Desiree Craig. I had formally presented these ideas for the first time on Temple's campus at the Center for Humanities at Temple (CHAT). The initial feedback that I received from Hilary Dick and Miriam Solomon was very useful. I was subsequently fortunate to be a year-long fellow at the CHAT where challenges concerning how I should and should not employ the concept of creolization were genuinely fruitful. For their central participation in these discussions, I would like to thank Liz Varon, Hilary Dick, Talissa Ford, Oliver Gaycken, Jeremy Schipper, Matthew Johnson, Byron Lee, Lior Levy, Holger Lowendorf, Nyama McCarthy-Brown, Nicole Noll, Chiaoning Su, Amy Woodworth, Andrew Diemer, and Janet Neigh. Requiring separate mention is Peter Logan, who is ultimately responsible for everything that takes place in that very special domain that he has cultivated on the top floor of Gladfelter Hall. For the tireless spirit with which he undertakes this organizational work from which so many of us benefited and for his terrific friendship, I thank him. Beyond the Department of Political Science and CHAT, the people who helped make Temple an intellectual home were Rebecca Alpert, Laura Levitt, David Watt, Ruth Ost, Paul Taylor, Terry Rey, and the members of the Committee on the Status of Women (CSW), especially Joyce Lindorff, Abbe Forman, Melissa Gilbert, and Nilgun Anadolu-Okur. Not part of the faculty at Temple but also residing in Philadelphia is Ros Dutton, whose insights and support have been the source of multidimensional growth indispensable to the completion of this work.

Since composing the initial manuscript that became this book, I presented the creolization pieces of it on two major occasions, first at the American Political Science Association conference in Washington, DC, in 2010 and then at the Western Political Science Association meeting in San Antonio, Texas, in 2011. I particularly appreciated the comments and questions posed at the first presentation by Laura Grattan and the conversation on and beyond the two-part panel at the second with Keisha Lindsay, Barnor Hess, Ed Barvosa, Michaelle Browers, Cricket Keating, Farah Godrej, and Rita Dhamoon. Bonnie Honig also read and commented thoroughly on these pieces with just the combination of enthusiasm and criticism that stimulated reflection that improved them.

Once there was a complete manuscript that had benefited considerably from the suggestions of two very helpful reviewers for Fordham, Rogers Smith, Jason Neidleman, and John Comaroff read the entire text, offering the insightful challenges and responses that are so characteristic of them.

Perhaps one of the clearest marks of age is the increasing simultaneity of moments of triumph with those of grave loss. The experience of the latter is intensified when it involves the very people who enabled and would have found the former *delicious*. This is particularly true of the much loved and missed Yvonne Patricia Solomon Garel, my beloved late mother-in-law. I began the reflections that led to this book in the shadow of her sudden and untimely death. Although she did not do intellectual work of this kind, I tried in my own very limited way to emulate the spirit in which she undertook everything else that she did do. I began graduate school with two very young children, one seven weeks old, and a thoroughly involved husband who was also a department chair and active scholar. Grandma Pat assured that I never felt the tension between work and mothering that remains an at-times impossible juggling act for most employed women. As her son, my husband, frequently says, when it came to what really mattered, she didn't ask whether something was possible, only how to make it happen. It is precisely because one knows how lucky one is to have any time with such a person that their departure hurts so indelibly. For her husband, Jack Garel, my late father-in-law, to carry on in its wake was not possible. His delight in watching his children and grandchildren enjoy themselves and in mundanely fixing his own home and that of others is a precious memory.

I was very thankful to have read Edwidge Danticat's stunning *Brother, I'm Dying*, which opens with the death of her remarkable uncle and her own first pregnancy before I, in the same phone call, received the news of the death of my mom's beloved cousin, David Levy, and the arrival of my brother's first child, my fabulous niece, Mila Bea Comaroff Wang Mi. The son of my grandfather's sister, David, bridged countries and generations, embodying in often-dreary Manchester, England, the humor and humanistic sensibilities of South African Jewish life that are worth carrying on. Although we try to sustain these deliberately through certain rituals and through nurturing relations between generations, it is striking how what we seek is often captured best in the smallest of gestures, and even then, in the minutiae of how they are done. Also among those missed is Don Belton—colleague, writer, magnificent storyteller, and kindred spirit—whose murder was the outcome of displaced anger unleashed out of confusion, fear, and self-loathing. When standing at Temple's food trucks waiting for lunch, I often would wonder what astute and hilarious comment he might have made. One of the many reasons I miss him is that I don't know what it would have been. There are also Gary Tobin, whose unique combination of brilliance, courage, humor, and impatience was and remains a genuine inspiration, and William R. Jones, who, in addition to his own momentous contributions to promoting the work of black intellectuals and developing black existential liberationist thought, officiated at my husband and my wedding, talking in the most moving of terms about the revolutionary power of committed love. Finally, there are two recent losses from the vibrant Hyde Park community that was my childhood home: Michel-Rolph Trouillot, whom I did not know personally but respected greatly and whose many insights punctuate the text that follows and Gabe Mitchell, who I remember as my brother's curly-haired, mischievous friend, who felt the world that swirled around him with a profundity that then and now makes me short of breath.

Profound thanks are also due to Drucilla Cornell, Ken Panfilio, and Roger Berkowitz for inaugurating such an important and exciting book series that I am very proud to join.

Last, to my transnational, diasporic family, who exemplifies the best of creolization as vividly as anything else: to Sylvia Crosdale, Jean and John Comaroff, Leonard Gordon, Robert and Marc Evans, Josh Comaroff, Shing Ong, Mila Bea, Leo, Mathieu, Jenni, Sula, and Elijah Gordon. And to my ever and always beloved, Lewis, with whom the past fifteen years together seem like an immensely pleasurable blink of an eye.

Introduction

> . . . with what eyes?
> —SAPPHO[1]

> . . . yet more inclusive than "and."
> —PAULA WILSON[2]

This book offers a reading of two central themes in the work of Jean-Jacques Rousseau through insights from the writings of Frantz Fanon. Through this effort, I hope to enrich discussions of the nature of methodology and requirements of democratic legitimacy and provide an example of the creolizing of political theory. In this case, it is a creolization of one canonical figure through the ideas of another as well as of central concepts in Western political thought. Why undergo such an undertaking?

Rousseau's unsettling challenges concerning the emancipatory potential of human inquiry and his infamous conception of the general will can be more fruitfully understood and further enlivened through drawing upon resources from the creolized thought of Fanon and, by extension, political reflection from the Global South. In particular, when using the typically abstract idea of the general will to explore how political theory can be put in the service of forging more legitimate democratic possibilities in diverse and unequal, colonized societies, one can envision creolization as the generalizing of political will or as the achievement of generality. Put slightly differently, creolization as articulated here might be understood as the operationalizing of the general will. If I am correct, this effort has broad implications for political theory. Among them is the advancement of political theory as a form of creolized thought, or one in which disparate disciplinary and methodological resources are brought together to create unique amalgams better attuned to addressing salient political problems and debates thrown open by the complexity of human institutions of power.

To achieve this task, I will first read Rousseau through Fanon, with preliminary definitions of the creolizing practice at hand and then offer a more detailed discussion of creolization. I hope to show in conclusion both the relation of creolizing political theory to a correlative approach that will no doubt be in the reader's mind—namely, comparative political theory and the study of politics more broadly.

Although a creolized political theory will not resolve all of the methodological and disciplinary problems involved in doing political theory today, its addressing of deficiencies of homogenous models and some misguided conceptions of heterogeneity should, in a modest way, further the cause of a political theory reflective of actual human practices and the more adequate instantiations of political legitimacy that might emerge from them.

Such are my goals.

For many readers, the words *creolization* and *creolizing* will be something of a mystery. For others, both terms will immediately bring to mind particular categories of creole people, most likely the descendants of mixed-race leaders who waged the first wave of independence movements from Portugal, Spain, and France in the Luso-, Hispano-, and Francophone Americas. In short, some explanation is in order.

Although the word *creole* first emerged in the sixteenth century to describe new groups of people and then unique linguistic formations, I am using *creolization* and *creolizing* in a way that is indebted to but distinct from these meanings. Its significance here, while informed by, is also discrete from the various positions in social scientific debates over what exactly transpired in the Caribbean communities out of which global modernity first emerged.

I am then using *creolization* and *creolizing* to name a particular approach to politics and to the engagement and construction of political ideas. In historical and social scientific literatures, creolization has referred to distinctive ways in which opposed, unequal groups forged mutually instantiating practices in contexts of radical historical rupture, ones through which people from elsewhere became indigenous to what had recently been foreign places by breaking with the trajectories that their previous collective genealogies would have anticipated. Although the progressive outcomes of such processes were in no sense assured, because creolization generally focuses on collective ends beyond those of basic coexistence and toleration, it draws attention to the mutual transformation involved in molding that which emerges as politically shared. It can therefore, I suggest, provide models for how enriched political structures, discourses, forms of identification, and thinking might be envisioned. If in actual empirical instances, processes of creolization are often hijacked by a small group of people who establish themselves as the highest embodiment of a principle of mixture and radical openness, when articulated as an approach to politics, creolization might offer a powerful regulative ideal of how better approximations of a conception of a shared, public good or general will can be constructed. In capturing what it is both to remain painfully aware of the most salient of meaningful differences while paying equal attention to how they might be effectively synthesized in solidarities of political action, the generalizing of political will might, through this lens, be understood as its progressive creolization.

As I will also explain at greater length, when turned to as a methodological approach or as a way of *doing* political theory, creolizing, in the language of Rousseau, seeks and at best embodies a general will rather than a will of all. Not simply an aggregation of strategies, commitments, or texts tied to interests of discrete actors and divergent disciplinary camps, creolizing is instead an effort to rearticulate the world and, in this case, the project of political life, that these different approaches share. When creolizing, one is galvanized by problems and questions that are envisaged as necessitating drawing from what have historically become discrete disciplines to create fresh ways of addressing urgent political debates. Unavoidably treating with suspicion the notion that the prerequisite for their supposed rigor is the growing insularity of academic disciplines, a creolized methodology then does not seek the opposite extreme. In it disciplinary syntheses and mixture are not pursued for their own sake. Instead, evident in a creolized method is the shelving of an aversion to cross-field frontiers through which access to the full range of scholarly resources would be jettisoned. As such, our scholarly endeavors when creolized can be undertaken more coherently since we are able to use materials that existing scholarly boundaries might encourage us to lack, enabling us to foster the stitching together of answers we could not otherwise fathom.

To reiterate, creolizing political theory is not achieved by aiming to exemplify inclusivity and diversification as inherent ideals but when cross-fertilization of distinctive disciplinary developments is not averted by a repugnance that would treat the products as crude, deformed impurities. The nurturing of this alternative sensibility in turn demands that the imperatives of the inquiry itself prevail over what might be mandated by dictates of disciplinary membership. Such forms of academic belonging are not rendered wholly irrelevant—after all, in addition to their central role in the political economy of hiring and promotion, disciplinary communities are sustained by substantive shared commitments and understandings of some of what constitute compelling foci for reflection. Still, creolization as a methodological approach reminds us that there is a point at which imperatives of loyalty promise to produce decadent scholarship. Frequently hiding the historical specificity and contingent emergence of particular disciplinary formations, reifying disciplinary identities can keep us from remembering that certain categories, epistemic goals, and forms of evidence and argumentation were developed to address a specific set of problems, in turn begging the question of whether there are moments when the desire for the ongoing use of such tools comes to trump their original purposes.

In sum, if, in political terms, we could understand creolization as the generalizing of a shared, public will forged by individuals as they articulate what they seek in and through collectivities that comprise a polity, we could understand the creolization of political theory as its generalizing as well. In this case, it involves rearticulating the shared world that is the condition of possibility of each partial perspective and to which all, in conflicting ways, refer. In other words, the political and methodological meanings of creolization, while distinct, ultimately merge since disciplinary narrowness cannot, as Rousseau and Fanon both contended, avoid having exclusive political outcomes. This is not only because each would necessarily hide from view essential dimensions of the full scope and meaning which political models should aim to express, but also because each would treat fault lines as fixed rather than precisely what is negotiated through political thought and action.

Readers familiar with the terrain of political theory—in associating creolization correctly with questions introduced by and associated with imperialism, colonialism, difference, and inequality—will no doubt wonder about its relationship to the politics of multiculturalism, discourses of hybridity, and intellectual work undertaken beneath the rubrics of interdisciplinary and comparative political theory.

As explored at greater length in Chapter 5, creolizing departs radically from the guiding ideals of most brands of multiculturalism. For, while internally varied, multiculturalism—as an approach to politics, to the development of school curricula, and to policy making—focuses on unequally located, often formerly colonized or enslaved groups by demanding that central political institutions offer opportunities for more meaningful enfranchisement through recognizing the distinctive cultural worlds in which each is embedded. The surest way to demonstrate respect for these, this paradigm advances, is through nurturing the conditions for their preservation, usually through maintaining their relative separation and semisovereignty. Without this, each would cease to be a position or site from which more hegemonic worldviews could be critically evaluated and potentially enriched.

By contrast, in processes of creolization, a given pressing aim or project trumps or prevails over principles that would in advance restrict by fixing a priori rules of engagement. In seeking to create viable forms out of what has been and is suddenly locally available, one assumes that each, while retaining some of its original character will, in being resituated and recombined, remain itself by becoming something new and distinctive. Additionally, unlike multiculturalism, which agrees to assume that political liberalism is a singular adequate model for the political present that might at best be tweaked or made more accommodating, creolization emerged where existing terms for social cooperation were absent, throwing into sharp relief the politically determined, relational, and malleable nature of the worlds of meaning to which *culture* refers.

Emerging after multiculturalism with the institutionalization of postcolonial studies in Western Europe and the United States and ethnic studies in the United States is the focus on *hybridity* and on *bordercrossers* associated with Gloria Anzaldúa (1987) and Homi Bhabha (1994) among others. As a challenge to the excessive crudeness of some brands of multiculturalism and an essentialism associated with nationalist anticolonial movements, discussions of hybridity emphasized not only the internal diversity and dissensions within particular cultures and communities but also the multiple, competing forms of belonging experienced by any one individual. Through a focus on the melancholic experience produced by the claims to, yet actual absence of, an isomorphic relationship between individuals and the groups of which they were a part, discourses of hybridity magnified the position of particular people whose contingencies of birth and identification produced experiences of unusually intense tugging demands of competing loyalties. Although the insights borne of this position were thought to extend more generally to illuminating the process of disavowing the constructed nature of membership and belonging and the disciplining and repressive capacities of both, hybridity often became more closely associated with the angst of specific individuals whose mediating role ironically reasserted the logic of pure, distinct groups through which they moved as a go-between. While the existential insight produced by this homelessness or permanent in-betweenness made for rich literary and philosophical reflection, it often was pitched against the spirit and forms of anticolonial and progressive politics that required, however open-endedly, defined collectivities through which people could struggle for more democratic conditions.

By contrast, while specific groups of creoles may have functioned in just this way, supposedly embodying unique mixtures of political possibility and epistemic insight through mediating between less or noncreolized groups, creolizing as a process leaves none of the poles that "in-betweenness" negotiates intact. Similarly, while creolization in literary criticism has been tied fundamentally to poststructural analyses of the repressive limitations of collective forms of identity and identification, as used here to describe an approach to politics and to political theory, creolizing does not stop in the moment of suspicion and critique that would create an impasse for most efforts at forging solidarities. Instead it aims to build from the insights of a wariness of the highly imperfect ways in which these have been pursued so that public identities might be better constructed.

These distinctions among multiculturalism, hybridity, and creolization are not only necessary for understanding the relevant terms of this text and the different stakes and priorities to which each is tied. They are also indispensable because the way in which *culture* is perceived overdetermines how *disciplines* are envisioned and maintained. For example, the most frequent contemporary response to a world (rather than only colonial outposts) of merging center-periphery relations has been to turn in cultural matters to multiculturalism and decreolization and in scholarly ones toward interdisciplinarity and hyperspecialization.

Interdisciplinarity, as opposed to transdisciplinarity and creolization, treats disciplines in the same way that multiculturalism treats cultures: as a smorgasbord of options illuminated through understanding their discreteness rather than the constitutive relations and tensions among them. If, by contrast, hyperspecialization acknowledges shared beginnings of now distinct endeavors, it is an instance of *decreolization*. For scholars of creole linguistics, decreolization describes the isolated trajectories of once only slightly different varieties of a single tongue that in their separate movements become less and less intelligible to one another. As they increasingly reflect the articulation of tinier, circumscribed fragments of experience, they come to lack the linguistic generality of a once shared genealogy. When made an orientation to scholarly endeavor, decreolization involves valorizing the deliberate move away from the generalization I have been describing. For the sake of making each academic niche more coherently itself, more rigorous through autonomous differentiation, each stakes out such distinct territories through specifying particular foci, forms of evidence, and methodologies that it prizes and through which it is definitively marked. Creolization, as I will explore further in the conclusion of this book, introduces a diametrically opposed trajectory, grounded in values and priorities understood fundamentally through the lens of politics and thereby through generality.

Still there is irony in the project of creolizing political theory: When explicitly sought as a political program and as a method, creolization can come to resemble its multicultural and interdisciplinary alternatives more than its advocates would allow. It too can become a celebration of diversity for its own sake, depoliticizing the challenge represented by such competing and conflicting sites of experience, insight, and identification. By contrast, processes of creolization are most pronounced when settled coordinates to which symbolic forms referred are radically interrupted and when factors that would render creolization impossible are made absent. With theory as with politics, creolizing will not emerge when it is deliberately pursued. It will instead be the inevitable outcome when we recall a larger *telos*, in this instance, a galvanizing concern with understanding, forging, and protecting a distinct domain of political life so long as we are not straight-jacketed by commitments that would frame creolizing itself (or the possibility of better realizing our aims and that which we are through the possibility of our becoming something other than what we've been) as illicit.

The juxtaposition of Rousseauian and Fanonian thought in which much of this book is engaged is made possible by a creolized as opposed to a comparative approach. Why?

As I explore in more detail in the conclusion of this book, within the US academy, no new development has created more disciplinary space for the project of creolizing political thought than comparative political theorizing. Still, for all of its inner diversity as an emergent subfield, the framework of comparativism, even if only strategically engaged, cannot entirely divorce itself from the suggestion that it offers an exploration of conflicts over terms of social cooperation from within discrete religious and moral traditions the boundaries of which remain distinct. Once the search for distinctness and clearly recognizable difference become a requirement, several other problems emerge. Among them are what can and cannot be made to appear as sufficiently similar and different. As I suggest, drawing on the work on disavowal of Sibylle Fischer and Susan Buck-Morss, even if we recognize and acknowledge the inevitable blurriness of such boundaries, this is not enough since it might be precisely out of the most creolized of circumstances that what we consider the height of intellectual contributions of any given empire or civilization in fact proceed. Indeed we might be masking the very insights about culture and politics that we are aiming to reveal in calling "Chinese" or "Indian" or "Iranian" what are actually rich examples of the greatest fruits of creolization. In them, distinct political insights are molded through articulating fresh generalities out of situations that interrupt longer, more continuous and traditional ways of understanding the many dimensions of projects of collective living. Exactly as previous genealogies are most strained and shown to be lacking in solutions, do people combine elements of these pasts, now resituated, with radically other ones in ways that produce political thought flavored enough by older forms to be recognizable but that is also disarmingly new. Still, if some of the work under the conceptual framework of disavowal cautions that any hegemony will be marked by the inevitable limitations that preceded them, creolization makes this worry an ongoing guide rather than an obstacle to forging fresh collectivities.

In other words, for a comparative political theorist, Rousseau and Fanon might for multiple reasons not be ideal candidates for shared exploration. First, they may be considered neither sufficiently similar nor sufficiently different. After all, while they are both products of the Francophone world, they were neither direct temporal nor spatial contemporaries. This does not present problems here, however, since the aspiration is not to show the relative distinctness of the respective worlds of each but instead what happens to concerns with the relationship of questions of method to those of political legitimacy in one and then the other for the sake of the world of both then and for us now.[3] In so doing, I do not explore the ways in which Fanon takes Rousseau's ideas only to apply them to a new terrain, producing interesting, historically specific insights. Instead I witness in Fanon the critical engagement of challenges introduced through colonial relations to explore their implications for Rousseau's conceptions of method and legitimacy. In so doing recognizable concerns—with decadence and inequality—are taken up and necessarily altered, forming a distinctive new part of a shared intellectual genealogy. It is because Fanon is *so much more than applied Rousseau* that I suggest that he might be understood as a kindred spirit and better intellectual heir than figures like Jürgen Habermas or John Rawls. Creolization, in this sense, need not always refer to what transpires in colonized settings or among the downtrodden and wretched. After all, unanticipated trajectories in the development of ideas and practices can transpire wherever there is literal or metaphorical migration. Still, the insistence that creolization not only involve distinctive syntheses, but those that would embody better generalizations, more meaningful approximations of the needs and hopes of the society at large, does imply an ongoing relation to those seeking progressive political transformation. Put differently, those who benefit from partial arrangements masked as benefitting all are more likely to oppose actively the appearance of more legitimate alternatives that clearly reveal their claim to generality as phony. As such, they are more likely to reject creolized products as illicit, impure, or otherwise undesirable.

Additionally and finally, this book is an exploration of creolization as opposed to its alternatives to the extent that it can be read as a sustained exploration of the meaning and implications of what Rousseau called "generality" or of how it is that what abiding differences have in common can be meaningfully articulated in and through political activity. As such I begin with Rousseau because while not the first to use the language of "the general" as the distinct scope of the project of politics, he was the one to explore most compellingly its requirements and possibilities. Part of this turned on articulating its fragility by outlining the ways of thinking, being, and acting that could nurture or undercut it in both his early writings on the nature of inquiry in the arts and sciences as well as in his later, explicitly political reflections. While Rousseau was not a creolized thinker in the sense for which I will argue, he was a genius of a generalist, contributing uniquely as he moved among and between a great variety of fields and media. Part of what distinguished him from other renaissance men of his day were the sensibilities that ran through all of his engagements.

Frantz Fanon, as I will show, provocatively suggested that politics and ethics described the relationship between selves and others while colonialism created selves and subothers and the mechanisms through which their nonrelations were administered. While Rousseau did not draw on and enrich his own ideas through the thought of such fundamental "subothers"—his engagements with them were imagined and projected—they were essential to his understanding of how one dislodged and upset the deceptive self-perceptions that created the greatest obstacles to regenerative thought and politics. If Rousseau introduced new ideas and orientations into the history of political reflection, exemplifying original syntheses of tremendous variety, these were not creolized in their own right. Instead they invited a creolization that could and would be undertaken by others, most especially, as examined here, by Frantz Fanon who shared the position that standards for intellectual and political legitimacy were intimately and inevitably interwoven.

To say that societies such as those in the (Franco-, Anglo-, Hispano-, Lusophone, and Dutch) Caribbean were creolized is to insist that their life practices were those that emerged out of situations in which previously unconnected people—a settler class, slaves, dwindling indigenous populations, and subsequent waves of laborers—whose mutual recognition was unprecedented, were thrown suddenly together in ways that abruptly disrupted previous more coherent and discrete orders of collective meaning. Out of such violent ruptures, new perspectives based largely on reinvention and recontextualization began to take shape. Strikingly, those who unequally occupied such societies did not remain sealed off neatly from one another but instead lived within relations marked by mundane dependency, antagonism, intimate and complex interpenetration. Perhaps most significantly, what resulted were *illicit blendings* or those that, unlike other instances of cultural mixture, referred to symbolic creativities combining contributions from those thought incapable of it *and* from those with greater power.

While creolization has been used to describe particular products—languages, music, and foods from Haitian Creole to calypso and gumbo—these more significantly turn our attention to the *process* of which they are an expression. In it, symbolic forms with previously distinct genealogies linked to disparate and conflicting political and structural locations converge to elaborate an indigenous human world in a locale previously home to few or none of the people so implicated. Remarkably, in the results one simultaneously recognizes the presence of both elements that previously had separate histories and the unique form born of their combination. In those instances when native populations did survive the processes of settler colonialism, the coordinates of their world—to which prior ideas, customs, and practices referred—were radically and permanently disrupted. As a result, while facing intense external and internal pressures to offer themselves as embodiments of unsullied authenticity and to index their autonomy accordingly, it was only through intermarriage, mixture, and creolization that such communities were able to survive.[4]

Given what has just been said, why would we *want* to take a concept that emerges out of the violent displacement of plantation societies of early global modernity and use it as a model for our approaches to constructive theorizing? Few, after all, would choose to occupy or mimic such situations. Why would what many have framed as the particularity of the Caribbean phenomenon offer insights to illuminate a now global predicament?

The explorations that went on under the name of creolization aimed to explain forms of mixture that were not supposed to occur. In the dread and curiosity that they thereby inspired, they also drew attention to seeming anomalies that proved, if in more rapid and intense terms, in fact to be prototypes for understanding what transpires more generally as stratified, displaced peoples converge. Capturing the closure and openness, sedimentation and fluidity, identification and nonidentification that efforts to illuminate the workings of culture consistently overemphasize in one direction or the other, creolization therefore offers a better account of the nature of the reality in which political life and theorizing proceed. We would therefore do well to have it inform our methods of inquiry because, as already stated, *however unwittingly, frameworks for understanding symbolic life overdetermine how it is that we conceive of the disciplines themselves.*

The discipline of political science, in what for many might be surprising, was historically heavily creolized. Drawing on the full range of resources relevant to understanding the political world, its early participants forged a shared field language through which those working on divergent questions could communicate their separate findings (even if incompletely) to one another. Many constitutive works in this area of inquiry could as easily be considered studies in history, psychology, or sociology as in theory. They could be defined in multiple ways precisely because their authors were less concerned with demonstrating subfield mastery or loyalty than with grasping problems larger than any single, historically contingent scholarly niche.

More recently, however, the various subfields that comprise political science have undergone processes of radical decreolization,[5] or, as I have already described, of moving along increasingly isolated (often also framed as autonomous) trajectories that cease to be mutually intelligible. Rigor and sophistication are ever more premised on fluency in specialized areas in which good work can only be meaningfully undertaken if one devotes oneself entirely to mastering its specific language and norms. The difficulties with this are many: Most immediately, it means that the larger synthetic work at which a more focused inquiry is supposed to aim is entirely lost to very complex treatments of increasingly smaller issues. In these circumstances, disciplinary languages become less the province of the development of concepts that facilitate broader comprehension and more the gatekeeping devices that assist in artificially narrowing the pool of who would dare enter.

To creolize political theory, by contrast, is to break with identity-oriented conceptions of disciplines and methods, those through which one aims to make oneself and one's work isomorphic with seemingly preexisting conceptions of what a disciplinary community indicates one must be and must not do.

The creolizing processes of New World plantation societies explored by social scientists operated differently in distinct domains. As Robert Chaundenson (with Salikoko S. Mufwene) has described it, "the centrifugal force" of the settler class was most pronounced in the linguistic terrain and in others most suffused with the written word. It is precisely this uneven quality of creolization and its legacies that informed Paget Henry's (2000) seminal *Caliban's Reason*: Henry observed that while creolization was fully evident in Caribbean folklore, music, and theater, when one turned to Caribbean philosophy, the same process was skewed and incomplete. In this "most quintessentially rational area of inquiry and work" (Henry 2000, 70), the ongoing presumed authority of Europe continued. In response, Henry argued, intellectuals needed to undertake a project of reenfranchising African and Afro-Caribbean philosophies, recentering long-concealed areas of the imagination and reestablishing their ability to accumulate authority. Rejecting "negative evaluations that block African and European elements from creatively coming together" (88), creolization, in this context, involved the act of deliberately indigenizing theoretical endeavors, of drawing on local resources of reason and reflection to illuminate local aspirations and assuming that the fruit of these particular endeavors could, as had proved true of their European counterparts, be valuable in themselves *and* to projects elsewhere.

Creolizing of political theory would thus preliminarily involve at least the following components.

First, a particular orientation toward historical work in political thought, in which we repeatedly ask if we are paying due attention to the geographies within which we situate our subjects, whether we are not reading back into them *post facto* conceptions of proximity and distance, actual and imagined discreteness, particularly when investigating sources of inspiration, relations of indebtedness, and other forms of influence. When creolizing political theory we must be sure that we are not naturalizing and simplifying once contested geopolitical relations only later (and even then incompletely) solidified. An excellent example of such an endeavor is Susan Buck-Morss's recent exploration of the implications of Hegel's more than likely scrupulous following of the events of the Haitian Revolution when crafting his most seminal formulation of the nature of freedom.[6] Creolizing both Hegel and a pivotal concept in the canon of theory, Buck-Morss (2000; 2009) explores why an obvious connection in its day (between the press surrounding abolitionist struggles that culminated in the first New World Black Republic and philosophical considerations of the progress of freedom in history) could subsequently be ignored with authority. Perhaps ironically, rooted in greater attention to the past and present of creolization, historians might unearth questions the answering of which would render their historicism more rigorous, even in its own terms.

Central clues for such work can be found by looking for traces of people rendered only in marks of their evasion. For example, when many readers encounter Niccolò Machiavelli's *The Prince*, they do not imagine the world from which it came as one that had been dominated by two Muslim empires whose lengthy presence in Southern Europe had led to extensive intermixing of people, cultures, and ideas.[7] Still, the *Reconquista* or expelling of the Jews and Moors by Queen Isabella and King Ferdinand is one of Machiavelli's examples of religion used effectively to consolidate political power. What happens as readers, if we move beyond pointing out the mere presence of this example, to reimagining what it means for understanding the conditions that fostered Renaissance republican theory?[8] At the very least, it would suggest a different way of narrating the situations that produced what are considered historic moments in the development of political theory. In this case, rather than an expression of a pure and unsullied, distinct Roman tradition (or of fifth-century Athens or early modern England for that matter), world-transforming insights were instead the fruit of efforts to address new dilemmas thrown open by the rupturing of genealogies of symbolic life that, under multicultural models and its sensibilities, are usually lamented.

Second, creolizing political theory (in emulating the situations that produced some of the richest moments in the history of such reflection) involves conceptualizing the task of theorizing in such a way that we create conversations among thinkers and ideas that may at first appear incapable of having actually taken place, that confound at least one conception of the dictates of rigorous scholarship. One example is this book, which suggests that one might trace a richer genealogy from Rousseau if one connects him to what has been called the black radical thought tradition than to those that move only from Western Europe to the Anglo–United States. Another example is Roxanne Euben's (1999) *Enemy in the Mirror*, which emphasizes the kindred character of the criticisms of European modernity within the continent and in the work of Sayyid Qutb.

Pivotal to this is a third defining orientation toward, in the language of Paget Henry (2009b), the concept of the knowing subject. It is one that necessarily rejects a structure that dominates most efforts at cosmopolitan theorizing, in which those from Western Europe and the United States are invited to places that together comprise the rest of the world. Visitors lend locals cultural capital, authority, power, and legitimacy through the fact of having visited from a small set of highly elite institutions in exchange for temporary encounters with intellectuals of the Global South who, engaged primarily as informants, offer their lives as evidence for the supposed authenticity of the purportedly more abstract, historic, and universal insights of their visitors. Such approaches remain reliant on what has been referred to by Michel-Rolph Trouillot as the "savage slot." At the core of eighteenth-century utopian and anthropological writings, Trouillot (2003) explains, was a turn to the life practices of people thought to occupy times and places stubbornly outside the otherwise inexorable progress of history. Evidence of the supposed nature of their lives was used in arguments among Europeans about what could viably be conceived as alternative futures. The "savage slot" was the ultimate empty signifier: it could be made to demonstrate that people were not necessarily hungrily materialistic nor egotistical, and that those living in modern Europe therefore need not, for instance, accept the inevitability of a capitalist future wrought with narrow individualism. To creolize political theory necessarily expands who is involved in the theoretical dimensions of such discussion and as such the structure of what functions as evidential. In this sense, the work of creolizing political theory, which is necessary to the articulation of a global future, is significantly more advanced outside of the Global North where, not always but often, scholars are compelled to follow and engage more hegemonic debates as well as critical responses to them that are local.

Finally, the implications of creolization extend beyond political theory to political science more generally. There is considerable recent discussion of the place of political theory in the larger discipline much of which assumes that work of our empirical counterparts clearly meets requirements to which we theorists are held and often found wanting. In one recent contribution to this ongoing debate, Andrew Rehfeld (2010) pointed out that those whose work has become most influential in the subfield are precisely those trained in a pure discipline external to political science. He mentioned as examples the philosophy training of the late Iris Marion Young and of Charles Mills and the historical one of Quentin Skinner. The same might be said of empirical political science: given the increased value placed on innovation at the level of hyperspecialized methods, one might be better equipped to contribute to contemporary political science if one were trained in advanced economics and mathematics and simply approached politics as one's field of application. This trend betrays a preference for a methodological purity that departs from the discipline's history. It is an ironic one in which legitimacy as a political scientist is a stamp imported from disciplinary locations outside of it and rigor and sophistication are associated with ever more specialized terms, even as these narrow the questions that can thereby be illuminated and the scope of people with whom findings could be discussed and explored.

Creolizing the study of political science would move in the opposite direction, toward rearticulating the world to which increasingly separate pieces of the field refer in ways that can embolden scholars and students to comprehend and participate in forging the shape of the political domain they are entering. If this, rather than narrower career-related concerns, is our primary concern, we would not see our work as better because it can only be understood by a tiny handful of similarly trained professionals also fluent in our respective disciplinary dialects. We would instead aim to take what is most valuable in respective approaches and use them to illuminate shared dilemmas in ways that would enable us to reenliven a broader field language through which we might articulate what might be done.

Creolizing theory and methods through which we investigate political life is not without its limitations as I explore in more detail in Chapter 5. Briefly stated here, creolizing processes emerge precisely in contexts of interruption and loss, in which continuities are broken and people must work with what remains to proceed. If one's approach to symbolic life and disciplinary formations is to try as comprehensively as possible to keep their many elements living through as close-to-perfect duplication as possible, creolization will offer little beyond the challenge to all forms of conservatism: that for anything to remain meaningful it must be transformed as it is resituated again and again in each new generation and circumstance. In addition, processes of creolization cannot themselves determine the conditions or content of creolizing convergences. No single person or group controls the contributory elements or the unequal ways in which they combine. Although, as scholars, in our own work, we are engaged in enterprises that are more deliberate and controlled, it is for this reason that I advance creolization as *necessary* to but certainly not sufficient for the project of a vibrant political theory for the future.

This particular instance of creolizing, although a particularly compelling example, is by no means the only one possible. After all, with Rousseau and Fanon alone, one might fruitfully creolize the former through engagement with Anténor Firmin or C. L. R. James or W. E. B. Du Bois or might explore the ways in which his political aspirations were critically resituated and reworked among New World formally educated creoles, such as Simon Bolivar, who studied these writings in spite of their legal prohibition (Lynch 2006, chap. 2). One might also creolize Mary Shelley through a coupled investigation with Fanon.[9] In other words, the enterprise undertaken here is intended as inaugural and inviting, not exhaustive.

While Rousseau was not a figure that one might single out for explicit, elaborated progressive explorations on questions of race or colonialism,[10] even his critics have considered him to be the thinker who introduced what it was to undertake a dialectical treatment of the project of modern life. The fundamentally ambivalent and melancholic character of the orientation of his writing—of being shaped by aspirations that one simultaneously incorporates, challenges, refashions, and transcends—is also a defining feature of the tradition of black radical thought, of which Fanon is a crucial and canonical member. In other words, we take up Rousseau, not to shield him from instances of necessary and useful criticism or because "he had it all right," but to suggest that evidence of the ongoing richness of his thought is that it is worth engaging and amending. Fanon offers resources for just this creative expansion.

In Chapters 1 and 2, I turn first to Rousseau and Fanon's challenging comments concerning method. Both urged writers and readers to grapple with their conclusions that our approaches to inquiry could never easily be separated from the worlds of which we are part. If for Rousseau, it was difficult for work in the arts and sciences to be anything but an expression of extreme decadence, for Fanon, they lent scientific credibility to colonial relations. From there, we turn to a discussion of Rousseau's general will and to Fanon's national consciousness, closing with a discussion of how the relationship between Rousseau and Fanon that I have undertaken is an example of creolization. I conclude with some suggestions about the broader applicability of creolization to discussions of comparative political theory and methods in political science at large.

1

Delegitimating Decadent Inquiry

They will begin, according to their customary practice, by establishing a different question according to their whim; they will make me resolve it as it suits them. In order to attack me more conveniently, they will make me reason, not in my manner but in theirs. They will skillfully turn the eyes of the Reader away from the essential object to fix them to the right and to the left; they will battle a phantom and claim to have vanquished me: but I will have done what I ought to do, and I begin.

—JEAN-JACQUES ROUSSEAU[1]

When Rousseau provocatively diagnosed the Enlightenment as one more example of the moral decay of empires and offered his challenging portrait of political legitimacy he reversed the geopolitical values of his day, suggesting that it was in Europe's backwaters where freedom and virtue had a present and future. He tied the alternatives that he prized not only to this periphery but to its greater reaches in the brown and black world, seeing in them the elements of the ancient political past that he hoped might still materialize, if now in modern conditions. Still, if cast heroically and as evidence of the universal equality of human beings, his was an imaginary Carib who, while offering an illuminating critical mirror, was a fundamental expression of Rousseau's highly European world. Rousseau's gestures toward creolized inquiry, clearly informed by his own real and imagined personal alienation, stimulated theoretical challenges unlikely otherwise to have emerged. Fanon's thought takes these where Rousseau could not reach, informing them with insights borne directly out of the contradictions and challenges of the creolized Francophone empire.

INTRODUCTORY PARADOXES

Rousseau lived for sixty-six years, all of which fell squarely in the eighteenth century.[2] Born in Geneva, when finding himself once again past curfew and locked outside of its gates, he fled his apprenticeship to wander the Swiss Catholic environs and those of Northern Italy. While a consummate traveler,[3] he moved to Paris at thirty and but for his brief time in Venice (as secretary to the French Ambassador Comte de Montaigue) and when seeking refuge in Neuchâtel and then England (initially through the arrangements of Scottish philosopher David Hume), he remained in and then just outside of it for the rest of his life. In addition to authoring *Julie or the New Heloise*, arguably the most widely selling novel of his century,[4] Rousseau composed several successful operas, pioneering work in autobiographical reflection, and enduring studies in music theory and botany. While responses to his controversial educational and political writings drove him into exile,[5] many revolutionaries sought to institutionalize their often-paradoxical spirit through the tumultuous events that culminated in the founding of the French Republic.[6] The challenging diagnoses and conceptual alternatives that he proffered remain the focus of extensive criticism, teaching, debate, and scholarship to this day.

Frantz Fanon, by contrast, began his thirty-six-year life just less than two hundred years later on the Caribbean and New World Francophone island of Martinique. Spending most of his brief adulthood in North Africa, his political writings became the primary articulation of the cause of anticolonial struggle as one of twentieth-century revolutionary humanism. The innovative practices developed and instituted under his directorship at Blida-Joinville Psychiatric Hospital, those that tied actively resisting mundane practices of dehumanization to the very possibility of mental health, became indispensable to subsequent research and practice in existential psychiatry. When he died under the name of Ibrahim Fanon in a hospital in Bethesda, Maryland, his body was carried to lie in state in Tunisia before being placed in a martyr's graveyard in Aïn Kerma, eastern Algeria. Had he been able to resist his body's rapidly spreading leukemia, he might have celebrated the culmination of the collective struggles through which Algerian men and women were to emerge as political subjects and therefore as "adults." However, the radicality of how he defined the ending of colonial relations would no doubt have put him in direct conflict with the newly powerful. Still, while remaining at best ambivalently engaged by most

French scholars,[7] Fanon has been canonized in the names of streets, schools, and health centers in much of the nonwhite Francophone world and in historic and ongoing fights for freedom in Iran and South Africa, Cuba, Brazil, India, Iran, South Africa, Palestine, and the United States.

Rousseau learned to speak, think, read, and write in the French language; his ingenious energies were devoted to French debates.[8] At the same time, he was, often in ways that he more emphatically emphasized than did others, very much an outsider. Having descended in childhood from the patrician class of his late mother to the artisan one of his father, and then having to support himself from his teenage years onward, he labored in various stations—from that of domestic servant, tutor, and music copyist to secretary for both the aristocracy and haute bourgeoisie—before becoming a recognized composer, novelist, and theorist.[9] He said of himself, "Without having an *état* of my own, I have known and lived in them all from lowest to highest, excepting only the throne" (quoted in Damrosch 2005, 235). On another occasion, he reflected, "The manner of life I chose, which was isolated and unpretentious and made me almost a nullity on earth, put me in a position to observe and compare all conditions from peasants to the great" (ibid.). Even when disavowed by his countrymen, Rousseau identified primarily with a mythologized rendition of the Swiss republic of his birth.[10] It was neither a place of big, urbane cities nor a history of making history. Perhaps as a result, its citizens' loyalties were local rather than cosmopolitan. As Jean Starobinski (1988, 333–51), another Swiss-French political thinker, would stress in the twentieth century, Rousseau embodied a prototype of a "doubly insider, doubly excluded" position, through imagination and in prose fashioning in terms of universal significance a political home more hospitable than the options in fact available to him.[11]

Fanon first left his home of Fort-de-France[12] to enlist in World War II so that he could fight directly for the restoration of the French Republic and through it for, as he is reputed to have said, "the cause of human dignity."[13] It was during his military service on North African bases (in Casablanca, Bejaia, and Oran) which brought together men from all reaches of the French territory, his subsequent studies in Lyon, and psychological work in the colony, Algeria, however, that he so acutely grasped that Martinique and the rest of the Antilles were indeed part of France, sharing its Parisian capital (Macey 2002, 32), but were, more specifically, among places inhabited by France's (internally variegated) *nègres*.[14] As the opening narration in Cheik Djemaï's film preview put it: as a Martinican, Fanon's encounters with French culture made him an Algerian revolutionary. As he would later explore in depth in his first book, *Black Skin White Masks* (hereafter *BSWM*),[15] Antilleans were forcefully cast as "the unconscious, liminal shadow, the repressed and undesirable side of the imperial European subject that has racialized its identity as white" (Henry 2005, 96). In spite of significant differences, this role of "the black" proved global, shared as much in Tunis and Fort-de-France as in Accra, Durban, Sydney, and Tripoli.[16] Thinking through the contradictions it uniquely revealed therefore proved of universal value.

Seemingly divided by centuries and oceans, in other words, Rousseau and Fanon in fact shared a geopolitical world that spanned time and space through the shape and project of the Francophone empire. If in substantively different degrees, Geneva, Martinique, and the colonies of North Africa all lay within its shadows.[17] Ironically perhaps, it was from here that so many quintessentially "French writers" would emerge—not only Rousseau and Fanon but also Jean-Paul Sartre (from Alsace-Lorraine),[18] Albert Camus, Jacques Derrida, and Jacques Rancière (all born in Algeria).[19] Anticipating this tradition, Rousseau and Fanon's sensibilities, if in divergent ways, were as fundamentally shaped by aspirations emanating from this center as by what it was to constitute its periphery.[20]

By Fanon's time, those of the "New World" had become France's old colonies.[21] In Rousseau's day, however, the tantalizingly incomplete bits of information that emerged from European confrontations with "newly discovered" societies were formative, pervasively impacting the consciousness of generations of eighteenth-century political and moral writers.[22] As Michel-Rolph Trouillot has provocatively suggested, the unquenchable thirst of French reading publics for such materials, "reports" from seemingly untouched domains, were sustenance for utopic longings.[23] Few cared if these had any accurate or well-observed basis, whether they were ethnographic or fantastic (Trouillot 2003, 14–18). For each promised to reveal the natures of radically other peoples who in their radical otherness could supply a defining affirmation of or contrast from locally sought-after possibilities. While the Cape of Good Hope was as ripe material as were feral children of Europe or native Greenlanders, few sites were as much the focus of French Edenic projection as the islands of the Caribbean, in particular those of the French Antilles.[24]

Still, while there were no modern European political thinkers whose work could remain unaffected by the many implications of their nations' imperial and colonial policies, it would be a mistake to describe the France of Rousseau's day as *avowedly creolized*. Indeed, great efforts were made to avoid the nation's creolization, to keep the influences of the colonies highly controlled and separate, discrete from local self-understandings. This was a remarkable feat when one considers that by 1780, half of France's exports to other European countries came from Guadeloupe and Martinique, Saint-Domingue (now Haiti), French Guiana, Louisiana, Île Bourbon (now Réunion) and Isle de France (now Mauritius).[25] Many French workers were employed in commercial exchanges with the colonies and tropical goods that had once been luxury items quickly became continental staples. In the 1630s the French colonies had grown tobacco through the labor of peasants who crossed the Atlantic as indentured laborers. When sugar replaced tobacco, small plantations grew into large establishments and France in the 1670s and 1680s entered the Atlantic slave trade. It would import four times as many slaves to the Caribbean as the British did to its North American (not including *its* Caribbean) colonies, with the sugar-producing island of Martinique alone importing more slaves than the US mainland states combined (Trouillot 1995, 17; Curtin 1969, 268).[26] Indeed, after Britain and Portugal, France was, in the eighteenth century, the third largest supplier of enslaved Africans to the Americas.[27]

While France's economy was radically transformed, in other words, its national self-perceptions were not. Indeed, the story of French New World holdings, besides those in Canada, remained largely marginal (Dobie 2010).[28] This was not accidental. Much theoretical and legislative energy was devoted to making what transpired across the ocean appear remote. Arguments over the moral significance of the physical differences of Africans abounded, for instance, along with the soon-after-mid-century fashion of women of high society replacing their domesticated parrots and *petit chien* (little dogs) with small black boys. Most especially on the rise, absent at the end of the seventeenth century, was the association of blackness with servitude and corresponding efforts to assure that blacks and whites remained separated through limiting the numbers of Africans, slave or free, within France itself: the royal edict of 1716 (in the year of Rousseau's birth) and declaration in 1738 stated that slaves could only remain on French soil for the time required for their religious education and apprenticeship in a trade.[29] Slaves of those who did not comply, it was threatened, could be confiscated and returned to the colonies. Failing to slow the stream, the *Police de Noirs* passed in 1777 (the year before Rousseau's death), prohibited the entry of all nonwhites onto mainland French soil.[30] Such policies proved effective:

the number of enslaved blacks registered with the admiralty of Bordeaux in France dropped from 1,098 to 102 after 1756. While the actual figures were surely larger, estimates suggest that in the late 1770s there were no more than four to five thousand enslaved or free blacks living in France in an overall population of 28 million while there were about three times as many in England, in its total population of 10 million (Dobie 2010, 6; Boulle 2007, 196; Noël 2006, 95; Braidwood 1994).[31] In other words, as the distinctness of France from its colonies became ever more difficult to disentangle, a series of theoretical and legal measures were enacted with the aim to shore up national and racial boundaries.[32] These were designed, writes Dobie, to keep slavery and slaves "out of sight and mind in safely distant 'offshore' locations" (2010, 5).[33] One legacy of such gestures, even if they could never be completely successful, is the ease with which one might with academic credibility distance a Rousseau from a Fanon in the subsequent study of both.

It was not that Rousseau and other eighteenth-century writers associated with the movements of Enlightenment did not write, often critically, about slavery. Indeed, as with classical republican thought, it was usually against (abstract, individualized, or ancient forms of) servitude and subordination to the arbitrary will of others that the very meaning of freedom and consent were elaborated. Some also emphasized the hypocrisy and cruelty of European imperialists[34] or were significantly influenced by sustained interaction with the writings or artistic work of major non-Europeans. Rousseau has been deservedly known as European modernity's first radical internal critic precisely because of his unrelenting indictment of the desirability of its model of civilization and progress. At the same time, he and his contemporaries were able to write from a geopolitical world that, if enlarged and changing, remained largely intact. If imperfectly and without full self-awareness, they could, for the most part, determine how and when it was that the literal or figurative Carib would enter. They could, in addition, opt for frozen references to him rather than to those of his effective decimation and retreat to the islands of Dominica and St. Vincent by 1755. It is in this sense that the France of Rousseau's day was markedly different from the heavily creolized Martinique in which Fanon was raised.

We still can and must ask in turning to Rousseau: How is it that a man who entered intellectual history by problematizing the possibility of progressive inquiry became one of the progenitors of the contemporary social sciences? Why was it he, a figure so antipathetic to conventional conceptions of the future who articulated hypotheses and dilemmas that carved scholarly terrains that would only blossom a century or two later? What are we to make of the paradox that a theorist who tried rigorously to locate himself outside of or anterior to Enlightenment civilization produced such a methodologically synthetic, if not creolized, body of work that the association that meets to engage his legacy today draws together members of such a broad range fields that they are not always mutually intelligible?

Many students of the human sciences aspire through the turn to method to make a science of the study of politics. They hope in so doing to arrive at law-like patterns and behaviors with predictive powers, taking the position that these are most likely to emerge when they eradicate the impact of themselves as human beings on the research they are conducting. This is not only impossible. It is ultimately undesirable, too. It is not possible because the best these efforts achieve is a humanly envisaged image of what it would be like to study the human world as unaffected by human beings. We cannot but perceive and reflect as embodied and situated creatures whose sense of meaning is fundamentally informed by our past and present individual and collective commitments. What is more, in such efforts we make the subjects of our studies no longer the people that they in fact remain and their interactions other than what they will of necessity continue to be.

Both Rousseau, on whom I will focus in this chapter, and Fanon, on whom we will soon devote more attention, aimed to illuminate the paradoxes faced by human beings, taking seriously, as socially embedded creatures, the challenge of distinguishing the necessary and inevitable from that which could be otherwise. In an effort to assure that they did not simply reproduce the coordinates of what existed as if features of the natural world, both figures sought critical distance from what Michel Foucault would later call the dominating *epistemes* of their day. Rousseau and Fanon were both weary of what were uncritically treated as authoritative or esteemed methods. Maintaining a skeptical view did not mean that the work they carried out was without method, however. Instead legitimate methods emerge in their work as synthetic and creolized ones or those that draw together diverse resources previously separated to form a unique combination attuned to specific, immediate, and complex political challenges.

Rousseau did not seek to erase his own subjectivity when engaging scholarly debates. He did aspire to separate himself from the self-congratulatory norms and values of his day, those uncritically celebrating enlightenment, civilization, and freethinking. He did so by putting himself outside of his time and place, framing himself as a barbarian through a combination of identification, will, and sheer assertion. From this location, he describes himself as having experienced a (divine) revelation about the fundamental relation of empire to inquiry: In short, those positioned in polities with resources to undertake work in the arts and sciences were least able to pursue them effectively. This extended more generally to colonial expansionary voyages. Those poised for firsthand encounters with previously unknown peoples, what Rousseau thought constituted radically unique opportunities for human study, had no interest in them. With very different driving priorities, they were more concerned to rationalize their own often-imperious actions. Still, as critical as he was of them, Rousseau was himself fascinated by travel writings. He took from them profound instances of refusal; moments when narratives of the inevitable desirability of French models were clearly and publicly rejected by people who faced being or already were colonized. Still, Rousseau was not able to move (at this stage) beyond critical refusal. Trapped in a singular Christianized classical teleology, the further one moved from originary moments, in this case ones that were only basically social, the further one moved toward decay. Indeed, even in *Social Contract*, Rousseau pins his greatest hopes on those places in which general wills were still emergent. Nevertheless, out of his fascination with insistent refusals to be assimilated into a single problematic norm and his valorizing of what others called "backward" as a lens through which to delegitimate unjust equalities, he cultivated a fruitful terrain in which many still profitably labor. Put differently, while he was not himself a creolized thinker in the sense for which I will argue, he introduced ideas and orientations into political reflection that invite productive creolization by others.

As I will show in Chapter 2, Fanon, in both the opening of *Black Skin, White Masks* and his life's practice and research, asked if what are framed as apolitical norms of specialized scientific research can ever be independent of the colonial world from which they emerge and within which they function as meaningful. For him, those interested in grasping human relations rather than political norms and practices that compromised them needed to make a question of method itself by demanding that work in the social sciences advance the cause of liberation. His political writings therefore emerged out of direct collective efforts to restructure Algerian society "from the bottom up." In so doing, he offered a portrait of how we might witness the emergence and generalizing of a formerly squelched political will. Indispensably aiding in its articulate forging was a critical orientation to the nature of inquiry and of truth.

PARADOXES OF IMPERIAL ENLIGHTENMENT

Rousseau's life as the man who was subsequently canonized began with his controversial reflections on the moral value of work in the arts and sciences.[35] His rendition of the initial, transformative impetus that culminated in this writing is frequently retold, often as "the illumination at Vincennes."[36] When walking on a belligerently hot summer day[37] to visit his then still close friend and editor of the *Encyclopédie*, Denis Diderot, Rousseau stopped briefly under the shade of a tree.

Diderot had been imprisoned by royal edict with neither a trial nor hearing for his irreverent *Letters on the Blind*. In it he had queried: If it is true, as the Church claimed, that the existence of G-d is self-evident to all who could through their eyes directly perceive the grandeur of the physical world, could not the blind man, without such access, legitimately refuse to believe?

Beneath the tree, Rousseau paged through an issue of France's most influential literary journal, *Mercure de France*, only to arrive upon the announcement of an essay contest sponsored by the Academy of Dijon. It asked for answers (that could be read aloud from start to finish within thirty minutes) to the question of "whether the restoration of the arts and sciences tended to purify morals." Rousseau described himself as having been thrown into a fit of reverie: Ideas streamed over him and, as if for the first time, he experienced a piercing clarity. His response, known to contemporary readers as his *Discourse on the Arts and Sciences* or simply *First Discourse*, offered a passionate and unremitting "no" that won him a first prize and generated three years of highly public, heated debate.[38]

Leo Damrosch has observed, that it "is curious that this rather obscure [Dijon] body of lawyers, physicians, and churchmen [among them, a hopeless alcoholic and a former musketeer] should have launched a great career" (2005, 215). Because the academy was only recently founded, bourgeois, and provincial, its goings-on rarely made news in Paris (Cranston 1991, 233). Furthermore, in what can be read as an affirmation of the *Discourse*'s arguments concerning the relationship between work that is rewarded and that which is of enduring quality, the essay itself is generally considered by later generations of scholars as one of Rousseau's least significant pieces of writing. In Robert Wokler's estimation, for instance, not only was the argument lacking in originality, much of its scholarship was also secondhand. Although it would be excessive to frame it as plagiarism, as a 1766 text by

Dom Joseph Cajot in fact did, words and passages of his intellectual heroes were more "recapitulated" than engaged constructively to build new arguments (Wokler 2001, 29).[39] Rousseau shared this negative assessment, calling the work the weakest of his writings, deficient in logic and order, balance and harmony.[40] Still, in it and in his exchanges with critics, one sees the first articulation of themes that he developed into what he called "the [true but distressing] System" (*CW* 2:184) of his subsequent political thought.[41] In addition, and as important, the orientation he staked out as a writer and thinker, which is our focus, was here inaugurated. It was, as I will explain shortly, as someone whose position as an outsider was indispensable to correctly diagnosing his times.

Rousseau wrote appreciatively of the kind of question that the Academy of Dijon had posed—one bound up with truths of human happiness rather than scholastic subtleties that plagued every branch of learning—and made clear that he anticipated that he would not easily be forgiven for what he dared to say. Offending all that was admired (including by some of his closest friends and later collaborators), he announces his readiness for blame.[42] He is able to do so precisely because he claims that his primary aim is not to please men of his century, country, or society. This distinguished him from most of his contemporaries who sought to be freethinkers and philosophers. Only seeking these ideals because they were fashionable, Rousseau swipes, most men fell far short of them. If born two centuries before they would have donned as quickly the mantle of Catholic fanatics tormenting dissenting French Protestants.[43] "They care very little about the sciences," he wrote, "provided that they continue to place the learned in honor. It is like the priests of paganism, who only supported religion as long as it made them respected" (*CW* 2:198n).

While the negative position that Rousseau advanced in answer to the Academy's question was not novel—a less creatively realized version of it was the conventional conservative response to many a new social development and the position of the Dijon competition's second prize winner—it collided with the self-image of the moment with what Peter Gay (1987, 1) described as an anachronistic moral sternness.[44] At the same time, its severity was conveyed with lyrical abandon, wrought in phrases and metaphorical flourish difficult to ignore and easy to quote (usually without reference to qualifying context).

In addition, the work did not align itself with any easy or obvious allies: Aristocratic interpreters read into its nostalgia an articulate assault on the bourgeois upstarts they resented. Diderot appreciated that its positive examples were entirely pre-Christian (Cranston 1991, 234), while the Academy awarded what they thought gave voice to their deploring view of a contagious secularism (Damrosch 2005, 215). The few people who Rousseau praised unambiguously were those who could not and would not defend or champion him. The stylized nations of the distant past, "savages" of the Americas, and the few citizens in nations of Europe that labored largely uncompensated—these were those peoples who he characterized as not valuing the work involved in leaving written or scholarly records of themselves. So busily involved with public life and social duties, their only legacy was in memories of their deeds conveyed usually by word of mouth to interested later generations.

However, Rousseau does not, as so many readers then and now surmised, scorn learning in a celebration of intellectual or cultural primitivism. Indeed the text begins with his emphasizing the beauty of human beings, through resources of their reason, stepping outside of shadows, "travers[ing], like the sun, the vast expanse of the universe with giant steps" (Rousseau 1987, 3).[45] He also, albeit briefly and almost in conclusion, singles out for special consideration a small group of men with rare intellectual gifts who, undeterred by the absence of teachers or societal rewards, could not avoid investigating the world around them.[46] In his *Second Discourse*, to which I will soon turn, Rousseau wished that men of this character and caliber had been poised directly to observe the peoples encountered on European expansionary voyages. They, he wrote with resignation, would have made full use of this completely unique opportunity for human study.

His brief list of examples included Verulam, Descartes, and Newton, men satisfied to labor without compensation beyond the inherent value of understanding. Almost always self-educated—spared the kind of "schooling" that imprinted the weaker mental habits of teachers on their students— "these tutors of mankind had none themselves" (Rousseau 1987, 21). Spurred on by obstacles intrinsic to inquiry, these men would "venture forth alone in their footsteps and to overtake them" (ibid.). It was they who could raise monuments to the glory of the human mind because doing so was not their primary aim. Still, since souls imperceptibly proportion themselves to the objects with which they are occupied, Rousseau argued that men of this kind should not merely "occupy a chair at some university" or labor for a modest pension from an academy. He asked pointedly, "Does anyone . . . believe that their works would not [feel] the effects of their condition?"

(ibid.). They should instead be among kings' counselors and given asylum in courts, receiving the "recompense worth[y] of them" namely "of contributing by their influence to the happiness of the peoples to whom they have taught wisdom" (ibid.). It is only then that we might see what could positively emerge from virtue, science, and authority working in collaboration. The separation of political power from enlightenment and wisdom confined learned men to the petty and princes to the less than noble with negative consequences for all.

The difficulty was that while the achievements of men like Descartes and Newton could be attributed to their individual idiosyncrasies, their rarity was instead the result of a larger paradoxical predicament that is the central focus of Rousseau's *First Discourse*: If arts and sciences, at their best, reveal and illuminate the nature of human beings and their physical and social world, this is hardest to do precisely where the conditions for such inquiry are most developed. In amply resourced circumstances, often the city centers of large empires, Rousseau contended, wealth, luxury, and idleness had nurtured and in turn been intensified by an increased affectedness, by a desire, at any cost, for people to please one another and gain mutual approval. Craving recognition and praise, informal and formal education were primarily devoted to refining taste and manners formulaically to secure it.

In such heavily crafted circumstances, while behavior is almost completely predictable, it cannot be treated as revelatory: One can never know whom or with what one really deals. Where social rules function so despotically, not only is it highly difficult to uncloak the nature of human beings, few will "follow their own lights" in the way that real inquiry demands. If the very situations that could support the arts and sciences therefore make the dispositions necessary actually to engaging in them scarce, it is, by contrast, in those places that Rousseau characterizes with moral states to see themselves and others where they are least likely to undertake such work. The values and priorities that make such people coarser, more transparent and independent, are the same ones that would discourage the sensibilities that would appreciate devoting time to meticulous and documented study. The implications? Those with the character necessary to engage meaningfully in artistic and scientific inquiry would esteem the activities and their products the least.[47]

Rousseau reminds readers who might wish to forget that the arts and sciences or "enlightenment" had been absent in Europe—after all, the question of the essay contest was formulated uncontroversially as the "restoration" rather than, say, "development" or "flourishing" of arts and sciences. What are now considered intellectual centers only centuries before lived in a state "worse than . . . even more contemptible than ignorance" (Rousseau 1987, 3). In a classically Rousseauian simultaneous recognition of indebtedness to often denied corners of the world while inverting more conventional orders of value, he writes that it was the fall of Constantinople that introduced through Italy into Europe works from the classical age. This brought about nothing less than a revolution set in motion "from the least expected corner," from the "stupid Moslem, the eternal scourge of letters, who caused them to be reborn among us" (ibid.). This formulation in fact rearticulates a highly misleading European myth: For the arts and sciences to be "*re*claimed" in Western Europe, it had anachronistically to be cast as part of a geography that united it with the Mediterranean world, with Greece and Rome and Italy, a way of conceiving of geopolitical relations that only emerged later. A more accurate formulation would have asked about the "introduction" of the arts and sciences into Europe's northern and western reaches.[48] Either way, the appearance of this "debris of ancient Greece" (ibid.) stimulated not only work in letters and then sciences, according to Rousseau, but a larger and more radical social transformation. The arts and sciences could not alone be blamed for such developments, but they did offer one of the clearest indices of what Rousseau considered the resulting depravity: Indeed he insisted that their perfection could be measured in direct proportion with the corruption of the vigor and health of souls.

Rousseau portrays two different possible trajectories: The first is of places where the arts and sciences are highly developed. They appear and would be mistaken by foreigners as replete with virtue. He laments, if only decency were the same as virtue, if official maxims were lived as rules, "if true philosophy were inseparable from the title of philosopher" (Rousseau 1987, 4). In fact what such polities have perfected is the cultivation of taste and politesse, of making the art of pleasing into repressive rules that cast minds into a uniform mold, transforming society into a herd.[49] By such measures, by which one "no longer dares to seem what one really is" (ibid.), eighteenth-century France no doubt surpassed any historical or present competitors. In cultures of contrived outward appearances, however, there is much uncertainty and little well-founded friendship, esteem, or confidence. Finery in all its varieties is, after all, an art, but one that in fact cloaks deformities and weaknesses that a strong and vigorous body and soul would neither need nor desire.

Significant examples of this alternative include what typically are considered the greatest of empires:[50] from "the first school of the universe," Egypt, to Greece, Rome, "Arabs, and finally Turks" (Rousseau 1987, 5), all places and peoples that beginning as humble shepherds, fieldworkers, or laborers illustrated that mores and virtues dissolved as wealth and arts progressed. (Their vigor had manifested itself as martial virtue through which territories had expanded and with them a reliance on other people that enabled them to become slack.) One cannot, Rousseau emphasized, have the arts and sciences where people do not treat what is done with time lightly. This was already a sign of danger. Writes Rousseau, "In politics, as in moral philosophy, it is a great evil not to do good, and every useless citizen may be viewed as a pernicious man" (12). Not only did such undertakings accelerate a turning from social and political duties to more self-directed and idle uses of hours, days, and weeks, it also required and then buttressed a concern to become rich at any cost. Politicians, who enunciate what is publicly esteemed in such societies, would speak only of commerce and money, estimating the value of their populace not according to their productive contributions but in terms of how much they could and would consume. Such men misled one another into mistaking luxury for the outward and indisputable sign of the brilliance of their empires, even though obsessions with it were likely to shorten and morally impoverish their reign.

Rich monarchies had historically been conquered by bands of men who, in economic terms, were humble and poor.[51] Some such nations had deliberately avoided the trajectory toward empire and decadent decay. Seemingly more coarse, with less affected manners and language, their actual characters and relations with one another were not concealed by ornamentation. Reminiscent of Hannah Arendt's (1958) later distinctions among labor, work, and action: rather than leaving the remains of elegant buildings and eloquent written language, *works* designed to last forever, their lives were those of labor and their legacies of heroic and glorious political *action*, worthy of being recorded in the memories of their descendants. As examples, Rousseau names the Scythians, Germans, and early Romans. In a note he mentions those of whom he claims not to dare speak, the "happy nations which do not know even by name the vices we have so much trouble repressing, those savages in America whose simple and natural polity Montaigne unhesitatingly prefers not only to Plato's *Laws* but even to everything philosophy could ever imagine as most perfect for the government of peoples" (Rousseau 1987, 7n17). Rousseau writes that Montaigne includes examples that many would not know how to admire. "'What!' he says, 'why they don't wear pants!'"

The Scythians, Germans, early Romans, and natural polities of "the savages" if not identical with, remained closer to an image against which Rousseau posits the decadent present which he urges his readers to recall: "of the simplicity of earliest times," "a beautiful shore, adorned by the hands of nature alone, toward which one continually turns one's eyes, and from which one regretfully feels oneself moving away" (1987, 15). While "innocent and virtuous men" were content to have "the gods as witnesses of their actions, they lived together in the same huts" (ibid.). It was when they sought to banish these "inconvenient spectators," that they either moved into what had been their prior residences or made their own homes indistinguishable from former temples.[52]

It is not trivial that from Egypt to Greece stories emerged that cast a god antagonistic to human tranquility as the inventor of sciences, as the one that indulged the "vain curiosity" in people. Moreover, it is with reason that nature shrouded her operations with a heavy veil (as a mother wrests scissors from the hand of a clumsy child).[53] Against the more noble "idea that one wants to form of it" and although it mortifies men to say so, the origins of human knowledge were in superstition, ambition, and avarice—from pride—and its objects were often also our defects—jurisprudence assumes the existence of injustice; history devotes itself to tyrants, wars, and conspirators. In other words, most people seek what become the sciences and arts for self-interested, vain motives and naturalize some of the greatest weaknesses and faults of human beings in their institutionalization. One cannot easily affirm that the very best of the learned produce much that is useful or that what are considered sublime discoveries—whether the ratios in which bodies attract each other in a vacuum or understandings of which stars can be inhabited or how insects reproduce—have made communities better governed. What then of the many others "who to no purpose devour the substance of the state" (Rousseau 1987, 12)?

The vast majority of people who pursue the arts and sciences have no talent for or intrinsic interest in them. Instead what motivates most artists, whom Rousseau assumed would be male, is first and foremost praise, particularly in the form of female attention.[54] The quality of their work and its aims are therefore entirely determined by what promises to elicit it. Few therefore even aspire to create work that would outlive them. The small number who do, in their own day, die in oblivion. For the same luxury that inclines us to live wholly in the opinions of others also erodes the ability to say that, however popular something might be, that it is, in fact, banal or crude, untrue or ugly.

Men who engage in the arts and sciences desperate for gaining distinction go to any length to make a name for themselves, often through callous, ill-reasoned, and contemptuous attitudes toward homeland and religion that they hope will make them appear clever or witty. Such work is also necessarily primarily sedentary and as many other occupations without physical exertion, weakens military virtues by enervating the vigor of the soul and the body.[55] How could men crushed by small needs and pains, face extreme hunger, thirst, danger, and fatigue? Rather than practicing virtue, men become content to study it.

The greatest expense and most severe consequence of flourishing arts and sciences, however, is the culture of ill-distributed glory that is ultimately antipolitical. In other words, people are rewarded for being talented rather than virtuous; eloquent rather than useful; pleasant rather than good. Wise men who might have had their virtue enlivened and made advantageous to society, therefore instead allow it to languish[56] with the result that one has societies with specialists of all varieties, whether chemists or painters, but no citizens. The few who remain live in the abandoned countryside, indigent and despised, producing bread and milk, daily sustenance, for others. The vast majority of people who would not be great sculptors or geometers might be highly useful in another more civically necessary occupation. Envisaging and accepting this alternative would be possible if they did not see it as a demotion, if they could be content with their own self-esteem and self-worth (rather than envying the glory of immortalized writers and thinkers). Satisfied with what Rousseau calls the "true philosophy" of aiming to act well, they could thereby spare state monies and make more politically relevant use of their precious time.

Rousseau momentarily entertained the critical suggestion that luxury might be necessary to provide bread for the poor, but he ultimately concluded that luxuries and poor people were produced together: the luxury that feeds a hundred poor people in the cities simultaneously allows a hundred thousand to die in the countryside; the money handed by the rich to various artists for what is superfluous is thereby not available for farmers to subsist. "And the latter has no clothes precisely because the former have braids on theirs . . . Gravy is necessary for our cooking; that is why so many sick people lack broth" (*CW* 2:116, asterisked note one). In claiming that the very meaning of luxury is zero-sum, that it is exactly to have what others lack in necessarily exclusive forms of conspicuous consumption, Rousseau frames himself as saying what is both true and indecent. His remarks were, he commented, tempered only by the constraints of language. He writes, "My adversaries are most fortunate that the culpable delicacy of our language prevents me from offering details that would make them blush for the cause they dare defend" (ibid.).

Rousseau later would modify his account of imperial decay, acknowledging that it was flawed political decisions rather than the flourishing of the arts and sciences that caused ruin; that the degeneration of mores was instead the outcome of multiple factors including climate, custom, temperament, governance, and law; that the presence of the arts and sciences was in fact a corollary rather than singularly decisive of a more fundamental path toward degrading decadence. It was in fact out of inequalities introduced through the creation and normalization of private property that wealth accumulated with relations based in dissimulation, dishonesty, opacity, and deceit between rich and poor, masters and slaves.[57] But at this earlier moment, Rousseau insisted that imperial wealth, luxury, and idleness emerge together, developing and developed by the arts and sciences (*CW* 2:48). Although these forms of inquiry and expression were less despotic, they were ultimately more powerful than both government and law: Rather than limiting the body, they captured the mind and imagination, leading us to embrace the curbing of our liberty as the condition of being civilized.

Less developed but as pertinent is another challenge made visible by Rousseau's admonitions about the (ultimately unbridgeable) gap between appearance and actuality. Namely, in associating behavioral conformity with societal wealth and decadence, Rousseau raises questions about cause and effect: If sciences, arts, and letters can only emerge in places wealthy enough to indulge their vices—among them an obsession with being pleasing that can be produced through formal and informal education—is what is studied as the "human nature" of individuals and larger collectivities in fact only a byproduct of one brand of societal development? Is the predictability that the social sciences seek and claim to illuminate in fact produced by the same condition that enabled it to be studied?

To the question of the relationship of behavior to social conditions for study, Rousseau adds that of empire to inquiry. While one does not, even in Rousseau's account, *need* imperial resources to investigate the world—he describes himself, when in isolation, naturally wanting to reflect and again there are the largely uncompensated men who should undertake work in the arts and sciences—"centers of learning," as opposed to individuals and small groups engaged in scholarly or intellectual endeavors, have historically emerged within empires. First through extraction and then through the requirement of training teams of bureaucrats to administer the imperial domain, empires then through their sheer magnitude and weight, like the sun, draw everything toward and into them. Many great minds, often from the peripheries of such terrains (and, in Rousseau's account, raised in environments marked less by the pathologies here described), flocked to them in search of kindred spirits and economies that could sustain their creative endeavors.[58] Writing that they and others produced could thereby be published and kept in print across multiple generations precisely because of their inclusion within one centralized collection. This does, as Fanon would make explicit, raise the question of whether most of what would be celebrated under the name of the pursuit of truth (rather than shunned as heresy, propaganda, or ideology), would not already be implicated in the process of legitimating the societies from which the conclusions emanated. At the same time, imperial societies are highly complex and internally variegated: Resources and "idle time" can be put to an array of uses, not all self-serving. Still, Rousseau would insist that it was a rare few that could remain focused on purposeful projects driven by their own questions, inured to pressures to please by remaining sufficiently trendy or audacious to hold an ever-fleeting public eye.

Rousseau's adversaries also raised more particular challenges to the paradoxical predicament he had portrayed. In particular, had Rousseau not been uncharitable in his depiction of scientists and artists? Were not these men the few who lived with alternative values, often choosing moderate lives, books, and opportunities to study over riches and ornamentation? Had Rousseau mistaken their patrons, the idle rich who profited from their industry, for artists themselves? Were scientific experiments not a substitute for the idleness he scorned? Why was he so willing to reduce men to admiring stupidly, rather than exploring, nature? Did not the cultivation of sciences lead societies to flourish through expanding the work of artisans, easing the labor of farmers, and creating roles for physicians and jurists? Were not the fruits of such work more ambivalent and ambiguous, producing evils and some of their remedies? In failing to achieve their intellectual objectives, had not some produced useful, even important, mistakes?

Rousseau never fully addressed all such challenges. He maintained, for instance, that many poor philosophers were angry that they lacked wealth and still devoted time to idle priorities. Most artists, he insisted, were neither simple nor modest. It was, after all, impossible for cultures of decadence and luxury not to affect all within their orbit, if in divergent ways. But these important considerations ultimately remained secondary to the primary epiphany that struck Rousseau on his way to Vincennes. It had everything to do with the irreverent questions that had landed Diderot in prison: could the blind, by virtue of their blindness, legitimately perceive the world in radically different terms, ones that provided sufficient grounds for refuting the greatness of G-d? Rousseau himself sought no such refutation, but asked in a secularized version, what happened to ultimate sources of authority and legitimation, to the societally sacred, if one framed value in profoundly different lights? Would seemingly self-evident grandeur dim? The answer seemed to be yes.

TEMPORAL PARADOXES

While Rousseau insisted on the radical unity of the human species—that visible differences soon called "racial" or "national" were the product of a range of contingent circumstances—he was fascinated by our internal variation. He saw it less as instances of distinctive "cultures," however, than as an array of particular moments that one might arrange along a teleological trajectory from multifaceted health and vigor toward decadent dependence and loss. It was typically assumed that it was only those farther along these developmental paths who were poised to assess all that came before, all that "they" had moved through and transcended. Rousseau, however, inverts these relations, suggesting that it was instead from the position of earlier points that one could critically evaluate, implicitly or explicitly, what were framed as the unqualified and inevitable goods of advanced civilizations. It was in allying himself with these earlier locations—through identification, willing, and mere assertion—that he could put himself at odds with his own time and place. This, he suggested, enabled him uniquely to think with an independence that could well lead to conclusions that would not be pleasing to others. It was only through such a break that he could correctly diagnose his day, seeing anew its self-congratulatory self-ascription as enlightened.

When Thomas Hobbes had introduced his astonishing *Leviathan* (in 1651 at the age of 63), he offered a brief statement about the nature of wisdom and how to ascertain the credibility of the political insights he was outlining. Repeating what was frequently stated in his own day, he affirmed that one does not become wise through reading books but by reading men. This was a more difficult feat than was commonly assumed, however: It was not enough to observe those around one and to show one's "wisdom" in disparaging them. Instead it was best achieved by taking pains to read oneself. Hobbes emphasized that he was not here echoing the challenging way that "reading oneself" was usually invoked—by emboldened men to their social and political "betters"—but by studying one's own thoughts, emotions and passions in a range of circumstances to gauge the reactions of others in similar and slightly modified predicaments. Doing so could enable one really to know one's few acquaintances. The task of those who governed far exceeded this, of course: they needed to *read* nothing short of humankind. Hobbes hoped that his treatise would lessen the burden: All the governing leader need do was see if he did not recognize himself in what Hobbes had written. If he did, this was the surest (in fact, only) demonstration for such a doctrine. Hobbes therefore assumed the radical predictability of human passions within and outside of constituted political orders, his having access to them, and that drawn sharply (even if the objects to which they attached varied with the particularities of individuals and their schooling), all would recognize their natures in his shared mirror. Although he wrote to all, he framed his treatise as directed to those at the reigns of political power, distancing himself from those that might challenge them.

Rousseau establishes his authorial authority in the *First Discourse* rather differently. Locating himself deliberately and emphatically as an outsider of both his space and day,[59] he suggests that the fundamental constitution of men can be sufficiently different across political time to make men of separate moments largely incomprehensible to one another.[60] His role as a thinker is to understand and make available through his writing the internal life of these varied instantiations of human being. The number of approving readers could not ascertain the credibility of his insights, however. In his "Letter to Grimm" (of 1751) he wrote, "I want in vain to make him understand that a single witness in my favor is decisive, whereas a hundred witnesses prove nothing against my sentiment, because the witnesses are parties in the trial" (*CW* 2:85).

It was the convention of his day not to include one's name on a title page. Rousseau followed this norm, only to break with it, identifying the author, himself, as "a citizen of Geneva" and by an epigraph from Ovid's

Tristia, "Here I am the barbarian because they do not understand me."[61] In fact, Rousseau lacked technical grounds for the former claim since he had renounced the Reformed religion in his conversion to Catholicism in 1728 (Cranston 1982, 236).[62] In addition, as Starobinski (1988, 337) has emphasized, Rousseau's form of identification made him "doubly a rebel" as "the myth of Geneva through which he attacked France became reason for dissatisfaction with Genevan reality." Still enabling Rousseau to speak from the position of foreigner with erstwhile loyalties, he emphasized, in a period antagonistic to it, both a desire for rootedness and certainty that the location from which one wrote really mattered. Unlike many who sought to make the particular place from which they thought irrelevant, he insisted on its determining effect on what he could and would not say. Rousseau would later, in a similar spirit, praise the Poles for being Poles, unlike the French, English, and Germans who he thought in becoming increasingly European could be "at home" anywhere that could satisfy their bourgeois preferences.[63] Here this performance of particular patriotism, of love of one country rather than of the world, would only have seemed anachronistic to his cosmopolitan contemporaries.[64]

Compounding his loud allegiance to a specific, nonlocal place, was Rousseau's announcement that he and the content of the essay would be taken for coarse, uncivilized, and primitive. To be backward (in the way of the barbarian), for Rousseau, however, was an achievement: It was to have circumvented being molded by the repressive civility sacred to and enshrouding his times. In his "Preface to Narcissus," he proudly wrote, "in spite of the politeness of my century, I am as crude as the Macedonians of Philip" (*CW* 2:187n1); to Grimm, he insisted, as if it were necessary and clarifying, that being a barbarian and a criminal were "two completely different things" (85). These very features that made him abhorrent were those that enabled him to see through deceptive masks, to diagnose our actual conditions. He reflected, "We finally come to modern peoples, and I am careful not to follow the reasonings that are judged to be appropriate on this subject" (124).[65] He later described himself as "not made like anyone" else he had ever met, a condition that he deplored and desired, that was his misfortune and greatest source of pride (*Confessions*, opening paragraph; Starobinski 1988, 124). Here, in an early public introduction, being an unsynchronized anomaly was an essential virtue, one through which he would reveal what were not mere epistemological concerns, but moral ones as well (4).

If a desirable future is understood in the singular, assuming that breaking with what is most easily accepted is indispensable to fresh thought and seeking truth by studiously avoiding efforts to gain public approval, would seem to require moving backwards. The only positive alternative to being contemporary therefore was to be of a prior moment not in historical time but in Rousseau's philosophy of history or developmental philosophical anthropology. Rousseau makes very clear in his exchanges with his critics and in subsequent writings, that his are not exercises in history but in theoretical, exploratory, or genealogical reasoning divided into a decadent present and a period before its emergence that, in lucky and exceptional instances, was extended into a period coterminus with the *now* of Western Europe.[66] From this vantage point, Scythians and early Romans are preferable to their imperial counterparts. Within his contemporary Europe, prized for their nobility are the poor who remain civic-minded, whether in their capacity to fight for a homeland or to supply it with food.[67] In other words, Rousseau could circumvent the paradox that he had identified, doing justice to the question of the effects of the arts and sciences precisely because he was not a "man of his century" but instead, if only through willful identification, rooted in a previous period of humankind either now lost or facing threats of extinction.

One would be struck by Rousseau's references to "the savages of America" had he not introduced his own authority as tied up precisely with being considered a barbarian—the term used by many early modern Spaniards for people who could legitimately be conquered in the Americas. It was as such that he thought he could uniquely admire the striking examples of these newly encountered societies, examples, he thought, of "true philosophy" and the enactment rather than mere study of virtue. He commented in his "Preface to Narcissus":

> I notice that there now reigns in the world a multitude of petty maxims that seduce the simple by false appearance of philosophy, and which, besides that, are very convenient for ending disputes with an important and decisive tone without any need for examining the question. Such is this one: "Everywhere men have the same passions: everywhere amour-propre and self-interest lead them; therefore everywhere they are the same." When Geometers have made an assumption that from reasoning to reasoning leads them to an absurdity, they go back on their steps and

thus demonstrate the assumption to be false. The same method, applied to the maxim in question, would easily show its absurdity: but let us reason differently.

He then turned to the question of the relative merits of "savage" and "European" man:

> Among the Savages, personal interest speaks as strongly as among us, but it doesn't say the same things: love of society and the care for their common defense are the only bonds that unite them: this word of property which costs so many crimes to our honest people, has almost no sense among them: among them they have no discussions about interests that divide them; nothing carries them to deceive one another; public esteem is the only good to which each aspires, and which they all deserve. It is very possible for a Savage to commit a bad action, but it is not possible that he take on the habit of doing evil, for that wouldn't be of any good for him. I believe that one can make a very just estimation of men's morals by the multitude of business they have among each other: the more commerce they have together, the more they admire their talents and industry, the more they trick each other decently and adroitly, and the more they are worthy of contempt. I say this with regret; the good man is the one who does not need to fool anyone, and the Savage is that man. (*CW* 2:194n)

Challenged by one commentator that there was no place in time or space where a group of people had achieved perfection—that the need for such an imaginary instance was a delusion rooted in Rousseau's envy and maladjustment—the critic advanced that if there were times without certain crimes there would have been other disorders. Without gold and ambition there might be *both* fewer crimes and fewer virtues. For every one simpler society that might be more equitable there were hundreds of others that were vengeful and superstitious (*CW* 2:125). Rousseau replied that he needed only one example and that "a virtuous people cultivating the sciences has never been seen" (ibid.).[68] All learned nations, without exception, had lost love and practice of glory and virtue. When a critic suggested that America "does not offer spectacles less shameful for the human species," Rousseau retorted, "Especially since Europeans have been there."

Disputing the view, found in Aristotle's discussion of the enslavement following war, that the ability to vanquish people cannot but imply some superiority of the conquerors, Rousseau suggested that technological sophistication evident in warfare and moral improvement were not only not synonymous but also in fact opposed. He asked:

> What were we, then, I ask you, when we made the conquest of America that is so greatly admired? Will I be told that the event indicates the valor of the Conquerors? It indicates only their ruse and their skill. It indicates that an adroit and subtle man can obtain by his industry the success that a brave man expects only from his valor. Let's talk without partiality. Whom shall we judge to be more courageous: the odious Cortez subjugating Mexico by means of gun powder, perfidy, and betrayals, or unfortunate Guatimozin stretched out on burning coals by decent Europeans for his treasures, scolding one of his Officers from whom the same treatment evoked some moans, and saying to him proudly: and I, am I on roses? (*CW* 2:125)

Still, Rousseau flatly rejected the depiction of his *First Discourse* as an anti-intellectual expression of a desire forcibly to move history backward. Against the accusation by Gautier that he sought to burn down libraries, abolish all cultural institutions, and reduce men to being satisfied with bare necessities (*CW* 2:128–29), Rousseau distinguished between forms of ignorance and the role of institutions in polities not or already corrupted. He explained that he had, from the outset, separated ignorance that reduces human beings to beasts—the exit from which he celebrated—from that through which we might restrain our curiosity in modesty appropriate to our limited faculties. Science was not intrinsically evil, he repeated. It is we, human beings, who have meager capacities to make good use of it. While we might acquire a share of supreme intelligence, we tend to mistake our "vain and deceitful knowledge for the sovereign intelligence which sees the truth of everything at a glance" (190–91).

Having already failed to contain the consequences, however, there was no easy solution: Suddenly to remove academic institutions in already corrupted Europe would do no good—fully developed, their immediate disappearance would plummet the society into further decay. Once having strayed, a people do not return to virtue short of a great revolution which one should not desire and could not foresee (*CW* 2:53). In such circumstances, as with medicine for an already dependent body, arts and sciences might function as a palliative: as giving food to tigers so they don't devour the children. After having "hatched the vices," arts and sciences cover them with a varnish that does not permit the poison to find a vent so freely (196).⁶⁹ Rousseau's aim, however, had never been to offer remedies; proposing policy, he stated unabashedly, was for those bolder than he (129). Having "discovered" an evil, he had only sought to illuminate it in a spirit consistent with his preference for being a man of paradoxes rather than one of prejudices.⁷⁰

PARADOXES OF SAVAGERY

In his *Discourse on the Origins of Inequality* (hereafter his *Second Discourse*), Rousseau modified and extended the charges of his preliminary writings in his critical reflection on the meaning of European expansionary voyages. From his vantage point, for all of the havoc and terror that such imperial odysseys wrought, they did, as W. E. B. Du Bois would say of the creation of an African-American population through institutions of enslavement, create radically unique opportunities for human study—a clarifying mirror into the nature of the human species through studying it in the fullest range of predicaments. Instead of encounters of open-ended inquiry, however, what travel practices and writings revealed, in his view, were nothing more than efforts to shore up *a priori* models and commitments most compatible with rationalizing colonial and evangelizing projects. Perhaps to the point of exaggeration, Rousseau highlighted against these, several instances of "savage" people from the northern and southern most reaches of the globe and from the Caribbean who explicitly rejected what various Europeans offered. What was rebuffed in Rousseau's view was nothing less than the desirability of the triumph of these models of civilization. What one witnessed more than "savages" clamoring to become European were individual Europeans who, if not stopping to craft the quality written records Rousseau sought, left the implications of their actions: they broke with the ventures that had brought them, wishing to leave the decadence of the continent behind by "going native."

Qualifying his earlier undialectical position on the nature of progress and artistic and scientific endeavor, Rousseau observed "how the burning desire to [be] talked about, the yearning for distinction, which nearly always keeps us outside ourselves, is responsible for what is best and worst among men, responsible for our virtues and our vices, for our sciences and our mistakes, for our conquerors and our philosophers; responsible, in short, for a multitude of bad things and a very few good ones" (*OC* 3:188–89). This assessment fundamentally colored the story of the emergence of human beings that he outlined in his *Second Discourse*.

Now emphasizing that the most useful and least advanced of human knowledge was that of *man*, he asked how we could understand inequality without knowing human beings themselves. Already obsessed with the question of inequality, observes Cranston (1982, 293), exploring the "origins" of phenomena was a method of inquiry that attracted him. He began by cautioning his readers: "O man, whatever may be your country, and whatever opinions you may hold, listen to me: Here is your history as I believe I have read it, not in books by your fellow men, who are liars, but in nature, who never lies. Everything that comes from her will be true; if there is falsehood, it will be mine, added unintentionally" (Rousseau *CW* 3:19). It is worth emphasizing that in authoring a history of the species, Rousseau here implies and elsewhere made explicit, that he accepted the monogenetic account of evolution rather than the far more widely supported polygenetic theories of many of his contemporaries (*CW* 3; Duchet 1971, 21; During 1994, 52). In other words, while many writers insisted and urgently sought data to cement claims that human communities emerged from multiple points of origin, from distinct constellations of ancestors in separate portions of the globe, Rousseau supported the view that the full range of human beings all must be originally linked to the same small community of early human beings. Rather than innate discrepancies in their potential capacities, observable differences, including traits most associated with racial difference, had external, environmental causes and could, therefore, be altered.

What Rousseau sought through discerning a *nature* of man, which unlike individual men, including himself, could never lie was to reveal what befitted human beings or both what we deserve and should not tolerate. In so doing, he went even further back than the historical examples of his earlier writings. Daring "to strip [man's nature] naked, to follow the progress of those times and things which have disfigured it," he compared "the man of man with natural man" to show that our supposed perfecting was the true source of our miseries" (*CW* 5:326).[71] Through it, he sought an independent point of view from which critically to explore his own times—to assure that the scope of his imagination, of his perception of the possible, was not circumscribed. This demanded understanding a *state* that no longer existed and that perhaps had never been.

Rousseau famously charged that other social contract theorists, who had also examined the foundations of society, had failed to reach them. "Speaking continually of need, avarice, oppression, desires, and pride, [they] transferred to the state of nature the ideas they acquired in society. They spoke about savage man, and it was civil man they depicted" (Rousseau 1987, 38). But these failures were symptomatic of the paradoxes at the core of the undertaking itself. Rousseau reflected, here echoing the *First Discourse*, "[since] all progress of the human species moves away from its primitive state, the more we accumulate new knowledge, the more we deprive ourselves of the means of acquiring the most important knowledge of all. Thus, in a sense, it is by dint of studying man that we have rendered ourselves incapable of knowing him" (33). To achieve where others had failed, of distinguishing what was original from the artificial in the known instances of humankind, most essentially required clarifying what constituted relevant questions and problems rather than rushing prematurely to resolve them. He stated: "Let us therefore begin by setting all the facts aside, for they do not affect the question. The Researches which can be undertaken concerning this Subject must not be taken for historical truths, but only for hypothetical and conditional reasoning better suited to clarify the Nature of things than to show their genuine origin, like those our Physicists make every day concerning the formation of the World" (*CW* 3:19). For Rousseau, addressing what it means to be a human being cannot be done through recourse only to facts all of which are gathered with reference to guiding hypotheses that may themselves be deeply flawed. He would soon after write of Grotius, who denied that human power was established for the sake of the governed, that "his most persistent model of reasoning is always to establish right by fact [with the effect that research on public right is often a history of ancient abuses]. One could use a more consistent method, but not one more favorable to Tyrants" (*CW* 4:132).

To get to the root of what we are therefore required a different kind of exercise, one in which we imagine how we became what we are through postulating the absence of our conditions of possibility, in this case of established, complex human societies. Jean Starobinksi describes this pursuit of self-knowledge as an act of reminiscence: the "history" that Rousseau (1988, 19) recounts is an interior distance that we must travel toward other incantations of the self. Although Rousseau, much like Hobbes and Locke, oscillates between using the state of nature as a theoretical device and suggesting that it was an empirical place or moment—with Hobbes asking if what he described as natural was not affirmed for the doubtful by the practice of travelers arming themselves and people locking doors before going to sleep, by the Americas contemporary to him, recent examples of civil war, and ongoing international relations; Locke also pointed to the America of his day as an example of a place in which land was not yet enclosed and still held in common for the industrious and rational legitimately to seize through cultivation—Rousseau emphasized that the state of nature was theoretically and structurally necessary for his argument, indispensable, as Emile Durkheim (1960) later explained, to accurate notions through which properly to judge our present state. Rousseau therefore offered a portrait of a world without sociality, of pre- or asocial creatures, with nothing but sporadic contact with other proto-human beings.

Rousseau describes an original state of nature in which largely self-sufficient and solitary people of strong and undomesticated physical constitutions had easily satiated needs. Without industry or fixed dwellings, they had ample leisure time, were completely absorbed in the present, and at home in themselves and the world. Over time, changes in the physical environment produced semipermanent living arrangements and small bands that together took on characteristic features due to shared foods and climates. In these rudimentary associations, small groups began together to procure conveniences for themselves. With these emerged the earliest instances of conjugal love, primitive conceptions of possession, and a gentler iteration of human being. Those so transformed possessed no corresponding awareness that in each minor step away from total independence was an inborn trajectory toward the softening of body and mind and a multiplication of "needs" that could only lead to potentially servile reliance on others.[72] Although emphasizing the problem of discerning the origin of language, or untying the knot of the formative relationship of speech to society, Rousseau ultimately describes the elaboration of speech as introduced by occupants of islands (which had been more densely and predictably populated for a longer time) into mainland collections of individuals. Without these expanded resources, Rousseau suggests, there had been some primitive thinking, but general ideas only occurred to minds with abstract terms with which to articulate them.

Once social and conceptual relationships had emerged, people—instead of making only crude, instrumental, and strategic comparisons between themselves and other nonhuman animals—began to estimate their relative value or how they compared with one another. This in turn nurtured an increasingly self-centered vanity that made siblings of shame and envy. Each wanted the public esteem that accrued to the physically strong or to the beautiful, to the gifted singers or the adroit. Each claimed an entitlement to this high regard and sought its assurance through the institution and policing of shared rules of civility.[73] These expressed a new sentiment: far worse than any physical injury was the harm of being held in contempt. Efforts to avoid negative appraisals drove a larger wedge between being and seeming, pressures to feign desirable attributes that one lacked, in ways that, for Rousseau, further broadened capacities for manipulated and opaque relations.[74]

Sufficiently touched by society, these men and women were no longer what they had been in "true youth of the world." All of what had been unnecessary and therefore latent natural intellectual and emotive capacities were now fully active: They possessed the faculties of memory and imagination, active reason, and the ability to pursue their own egocentric interests. Exemplifying a unique developmental possibility that singled them and the meaning of their freedom out from all other nonhuman animals, human beings exemplified the faculty of self-perfection. Indeed the driving point of Rousseau's exploration is that what might be perceived as the perfecting of man could, from another vantage point, be considered his degeneration—the cause of all of his misfortunes; that which gave rise to errors through which he became a tyrant over himself and nature (1987, 45).

The basic equality of these nascent stages of society eroded, in Rousseau's account, with the emergence of conditions that made natural inequalities consequential. With the dividing and cultivating of land for agriculture, the discovery and uneven use of iron, and the introduction, normalization, and consolidation of private property (through it feelings of possession of family and huts extended into those of land), Rousseau wrote, "Vast forests were transformed into smiling fields which had to be watered with men's sweat, and in which slavery and misery were soon seen to germinate and grow with the crops" (*CW* 3:49). Some came to depend upon the exertion of multiple others and minor differences in physical endowments of one generation—of how quickly or extensively one could labor—compounded, over-determining the fate of their descendants.

What was essential for Rousseau was less the fact of inequalities and disparities of wealth as the relationships among people that they inevitably produced. Most, argued Rousseau at the end of his *Second Discourse*, would have to ingratiate themselves to others who would denigrate them precisely because they relied on their labor. Cunning, self-deception, avarice, and cultures of violence would become normal behavior, and the ability to perceive the shared conditions of collective thriving, the core of public-spiritedness, would corrode. In antagonistic relations that were effectively a perpetual state of potential war and unhappiness, each individual saw in others only limitations to their own enrichment.[75]

On the brink of ruin, the rich felt that this situation was particularly disadvantageous to them—that all that they had acquired by force could be removed through the same means. Bereft of justified reasons and means by which to defend themselves individually, they "conceived," Rousseau writes, "the most thought-out project that ever entered the human mind" (1987, 69). They aimed to use the strength of those who might attack them, by transforming these adversaries into their advocates through instilling maxims in the creation of political institutions that could secure what claims to natural right could not (ibid.). One rich man made vivid the horror of his own situation to his neighbor, who similarly held possessions that were as burdensome as his needs, demonstrating that safety could be found neither in wealth nor poverty. He urged all to unite, to institute rules of justice and peace that would bind the strong and weak in mutual obligations, making special exceptions for no one. "In short," wrote Rousseau, this man proclaimed "instead of turning our forces against ourselves, let us gather them into one supreme power that governs us according to wise laws, that protects and defends all the members of the association, repulses common enemies, and maintains us in an eternal accord" (1987, 70).

Rousseau comments that far less than this must have been required to convince people who were so easily seduced, who lived in constant dispute, and who were slaves to their own and others' greed and ambition. They ran into their own chains, believing that they would thereby secure their liberty. The few who could foresee the dangers were those who had already planned to profit from them.[76] These arrangements "gave new fetters to the weak and new forces to the rich" (1987, 70). In such societies, political institutions and laws frequently failed to create a genuine alternative to rule by force. Although less immediately corporeal in their effect, they transformed usurpation and theft into a right of whoever was best disposed to impose their will over and against others. "The profit of a few ambitious men [thereby] henceforth subjected the entire human race to labor, servitude, and misery" (ibid.). The establishment of one society made the creation of others a necessity. These multiplied, covering "the entire surface of the earth," spreading national war, battles and reprisals in their wake (ibid.).[77] Rousseau emphasizes that it is not possible to return to nascent society or primitive anarchism. In his *Discourse on Political Economy* and *On the Social Contract*, to which i will turn in Chapter 2, Rousseau instead sought to reconstitute these depraved men and women through an act of legitimate rather than counterfeit political association.

But more immediately worthy of emphasis is how the capacity of making comparative evaluations which opens with the distance between being and seeming is both indispensable to the emergence of inequalities and the possibility of curbing their detrimental consequences. In other words, the same abstract thinking necessary to political life—specifically, the work of understanding how sociality mediates individual and collective needs suggested by the notion of a common good—enables us simultaneously, and far more frequently, to distance ourselves from ourselves and others in alienated relations that rely upon submerging empathetic repugnance at the suffering of sentient others that, in Rousseau's story of the species, once arrested us.

Ernst Cassirer, in outlining a philosophy of human culture, insists that what sets apart human from nonhuman animals is not the ability to read and respond to (at times, complex) signs which nonhuman animals can also decode and detect, but our inhabiting a *symbolic world*.[78] A study of the anatomical structure of a particular animal species offers, through a view of its inner life, insight into its outer one as well since for all intents and purposes these are joined respectively as the receptor and effector which form a functional system through which the animal is fitted to its physical environment. When one turns to human beings, this circle is not only quantitatively but also qualitatively enlarged. Writes Cassirer, "Man has, as it were, discovered a new method of adapting himself to his environment. Between the receptor system and the effector system, which are to be found in all animal species, we find in man a third link which we may describe as the symbolic system" (1944, 24). This does not only open a broader but "new dimension of reality." Unlike organic reactions to external stimuli are human responses that do not only offer delayed but considered answers to such prompts.

Here, considering Rousseau, Cassirer emphasizes that "at first sight such a delay may appear to be a very questionable gain," unambiguously a deterioration of human *nature* or of what might, in principle follow from our raw physical potential (1944, 24). But, as Rousseau at times reluctantly conceded, we cannot escape from this achievement. We, as the anatomies of nonhuman organisms, cannot but adopt the conditions of our lives—a physical *and* deeply symbolic universe. The latter imbues all that it envelops with mediation. "No longer," Cassirer explains, "can man confront reality immediately; he cannot see it, as it were face to face. Physical reality seems to recede in proportion as man's symbolic activity advances. Instead of dealing with the things themselves man is in a sense constantly conversing with himself" (25).[79]

To understand the full import of the claim that it is symbolic thought and behavior that are the most characteristic features of human life and that what we understand as our progress is based upon the conditions they enable, Cassirer (1944, 32) emphasized, that it is crucial to understand the difference between signals—which belong to the physical world of and have substantial being—and symbols which belong to the human world and have only functional value. A sign is related to the thing to which it refers in a fixed way; one sign refers to one individual thing. By contrast, a human symbol is marked by its versatility and mobility—one can express the same meaning in various languages or with multiple terms (36). With them, one can develop general categories and talk in abstractions rather than only of concrete facts and immediate situations or circumstances (41). Without such symbolism, in other words, we would be confined to biological needs and practical interests without access to an ideal world.

It is between the dangers and possibilities of this predicament that Rousseau writes. At once, he emphasizes that were it not for our ability to think in general terms, political life—or a domain that seeks to break into, interrupt, and introduce a new logic within relations otherwise overdetermined by cyclical relations premised solely upon might—could not emerge. It is our ability to connect particular instances of forms of life or phenomena with larger structurally similar groups and categories that enables us to envision forms of communal and collective life; that makes it possible for us to introduce through acts of our moral freedom our own principles for shared conduct. At the same time, the spaces opened up by such mediation also suggest a world of being literally entrapped by ourselves—of everywhere encountering only our person.

It was precisely this weakness that struck Rousseau most about the writers and readers of travelogues of European explorers and colonizers of his own day, writings on which he drew heavily and that were treated by many distinguished philosophers as legitimate empirical data on African, Asian, and New World peoples. As mentioned earlier, the hunger for these was profound: Lahontan's 1703 *New Voyages to North America* went through twenty-five editions by 1758, shaping impressions of New France and through them discussions of nature and freedom (Dobie 2010, 177). Foreshadowing Rousseau, Lahonton positively depicted the distaste of the Hurons for private property and European technological advances, claiming that they looked down on the hierarchical relations of French society that required an obedience befitting slaves (179). In addition, a subgenre of fiction had developed in which Native North Americans engaged in dialogues with travelers, criticizing European mores from a primitivist perspective (180).[80]

For Rousseau, in spite of his personal fascination with them, the travel accounts themselves betrayed an incapacity on the part of their writers to perceive the most meaningful and important forms and implications of human difference. He stated:

> For three or four hundred years since the inhabitants of Europe have inundated the other parts of the world, and continually published new collections of voyages and reports, I am persuaded that we know no other men except the Europeans; furthermore, it appears, from the ridiculous prejudices which have not died out even among Men of Letters, that under the pompous nature of the study of man everyone does hardly anything except study the men of his country. In vain do individuals come and go; it seems that Philosophy does not travel. (*CW* 3:84)

Philosophy with a capital P was the kind that he criticized in his *First Discourse*. Unlike philosophy or critical reflection, its sources and products were vanity and vice, the rationalization of political worlds that were fundamentally illegitimate. Rousseau distinguished the role of Christian missionaries from the sailors, merchants, and soldiers who also undertook such voyages. In particular, he suggested that the skills of the former were not the same as those necessary to undertake work in the human sciences since they seemed able to articulate the worthiness of potential converts only by likening them to one, undifferentiated European notion of human character. In other words, on this model, equality had to be based on uniformity or sameness. This was precisely the criticism that Tzvetan Todorov made of Bartolomé de Las Casas. Although surely to be celebrated for arguing against the most brutal policies of Spanish colonial armies, he could only make such defenses by minimizing genuine differences between himself and the indigenous communities he encountered, by constantly indexing them in terms of their potential moral salvation. By contrast, writers like Juan Ginés de Sepúlveda, who assumed the radical inferiority of the indigenous people of Mexico and the Caribbean, in efforts to garner evidence, documented their distinctive ways of life (Todorov 1999, 151–17). Rousseau wrote:

To preach the Gospel usefully, zeal alone is necessary and God gives the rest; but to study men, talents are necessary that God is not obligated to give anyone, and that are not always the lot of Saints. One does not open a book of voyages without finding descriptions of characters and morals. But one is completely amazed to see that these People who have described so many things have said only what everyone already knew, that they have known how to perceive, at the other end of the world, only what it was up to them to notice without leaving their street; and that those true features that distinguish Nations and strike eyes made to see have almost always escaped theirs. (*CW* 3:85)

He imagined if instead a Montesquieu or a Buffon, a Diderot, a d'Alembert, or a Condillac were to visit Turkey or Egypt, Morocco or Guinea.[81] "Let us suppose that these new Hercules, back from these memorable treks, then wrote at leisure the natural, moral, and political history of what they would have seen: we ourselves would see a new world sally forth from their pen, and we would thus learn to know our own" (Rousseau 1987, 100n10). These men, we might conclude, would in so doing, act as if Newton had been at the armchair of the political leaders of his day. By contrast, it would be "terribly simple-minded" to take at their word the conclusions of "unsophisticated travelers" (ibid.).

Rousseau concluded that although Europeans had set themselves up as the world's judges, sometimes with the best, if moralistic, of intentions, their understanding of the peoples that they relegated to lower order species was at best superficial projection. They had missed a unique opportunity to engage in human study. Their bodies had traveled miles but they were incapable of perceiving that human beings could forge alternative life worlds, could think, act, and aspire otherwise. In their failures to see these larger possibilities, they had also missed an important opportunity for *self*-clarification. As Roxanne Euben observes, while travel for many betokens the possibility through unpredictable exchange of transformed imaginaries and identities, senses of "self, knowledge, time, and space . . . transfigured by the doubled mediation between [the] familiar and unfamiliar," it is unpredictable whether one's disposition will in fact be open to such enlightenment (2008, 12). Physical movement on its own is no assurance. Indeed it may encourage the petrification of unreflected upon identities and imaginaries.[82]

Rousseau considered this to have been the case with the writings he engaged here: The aims of travelers had not been actually to encounter the people about whom they felt compelled to write, but instead to aggrandize themselves and offer rationalizations for illegitimate self-enrichment: "We know nothing of the Peoples of the East Indies, who have been frequented solely by Europeans more desirous to fill their purses than their heads. All of Africa and its numerous inhabitants, as distinctive in character as in color, are still to be examined; the whole earth is covered by Nations of which we know only the names—yet we dabble in judging the human race" (*CW* 3:85–86). None, Rousseau suggested, had genuinely considered a phenomenon that contradicted the reasoning at the core of narratives of imperial enlightenment: "that [while] the Europeans torment themselves in order to acclimate the savages of various countries to their lifestyle, they have not yet been able to win over a single one of them" (1987, 106n16), that those they encountered constantly refused to imitate the Europeans or to covet their displays of luxury and wealth while there were countless examples of the reverse: of French and other Europeans who in more contemporary parlance "went native," taking refuge in these other nations, "no longer able to leave so strange a lifestyle" (ibid.). For Rousseau, the idea that cultural mixing (or creolization) might positively result from such encounters was unfathomable. The best possibility was that Europeans, moved by the people they encountered, attempted to peel away their own corrupted ways of life.

As Anthony Pagden writes, "[Rousseau's Caribs] are contemporary with the reader, yet they belong to a period of human infancy. It was a paradox for all those who saw in this new land the image of a world which man, in his progress from the state of nature to civil society had had to abandon. They, these 'savages,' are not like us as we are now, the argument went, they are like us as we once were" (1993, 117). For Rousseau, such people are most significant as evidence that the developments he describes are not inexorable; he sees in them highly significant acts of refusal: Although in the notes rather than the main text, and even there, as almost a final thought, Rousseau (1987, 106n16) claims, "It is something extremely remarkable that . . . [n]othing can overcome the invincible repugnance they have against appropriating our mores and living in our way." If they were as miserable as was claimed and the European alternative so unquestionably preferable, why did they refuse to imitate Europeans?

Rousseau goes on to describe "savages" brought to Paris and London who showed no excitement about displays of luxury, wealth, or "curious arts" (1987, 106n16); people from Greenland and Iceland raised and fed in Denmark who died of sadness and despair; the failed efforts of the Dutch to convert a single Hottentot—even when taken in infancy and raised with European customs and Christian principles—who, finally in a situation in which he might make a choice, decided to renounce the clothing, religion, and ways of life into which he had been socialized, keeping only what connected him emotionally to his individual relationship to the governor himself (ibid.).

All of this presents a paradox, however: if we rigorously follow Rousseau's reasoning, the Caribs and Hottentots when presented as original men ("which of all existing peoples has so far deviated least from the state of nature") who have not yet been transformed by sedentary living, appear, at least in the main, to be without the capabilities of complex reasoning that make both willing and moral freedom and full-fledged alienation possible. He wrote:

> All the kinds of knowledge that demand reflection, all those acquired only by the concatenation of ideas and perfected only successively, appear to be utterly beyond the grasp of savage men, owing to the lack of communication with his fellow-man, that is to say, owing to the lack of the instrument which is used for that communication, and to the lack of the needs that make it necessary.... [S]ince they depend exclusively on bodily exercise and are not capable of any communication or progress from one individual to another, the first man could have been just as adept at them as his last descendants. (1987, 87n6)

At the same time, here are individuals whose full abilities presumably are now active, if nothing else, through the arrival and imposition of Europeans. And they do, at least as individuals, choose to reject what is on offer. One might qualify that Rousseau does state that decisions over happiness are reckonings made by the sentiments rather than by reason; that these natural men can sniff the dangers on the horizon (1987, 107n16). Still, it is hard to conceive of opting for what constitutes Europe's prehistory as nothing more than the work of instincts. It seems instead, even if contradicting Rousseau's efforts to valorize these men precisely because they are more natural and uncorrupted by the influences of culture, as a *decision*, an outgrowth of comparison and reflection.

Even then, however, the possibilities linked to this signal "no" prove limited. As Pagden comments, "[The savage] has been driven forward by his 'discoverers' and up the temporal scale, to confront a world he finds abominable. But it is also, as he sometimes recognizes, a world that will one day be his own. He can only escape it . . . by returning to the woods. Only there can he hope to live for a while unmolested. . . . His society . . . as readers could not have failed to be aware, is in the process of being absorbed into a European one . . . and they are themselves in the process of being colonized" (1993, 138–39). Pagden concludes that this produces a despairing conclusion: that "the 'savage,' however defined, could ultimately have no place outside a world system whose character was already markedly European, yet could never survive *as* a 'savage' within it" (188).

In his *Social Contract*, Rousseau would describe both conquest and enslavement as impossible to articulate in terms of political right. The former could create a subjugated multitude or an aggregate but neither an association, polity, nor people. Both turned on the so-called "right of the strongest" or the claim that any individual or people who overcame others did so legitimately. Rousseau contended that force could elicit little more than acts of necessity and prudence. Without independent acts of consent, these simply set one person's private interest up against those of others, reflecting a readiness to divide the human species into "herds of livestock, each with its leader, who tends it in order to devour it" (*CW* 4:132, 137).[83]

Rousseau's "prehistory" challenged the inevitability of this outcome, first by offering a portrait of more fully satisfied, if less resourced people and communities, and secondly, through his turn to supposedly empirical examples of "real" natural men and women.[84] Though he formally posited such people as occupying the middle stage of his conjectural history, he also referred to them when characterizing the capabilities of original natural people both before the emergence of sedentary living and in more primitive places encountered by European explorers as examples of the vigor of less domesticated people able to be absorbed primarily, if not wholly, in an eternal present.

INSIDE-OUT PARADOXES

Because of the governing theodicean framework of Rousseau's analysis, one might accurately surmise that much of Rousseau's writings was an expression of nostalgic longing—of wishing to return to that which he could only access through imaginative and creative endeavors. However, there is an interesting irony: Rousseau's prizing of that which was disdained as backward was generative in ways that transcended his own life and writing. Not only have his *Second Discourse* and *Essay on the Origins of Language* been credited as founding works in anthropology, sociology, and linguistics, his early *Dissertation on Modern Music*, which challenged the adequacy of European theories of harmony for describing the full range of world music, is considered fundamental to the development of the field of ethnomusicology. In other words, if Rousseau's ideas about human difference did not reflect the possibility of creolization, his methods or approaches to his own inquiries, which were heavily synthetic, surely did. Not only did his explorations traverse the vast domains that comprise human symbolic life, he turned ecumenically to whatever resources he could find in music, the study of language, literature, philosophy, and natural history. Crucially, in addition, his investigations were always colored by a melancholic challenge to the injustices that he thought were expressed in and the result of the unambiguously positive qualities ascribed to what were called both enlightenment and civilization.

Emphasizing the losses of each developmental stage that culminated in what was seen as everyone's future, he came upon paradoxes and dilemmas that revealed some of the most difficult and interesting questions of what it meant to be a human being. While there are reasons for qualifying the view that Rousseau was a political radical, there is no doubt that he was a radical thinker: Nothing excited him more than tracing roots and origins that demanded grand explanatory stories. No questions or considerations encountered en route were too off-putting to go without mention. While asking whether those poised to undertake scholarly work in fact possessed the independence of mind to do so, his allegiances to disavowed spaces and times enabled him to break from monopolizing concerns, embracing (perhaps even enjoying) blame and shame over trying to please his contemporaries.

Although this disposition, of remaining the radical outsider while fomenting lively public debate, proved harder rigorously to embody than he might have initially thought, as a commitment, coupled with his vast creative breadth, daring imagination, and brilliant craft, it proved highly generative. Indeed, as stated earlier, when the association founded in his honor meets critically to engage his rich legacy, the range of scholarly fields that converge is impressive. His work, in other words, synthesized domains of life and study that have since splintered into autonomous areas of inquiry. We might ask, in a Rousseauian spirit, whether the development toward such specialization has not brought significant casualties in its wake.

It is not accidental that Rousseau reserved some of his most acerbic remarks for his references to academic posts and positions. Read through his subsequent writings, and some of his early comments about philosophy, one can conclude that added to his other fears about arts and sciences was a sense that with academies develop distinct classes of scholars, who might, as government representatives he would so fiercely criticize, develop their own partial, self-preserving group will. As he later made clear, in both the *Second Discourse* and his controversial collisions with D'Alembert over the potential institution of a theater in Geneva,[85] Rousseau ultimately concluded that stark and sedimented divisions of labor easily became entrenched. Reproducing over generations, they then over-determined group situational differences that became near impossible to mediate in political life or reconcile into a shared, general will. Scholars, one might also surmise, would develop their own excessively specialized language that rather than enabling unique political forms of communication among assembled citizens become a gatekeeping way to secure their own privileged role. Tracing the development of language, Rousseau would argue that what began in gestural expressions of want, it was only with the rise of trade that human beings needed phonetic and easily translatable and legible alphabets that, once modernized, became writing. As the communication of feelings was displaced by that concerning abstract ideas, most developed forms of languages became those best designed for exchanging money and arms, that, in George Orwell's 1946 observations, could "make lies sound truthful and murder respectable" (2005, 120). Finally, steeped in norms of abstraction, Rousseau suggested that those devoted exclusively to mental work developed thicker skins—one's within which it was far easier to ignore or evade otherwise visceral experiences of other people's suffering.[86]

At the same time, as the breadth and originality of Rousseau's own life work indicates, he did not contend that all study must be narrowly instrumental, demonstrably advancing a clearly or immediately known good. (Indeed, some subsequent scholars have suggested that it was precisely the ambiguity of his writings that contributed to their timelessness [Swenson 2000]). If this were so, there would surely have been no room for the tortured, dogged acknowledgment and exploration of contradictions. Still, the work did aim to illuminate the alienated condition of humankind.[87] After all, Rousseau's own early aims were to restore an image of a pure, uncorrupted person on the basis of which he could explain the origins of inequalities and challenge their legitimacy as "natural."

In doing so, however, Rousseau engaged in what Nelson Maldonado Torres (2009) has called an "anti-European Eurocentrism": while problematizing Europe's governing values and valorizing the Caribs and Amerindians and Hottentots as remaining in more primitive states that we would all more happily occupy, he in fact denies these groups, as we have seen, "all the kinds of knowledge that demand reflection, all those acquired only by the concatenation of ideas and perfected only successively" (Rousseau 1987, 87n6). These are the very capacities that prove indispensable to the acts of willing at the core of the moral freedom that is distinctively human. While their earlier points on a singular trajectory are not framed as a natural failing, but instead the result of a complex of environmental accidents, he does not entertain that these groups might have collectively (rather than in individual acts of refusal) chosen to reject the introduction of private property or unequal political relations or adopted both along with institutions to counter their greatest dangers. Instead, as Sankar Muthu (2003, 8) has demonstrated convincingly, while Rousseau's scathing criticisms of Europe and account of people as "self-making creatures" whose freedom can entrench alienation or secure its antithesis informed the explicitly anti-imperial writings of Diderot, Kant, and Herder, he remained as Anthony Pagden (1993, 142–43) has shown, squarely in the noble savage tradition of Michel de Montaigne, looking for empirical evidence of living primitives, free from artifice.[88]

These interpretations of New World people *did* challenge the more widespread ones that assumed their genetic, behavioral, and cultural inferiority that were taken to legitimate well-entrenched and expanding colonial activities. Still, in Muthu's estimation, they collapsed into paradoxes that made "the possibility of meaningful commiseration remote" (2003, 13). For while turning "presumed savagery into a badge of honour," this "ultimately cast them as lacking the cultural agency that would have made them recognizably human" (23). Muthu emphasizes, here with Starobinski (1988, 327), that in trying to emphasize the distance that human beings have traveled from their supposedly natural to corrupted state, Rousseau lands up humanizing certain animals—insisting that orangutans belong in the human species—and animalizing certain human beings (Muthu 2003, 43).

In this context, one might consider several lines from Fanon: Emphasizing that he had no mercy for former governors or missionaries, he wrote, "To us, the man who adores the Negro is as 'sick' as the man who abominates him" (1967, 8). Both ultimately engaged in processes that he considered disastrously dehumanizing: First, the creation and then demanding expectation that colonized people not make meaning for themselves, but exemplify and embody a role "already there, pre-existing, waiting" for them (134) and that "this role is always a comparative and relative, rather than inherent one" (211). However noble Rousseau's intentions and ultimately significant for subsequent developments in the human sciences, the meaning of the Carib, the Hottentot, and the Amerindian exhibit all of these orientations: a priori admiration (the inverse to the "black problem"); a priori purposes posited from without; a priori comparative role in a discussion in which the setting of the terms were entirely monopolized by the relevant outside interlocutors.

There is, however, a striking irony. Even if it was not as author of the prize-winning *First Discourse* but instead of the *Second Discourse* (which was not even seriously considered by the Academy of Dijon),[89] "Rousseau has both been held responsible for the French Revolution [by Edmund Burke, Napolean Bonaparte, and G. W. F. Hegel, among others] and acclaimed as the founder of modern social science" (Cranston 1991, 293). The *Second Discourse*, in addition to offering a theory of the evolution of human beings that anticipated Darwin and propelled the study of anthropology and linguistics in new directions, did add to his earlier reflections both subtlety and a conjectural history of the origin and development of inequalities as intertwined fundamentally with the very emergence of human societies. While most of his contemporaries optimistically affirmed the naturalness of both sociality and reasonable collective life on the one hand, and inequalities on the other, Rousseau outlined a secular theodicy in which the most pertinent and destructive differences among people were not those of nature, but produced through social conventions or through how we, as human beings, live within society.[90] And throughout, as we have already seen, what enabled him to diagnose "developments" as moments of degeneration were the critical juxtapositions embodied by the figure of the Carib.

CONCLUDING PARADOXES

Few social theorists, especially French or Francophone ones, writing after Rousseau have failed to comment on the significance of his method to the development of their respective social scientific fields of inquiry. Emile Durkheim (1960), for example, in his "forerunners to sociology" book, credited Rousseau with correctly formulating the relationship of nature to society—that the latter did not emerge "naturally" from the former but was accountable to both what it indicated about human being and how, from its vantage point, society could be judged. For French philosopher and anthropologist Claude Lévi-Strauss (1966), Rousseau was the "father of ethnology," who had grasped in his *Essay on the Origins of Languages* that "to study men, one has to look close by; but in order to study man, one has to learn to cast one's eyes far off; first one has to observe the differences in order to discover the properties" (Rousseau 1998, 305). For Marxist literary theorist Fredric Jameson, what is most useful in Rousseau is not his particular ideas or opinions, but *how* he engages in political reasoning. For Jameson, Rousseau "is prepared to follow his own thinking into the unthinkable . . . [in a] process, in which confidence in reasoning leads the thinker on fearlessly into a cul-de-sac" (2009, 306). In these astonishing displays, one witnesses "a reasoning so self-punishing in the demands it makes on itself that it renders the problem insoluble and in effect incapacitates itself" (ibid.). Crucially, however, "[this] does not demonstrate the weakness of Rousseau's capacity for thought . . . so much as . . . [its] power and his frightening resolve to follow his own reasoning wherever it leads him" (307). In it, thought arrives "neither [at] impossibility nor diachronic incoherence . . . but rather [at] contradiction, the very motor power of the dialectic itself" (308).

By contrast, for Haitian anthropologist Michel-Rolph Trouillot (2003), it was Rousseau, together with the Spanish New World theologian and writer, Bartholomé de Las Casas, who most effectively mobilized "the savage slot" to implore fellow Europeans to imagine that the modernity that they tried to establish as the singular future was neither inevitable nor necessarily desirable. Rousseau, in other words, more explicitly than countless others, used a state of nature and the figure of the natural man to shore up legitimate grounds for criticism aimed at his own European contemporaries. This was powerful precisely because the stakes were clear and the arguments were explicitly counterpunctual and highly public (Trouillot 2003, 135). Their moral optimism was "sharpened . . . by Rousseau's social and political skepticism" (ibid.). Trouillot suggests that this kind of optimism, increasingly disavowed by anthropologists, was in fact the field's greatest strength. In an effort to deny the observer rights to sensibilities, many suggest that moral optimism is the same as social optimism and naïveté (135). Still, he writes, there is a need to hang on to this aspect of the history of the field since, simply put, "the alternatives are lousy" (139).

For empiricists skeptical of Rousseau's heavily inductive approach, it is worth bearing in mind, as Robert Wokler has emphasized, "No one before Rousseau came closer to conceiving human history as mankind's descent from an ape. His entirely speculative portrait of the orangutan as a kind of speechless savage in the state of nature happens, moreover, to have been coincidentally drawn with greater empirical accuracy than any description of that animal's behavior for at least the next two hundred years—that is, until the fieldwork undertaken in Southeast Asia since the late 1960's by Birute Galdikas, John MacKinnon, and Peter Rodman" (2001, 62). Buffon had insisted on a radical break between nonhuman and human animals, or on a "break in the chain of being." Pivotal for him, especially in the case of orangutans, was that they could neither speak nor reason. For Rousseau, human beings were uniquely spiritual, but language, which was long in development and had painstakingly to be learned and mastered, could not be definitive proof for humanity of people and lack of it in other creatures. The only way of showing definitively that orangutans were not protohuman was through observing the fertility of the progeny of a human-orangutan union. Although Rousseau was convinced by the fixity of species created by G-d, his controversial questions about orangutans, the closeness of savage man to animals, and portrait of radical shifts in human nature in our development, stimulated investigations into whether distinct species might be genetically similar or linked in sequential relations, research that eventually replaced the fixed species view with one of metamorphosis and transformation (58–62).

Finally, in the study of ethnomusicology, Rousseau is also cited as a founding figure (Nettl 1964, 13) for his inclusion in his well-known encyclopedia of music of examples of folk, Chinese, and Native American forms and more general rejection of the view of music as sound in favor of one through which it is conceived as comprising unique forms of culturally situated communication (Scott 1998, xxxviii). Rousseau's first published work was a song. He did first go to Paris with a new system of musical notation that he thought would ease transposing and the learning of beginners. His central involvement in debates over the relative merits of French and Italian opera generated as much notoriety as his *First Discourse* while his opera, "Le Devin du village," was performed four hundred times in fifty years, including as the first work following the reopening of the Paris Opera after the fall of the Bastille. In addition to writing most of the entries on music for Diderot's *Encyclopédia*, when he referred to "his trade" it was as a music copyist, a role through which he transcribed 11,200 pages of music in the final 7 years of his life. Finally, his "Chanson Nègre," a melody he wrote to creole folksong lyrics given to him by a gentleman named Flamanville from Normandy, who had never traveled to the islands, is seen as having offered definitive evidence that creole languages of the Francophone Caribbean developed as early as the late 1600s, significantly earlier than many scholars had previously surmised (Aurenche 1921, 13–37; Bernard 1996; Confiant 2009; De Beer 1972; Kein 2000).[91]

How is it that a figure who announced himself as challenging the moral value of work in the arts and sciences could have such a legacy? As the strands of argument that combine in this chapter hopefully suggest, Rousseau was profoundly ambivalent about the uniquely human domain of symbolic life described by Ernst Cassirer. Wishing for an ever-elusive transparency so that one might directly encounter oneself and others, he pinned such clarity on peoples who had been framed as backward. With a sense of the injustice at the misperception of the relative merits of their versus his own society, he imagined alternative possibilities, ones he considered to be less alienated. Although his framework suggested that those he praised were in fact people with incompletely realized latent faculties, including those through which political freedom is articulated, in so doing, his moral optimism combined with a sharp social pessimism producing a sense of possibility that was not naïve. Always heavily inductive and seemingly idiosyncratic, while he set much store on his efforts to be radically outside of the social worlds he inhabited, it was his syntheses of the multiple ways he occupied them that instead produced such bold and fruitful questions and ideas.[92]

In spite of the radical creativity of Rousseau's many undertakings—his genius as a generalist—if Rousseau remained only with the "noble savage," with the difficult and ultimately limited efforts to think beyond Europe by thinking before it, there would be little reason to try to creolize his ideas. He moved, if not completely, beyond this position in his *Social Contract*, suggesting that while some general wills have become mute and decayed there are others that are still emergent. He pinned such unique opportunities for legitimate governance outside of Western Europe. These gestures toward what we are calling a creolized inquiry, clearly informed by his own real and imagined personal alienation, stimulated forms of political reflection unlikely otherwise to have emerged. At the same time, Fanon's thought takes these ideas where Rousseau could not reach, exploring them in and through insights borne directly out of the contradictions and challenges of the creolized Francophone empire. Offering distinct descriptions of colonial encounters and their effects, Fanon's insights grow out of the ability to incorporate seemingly incompatible and closed but in fact porous sources of knowledge more adequately to grasp the ever-shifting terrain of human reality. These are marked by methodological, theoretical, political, and disciplinary generality in which traces of the sources from which they are derived remain evident but are not genealogically reducible to them. As such they offer a counter model to the form of political and academic retrenchment which hinders the ability to make productive juxtapositions that, often emerging out of cultural confrontation and historical rupture, can lead to more adequately universalist political postures.

2

Decolonizing Disciplinary Methods

To state reality is a wearing task.
—FRANTZ FANON[1]

Although Fanon never explicitly engaged Rousseau—he only names Rousseau once along with other liberal French writers that he mocks—Fanon shared with Rousseau an effort to challenge the ways that reason had been used to advance the singularity of particular models of desirable political arrangements and ways of being human.[2] Much like Rousseau, Fanon sought out the points where preferred frameworks confronted their opposites. However, if with Rousseau there were men and women ready to affirm themselves in refuting these approaches, for Fanon the advance and normalization of colonial relations pushed the colonized into a complex complicity. Indeed it was only when people deliberately shut out of political life and history rejected this liminal or damned location through directly challenging their unfreedom that imposed projects could be effectively resituated as one of many.

UNWELCOME ARRIVALS BEARING TRUTHS RATHER EVADED

Much like Rousseau, Fanon became a public figure through published writing bearing unwelcome truths. His *Black Skin, White Masks* (hereafter cited as *BSWM*), written in energetic bursts between 1949 and 1950, echoed Rousseau's challenges to scholars and writers driven by desires for flattering public opinion. Not focused on scholastic subtleties but questions of disalienation with ramifications for everyone, Fanon frankly stated, "No one has asked for this book, especially not those at whom it is directed" (*BSWM*, 7). Indeed, in a paradox resembling those of the previous chapter, the sign that what it offered was necessary could be measured precisely by the degree to which it was *not* sought.[3] Here and elsewhere, as I will soon explore in more detail, Fanon writes as a psychiatrist who knows that when one nears the "real issues," or those that decisively determine the situation of the relevant subjects, those most in need of facing them mobilize all of their resources of evasion.[4] Central among these, of course, is reason. Aiming at something quite different from pleasing readers, he writes, "because there are too many idiots in the world and having said that I must prove it" (*BSWM*, 7). He proceeds to treat idiocy as a symptom of widespread social and political pathologies that must be understood lest they be mended.

Whereas Rousseau had pinned his theoretical orientation and credibility to his peripheral location through which he identified with margins more generally, Fanon was a product of Lycée Schoelcher in the French territory of Martinique and of qualifying training in psychiatry in Lyons. Still, the man Fanon and his writings were, without any of his own encouragement, perceived to have come from a nowhere for which no one was prepared. Indeed, from the moment of its publication in 1952, *BSWM* was revolutionary. "Insofar as questions about blackness figured at all in the discourse of the early 1950s," writes Fanon's former intern and biographer, Alice Cherki, their discussion "was the purview of a white intelligentsia." While those who occupied the world of ideas could contemplate debates over the nature and meaning of racialization, they were "deeply unsettled when a black man took it upon himself to enter the discussion" (Cherki 2006, 26). It was not that there was no established place for black novels and poems. Francophone creative writing was emerging in the postwar period as a genre of "exotic literature" (Macey 2002, 160). Fanon's, by contrast, was a theoretical and analytical work that received a "baffled, even indignant reception."[5] Not only a "thorn" for all but the progressive Christian publications (Macey

2002, 27), it also shocked his fellow Antilleans whose largely assimilationist politics was not one that emphasized or embraced questions that drew attention to their blackness.[6]

Rousseau, as I have argued, pinned much on moments when colonized individuals symbolically rejected the offerings of supposedly irresistible French modernity.[7] These figures, without the gaps between being and seeming that defined the decadent, offered a comparative lens to gauge the losses of what were presented as desirable forms of development. In Rousseau's account, their refusals appeared as adamant as they were reflexive and unambiguous. For Fanon, the acts that Rousseau sought proved very rare. Indeed *BSWM* offers a consideration of the false dilemmas that make *choosing* alienation almost inevitable. Efforts to evade the necessity of disalienation or of dismantling these governing terms could only produce multiple failures, all of which express what it is to live in conformity with a category that one plays no role in constituting.

Fanon, like Rousseau, wrote of a world in which people were overdetermined from without. As if echoing Rousseau, Fanon reflected, "What I call middle-class society is any society that becomes rigidified in predetermined forms, forbidding all evolution, all gains, all progress, all discovery. I call middle-class a closed society in which life has no taste, in which the air is tainted, in which ideas and men are corrupt. And I think that a man who takes a stand against this death is in a sense a revolutionary" (*BSWM*, 225). Still, repressive social norms of politesse, however life-evacuating, were not his primary focus. It turned more to a particular form of racialized categorization that prematurely foreclosed both the being of the particular black and white person and their relations with others. In other words, to the sharp economic inequalities that nurtured and reproduced opaque and alienated relations of masters and slaves, Fanon adds explicit projects of dehumanization through which it is not only labor and land extracted from the colonized, but their full position as people with agency.

While one hears, Fanon remarks, that the Negro makes himself inferior, the truth is that he is made so (*BSWM*, 149). Central to this process is the governing expectation that one conform with a category "that identified [one] from a distance, without inquiry, without exchange of a single word" (Ehlen 2001, 87). In what Lewis Gordon has called a "perverse form of anonymity,"[8] these prescriptions were ubiquitous, evident as much when policemen, teachers, or employers, would say without any necessary sense of qualification, that they "knew blacks" or when physicians would address all North Africans in pidgin, angry if the relevant man or woman expressed a sense of insult in standard French (*BSWM*, 32).⁹ Indeed, Fanon emphasizes that in colonial societies, there is much greater comfort in confronting people from the colonies who offer opportunities for charitable shows of good will. While seemingly generous, however, such displays in fact cautioned the colonized person to keep his place;¹⁰ fastening her to a Negro effigy (*BSWM*, 35).¹¹ "Willy-nilly," Fanon writes, "the Negro has to wear the livery that the white man has sewed for him" (*BSWM*, 34) out of a thousand details, anecdotes and stories (*BSWM*, 111), the "Negro is a toy in the white man's hands" (*BSWM*, 140).¹² As laboratories tried earnestly to produce denegrification serums, Fanon observed that being black was not provided by "residual sensations and perceptions primarily of a tactile, vestibular, kinesthetic, and visual character." It was instead the product of a particular set of commitments: "Let us have the courage to say outright . . . the racist creates his inferior—the feeling of inferiority of the colonized is the correlative to the European's [whether he be in Martinique or South Africa] feeling of superiority" (*BSWM*, 93). Although he had originally planned to confine this exploration to the Antilles, he was compelled to see that in spite of the variety of nationalities embodied in black, wherever he or she went, the Negro remained a Negro (*BSWM*, 172–72). Fanon commented, "the Negro is in demand . . . but only if he is made palatable in a certain way" (*BSWM*, 176).

Ontological studies of the condition of the black person could not illuminate it, Fanon challenged, "not only because the black man must be black in relation to the white man"—as racial positions are necessarily relational and incoherent when divorced from these constitutive frameworks—but also because the relation of the black to the white person "does not have a converse" (*BSWM*, 110). The categories and positions "white" and "black" while complementary are not symmetrical: For the black person in the colonies, the only *real* eyes are white. It is under their gaze that this new genus, the Negro, appears.¹³ White men and women, by contrast, need not "meet the black" person's eyes or, by implication, see themselves with a black third-person consciousness. "[Alterity] for the white man is always another white man," never a black person, who is not an Other but only a space of projection (Cherki 2006, 32).¹⁴ In particular, the form that projection takes is a mechanism through which "anything that I find in myself that is reprehensible or embarrassing, I ascribe to someone else" (*BSWM*, 97). As a result, all that is repressed and undesirable, incompatible with an idealized racial white identity, together form a caricature "Negro" that amounts to a psycho-existential deviation or "aberration of the affect in the psyche of Africana peoples" (Henry 2005, 97). Marilyn Nissim-Sabat (2010) insists that the assimilating of whiteness, a contingent category, to the very definition of what it is to be essentially human, is at the core of antiblack racism. It tells people who know themselves to be otherwise to live a subhuman status in relation to that of whites.

At the core of colonized black subjectivity, then, is the necessity of negotiating a terrain in which one is *a real person* in direct proportion to one's ascent toward (absent) whiteness and renunciation of one's blackness. Whether through language or relations of love, one might, as a Negro, try to move away from the subordinate position attributed to him or her through assuming French culture and through it the "weight of civilization" (*BSWM*, 18). In colonial situations in which a people experiences "an inferiority complex . . . created by the death and burial of its local cultural originality" (ibid.), from black to white "is the course of mutation. One is white as one is rich, as one is beautiful, as one is intelligent" (*BSWM*, 51–52).

One does not encounter, in other words, Rousseau's expectations of the readily resistant "savage" or even Jean-Paul Sartre's that black poets would turn against the French language. Instead, Fanon writes plainly, "It is normal for the Antillean to be anti-Negro . . . [having] taken over all the archetypes belonging to the European . . . There is no help for it: I am a white man. For unconsciously I distrust what is black in me . . . When I am home, my mom sings me French love songs in which there is never a word about Negroes. When I disobey . . . I am told to 'stop acting like a nigger'" (*BSWM*, 191). In every society there were magazines, games, and films that directed expressions of aggression. In Europe and its colonies, these were written by white men for little white men. Showing explorers, adventurers, and missionaries facing the danger of being eaten by wicked Negroes;[15] these were similarly read by black children who identified equally intensely with the protagonists and victors (*BSWM*, 145).[16] Fanon writes that in Europe the Negro has the function of symbolizing the lower emotions and baser inclinations, the dark side of the soul. Indeed the color black symbolizes evil, sin, wretchedness, death, war, or famine; all birds of prey are black. When one taps the unconscious of most white men and women, the black emerges as the torturer, as Satan, in association with shadows and with dirt, with sin and bad character, with darkness, abysmal depths, with the ruining of reputation. He writes, "In Martinique, whose collective unconscious makes it a European country, when a 'blue' Negro—a coal-black one—comes to visit, one reacts at once: 'What bad luck is he bringing'" (*BSWM*, 190–91). Still this collective unconscious is not a function of "cerebral heredity . . . [but] the unreflected imposition of a culture." Antillean boys would talk constantly of the dangerous Senegalese, only realizing, when in Europe, that "the Negro" included them too (*BSWM*, 148).[17]

Between insignificant black insularity or the only way out "into the white world" (*BSWM*, 51), if appraised solely in terms of his assimilation, the Antillean desiring to stand with the real and universal will of course take on the French language and manner, wanting "to emphasize a rupture" (*BSWM*, 36).[18] He cannot avoid a choice: "The white man's language gave honorary citizenship"; French was the key that promised to open barred doors.[19] The rare Martinican might cling to his dialect, "knowing where he is from," but doing so trapped him in a sequestered particularity synonymous the world over with barbarism. It was no different in matters of love, where proverbs and petty rules from childhood onward governed choices. These were well captured as enunciated publicly by teachers and mothers in the following characteristic words, "It is always essential to avoid falling back into the pit of niggerhood, and every woman in the Antilles, whether in a casual flirtation or in a serious affair, is determined to select the least black of the men" (*BSWM*, 47–48). Antillean women who traveled to France without any reservations equated marrying a black man with impossibility: "Get out of that and then deliberately go back? Thank you, no" (ibid.).[20] It was not that individual black men did not have good qualities, it was just so much better to be white.[21] For all this, of course, few such women would ultimately find that for which they waited.

Perhaps in the most painful of contrasts with Rousseau is Fanon's figure of Jean Veneuse, the protagonist of René Maran's 1947 autobiographical novel, *Un homme pareil aux autres*, and one of many "little Hottentots whose parents, in the hope of making real Frenchmen out of them, transplant them to France too early." For "their own good" weeping parents turn them over to "gloomy" schools in the French countryside. In Veneuse's case, it was "to this schooling that [his] character [owed] its inner melancholy" and fear of social contact (*BSWM*, 74). A negative-aggressive type, nursing past disappointments and cultivating a secret zone of bitterness, he assured the near impossibility of positive experiences that could compensate for the past lack of self-esteem. With an obsessive feeling of exclusion, he was always ready to be rejected, subconsciously doing everything to achieve just that catastrophe. Because experiencing his parents' choice as a form of abandonment, he dreaded showing himself as he actually was for fear of being disappointing and maintained an insatiable desire for proof of absolute and incontrovertible love (*BSWM*, 77–78). Although Veneuse was an abandonment neurotic who happened to be black, who would, in the absence of antiblackness, have manufactured principles for his own exclusion (*BSWM*, 80), his initial turning over to the school was overdetermined by racialized conditions in which his parents (and many others like them) conceived of what it meant to create opportunities for their children as entrusting them to boarding schools through which it could be assured that they would remain untainted by the potential liabilities that were their birth parents.

Veneuse is a primary example of a more general observation by Fanon, one that would again disappoint Rousseau: If his psychic structure is weak, when a Negro comes in contact with the white world there is a collapse of the ego. He will stop being an actional person. His goal instead will be for the Other (in this case necessarily a white Other, since all meaningful Others, by definition, are racialized white) to give him worth or self-esteem. This is the condition of the Negro as opposed to the black man or woman, as already suggested. As the site of projection, the Negro *is* comparison. For the vast majority, this means to be constantly preoccupied with self-evaluation and questions of merit when encountering another. Fanon writes, "The Antilleans have no inherent values of their own, they are always contingent on the presence of the Other" (*BSWM*, 211). This Antillean will ask if the other is more intelligent or darker skinned or more respectable with the implication that one has no inherent worth. Instead one's own position is based on relations of dependence. Greedy for security, others appear as mere instruments that should enable "me to realize my subjective security" (*BSWM*, 212). In sum, "Everything that an Antillean does is done for the Other . . . because it is the Other who corroborates him" (*BSWM*, 213). Fanon emphasizes that if there are some exceptions, this phenomenon is too widespread and predictable to be understood as an individual failing. It is rather a function of a particular environment, of a neurotic society of comparison.

Where being, value, reality, and possibility are white, it is inevitable to try—in whatever ways might be available, whether through one's chosen language or desired lover—to move in that direction, even if it is, by definition, not ultimately accessible to one. In such circumstances, even when a particular dilemma or issue is not racial, because of the racialized nature of meaning, everything becomes racially encoded. Fanon observes that it is only if one has been challenged as a man or woman that one begins to ask if one is a man or a woman.[22] Similarly, "I suffer from not being white" only to the degree that as a black or colonized person I am "a parasite on the world . . . a brute beast, that my people and I are like a walking dung-heap that disgustingly fertilizes sweet sugar cane and silky cotton, that I have no use in the world" (*BSWM*, 98). Then I will try to make myself white, to try to compel others to acknowledge that I am human. Still, the infernal circle is inescapable: "I am liked in spite of my color and so too when I am disliked" (*BSWM*, 117).

The sad irony of course is that those who exceed racialized expectations have it no easier. Those who "speak well," Fanon observes, are treated with suspicion; the black who quotes Montesquieu appears "to be starting something."[23] Although such men and women and black professionals more generally seemed the obvious contradiction to statements such as "Negroes are savages; Negroes are brutes or illiterates," Fanon wrote that a particularly contractual relationship clung to them. For one, their exceptional status was always remarked upon: they were not doctors or teachers but the "Negro doctor" or a "Negro teacher" but, even more significantly, their post came with an implicit warning: if they made any mistakes, there would be no such future opportunities for *any* blacks. As Fanon put it, "As long as everything went well, he was praised to the skies, but look out, no nonsense, under any conditions!" (*BSWM*, 117).[24] While white men and women succeeded as a race and failed as individuals, with black or colonized people, it was the reverse.

STANDING OUTSIDE OF TIME AS PETRIFICATION

Fanon, unlike Rousseau, declared himself to be "irreducibly" a man of his times. He could and would not try to step outside of them, instead engaging in the opposite extreme. Rather than always being the foreigner, writing from elsewhere, to the dismay of some and delight of others, he made the places to which he moved his own. Not only through identifications expressed in descriptions of himself as the Martinican-Algerian revolutionary psychologist and philosopher, he also took direct responsibility for and put his manifold insights and skills in the service of what his new homes would become.[25] Whereas Rousseau had longed for the position of those occupying earlier moments in his secularized theodicy, Fanon saw the unique predicament of the colonized as having been thrown outside of historical time into a liminal condition of damnation. He was in fact exploring the conditions for reentering precisely this temporal flow, of being resurrected from the unique petrification that accompanied imperial projects for the vanquished. He thus emphasizes from the outset of *BSWM*: "Every human problem must be considered from the standpoint of time. Ideally, the present will always contribute to the building of the future. And this future is not the future of the cosmos but rather the future of my century, my country, my existence. . . . The future should be an edifice supported by living men" (12–13). To be an agent, capable of being actional required literally "being present" to all of what Rousseau rejected in the name of independence. This is opposed to being stuck in another's time or drama. Indeed, as Ato Sekyi-Otu has emphasized, the lamentation at the core of dehumanization is not over the "damage done to antique particulars in their ancestral and wondrous uniqueness" but instead the "deviation from the regular predicament of human intercourse, normal prospects" (2011, 50).

This was one of the many difficulties with the Négritude movement, as Fanon understood it. Turning to it followed his much cited account of an encounter with the young boy who pointed him out, declaring, "Look, a *nègre!*" Up to this point in the text, Fanon traced effort after effort to evade being the "two-dimensional object" of colonial reasoning.[26] Frozen by the words of the child, he is suddenly "imprisoned in this overwhelming objectivity" (*BSWM*, 109). Collapsing under the weight of cannibalism, slave-ships, tom toms, into a negrified thing, he seeks refuge. Rather than refusing negrification, he assigns it oppositional value that he embraces. If emotion, affect, corporeality, and spirit were what it was to be black, so be it! Fanon and the black person struggling to be a human person about whom he writes will *be* the essence that is supposedly theirs, that at which, because of their supposed nature, they can excel. In so doing, Fanon challenges at once a supremacy of a version of whiteness that supposedly is without this black character and affirms a version of black superiority in a "descent into blackness" that emphasized the limitations of European, colonial man.

A prime response to the racialization that I have been describing, Négritude refurnished that which was ascribed to blackness through renouncing the imperial present and future in the name of a mystical past that antedated them (*BSWM*, 14). Fanon emphasizes how much he *needed* Négritude; that as he groped after a reason that kept eluding him, it hailed him, offering a bath in the irrational. "Since no agreement was possible on the level of reason," he describes throwing himself back toward unreason in the form of a challenge: "It was up to the white man to be more irrational than I" (*BSWM*, 123–24). Going back "no longer to sources but to The Source" (*BSWM*, 126)[27] in a rhythmic attitude of ruling the world with intuition in an abandon or state of communion, Fanon writes, "The white man wants the world; he wants it for himself alone. . . . But there exist other values that fit only my forms. Like a magician, I robbed the white man of 'a certain world,' forever after lost to him and his." Here, much as with Rousseau, Négritude emphasized the losses inherent in European modernity and civilization, in the move toward complex societies and increased cerebreality. Blackness remained, by contrast, all that had, in such movements "forward" been left behind. Such a move, if only for a brief moment, rocked the "white man backward . . . as I was told by a friend who was a teacher in the United States, 'The presence of the Negroes besides the whites is in a way an insurance policy on humanness. When the whites feel that they have become too mechanized, they turn to the men of color and ask them for a little human sustenance'" (*BSWM*, 129).[28]

The victory was, however, fleeting. Although "rummag[ing] through the antiquity of the black man" demonstrated that Fanon "belonged to a race that had already been working in gold and silver two thousand years ago" and that knew how to "build houses, govern empires, erect cities, mine for metals, weave cotton, forge steel," previous Negro civilizations, however grand and anticipatory, did not confer patents of humanity on contemporary black people nor guide them through the present moment (*BSWM*, 225). What is more, even in such civilized forms, blackness here occupied the place of the species' infancy, Europe's prehistory—something for which, from the distance of transcendence, one could feel a fond affection. Fanon writes, "I will be told, now and then when we are worn out by our lives in big buildings, we will turn to you as we do to our children—to the innocent, the ingenuous, the spontaneous. . . . You are so real in your life—so funny, that is. Let us run away for a little while from our ritualized, polite civilization and let us relax, bend to those heads, those adorably expressive faces. In a way, you reconcile us with ourselves" (*BSWM*, 132). The very transparency that Rousseau sought is here reinscribed in the most patronizing of terms. Perhaps worst of all, Fanon's unreason was countered with "real reason" (ibid.) revealing Négritude in its relativity (*BSWM*, 133), as a dependent point of comparison with the terms it sought to counter.

WHEN WORLDS OF MEANING ARE COLONIAL WORLDS

Fanon, like Rousseau, revealed an evil that he has discovered, but his purpose in portraying it was explicitly to clear the ground for its destruction. Doing so required making use of scholarly resources, but ones, he suggested, that had been colonized. Not only was reason never wholly independent, abstract, or apolitical, it was also necessarily part of the meaningful world of empire, one that sought to make human beings determined and predictable, rather than contingent creatures who could will for things to be otherwise. Fanon sought in describing these phenomena and dilemmas to make others also *feel* them. What led some to call his *BSWM* eclectic exemplified for others precisely the improvisational attitude necessary to capture the multidimensionality of human lived experience. Fanon writes, "What are by common consent called the human sciences have their own drama. Should one postulate a type for human reality and describe its psychic modalities only through deviation from it, or should one not rather strive unremittingly for a concrete and ever new understanding of man?"

Like Rousseau, Fanon was concerned about the ways in which the supposed authoritativeness of some brands of empiricism, of dubiously collected facts, could block the larger project of understanding human beings, obscuring the clarifying of what it was, in fact, that we should be endeavoring to understand. If with Rousseau, fact was pitted against right for the sake of legitimating despotism, in Fanon, these were linked to problematic hypotheses that naturalized and biologized racism, suggesting that feelings of inferiority were lying dormant within black bodies, activated, not created by colonization (*BSWM*, 99). Fanon emphasizes, "What matters for us is not to collect facts and behavior, but to find their meaning" (*BSWM*, 168). In the absence of such meaning, one participates in "an endless task, the cataloging of reality. We accumulate facts, we discuss them, but with every line that is written, with every statement that is made, one has the feeling of incompleteness" (*BSWM*, 172).[29]

This was achieved with the assistance of the mistaken pursuit of a particular brand of objectivity, one that tied rigor to rendering human beings mere mechanisms without the agency that could introduce either contingency or meaning into the social world or a capacity to undertake its deliberate transformation. Fanon explicitly rejects this central tenet (and with it any valorization of human beings as least corrupted when acting most instinctively), that "lead[s] only in one direction: to make man admit that he is nothing, absolutely nothing—and that he must put an end to the narcissism on which he relies in order to imagine that he is different from the other 'animals'" (*BSWM*, 22). Here we are reminded of Rousseau's earlier challenge: whether what we might reveal under the name of "science" is not a product of the very social forces that also make such investigations possible. Fanon refuses to so surrender, "grasping [his] narcissism with both hands, [he] turn[s] [his] back on the degradation of those who would make man a mere mechanism" (*BSWM*, 23).

One might sum up Fanon's reworking of the most central problems posed by method in Rousseau in one of his closing Marxist pleas: "That the tool never possess the man" (231). Indeed he prefaces the text in a spirit much like the opening of Rousseau's *Second Discourse*: "It is good form to introduce a work in psychology with a statement of its methodological point of view. I shall be derelict. I leave methods to the botanists and mathematicians. There is a point at which methods devour themselves. . . . I believe that the fact of the juxtaposition of the white and black races has created a massive psychoexistential complex. I hope by analyzing it to destroy it" (*BSWM*, 12). In spite of the exhaustiveness of much psychological literature, its authors often, in seeking lawlike rules and formulas, eliminated precisely what makes the human subject peculiar. In so doing, such practitioners cloaked the very contorted agency that Fanon sought to uncover in the most constrained of conditions. As Peter Caws aptly described: "One convenient way of escaping responsibility for unfortunate social facts (private property and wage labor, for example) is to regard them as relations between people and things: The capitalist is related to his property, so the expropriated worker vanishes from the equation; the worker is related to his work, so the factory owner similarly vanishes. Marx insists that both are disguised relations between people and other people: The owner of private property deprives, and the wage slave is enslaved to, human beings in flesh and blood, not economic abstractions" (1992, 296).[30]

Race is one such abstraction, a key element in "an obdurate material social reality . . . which . . . reordered the world . . . [penning in the racially subjugated] to an unwilled particularity" (2011, 53). Its efficacy was reason for special caution, to keep it from being "permitted to provide the final vocabulary for self-understanding and moral reasoning" to mask the "important [and distinctly human preoccupations] beneath what is contingent" (53). As Lewis Gordon describes, "In Fanon's view, however universal the hostile structures against black presence may be, we must also remember that all of those structures are *situationally* lived by people of flesh and blood" (45). Just as flesh and blood play an indispensable role in maintaining them, they might choose not to. It is not that such a task is ever easy or certain, only that recognizing our freedom and agency requires also seeing how we might help to cement arrangements we would not devise. Such an attention to responsibility, even when heavily mediated by institutional norms, extended crucially to the role of scholar and writer. Fanon exhibited precisely this orientation when he asked in "The North African Syndrome" (1967d, 3), "Have I not, because of what I have done or failed to do, contributed to an impoverishment of human reality? . . . Have I at all times demanded and brought the man that is in me?"

The challenge with such a humanistic standard is that it is pursued within imperial societies, those that in dominating others cannot avoid convincing themselves of the latter's rightful subordination. Fanon insists, "It is not possible to enslave men without logically making them inferior through and through. And racism is only the emotional, affective, sometimes intellectual explanation of this inferiorization" (1967e, 40). Remarkably, the outcomes are usually highly rational. Indeed, Fanon states plainly that the racist in a culture with racism is normal, someone whose economic relations and other ideas are in harmony. It follows that in colonial circumstances, those who are antiracist are an aberration that cannot be treated as a rule. One cannot, writes Fanon, require that men be against the "prejudices of [their] group," that they, through principles or abstract commitments, deliberately embrace disharmony. To do so would be irrational. Avoiding treating racism as a consequence of the "flawless logic" of needing to rationalize one country drawing its substance from another is to individualize relations overdetermined by conquest and to seek behavior change that misses the more basic point that within colonial circumstances (41), "Every Frenchman in Algeria is at the present time an enemy soldier" (1967c, 81).[31]

Processes through which conquered groups are made inferior rely centrally on what Fanon calls *deculturation*. "[The] negative of a more gigantic work of economic, and even biological, enslavement" (1967e, 31), the devaluing of language, dress, and culture of the oppressed is too consistent to reduce to the behavior of individual psyches encountering the unfamiliar (33). Involved instead—parallel with raids, expropriation and bloodshed—is the systematic demolition of indigenous systems of reference. For in the "sacking of cultural patterns," is the "destructuring" of "social panoramas" or of independent collective orientations and viable distinct points of view (ibid.). Fanon emphasizes: "The setting up of the colonial system does not of itself bring about the death of the native culture. Historic observation reveals, on the contrary, that the aim sought is rather a continued agony than a total disappearance of the pre-existing culture. This culture, once living and open to the future, becomes closed, fixed in the colonial status, caught in the yoke of oppression. Both present and mummified, it testifies against its members. . . . The apathy so universally noted among colonial peoples is but the logical consequence of this operation" (34). To reproach colonized communities as "inert" is, in Fanon's estimation, "utterly dishonest." Settlers erect archaic institutions patterned after caricatured versions of "formerly fertile institutions" (ibid.). Appearing to embody respect for the "personality of the subjugated people," these are "tantamount to utter contempt . . . elaborate sadism" (ibid.). For "honoring culture" in such instances is to practice ongoing mummification that undercuts the possibility of creating conditions that allow for open, permeable values "incarnated by men." Recognition here instead reflects a deliberate effort "to confine, to imprison, to harden" through a maximal objectification and simplification that renders cultural confrontation impossible. What is rather achieved is a juxtaposition of a colonial culture that is dynamic, growing, and coherently structured against an amalgamation of curiosities, characteristics and habits, decontextualized and without structure—the kind of "retentions" that, in Nigel Bolland's account, creolization seeks to avoid making the primary representative of New World black cultures.

In such a cultural battlefield, generations of colonized people faced the "choice" between "retraction of one's being" into a contrived traditionalism and a "frenzied attempt at identification with the colonizer" (*A Dying Colonialism*). It is only with the forceful positing of an alternative trajectory that seeks to move beyond colonial stability, that the coordinates of complicit cooperation and unilateral resistance will be dislodged and with it the inability of colonized people to be sources of independent signification who can ascribe meaning to particularly symbolically charged cultural elements from the head scarf to instances of Western medicine.

Fanon documented examples of work that while honestly studying colonial societies in accord with existing standards of rigor was completely divorced from an understanding of the real nature of such predicaments. It is worth emphasizing that like W. E. B. Du Bois, Fanon did not take the position that a subjective experience is the unique monopoly of any one group. Indeed he writes, "it would give me no pleasure to announce that the black problem is my problem and mine alone and that it is up to me to study it" (*BSWM*, 86). It is precisely because such understanding is possible that he offers so scathing an assessment of Octavio Mannoni's *Prospero and Caliban: The Psychology of Colonization*.

It was not a question of what Mannoni had failed to gather. If anything, it was his conception of objectivity that threatened to lead him into error. As Fanon says of him, it seemed that he had "not tried to feel himself into the despair of the man of color confronting the white man;"[32] that he had not grasped the dilemmas that we have begun to consider. It is clear, observes Fanon, that the Malagasy has only two choices: to be dependent or suffer from an inferiority complex: either he stays in his place or he aspires to assimilate and is rejected for doing so (*BSWM*, 93). While legitimately concerned with redressing the shortcomings of earlier ethnographic work, Mannoni, argues Fanon, proceeded in his own right to seal the Malagasy into their own customs with their dependency on their ancestors and strong tribal characteristics, deliberately ignoring that "since Gallieni, the Malagasy had ceased to exist" (*BSWM*, 94). Indeed if Martians were to colonize Earthlings—and Fanon emphasizes, "not to initiate them into Martian culture but to colonize them"—we would be doubtful of the persistence of "any earth personality" (*BSWM*, 95). Herein lies Fanon's larger claim: where colonization rather than simply domination is the aim, prior horizons and psychological mechanisms are shattered. From this point forward, other Malagasy cannot constitute a legitimate point of view, a defining other. It is only colonizing eyes that bestow reality. However generous or humane French pioneers may have been, this formed the structure of their arrival: with it, one became French or disappeared. However, achieving Frenchness for the colonized was never fully possible. Without an analysis of this, Fanon wrote, analyses like Mannoni's were "condemned to falsehood, to absurdity, to nullity" (*BSWM*, 97).

Not only failing to problematize how colonialism radically interrupted symbolic worlds, Mannnoni also exhibited precisely the form of imperial reasoning that we were just discussing, placing responsibility for their colonization on the vanquished, suggesting their political fate was, in a sense, welcomed. For Mannoni, after all, not all peoples could be colonized, only those who experienced a need for dependency. The implication was that wherever Europeans successfully founded colonies these outcomes had been unconsciously expected or desired, even foretold in local legend. By contrast, those who landed in the role of settlers were driven by an authority complex that led them constantly to seek to flee worlds of Others who had to be respected and engaged. Wanting instead a world without men (*BSWM*, 108), with creatures beneath their own status, they found those who sought instead only to be obedient, in relations that satisfied all parties (*BSWM*, 99). No, says Fanon: how can welcoming European guests and even suggesting that their arrival was anticipated amount to the unconscious awaiting of a white master? This conclusion could only be one overdetermined by *ex post facto* outcomes and their conceptual arsenal.

Central to problematizing the way sciences were used to lend credibility and authority to exploitative projects was to rearticulate them as always already enmeshed in political contestation. If Rousseau sought to illuminate the decadence of eighteenth-century France by juxtaposing it with the "savage" conceived as its prehistory, Fanon, as Nelson Maldonado Torres (2008) has suggested, illuminates the human being and the human sciences through the questions and circumstances in which subhumans are created. Still, Fanon's orientation toward scholars like Mannoni and to many of Europe's leading philosophical minds—Freud, Lacan, Hegel, and Sartre—was not one of reaction. He drew on these theories where illuminating at the same time as pointing out where they in fact became particular or where they failed to realize that what they described of elements of the life world of Europe did not extend to its underside. But, Maldonado Torres insists, this was far more profound than a relativist upsurge and in this sense not the equivalent of the Négritude that Fanon had embraced and then challenged. The aim was not to point out that what "may be valid 'there' in the territory of the colonizer" was "not 'here' in the territory of the colonized." Instead it was to reveal the codependence and mutual reliance of the two in ways that most scholarship obscured by exposing a double world of theorizing. Maldonado Torres states, "Dominant European approaches are generally mistaken not only because they do not apply in the colonies, but also, and more fundamentally, because they cannot even register how the very condition of coloniality reveals another side of themselves" (2008, 99).

This brings me back to my discussion in Chapter 1 of the feat of restructuring an economy around colonies that remain absent from one's national narratives; of the triumph of divorcing what are framed as quintessentially Enlightenment ideals from the international slave and colonial routes through which they spread through the globe. For Fanon the work of intellectuals must be to unravel the terms that make these victories appear natural or inevitable. The colonial condition therefore is, as Maldonado

Torres writes, a fundamental "axis of reflection" since it is within the colonial condition that "humanity itself produces its opposite . . . it serves as a referent to test the radicalism of ways of thinking and behaving that aim to give expression to what is most distinctively human" (2008, 100). In other words, against Rousseau, for Fanon, the colonized person is not a key subject of study because somehow untouched. It is precisely the opposite: It is in the relation of the colonizer to the colonized and the worlds that erupt between them that we begin to understand what becomes of the human being in the modern world and what, under such circumstances, can be done to and with freedom.

FORGING METHODOLOGICAL ALTERNATIVES

The implications of this are not, however, as is so frequently assumed, particular to one or even most communities of color. No, the liberation of the person of color is inseparable from the rearticulation of the project of all humankind, from forging a decolonial humanism. As I have already stated, racial identities are coconstituting, making little sense in isolation from one another. The project of unraveling their structure therefore demands meditations on reason and the uses to which it has been put through a dialectical demonstration of how one studies and understands what it is to live in a multiracial world in which the singular normative standard is white. Much like Rousseau, Fanon's orienting skepticism to the spirit and aims of most of the social scientific work that surrounded him formed the basis for his own methodological innovations. To illuminate his predicament, Fanon must take the reader through stages of failed efforts to live with dignity without undertaking the more fundamental project of "restructuring the world." The neat application of methods derived from the natural sciences and even the resources of brands of philosophy that are tone deaf to the cultural specificity of the worlds out of which they emerged cannot be adequate for exploring the nature of such ambiguities and how it is that they are suffered through. Colonial worlds like racist ones are in fact highly rational, with rules and logics that are discerned and negotiated. Fanon's aim here, as with Rousseau, is not simply for one to register the logical cogency of what is said, but to be moved by it in ways that alter one's relationship to the people and world around one.

Fanon had found for all his efforts to be a good tactician, aiming to rationalize the world and show white men and women how they "were mistaken," victory was elusive. Even as scientists reluctantly conceded that black people were human with the same morphology and histology as others, with a heart on the left side, the concession was highly abstract. As Fanon put it, "on certain points the white man remained intractable. Under no condition did he wish any intimacy between the races, for it is a truism that [race] mixing lowers the physical and mental level, should be avoided until we understand it better" (*BSWM*, 119–20). Fanon described this result as making clear that he had to change his tune; the victory of reason played cat and mouse with and made a fool of him. Truth itself, perhaps here parting from Rousseau, could not be apolitical. As Nigel Gibson writes, "Indeed the colonized can respond only to the living lie of colonialism with another lie. The colonizers are liars because they refuse to tell the truth. For Fanon, by this denial the colonized remain true to themselves. Fanon claimed no Truth; truth was commitment—truth was to take a stand against the oppressive 'reality'" (2011b, 7).[33] He does not, however, as some Négritude writers might have it, pose against this a black truth, but instead aims to dismantle the entanglement of truth and race or the politics of truth in a colonial context (ibid.). Without such reconstruction, objectivity is always directed against the colonized.

While we have seen that he introduced his first published book with an explicit challenge to method, with problematizing how one undertakes endeavors of inquiry through emphasizing the uniqueness of human being, it would be misleading to suggest that Fanon's inquiries were then *method-less*. Having initially submitted the text that became *Black Skin, White Masks* as a thesis to complete his medical school training entitled, "Essay for the Disalienation of the Black,"[34] he was met with discouragement: Writes Ehlen, "Their idea of a clinical study did not entail observing one's own subjective conscious reactions and extrapolating these to a generalized pathology . . . furthermore Fanon's ideas of racial psychology were far too radical to be appreciated by a standard psychiatric faculty in 1950" (2000, 97–98). While initially disappointed, he quickly revised the manuscript as a book that he submitted for publication by Seuil,[35] choosing another topic for his thesis.[36] At the time, it was determined that he would need a preface for the book as he was not much known outside of Lyon. His first choice was Francois Jeanson, then twenty-nine and a contributing editor to *Les Temps Modernes*. Jeanson, as recounted in his afterward to the 1965 Seuil edition, later relayed, "Having found [Fanon's] manuscript exceptionally interesting, I committed the error of telling him so" (Ehlen 2000, 102). When Fanon indignantly replied, "You mean, for a Negro, it isn't so bad," Jeanson showed Fanon to the door which increased Fanon's respect for him. The two became lasting friends.

Today some view the work as juvenile (Cherki 2006, 25); others at the time of publication and subsequently found it opaque, difficult to categorize in terms of genre (Macey 2002,160–61), or too reliant on psychoanalytical literatures to make for comfortable or easily digestible reading (ibid.). Macey, drawing on Lévi-Strauss, decribed it as an exercise in bricolage, a term "used to describe how myths are assembled from the material that are at hand: the word literally means 'do it yourself'" (162); in this case, drawing from the phenomenology of Sartre and Merleau-Ponty, the Négritude writers, the psychiatry in which he had just trained forging syntheses that some call "seamless" (Henry 2005) and others as "far from being smooth" (Macey 163).[37] Aiming not only at elucidating particular arguments but at moving his readers, Fanon proceeds at both philosophical and psychoanalytical levels, in what Paget Henry has called a "complex and synthetic methodology" (2005, 96), that Maldonado Torres describes as "a transdisciplinary endeavor that requires the reformulation and reconfiguration of existing disciplines and the creation of new ones" (2008, 129). Henry Louis Gates observes, "It may be a matter of judgment whether his writings are riven with contradictions or richly dialectical, polyvocal and multivalent. They are in any event highly porous to interpretation [so that] the readings they elicit are . . . of unfailing interest" (2010, 86).

Few who seriously engage it do not emphasize what he called his "sociogenic" analyses. Rather than offering a portrait of the origin of the species as we saw in Rousseau, these analyses aimed to elucidate the constitution of meaning by emphasizing the coconstitution of social structures and individual choices in the larger rejection of the view that societies can be studied like inert beings[38] and that tried in its very approach to the human subject to capture our features—multidimensional and free, even if highly determined.

If Rousseau's primary concerns were with the curbing of freedom and erosion of morality, Fanon makes liberation his first philosophy (Maldonado Torres 2008, 130). He writes, "I will say, however, that every criticism of that which is implies a solution, if indeed one can propose a solution to one's fellow—to a free being. What I insist on is that the poison must be eliminated once and for all" (Maldonado Torres 2008, 62). It was erroneous to distinguish among or rank forms of exploitations since all were applied "against the same 'object': man."³⁹ Exploring their structure abstractly was to "turn one's back on the major, basic problem, which is that of restoring man to his proper place" (*BSWM*, 88).

Although Fanon suggests that he had waited for his ideas to cease smoldering before writing them down, since he wanted neither to hurl them nor ignite fervor (which brings fire, famine, and contempt for man and is the weapon of the impotent), he does write in a way that he ascribes to Jean-Paul Sartre of "[grabbing] you by the guts" (*BSWM*, 228), so that to reveal is the beginning of the process of annihilating what is described (*BSWM*, 2–3). It would be dishonest, he writes early on (*BSWM*, 86), to pretend that he is objective, if objectivity presumes an orientation of affective neutrality. He describes his own text as a "mirror with a progressive infrastructure, in which it will be possible to discern the Negro on the road to disalienation" (*BSWM*, 184).

Fanon therefore suffused his studies with the touch of the human subject.

It is remarkable that much has been said about the lyrical quality of the writing of both Rousseau and Fanon. Commentators like Peter Gay have suggested that Rousseau "wrote too well for his own good"; Fanon's writing, many said, could not leave one unchanged. In fact, both men, considered two of the best writers in the canon of political theory, composed in much the same way: through dictation.⁴⁰ Rousseau often froze with pen in hand. He would compose easily as he strolled or craft and recraft sentences and paragraphs in his head when enduring yet another night's insomnia.⁴¹ In the morning, Therese Levasseur's mother (his mother-in-law of sorts) would take it all down. Fanon also would speak aloud as he paced, while his wife Josie typed, trying to capture "the rhythm of a body in motion and cadences of the breathing voice" (Cherki 2006, 27).⁴² When Jeanson had suggested that Fanon clarify a particular phrase, Fanon replied, "I cannot explain that phrase more fully. When I write things like that, I am trying to touch my reader affectively, or in other words irrationally, almost sensually. For me, words have a charge. I find myself incapable of escaping the bite of a word, the vertigo of a question mark" (quoted in Macey 2002, 159). He went on to say that, like Césaire, he wanted "to sink beneath the stupefying lava of words that have the color of quivering flesh" (ibid.).⁴³ Cherki writes, "The profound singularity of this work, its subject matter notwithstanding, arises from the writing itself. Its originality follows from its urgency to convey an experience by going one-on-one with words . . . [he] wished to write inside the sensory dimension of language in order to give rise to a new way of thinking that would depend on something more than conceptual jockeying" (2006, 27). In other words, what both sought to convey was better communicated through spoken language, through bringing the reader into a living conversation, with the urgency and precision absent in the quiet composure of the individual study. Writing in such a way embodied a form of invitation. One could not simply put the text down and ponder. Instead the work awaited one's answer, one's contribution to an unfolding and open discussion.[44]

For Fanon, this offered an alternative form of education, one that sought "to teach the Negro not to be the slave of their archetypes" (*BSWM*, 35).[45] He reflected, "The white world, the only honorable one, barred me from all participation. [I] was expected to behave like a black man—or at least like a nigger. I shouted a greeting to the world and was told to stay within bounds, to go back where I belonged" (114–15). To the crippled man who advised Fanon's brother to resign himself "to [his] color" the way he had adapted to his stump (140), Fanon refused. He therefore would also tell the drawn and quartered Martinican man of comparison that it was the environment that was responsible for his delusion. The obvious implication? Simply stated, "the end of the world" (216) or, in actual fact, of *this* and other worlds constructed around the preservation of overly constrained false dilemmas. Fanon would say much the same to the waiting lighter skinned black women who sought to transform her condition by ascending the hierarchy of pigmentations: this is not a personal flaw best responded to with moralism; instead, "another solution is possible" (82).

Rather than acting out the inevitable, in what simultaneously constituted "normality" and "failure," the answer was to eradicate the foundational terms of the dilemma (*BSWM*, 100). Fanon writes, "There are two ways out of this conflict. Either I ask others to pay no attention to my skin, or else I want them to be aware of it. I try then to find value for what is bad. The other is to terminate this neurotic situation, in which I am compelled to choose an unhealthy, conflictual solution, fed on fantasies, hostile, inhuman" (197). This demanded rising above the "absurd drama that others have staged around me," "rejecting the two terms that are equally unacceptable, and through one human being, to reach out for the universal" (ibid.). He, and by implication other "Negroes" and white people would be disalienated as they refused to seal themselves away "in the materialized Tower of the Past" (226). This in turn meant rejecting the present as definitive (ibid.); of demanding human behavior from others and not renouncing freedom through one's choices; reminding oneself "that the real leap consists in introducing invention into existence." After all, Fanon reflects, what "I wanted [was] to be a man among other men . . . to come lithe and young into a world that was ours and to help build it together" (112–13).[46]

Fanon is often described as the man who made a plea always to remain someone who questions. Here was not only an orientation to the future but also to every dimension of the present. Lewis Gordon has described Fanon as having achieved this when it came to questions of inquiry, by making our methods themselves a question. He does this in a way reminiscent of Rousseau: If colonization leaves nothing untouched, determining not only race, gender, class, and ethnic relations but also how time and space, the sacred and profane are understood, if, in other words, colonization is a form of cultural life with its own distinctive and self-protecting logic, how could it fail, in a most determining way, to shape the epistemic conditions of social life as well? How could one assume that methods, procedures through which research projects are designed and expected to be pursued and evaluated, could remain untarnished by its brush? How could they do so and still be meaningful or even comprehensible to those who would undertake and read them?

Still, for Fanon, to be capable of posing such questions affirms that we can remain self-reflective, that we can ask about how independent our thought manages to be so that we are not dogmatically duped robotically to replicate racist rationalizations. As Fanon wrote, "The prognosis is in the hands of those who are willing to get rid of the worm-eaten roots of the structure. . . . Reality for once, requires a total understanding" (*BSWM*, 11).

PATHOLOGIES OF LIBERTY

Indeed for Fanon, questions of mental health and sickness could not be divorced from the social world of which they were a part; "mental disorders" were therefore also a "pathology of liberty" (Bulhan 1985, 227), instances in which the agency of human beings was distorted and self-destructive in ways that could not be restored without altering their relations with others.[47] Even when not mechanistically their result, it was impossible for sickness not to be expressed within the terms of meaning of the patient, not to latch on to the coordinates of his or her social world. Psychiatry, as Fanon emphasized in his resignation letter from Blida-Joinville, was the medical technique that aimed to enable man no longer to be a stranger to his environment.[48] However, if in European societies, medicine was respected and the doctor-patient relationship sacred, in the colonies Western medicine was associated with the intensification rather than the alleviating of pain (97).[49] Often, in North Africa, working for the army, doctors were seen as an extension of colonial intrusions. Still if depoliticized science may have been impossible, science in the service of the people was not.

France had, as Macey emphasizes, conquered Algeria with a gun in one hand and quinine in the other. The expeditionary force that landed east of Algiers in 1830 included 167 surgeons and doctors. As towns fell to the French, hospitals staffed by military doctors popped up so that by 1876 even the most remote tribal areas had resident military physicians. In addition to prevention and cure, these men and women elaborated "the view of humanity from a racial standpoint," sending their studies back to France contributing in important ways to perceptions of the new colonial subjects. Algeria had proven to be home to two races: an Arab majority and a minority of tribes, including the Kabyles who lived in the harsh mountains. Although Fanon would define "Algerian" ecumenically, subordinating ethnicity to a nationalism of the will, French colonial discourse distinguished the "bad Arab" from the "good Kabyle." The former was the real focus of the Algiers School that aimed from the earliest stages of conquest to explain the "Arab mentality" in terms that slipped between metal pathology and ethnic psychology. As Phillipe Lucas and Jean-Claude Vatin put it in the introduction to an important anthology of anthropological writings on Algeria, "What mattered was not so much the native himself, but what would be said about him. The Algerian disappeared behind his appearance, behind the image of him that the colonial majority wanted to give of him" (quoted in Macey 2002, 219). Fanon summed up the way that Algerians were encountered in hospitals in the French world as bearing "the dead weight of all his compatriots" (226), spontaneously submerged within pre-existing frameworks. European psychiatry's history in Algeria was longer and more sustained than in most other African colonies, largely due to the degree of penetration of French settlements there.[50] One result was an early presence of Algerians suffering mental disorders in France. Sent to asylums, systematized observations of them soon emerged. These moved from suggesting that the colonized had no culture to the claim that they ranked at the bottom of a hierarchy of distinct cultures. Early psychological accounts were of primitive creatures that were primarily vegetative and instinctual, prone to act in hordes, with infantile curiosities (Bulhan 1985, 220).

When Fanon came to Algiers, he encountered the theories and practices of the Algerian School of Psychiatry, one counterpart of a larger pattern of colonial powers employing behavioral scientists to explain the psyche of the colonized which, in Bulhan's words, "often just gave scientific trappings to prevailing bigotry" (1985, 228). In this they were not unique, of course, but instead one wing of a larger, global project. Stephen Jay Gould's (1996) *The Mismeasure of Man* documents a whole US culture in which authoritative and excellent science was that which legitimated hierarchical ordering schemes that guided and rationalized genocidal policies and then those of enslavement. Fanon described a unique malaise produced by institutional racism that resulted in an inability of standard medical practitioners to treat the oppressed. Doubting the veracity of their illness based on their vague and amorphous complaints, the doctor usually patronized his patients, relying on and buttressing prevailing stereotypes.[51]

To assure that science and reason were not simply additional instruments of imperial endeavors, and that his work, as *chef-du-service* was not so complicit, Fanon attempted to understand the symbolic life of colonized communities, to be sufficiently saturated by an understanding of local conditions that he might be productive. From the start, however, here breaking with subsequent work in ethnopsychiatry, Fanon assumed that "culture" could not be treated apolitically. Much research of this kind followed the logic I mentioned in my earlier discussion of Trouillot's account of the "savage slot." In it, researchers sought out remote societies to generate evidence to settle internal European debates. First with Dr. R. Lacaton on the question of the meaning of confession and then Dr. François Sanchez on distinct conceptions of madness and their implications for treatment, by contrast, Fanon undertook to grasp the ways in which the experience of the oppressed was informed by politically antagonistic conceptions of their situation.[52] Fanon insisted that one could not understand how people negotiated and attempted to make sense of colonial situations without seeing them as ones that pitted groups against one another, constantly testing their allegiances. Such conditions fostered extensive mutual incomprehension. Few began with Fanon's conclusion: that a normal black child growing up in a normal family "will become abnormal on the slightest contact with the white world" (*BSWM*, 143).[53]

When Fanon had first arrived at Blida-Joinville Psychiatric Hospital, he instituted a range of radical changes that some have described as literally unchaining existing patients. Much as with his political writing, his approach to psychotherapy was an eclectic combination governed by the larger, uncompromised aim of being efficacious. Blending psychoanalytic psychotherapy, behavioral therapy, and existentialist-oriented psychotherapy, doctors took active and involved roles, using both individual and group methods and socio-drama in which a patient recounts personal experiences to others who offer their responses. Patients did not pay the therapist since this modified the quality of transference and countertransference and every effort was made to minimize the prisoner-jailer quality of traditional approaches that attenuated sadomasochistic relations through confinement and isolation in which patients might aim to make of themselves the objects that those who controlled their conditions sought. Instead, Fanon tried always to move toward meetings of two free people. He therefore removed barbed wire surrounding the facility, desegregated the wards, removing images of Paris in leisure rooms that were supposed to suggest a sense of "home" to patients who had never wandered through the Champs Elysées, and created mechanisms to foster direct participation in particular forms of decision-making. A newspaper was instituted, as were soccer teams. Always closest to his interns and indigenous nurses, Fanon remained firmly committed to the being of the patient and to aiming to restore freedom where it had been lost: undermined psychologically by anxieties, obsessions, and inhibitions and socially through victimization, rejection, and coercion. He assumed throughout that the function of medicine was to make men at home in their environments and that the purpose of social structures was to serve men's needs (rather than driving them to desperation).

Still, Fanon found that such humanistic innovations, ones with which he had become familiar during his training, were far more effective with European women patients than with Algerian men. Some of this was a function of linguistic barriers: with the latter, Fanon worked through translators, mainly Algerian male nurses, but some was the error of assuming that what had worked with the pioneering Catalan psychologist François Tosquelles during Fanon's residency in Saint Alban in central France would be appropriate in this rather different context.[54] After a year of work, he realized that he would have to be "timid and attentive" in his efforts to understand the situation of native patients.

As examples, Fanon described the moment when a colonized person had committed a crime and needed to be judged. He argued that the nature of their confession could not be understood without qualification:[55] normally, in confession, a person takes individual responsibility for their wrongdoing, affirming the values that he or she has violated in this individual act, and in the act of apology gives the ransom for his or her reinsertion in the group. But where oppression enters, such confessions are largely coerced. Even when they are not, the reciprocal recognition, which underpins their effective logic and meaning, is absent. The verdict and what follows, however, can be neither just nor rehabilitative if the accused is unwilling to appropriate the act, to accept the validity of the rules it has violated. But even more important, why would he when he knows full well that he will not, cannot, be "reinserted" into a community from which he is excluded? What if "the crime" was, from the very start, a rejection of the condition of being marginalized in one's own home?

The logic of the confession was one that assumed intact communities of relative insiders and equals with shared rules and norms and similar understandings of what it meant to belong. These analyses did not consider the situation of people suddenly shut out from the political community, whose presence in the place they had always lived represented a form of crime. If they were to accept the conditions and norms of the prevailing society, what they in fact conceded to was the acceptability of their nonbelonging. What, in such circumstances, becomes of innocence and guilt, or the pursuit of justice? What is the person who must negotiate such a system to conclude about his or her own "liberties"? As Renault has commented, "The objectivity of values is illicitly translated by the colonizer into a legitimization of domination . . . Telling the truth is showing allegiance to those who hold them in their power" (2011, 109). The colonized will not confess in the presence of the colonizer, then, not because he is primitive or illogical, but because true and false both turn on a logic to which he is opposed. It is in the colonial context therefore that he *learns* to lie. Before the struggle for independence, truth consists in retraction and unqualified rejection. In the midst of it, the aim is to liberate appropriate truths, ridding them of their colonial properties in acts of quasi-invention through which "one can borrow from Europe" if she is "provincialized" or creolized (111).

With madness, Fanon and Sanchez insisted that institutions for dealing with it in the Muslim world predated any European counterparts. These were not, as so many writers claimed, communities living outside of history, brought willingly or against great odds, into its moving stream. In such an act of Europe's provincialization, they documented that within it, madness was treated as a disease that alienated the victim from herself and others but one for which the ill person was framed as responsible. Blamed for its consequences, the mad woman was depicted as a social parasite who exploited her illness for ill-begotten ends. North Africans, they explained by comparison, saw the mad person as an innocent victim of spirits over which he had no control. His situation was accidental and could happen to anyone, since agency ultimately lay with the spirits who the community together had to appease or confront. The affliction was not confused with the person and the remedy was a necessarily collective one in which responsibility was shared.

For Fanon, in both instances, his aim was to correct European caricatures of North African behavior, to develop an approach appropriate to the context within which he worked, to identify indigenous conceptions that remained relevant to his own practice, and to combine these with effective innovations that he observed elsewhere. He aimed, in other words, not to miss the opportunities for human study not only made available by contact with a diverse range of human communities but that followed from the nature of colonial contact. What he exemplified here, however, did not only follow the rule of ethnology, but also his own creolized psychological approach: As Bulhan states, "The colonialism of Europe did not confine itself to economics or politics; it also permeated psychiatric concepts and practices. Fanon therefore endeavored to pioneer a psychiatry of liberation" that was appropriate to the needs and realities of his North African patients. This required that he combine methods both foreign and local in a fusion that met indigenous needs of challenging individual and collective unfreedom. In particular, it necessitated taking seriously that precolonial forms of meaning remained, if petrified and fragmented, and that recognizing the existence of these was part of the process of recognizing the humanity of the colonized. At the same time, to treat these as complete, rather than part of a world that had been radically interrupted, would be equally problematic. The people themselves had to negotiate this past in light of the larger aim of altering their present circumstances so that they could reemerge as meaning-making beings, responsible for the social and political world they occupied.

It was in and through such orientations to research and practice that Fanon effectively forged new methods. In Lewis Gordon's terms, he engaged in a "teleological suspension of disciplinarity" through which he was willing to go beyond disciplinary conventions and rules (in both determining legitimate questions and the execution of their answering) in the production of knowledge, making tools of whatever proved most useful (Gordon

2010a, 8). In other words, his scholarly aims were not to endear himself to a community of people with the same credentials as he; to affirm that he did in fact belong and to offer up his writings as proof of deserved membership. Instead, he was driven by the very questions at the heart of psychology and psychiatry, so much so that he might use resources outside their brink to illuminate and reenliven them.

In his *Les Damnés de la terre* or *Wretched of the Earth* (hereafter *WE*), Fanon turns to an exploration of the context of colonial alienation, one of political illegitimacy and coercively created and maintained inequalities. These are not simply those of masters and slaves whose relations are necessarily manipulating and deceptive. They describe instead the construction of a Manichean world, what one violently divided in two—one strongly built of stone and steel in which garbage disappears and people, white and foreign, are well-nourished with covered feet; the other densely populated by people who are dark and hungry, who seem to crouch with envy—does to human relationships. This is precisely the culture of dependence that Rousseau condemns but here theorized through imagining what Karl Marx (1976, part 8) later called the first moment of primitive accumulation, not as a singular, precursor moment but extenuated, as Rosa Luxemburg argued (2004, 32–70), to define global relations created through colonization and enslavement.

Fanon offers a phenomenological portrait of both sides, of what it means to see oneself as bringing values and civilization to outposts and backwaters, as making history, creating an epoch, embodying an absolute beginning and what, in contrast, it means to be treated as "a negation" of or "the enemy" of values, as corrosive, a deforming element that disfigures all that is beautiful or moral; what it is to be the *telos* toward which others hope to move, to define the terms of their development and what, in contrast, it is to be referred to in zoological terms, as reptilic, stinking, and gesticulating within what many would think, if left uninterrupted, would have remained a prehistoric vacuum. These depictions are rich accounts of the very kind of relations that Rousseau insisted made perceiving shared conditions of well-being, a general will, impossible, where instead the right of the strongest prevailed through which some enriched themselves clearly at the expense of others and maintained their ability to do so through brute, ongoing force. How could these Manichean poles meet to discuss anything shared? The thought of the possibility is patently absurd—under the guise of order and peace, this is, as Rousseau said of slavery, in fact a protracted state of war.

Fanon adds insight to Rousseau's claim on the one hand that there is no right to slavery and that the slave should escape as soon as he or she could and on the other that slavery creates "natural slaves" or habituates people to a set of conditions that make their legitimate exit extremely difficult to achieve. While underscoring the form and nature of these constraints, that one risks death and humiliation if one aims to challenge the coordinates of a Manichean world, Fanon writes that the "native admits no accusation," that he is "overpowered but not tamed," "treated as an inferior, but not convinced of his inferiority" (*WE*, 53). He lives in a permanent dream to switch places, with the basic insight that "the showdown [between the colonizer and colonized] cannot be put off indefinitely" (ibid.). Until such time, however, members of the colonized community do live with an anger that is perpetually lit—with sensitivity at the surface of open skin that flinches from a caustic agent—without any outlet. The explosions are inevitable but the targets the undeserving in battles that are ultimately displaced.

CONCLUDING COMPARISONS

Both Rousseau and Fanon tie their efforts to explain unfreedom to the origins and causes of inequalities and the ways in which they alienate human beings from themselves and each other. In doing so, both announce that they set themselves at odds with prevailing conceptions of authoritative reason that they demonstrate have been used far more to justify the curbing of human liberty than to aid its deepening or expansion.

In revealing the ongoing toleration of what he considers as amounting to despotism, Rousseau engaged in hypothetical reason that sought to distinguish what was original and artificial in man so we can see our natural selves. Developing his feelings of being an outsider into an epistemological and moral orientation from which critically to view his own and other European societies, he aimed to be independent of (rather than reliant on) the trappings of his social world. First endeavoring to write from an earlier moment in political time, then taking on, to the best of his abilities, the position and voice of nature, he elevated precisely those who were denigrated, putting in their mouths his own feelings and estimations, suggesting that they were able, because unencumbered by societal expectations and moldings, to transcend what the highest exemplifications of European reason could fathom. In doing so, he drew repeatedly on travel writings that he otherwise criticized to mobilize the evidence he ascribed to "earlier," less corrupted peoples and their counterparts in the Hispano- and Francophone colonies, as seeing through the supposedly inarguable allure of European modernity and civilization. The utter disinterest in grappling with these moments of rejection was symptomatic of a more profound unwillingness to see global exploration as an opportunity to understand humankind through engaging with their continuities and differences and through them the relationship of the contingent to the more permanent. Instead what most travelers keenly perceived were opportunities for personal enrichment, whether in the form of literal gold or its spiritual counterpart in potential converts.

While Rousseau inverted the usual value assigned to "primitives," because he was himself wedded to a singular developmental trajectory through which he aimed to show the radicality of human transformation through the emergence of private property and complex unequal societies, Rousseau ultimately framed these men and women as examples of man in his infancy. We might feel nostalgia for the imagined distance we have traveled from this way of being, but what are depicted as its living embodiments might struggle to elicit sympathies given their supposed absence of complex, comparative thinking and reliance solely on instincts that cannot form the scaffolding of moral freedom. The alternative that they *embody* therefore cannot be considered as a meaningfully articulated one but instead as a tragic, soon marginal, symbolic rejection. While a refusal of a very radical kind, whether because of Rousseau's strong identifications with the dispositions of the ancients, sympathies with displaced aristocrats or trappings by the episteme of his moment, he could not posit this as the basis for other courses of action beyond a return that he conceded was not ultimately possible. He later would try again in his *Social Contract*, still a highly ambivalent document, that he characterized as his effort to square the circle.

Although Fanon did not *explicitly* engage Rousseau and Rousseauian ideas, he was moved by similar orienting problems and concerns. In his hands, however, these were suffused with hopes that he and subsequent generations would make themselves agents of their times. What this meant was that what literally sickened them was also that for which they were responsible. Devoting themselves to revealing its multiple valences and coordinates was not separable from trying to do something about it. Like Rousseau, Fanon turned to the colonized, but not to point out that they too were human thankfully still relatively untouched. Instead he illustrated that one cannot disentangle the colonized from the colonial, that these make and are made by each another, forged at once. For Fanon, there was nothing ideal about the lives of men and women whose lives were only recently interrupted by the arrival of Europeans. Indeed, they only entered into the consciousness of Europeans because their worlds had been so shattered. They could not return to a moment prior to this, although, as I will explore in further detail in Chapter 4, many would try to do just that: to cope through finding refuge in a petrified version of the precolonial past. Such men and women were, however, never without history and culture or political conflicts over how best to live collectively. Framing them as such, even if in the most positive terms, obscured precisely that which was at work since it mistook the very processes that pushed people toward their own mummification for that which supposedly precipitated their entry into historic time.

Waging such critiques and fashioning alternatives could not abandon resources of reason and scholarship, even if these still needed to be held in suspicion, precisely because, as noted by Bulhan, worlds of colonialism aimed, however imperfectly, to be total. In such circumstances, many of the most essential questions—those of what happens to agency when its coordinates are so overdetermined; when *resisting colonialism* can mean little more than devoting one's energies to resurrecting a world that is no longer—are exactly those that are treated as settled starting points. However elusive the workings of reason, engagements with them enrich the lives of human beings, enabling us to explore that which we uniquely, as symbolic creatures, might do and be.

Unlike Rousseau, then, for Fanon, moments of refusal and rejection, while essential to nurturing the kind of self that can work with others to forge legitimate political alternatives, remain those of negation that must ultimately be surpassed. While his friend and interlocutor Jean-Paul Sartre first offered this unwelcome conclusion to him, Fanon ultimately agreed that he could not remain in the "night of the absolute" (*BSWM*, 133–34). Although the turn to Négritude was necessary in a way that Sartre had failed to grasp, he had to move through it to face his situation. More explicitly and unambivalently than in Rousseau, integral to Fanon's theory is an account of how this is done, of how people not only refuse habituation but seek to become the kinds of subjects that can create the political relations they deserve. It is to these legitimate alternatives that I turn in the next two chapters.

Although not intentionally, Fanon critically engages some of Rousseau's core ideas through creolizing them or by revisiting their problematics in light of the contradictions of the world he magnified as the unique situation of those seeking mental health within colonial conditions. In so doing, Fanon takes them in directions in which Rousseau could not go himself. Fanon creolizes these to the extent that he reemploys languages, concepts, and aspirations borne of a much older European world (that was already more diverse than conventional accounts would have it) and makes them speak anew in grappling with challenges that are fresh and familiar, distinctive and broadly shared.

3

Rousseau's General Will

I had perceived everything to be radically connected with politics, and that, upon whatever principles these were founded, a people would never be more than that which the nature of the government made them.

—JEAN-JACQUES ROUSSEAU[1]

Rousseau's and Fanon's interests in questions of method and inquiry, as I have shown, were fundamentally tied to their diagnoses of illegitimate politics. For Rousseau, the possibility of an alternative was easier to envisage than to realize. Still, trying to imagine people as we are and laws and institutions as they might be, he offered his effort "to square the circle" through the idea of "the general will" the pursuit of which, he insisted, was the only legitimate basis of government.

DEFINING THE GENERAL WILL

Rousseau made the general will famous and infamous in several fateful strokes. Although a concept with a prior life in sixteenth- and seventeenth-century French theological debates concerning the will of G-d to save all men (Riley 1988; Rosenblatt 1997), Rousseau recast it in evocative terms that have inspired, puzzled, and frustrated readers ever since. The centerpiece of his social contract constituted his effort to outline *philosophically* what could make politics something other than masked force and a citizenry, people, and body politic out of an amalgamation of individuals. Key to it was the conjoining of two of the most relevant categories for modern and contemporary politics, the *general* and the *will*.² Between what Patrick Riley (1988) has called the "minute particulars" and the universal, the *general* is appropriate to the domain of the *polis* rather than the *kosmopolis*. It is and must be limited by permeable and shifting boundaries. As opposed to both a reified particularity that would fix its borders as stone and to the search for an absolute, limitless universality, the general seeks within certain bounds to integrate meaningfully abiding differences. And to do so with the full recognition that generalities are always multiple and dynamic because politics itself turns on how thinking, decisions, and activity emerge out of variegated collectivities.

The need for political life, after all, is born from the unique features of what it is and means to be a human being. We are, as Aristotle observed, distinct from both gods and beasts: We feel and think in ways that are informed by but not reducible to our instincts. We can recognize cravings or even yearnings without looking at their evidence in actions already undertaken. For the divine, action is neither a unique domain nor challenge of life; to have a thought is to bring it into being.³ We, by contrast, are able to imagine meanings of justice, reason, and generality, all of which Rousseau claims emanate from the gods, but cannot translate them straightforwardly into rules for living. If we were like gods, we would need neither law nor politics. If we were no different from nonhuman animals, to seek these would be patently absurd.

But we are deluding ourselves, Rousseau argues at the start of his *Discourse on Political Economy*, if we compare our leaders with idealized fathers. The people who rule over us have no innate reason to love us. They may actually delight in our misery. It is highly unlikely that they feel any impulse for our care. If they do experience any guidance or direction as instinctive, they must actively root it out (Rousseau 1987, 113). It would be disastrous for them to consider the polity as their family only enlarged. Political leadership is necessarily and distinctively unnatural.⁴

And so we begin with one of the many sober requirements of political life. We may not try to enter or inhabit it as underdeveloped children under the care of a nurturing father who is ultimately responsible for our actions. It is just as misleading to imagine political adulthood as an option that we might refuse. We, as adults, are already elements of a single body the health and life of which depend on figuring out how it relates to itself.[5] For collective self-rule or popular sovereignty begins with a formal commitment to root out theocentric and hereditary conceptions of authority in search of more egalitarian alternatives. It turns the gaze to the ruled, the subjects, and attempts to make explicit that within these regimes they, or we, are the only resources available. This, in turn, makes collective life a project and a question rather than a task with a preordained design or ready outcome.[6]

Rousseau claimed in the *Social Contract* that we become moral through the civil association that forms the body politic. If it were not so frequently a site of abuse, he suggested, it would be blatantly obvious to us all that it is through the body politic alone that we become intelligent beings and persons, as opposed to limited beasts and slaves. But if we pursue popular sovereignty in search of the conditions for the emergence of our own aspiration for political right, we must ask: How can legitimacy emerge within political life, from politics? We know how moral considerations or ethical concerns can generate norms that we can adopt as ideals or standards *for* politics. But what happens if we seek *political* legitimacy? What would it look like? Would we recognize it? What would bring it into being?

Although generations of modern and contemporary political theorists from Kant to Rawls and Habermas have asked these questions, they do so within a terrain carved out by Rousseau, by one that defined the general will, republicanism, and political legitimacy together.[7] In Rousseau, the general will, simply stated, is the reflective expression or will of the people as citizens considering the necessary grounds for their ongoing shared existence, for what has made possible and will sustain their transformation from the aggregate they once were into "a public, moral person," or body politic. Authentic acts of the general will are therefore acts of sovereignty, conventions of the body with each of its members based on the social contract common to all and backed by their collective public force. Aiming at the common good, general well-being, and common conservation, it is a set of positions with which one cannot disagree without having been fundamentally misled. Tending toward equality, the general will is contrasted with the will in general or the sum of the private interests and preferences of individual men. It does not seek to eliminate these more particular interests but frames them as secondary and subsidiary to a shared will that sustains a domain of general life. Not then "some mystical faculty of a collectivity that exists independently of the individual wills of its members" (Noone 1980 73), the general will is instead the basis for the achievement in political life of a kind of freedom that requires a mutuality and reciprocality rooted in consent that can be both given and retracted.

We may evade the general will. We can hide from its nagging expectations, pretending that they are themselves partial and particular. But it does not die or disappear in such instances. Legitimacy and politics do.

ELABORATING THE GENERAL WILL

We cannot know in advance if political legitimacy is, in fact, possible. We can inquire into its nature. We might imagine its form. We may attempt to foresee the challenges to its realization or the imperatives that it would have to reconcile. But even our most penetrating written accounts still do not themselves bring it into being. Its actual shape can only emerge out of political life itself. And so Rousseau opens with the question, "I want to inquire whether there can be some legitimate and sure rule of administration in the civil order . . . I will always try in this inquiry to bring together what right permits with what interest prescribes, so that justice and utility do not find themselves at odds with one another" (Rousseau 1987, 141). We are equally uncertain about the purpose served by such theoretical considerations. Rousseau states, "It will be asked if I am a prince or a legislator, that I should be writing about politics. I answer that I am neither, and that is why I write about politics. Were I a prince or a legislator, I would not waste my time saying what ought to be done. I would do it or keep quiet" (141). One writes about politics if doing so is not a substitute for other forms of consequential action. One writes if one does not face a calculus of enacting deeds or remaining in silence. Such reflection is appropriate for free citizens and members of a sovereign who can and should linger with the "oughts."

That social orders are not natural *is not* a question for Rousseau, since, he states without qualification, *they do not come from nature*. They are, however, in his words, "a sacred right," and the foundation for all other rights. Founded upon conventions arrived at without coercion, they are the only formations through which right and justice can be pursued. The most severe obstacles to their creation and sustaining are what Rousseau regards as absurd conventions, which, mistaking custom with right, would have us believe that some men possess natural authority over others or that the obedience to the conqueror by the vanquished and enslaved is more than merely prudent.

The "right" of the strongest, a primary example of what defines absurd conventions, is also what most characterizes the political illegitimacy against which governance by the general will is posited. Evident in familiar equations of sovereignty with force, Rousseau rejects this commonly held account by emphasizing the fundamental insecurity of such misleading conceptions of power. Explaining that the strength implied by potential violence can never be strong enough to secure mastery unless it is able to transform itself into something independently compelling, into that which elicits a sense of duty from others. In its absence, if one can disobey the strong, one does so legitimately. Rousseau writes, "Since the strongest is always right, the only thing to do is to make oneself the strongest. Clearly then, this word 'right' adds nothing to force. It is utterly meaningless here" (Rousseau 1987, 143). Obligation rests in a capacity to inspire more than the fear born of coercion or terror. It is therefore also, at least potentially, more permanent since linked to faculties beyond our basic instincts to survive.

This indictment of rule sustained only by threats or actual physical force extends to its institutional instantiations in both slavery and colonization. Both turn on relationships that require some—in losing their liberty, rights, and duties—to renounce their dignity as people. To lack a free will is to cease to be capable of moral action. Such an individual cannot be party to any but a vain and null convention: One cannot, after all, commit to someone from whom one can demand everything since even their right of protest thereby belongs to another.[8] Slavery and right are, for this reason, contradictory and mutually exclusive (Rousseau 1987, 146). This extends also to Rousseau's insistence on the radical difference between subduing a multitude through an act of colonization (which creates an aggregation) and legitimately governing a society (which involves the creation of a body politic that aims at a public good). In slavery and colonization, as with the more general notion of the "right" of the strongest, peoples' lives are made up only of strategic calculations. They presuppose the continuation of a state of war and impossibility of the social life upon which politics is based and to which it gives expression.

The desire to live less precariously through expanding one's powers, if impossible to accomplish in a long-term way through ongoing physical domination, necessitates the challenge of political association.[9] The unarticulated wish underpinning all such projects is to be fully protected by everyone else while obeying oneself as freely as before. Indeed Rousseau goes so far as to see this clause as implicit in the act itself to such an extent that it would be accepted everywhere by everyone. To fall short of it—which we, with any but transformed selves, will inevitably do—is, without announcement or warning, to return to a state of natural liberty.

It is in this context that Rousseau first mentions the general will: "*Each of us places his person and all his power in common under the supreme direction of the general will and as one we receive each member as an indivisible part of the whole*" (Rousseau 1987, 148; italics in the original). It is framed as the alternative—to the state of nature, to cycles of the "right" of the strongest—to our situation under illegitimate governments. Without some artistry, there is a tendency for all relations to collapse into sheer contests of willful force. What sustains any- and everything else is the possibility of a less fragile reciprocity. Rousseau writes:

> The first and most important consequence of the principles established above is that only the general will can direct the forces of the state according to the purpose for which it was instituted, which is the common good. For if the opposition of private interests made necessary the establishment of societies, it is the accord of these same interests that made it possible. It is what these differences have in common that forms the social bond, and, were there no point of agreement among all these interests, no society could exist. For it is utterly on the basis of this common interest that society ought to be governed. (Rousseau 1987, 153)

Antagonistic, competing interests of individuals and families create difficulties for which the formation of societies appears to offer a solution. Actually to form these draws on the accord above or beneath these warring interests, on the shared desire for amelioration through organized association. In this sense, all states are instituted to pursue a good that is common. To retain this founding purpose, the general will must direct their forces. It is what the differences have in common and undergirds social bonds. It must furnish the basis for governance.

To forge the polity demands what Rousseau's critics find most alarming: "the total alienation of each of us to the entire community." How could such a radical move not be disastrously dangerous?

Rousseau offers: if everyone gives himself entirely, the condition placed on all is equal. If any rights were retained with private individuals, some among them would remain as private judges distinct from the polity. What is more, in giving myself to a unit of which I am a part, I give myself to myself and to no individual, particular person. What is more, as part of the political whole, fundamentally implicated by it, I cannot wish for others what I would not for myself. This prescription therefore unites individuals into a single body making infliction of isolated harm impossible.[10]

This further encourages people in both their capacities, as members of the body and men, to be moved by both duty and interest to come to each other's aid. The aim, in other words, from its very foundation, is to create a palpable sense of unity—in which I am affected similarly to you and we are all mutually implicated—that is a living, rather than purely formal reality to members. What they together form through the act of convention is the state when passive, the sovereign when active. We act as citizens when part of the sovereign people who make law through articulating the general will. We are subjects when we make these our guides. We therefore live politically with both public and private selves the different directions of which we are to hold together.

Following the initial act of convention, Rousseau does state that nothing can be demanded of individuals that is not of use to the community and that what is not can be disposed of at will. Indeed Mark Cladis has recently argued that the line that Rousseau draws between the public and private spheres, between what may be demanded and regulated and what left alone, continues to be a useful guide for thinking about religious rights in the United States and abroad (Cladis 2003).

When people who once lived in the state of nature enter the political community in the writing of Thomas Hobbes or John Locke, it is their situation rather than they who are transformed. They continue, in the former, to be as vainglorious as before but now making their predictably self-interested calculations with the leviathan's potentially punitive hand in mind. They persist, in the latter, in their rational industriousness but now knowing that there are courts of law that will contend impartially with beastlike trespassers. With Rousseau, as evident in chapter 8 of Book I, the story is rather different. Through forming a polity we are transformed from stupid and limited, if highly independent, animals into intelligent beings. When living within polities "the voice of duty replaces physical impulse and right replaces appetite . . . man, who had hitherto taken only himself into account, finds himself forced to act upon other principles and to consult his reason before listening to his inclinations. Although in this state he deprives himself of several of the advantages belonging to him in the state of nature, he regains such great ones. His faculties are exercised and developed, his ideas are broadened, his feelings are ennobled" (Rousseau 1987, 150–51). However, Rousseau adds an important cautionary note here also in the spirit of Aristotle: when political relations are abused, this elevation of our souls is not only absent but inverted, lowering us, as was evident at the close of the *Second Discourse*, beneath our natural status.[11]

Rousseau adds, in a very different tone than the one through which he introduced himself and his work to public life: "To the proceeding acquisitions could be added the acquisition in the civil state of moral liberty, which alone makes man truly the master of himself. For to be driven by appetite alone is slavery, and obedience to the law one has prescribed for oneself is liberty" (Rousseau 1987, 151).[12] We are freed through collective life since it alone can set the conditions through which we could again become masters of ourselves now through authoring the laws under which we live. This moral liberty or legislative power extends beyond freedom from constraint or negative and natural liberty to the freedom to determine how we should relate to one other, how to secure the political equality that makes liberty meaningful, how to foster and maintain a form of society that might be the site through which we transcend alienation from ourselves and others.

If legitimate governments are those in which the general will directs the body politic, what is it? Rousseau offers several coextensive definitions.

First and perhaps most obviously, the general will, as we have already mentioned, conjoins willing, which is focused on active self-determination, with generality. It is what emerges when the whole community considers questions as they pertain to the whole community. Rousseau writes, "Sovereignty is indivisible for the same reason that it is inalienable. For either the general will is general, or it is not. It is the will of either the people as a whole or of only a part" (Rousseau 1987, 154). Sovereignty and generality are defined together. As Lester Crocker (1995) objected, only the people as a whole are "the people" in the sense of the source of legitimacy. The very meaning of sovereignty, or the general will, is the project of sustaining that generality. No one may be structurally excluded since it would be a preemptive "breach of generality," in what would, from the start, differentiate the foundational, shared interests that the state is to realize through its institution (Rousseau 1987, 154n1).

Second, the general will is what we discern when we think as citizens about the conditions necessary not only to sustaining our generality but also relatedly our shared well-being. Some, with good reason, have framed the general will as metaphysical. It is not impossible to draw this conclusion when it seems to have an existence independent of people's ability to grasp it.[13] At the same time, Rousseau makes it clear that the general will is in each citizen and that it must be realized locally, expressing the needs and possibilities of a given, limited, if permeable, community. In this sense, the general will also describes the scope of political identity. Between the universal and particular, what is general to a people is determined by the common context of their lives. This can be defined in the negative, as Max Weber outlined, when he wrote that a people recalls itself as such when attacked in war with other nations (Weber 1994, 1–28). It is also conceded when people defend the need for domestic infrastructure, for roads and technology that reliably enables communication and transportation, and for minimizing the decimation of necessarily shared natural environments.

Third, indispensable to the life of the general will is retaining active legislative power through periodically assembling everyone in the polity. Against those who might see this as unviable, Rousseau cited instances in the Roman Republic when citizens voted from rooftops. To secure such assemblies, he insisted that the people prearrange dates when they would be held that members of the government could neither postpone nor cancel. As has been widely noted, reading Rousseau as a forerunner to the deliberative democratic project does require separating some of his writings from the spirit that runs through them: He did fear public deliberation, fundamentally linking it to opportunities through which people could easily be corrupted or misled by leaders of fractious partial associations. When it came to voting, or expressing what each citizen thought properly expressed the general will, he preferred that people quietly consult the voice of their own conscience, the same one that he had identified in the *First Discourse* with the true philosophy of which most citizens were capable. Still, evident in this prescription is Rousseau's deep antagonism to political representation. Although he did admit that it was unavoidable in some instances, he ultimately pinned the decay of healthy polities or the efficacy of the general will on the partial will that undoubtedly evolved with and would be prioritized by members of a governing class.

Fourth, the initial moment of forming the compact had to be unanimous, but following that, what emerged as the majority opinion of what constituted the general will could suffice. If decisions were highly consequential, such as involved in the amending of law, one needed a significant majority. Where expediency could be the primary concern, a simple majority would do. Even then, however, voting on the general will involved a particular disposition and kind of activity. In particular, when casting their ballots, what citizens expressed was not their interests or wishes as private citizens, but what they were convinced was the exemplification of the general will as we have already defined it. In healthier polities, Rousseau suggested that these outcomes would be largely self-evident so that formal laws would be few and would simply enunciate what "everybody ha[d] already felt" (1987, 204). Still, in those cases when its content was murkier, if it turned out that some citizens' views did not prevail, they were to surmise that they had been in error. If anything, they would be relieved that others had corrected their mistake, preemptively curbing its potential destructiveness.[14] Rousseau writes of these cases, "If my private opinion had prevailed, I would have done something other than what I had wanted. In that case I would not have been free" (206).[15]

Fifth, while suggesting in these cases that the general will can be arrived at numerically, Rousseau goes on to offer some qualification: "It should be seen that what makes the will general is not so much the number of votes as the common interest that unites them, for in this institution each person necessarily submits himself to the conditions he imposes on others, an admirable accord between interest and justice" (Rousseau 1987, 158). The general will, as already mentioned, is what the differences have in common, what remains when "the pluses and minuses" of particular interests "cancel each other out." But what does this mean? Rousseau admits that shared interests may be felt precisely because of the existence of different, even sharply divergent ones. If there were none, he comments, everything "would proceed on its own and politics would cease being an art" (156n2). What is more, he cautioned that where unanimity reigns, it is a sign of an absence of liberty or will. Voting, in such instances, is nothing more than the culmination of fear or flattery in acclamation. Rather than seriously consider, people adore or curse (205). In other words, the identification of similarity requires not obliterating but skillfully negotiating differences. Still, the general will then, though general and necessarily shared, is not identical with a simple majority. The general will must always come out of the majority, but it alone is not sufficient.

Sixth, there is a difference already implied between what Rousseau designates the general will and the will of all. The latter is the sum or aggregate of each private citizen considering his or her private interest while the general will, as I have just said, is the answer one gives when considering the general interest or common good. In healthier polities the general will and the will in general are more likely to coincide, since in these instances, individual citizens maintain a clearer sense of how intertwined are their own and the community's needs and concerns. They sustain a mutual identification, a sense that they are joined not only by shared functions, but a common existence.

Seventh, the general will is not foreign or alien to us. We have a sense of it, however vague, since it is, as mentioned above, one of the many wills that we feel. It can also, for this reason, often be muted or trumped (Rousseau 1987, 150). Fidelity to its implied demands is never assured. Writes Rousseau:

> In fact, each individual can, as a man, have a private will contrary to or different from the general will that he has as a citizen. His private interest can speak to him in an entirely different manner than the common interest. His absolute and naturally independent existence can cause him to envisage what he owes the common cause as a gratuitous contribution, the loss of which will be less harmful to others than its payment is burdensome to him. *And in viewing the moral person which constitutes the state as a being of reason because it is not a man*, he would enjoy the rights of a citizen without wanting to fulfill the duties of a subject, an injustice whose growth would bring about the ruin of the body politic. (Ibid.; italics added)

Private interests appear to private men as natural and absolute. Calling out loudly with a piercing clarity, they make all other kinds of needs appear elusive, mystical, and suspect. The defining mold of interests becomes those that we would think we could satisfy on our own, with no social or political mediation. From this vantage point, arrogant with a sense of independent competence, common concerns, and shared causes, "the moral person" or "being of reason that is the state," seem unnecessary or deceptive. The quotidian and seeming individual quality of the experience of meeting some needs allows one to imagine that these really are discrete from the grander and more illusive collective sort, the return path of which is circuitous and highly complex. The diffuse nature of politics, sociality, and shared living, combined with intense ideological work that suggests that one can meaningfully be an individual apart from public life, allow us to think that we are not actually interdependent. The fact that neither politics nor sovereign power nor the conditions of reciprocity that can secure liberty are embodied in one man to whom we might point, enables many to think that what maintains our freedom is in fact an infringement on it. The amorphous nature of actual sovereignty, Rousseau here concedes, anticipating subsequent charges made by critics, endangers it for those for whom that which is real must be more concretely material. Its ruin comes of the belief that leads to acting as if the grounds indispensable for freedom are not themselves necessary. It is easy for each citizen to minimize the significance of his or her disinvestment from political life and to see idiosyncratic preferences as a more significant expression of who they were.

In addition, when we in fact try to act from the general will, we may do so in ways that are "unenlightened," misdirected, or too narrow. When sufficiently well informed, "with no communication among themselves," deliberations would always be good. By contrast, with the growth of intrigues and partial association, the will of each of these, particular and less comprehensive than the polity itself, is felt by subgroup members to be synonymous with the general will (Book II, chap. 3). Rather than an array of individual voters, wills coalesce around these factions, reducing their overall number and assuring that each citizen does not make up his or her own mind (Rousseau 1987, 156). When this happens in the extreme, Rousseau insists, in a way almost always ignored by most of his readers, the response must be to multiply their number and to prevent inequalities among them (ibid.). In other words, the differences must be rendered less fractious, so that they do not, in a definitive way, undercut the possibility of a will as broad as the polity itself. The difficulty with partial societies is neither membership in nor loyalty to them, but that we tend to narrow our focus beneath full generality, enabling us to conclude, usually at the behest of tricky leaders, that pursuing this restricted will alone is sufficient. Doing so renders each of these divergent interests less negotiable or mediatable, more likely to be treated as an exclusive, antagonistic end. Still, Rousseau insists, "If there were no different interests, the common interest, which would never encounter any obstacle, would scarcely be felt" (Rousseau 1987, 156n2).[16]

This is why Rousseau insists that we must agree in advance to the necessary grounds for politics, why we give an a priori "yes" to the general will, a commitment to the recuperation of the public spiritedness that will inevitably be in decline. This insight underpins the infamous passage that, together with the demand (qualified subsequently) that we alienate everything in the initial act of convention, is the basis of many of the staunchest objections to Rousseau's political writings. He states,

> Thus, in order for the social compact to avoid being an empty formula, it tacitly entails the commitment—which alone can give force to the others—that whoever refuses to obey the general will will be forced to do so by the entire body. This means merely that he will be forced to be free. For this is the sort of condition that, by giving each citizen to the homeland, guarantees him against all personal dependence—a condition that produces the skill and the performance of the political machine, and which alone bestows legitimacy upon civil commitments. Without it such commitments would be absurd, tyrannical and subject to the worst abuses. (Rousseau 1987, 150)

Private interests will always be in greater supply than the public spiritedness required to sustain the body politic that alone can diminish our dependence and encourage the civic skill and participation that can keep our relations from devolving into tyrannical ones. We assent in advance to being pulled back into our shared role as sovereign for when hiding from this, we diminish sovereignty itself, compromising its generality. What we agree to, then, is sustaining our role in the project of our shared autonomy.

There is great risk that assurances of legitimacy will be only empty formulas, the written dreams of outsiders that meet the requirements of logic or style, but certainly not of politics. Dagger (1997) argues that having made laws in one's capacity as a citizen that aim to enable social cooperation, one must share the burden of following them. It is not enough for the people to have constituted the state through sanctioning a series of laws or establishing electoral mechanisms (Rousseau 1987, 195–96). Their shared authority *is* the state's heart (194). As Rousseau writes, "The brain [which he compares with executive power] can fall into paralysis and yet the individual may still live. A man may remain an imbecile and live. But once the heart has ceased its functions, the animal is dead" (ibid.). Freedom requires people continuing to enact their collective sovereign power, actively associating, negotiating, and potentially reconciling their shared and disparate needs in a general will. If this is not genuinely general—if it is instead a particular will of a factious group presenting its concerns and aims as of more abiding importance—the "political machine" will begin to reinstate the cyclical life of the "right" of the strongest. Rather than abetting, it will foment dependence and its exploitation.

Eighth, when we seek to instantiate or discover the general will, we are articulating or sanctioning the laws of the polity that must be general in their content.[17] The aim is for us each to be sufficiently equal that they affect us all in comparable ways, benefiting and harming us similarly. Rousseau did not think that polities could achieve absolute economic equality because trying to create and sustain it would nurture sharp resentment and unmediatable friction. He did stipulate that inequality should not be so pronounced that one person could buy another or that another would have need to sell himself. For under those conditions, as I discussed in Chapter 1, the interests of each party would become fundamentally opposed. There would be no overarching general will that could incorporate both. This had been the case in Rome in which the patricians and plebeians in fact formed two cities in the physical space of one (Rousseau 1987, 205). Rousseau emphasized that the equality he sought was not a natural outcome, but this did not mean it was mere "speculative fiction" either (171). If abuses were inevitable, they could and should be regulated. "It is precisely because the force of things tends always to destroy equality that the force of legislation should always tend to maintain it" (171). The general will is therefore invested with the role of counterweight, of preserving the very fragile and always endangered circumstances that make it possible to resolve differences according to principles of right as collectively articulated.

Many writers have criticized Rousseau's emphasis on the indispensability of political unity to legitimate governance as potentially repressive. Citing lines in which he encourages contracting citizens to alienate everything, that express disdain for membership in partial associations, that make casual reference to forcing citizens to be free and that demand that members of the polity distinguish private from public willing, many see in Rousseau's writings dangerous formulas for intolerant, majoritarian societies with no room for dissent or innovation. It is true that Rousseau sees collectivisms that can prove dangerous as indispensable to political legitimacy, trying to counter their inherent extremes rather than banishing them from public life. But it is worth recalling the forms of difference that Rousseau feared. They were not of a primarily cultural, racial, or religious nature—indeed in the *Social Contract*, he is most intolerant of the religiously intolerant. He did fear polities seeing value only in what came from elsewhere, trying always to be other than what they were rather than developing themselves.[18] Still, the forms of difference that he thought would erode the general will were very particular, focused on radical economic inequalities and heavy-handed and censorious religious authorities. When he spoke of individuals who would manipulate the language of the commons through "personal trust" and eloquence (115) to seduce other men, it was always for the sake of their own narrow private profiteering.[19]

At the same time, many criticisms have been made of Rousseauian equality. From the perspective of Judith Shklar (1988, 260–73), the demand that law affect all comparably remains absolute in a way that is unachievable. Although Rousseau helps us more fully to understand the difficulties of creating equality through politics, he should, yet does not, fashion rights to protect the inevitable existence of unequal minorities. The question should not be if legitimacy (and equality) is present or absent, but the inevitably imperfect degree to which it is positively realized. John McCormick (2007; 2011) also warns that we be alert to the absence of institutional safeguards but with very different consequences. Against Shklar, he considers the reading of Rousseau as the prophet of egalitarian democracy ironic, for without offering institutional blueprints to curb material inequalities, McCormick cautions, he is, more accurately, the architect of a legitimated oligarchy.[20] While it is true that Rousseau offers few helpful suggestions about creating or maintaining the rough economic equality that he demands, it would require stretching him to a point of unrecognizability to frame him as suggesting that oligarchies could be legitimate in his terms. When Rousseau does offer suggestions about how best to realize the carefully calibrated portrait he offers—one that combines the focus on deliberation with the correct outcomes of more justice-oriented models; a language that sounds communitarian with one that treats the individual as its basic unit—they are normally backward-looking: trying to avoid the introduction of the new and destructive, since once eroded, in his view, polities cannot be mended. For this reason, it is more useful and instructive to read the work as offering a regulative ideal and normative theory.

Emphasizing the republicanism of Rousseau, Maurizio Viroli (1988), has drawn attention to the original front piece of the *Social Contract*, to the quote from Virgil, "let us provide them with equitable laws" (*Aeneid*, Book 11) and a drawing of the cat which Rousseau admired for its determined protection of its liberty. Viroli insists that liberty for Rousseau is the opposite of the servitude of being subject to the whims of another man. His aim is for none to owe obedience to a single person, for all to be equally subject to the law of their own making. Viroli writes, "Moreover, these passages which are often used to present an image of a 'totalitarian' Rousseau opposed to freedom must, on the contrary, be considered as so many affirmations of the principle of liberty as total independence of the will of any other individual"

(1988, 151). For in contrast to men who always seek distinction, "the law . . . will brook no special case" (191).

Rousseau concludes Book I of the *Social Contract* with the following: "It is that instead of destroying natural equality, the fundamental compact, on the contrary, substitutes a moral and legitimate equality to whatever physical inequality nature may have been able to impose upon men, and that, however, unequal in force or intelligence they may be, men all become equal by convention and by right" (Rousseau 1987, 153). Although there are no human worlds without symbolic content, there are those in which, highly fractured and diffuse, these do not map neatly or coherently onto the physical landscapes through which we move. One must imagine, absent shared meanings, what a world in which one's fate is sealed by one's physical endowments would be like. If not constantly violent and deadly, as Hobbes surmised, it is clear that the mundane living that is borne of stability and certainty would be impossible and with it most other attributes and products of culture and civilization.[21] The state of nature, the metaphorical beforehand to which one might constantly return, is not preindustrialized Europe or North America before the arrival of colonists. It is instead the ongoing potential for a collapse into asocial living, for the disintegration of politics into battles of the "right" of the strongest or war. An apt metaphor for these kinds of devolution is moving through a no man's land or travel in a time of war. One might, along a dusty, broken road, or a set of tracks, encounter an ally, who is also trying to locate medical supplies, weapons, or his wife. One would as easily confront a national enemy similarly stranded. All are likely to be desperate. Why else would one undertake a voyage through an unknowable terrain? One might, with luck, in fact arrive at one's destination, but the series of events of the physical journey may have completely altered the course of one's life. It will have required making a deal at a checkpoint, making or losing a companion, a safe route that took one fundamentally off course.

José Ortega y Gasset (1932) has described the "ever–present problem" of the relation between artificial civilization and self-supporting nature. Reminding readers of the insights of the Romantics, he points toward the wild vegetation that can only briefly be stifled by the scythe and geometric stone. The Romantics and Ortega seize on the insight that everything is ultimately earth, pointing to majestic monuments now overgrown with moss, mold, and vines. Civilization requires constant upkeep, ongoing artistry. If one wants its fruits, one must inherit and take on anew the project of its upholding. Otherwise it can and does vanish quickly. Indeed Ortega's fear was that modern men treated civilization as if it grew up as spontaneously as a forest and thus inhabited it as if primitive men in a state of nature (88–89). Exhibiting neither interest nor affinity with the values that were the base of its construction, such men would, as we saw in Chapter 1, valorize the archaic and primitive.

Such sentiments could not be more antithetical to the impulse at the core of politics and the *polis* that we have been exploring. For, writes Ortega, these begin with the creation of a new kind of space that is fundamentally different from, and often opposed to the open country:

> The Graeco-Roman decides to separate himself from the fields, from "Nature," from the geo-botanic cosmos. How is this possible? . . . . Where will he go, since the earth is one huge, unbounded field? Quite simple; he will mark off a portion of this field by means of walls, which set up an enclosed, finite space over against amorphous, limitless space. Here you have the public square. . . . [I]t is purely and simply the negation of the fields. The square, thanks to the walls that enclose it, is a portion of the countryside which turns its back on the rest, eliminates the rest and sets up in opposition to it. This lesser, rebellious field, which secedes from the limitless one, and keeps to itself, is a space *sui generis*, of the most novel kind . . . an enclosure apart which is purely human, a civil space. (1932, 152)

Finally, as I stated at the outset, while the general will is fragile in the sense that it can be evaded, trumped, and ignored, even then, as the aspiration that could sustain the spirit that leads to the formation of political associations, it does not die.

RECONCILING WHAT IS CONSENTED TO WITH WHAT IS RIGHT

The general will, as Nancy Hirschmann (1992, chap. 2) aptly put it, must be chosen and it must be right. It seems straightforward that the general will tends toward public utility, toward a good that is common. This is its purpose. Its meaning is the same as the actions that might achieve this aim. But in what sense is the general will always right? The general will has normative force: it always has the right and is legitimate, for it is the people as the source of legitimation seeking their own common good. But it is also supposed to be correct in an epistemological sense.

To assist citizens, enlightening rather than misleading them, Rousseau looks in the *SC* for assistance in the figure of the legislator and to civil religion.[22] Less explicitly than in other writings, he also outlines a pedagogical view of politics, one in which ongoing opportunities to participate in civic activities would give the public life a tangible reality, anchoring our orientation toward its sustenance. On the question of law and the legislator, Rousseau reflects, "Whatever is good and in conformity with order is such by the nature of things and independently of human conventions. All justice comes from God; he alone is its source. But if we knew how to receive it from so exalted a source, we would have no need for government or laws. Undoubtedly there is a universal justice emanating from reason alone; but this justice, to be admitted among us, ought to be reciprocal" (1987, 160). Although the social orders through which justice and right may be pursued are based in human conventions, what is good or in order is so independently of these, with their existence discrete from their empirical instantiation in a particular time or place. Justice's source ultimately is G-d, however, through reason, we can fathom its universal form. But how do we give it more than conceptual life? How do we bring about *political* justice? It does not suffice for each of us to act on what we tenuously grasp as divine. This may be equivalent to acting ethically, but in the absence of institutions to assure that conditions of association are honored reciprocally, laws of justice will be observed by the good and flouted by the wicked. The former's credit of grace may increase, but, in worldly terms, in the absence of legal institutions, taking ones cues from domains of the divine may be to act the fool. It could be politically astute to be the liar or cheat. We must therefore aim to craft laws that admit more infinite standards among us. For these to be efficacious turns on assuring that they are framed by an entire populace considering only and all of itself.

But, asks Rousseau, how would such an accord emerge? By sudden inspiration? "Who will give it the necessary foresight to formulate acts and to promulgate them in advance or how will it announce them in time of need? How will a blind multitude . . . carry out on its own an enterprise as great and as difficult as a system of legislation?" (1987, 162). We all, as both private individuals and citizens, need guides. Rousseau concedes from early on that as private individuals we see the good that we reject (usually in treating our individual private wills or those of partial societies as more real and urgent than the public ones that set the condition for their realization) and that as citizens we want a good that we do not see. There are instances in which the general will is self-evident. In many other cases, it is difficult to discern its shape in one alternative as opposed to another.[23]

Rousseau comments on the dilemma: for an emerging people to grasp sound maxims of politics and rules of statecraft, they would need already to possess the "social spirit" that the institution is to produce in them. Men would before the creation of laws be what laws were to enable them to become. And so, he reflects, one would need gods to give men laws. Or foreigners. Or religious and republican prophets, including Moses, Mohammed, or Lycurgus. What characterizes all three categories is that members of them behold the passions of men without feeling them and have no affinity with our "nature" which they know thoroughly. Their potential glory is of another sort, in legend or immortal memory. In other words, their labors could not be more different than those of artists and scientists in Rousseau's *First Discourse*: they instead resemble the few whom he there prizes.

These individuals then serve as catalysts or midwives for the transformation that Rousseau has already described as following from the creation of the social compact. But it would be dangerous to give administrative powers to those seeking such a massive and radical undertaking. This is why they must, as did the first of human languages, "compel without violence and persuade without convincing" (*CW* 7, 296). But how? They will speak of dilemmas that are untranslatable, of aspirations so general and distant to be beyond grasp, and in language that must be understood by people who see the future as chimerical. Does this sound miraculous? It is. These figures, ones that Max Weber described as the charismatic founders of countless movements and nations, often claim to speak for the gods, but unlike the "false" messiahs or upstarts of each generation, they effectively move the relevant people, giving them an identifying purpose across generations. Rousseau insists that this does not mean that the objects of religion and politics are identical. Only that they must work in tandem at the start of nations.

For some readers, the introduction of the figure of the legislator is an admission of failure on Rousseau's part, a concession to the impossibility of the emergence of the kind of people required to pursue and sustain a general will. Surely, if it relies upon the appearance of another Moses (both someone with his features and recognized positively for possessing them), moments of foundation will be very rare. Arash Abizadeh has argued that we are misled by trying to imagine that these first laws of establishment, those that enable us to envision ourselves as an interdependent body with common purpose, are arrived at through the exchange of argumentation and evidence. A better metaphor, he insists, is made with music.[24] These laws seem to appear and to appear as right in the way that a melody is simultaneously played and heard,[25] made and recognized as made right.[26] Margaret Ogrodnick (1999) interprets the role of the legislator rather differently, however. She reflects, "The impossibility of finding such a suprahuman figure . . . reinforces the responsibility for self-transformation that stands behind [Rousseau's] ideal of collective self-rule" (123). In other words, it clarifies both the qualities, dispositions, and self-understanding required of people capable of collective self-governance and our distance, even in regimes called "democratic," from embodying them.

But none of this can resolve the demands of actual action. For beyond legislation and active legislative power, there is still a need for a body that can unite legitimate willing with the force required to do its bidding. Government, Rousseau writes, is the intermediary between the people in their capacities as sovereign and as subjects, and is to do for the public person what the union of soul and body achieves in man. It is the sovereign's minister, loaned its power for the sake of executing laws, applying their spirit and principles to deal with particular matters.

And yet although this conception of the relationship of sovereignty to government remains consistent, the appropriate form of government will depend on a particular place—the size of its population and distribution of its wealth and resources. Each regime has its weaknesses. The greatest flaw of democracy, for instance, is that, more than its alternatives, it frequently leads to the confusing of sovereignty with government when liberty depends upon this conceptual and practical separation. If the majority of people, as the term *democracy* classically suggests, were actually to execute public policy, this would require that many among the sovereign people would turn from a focus on maintaining a general perspective to a preoccupation with particular people, relations, and objects, making it increasingly difficult not to treat private interests as the business of public affairs. Democratic governance could also, as Aristotle had cautioned, have the effect of displacing the sovereign general will with nothing more than a magistrate (if now made up of many people enacting a unanimous whim) pronouncing decrees (Rousseau 1987, 162). The distinction between sovereignty and government requires that we consider whether the presence of institutions associated with democratic rule ensures that the legitimacy associated with the aspiration to self-governance is in fact present.

That is why, Rousseau insists in ways that most dismiss as outmoded and romantic, that the tasks in which politics consists cannot be abrogated. They will be. Public service will cease to be the chief business of citizens. Mercenaries and political representatives will signal ailing polities. In assemblies, people will answer "a different question from the one [they were] asked" (Rousseau 1987, 204). Instead of voting for that which is advantageous to the state, they will weigh in for the advance of this man or that party or another opinion. In these cases, rather than running to assemblies, as citizens do in well-run cities, people will fiercely avoid them. Knowing and resisting a process through which the general will is sure not to predominate, in its name, bad laws will breed worse ones. Rousseau declares, "Once someone says *what do I care?* about the affairs of the state, the state should be considered lost" (198). Patriotism will dwindle. Private interests will appear as all that remains. States, in the sense of living polities, will die.

But perhaps this sounds really silly. Through its lens, most of political history would then be that of dead states and much that is called politics would instead constitute its abrogation. What would remain as politics would be too narrow to be of any use. It would only refer to exceptional moments when fallible and limited men and women act like gods, or resemble prophets.

To conclude this, however, would be misleading. Politics must be about what is general, what can emerge as shared in a context of permanent and abiding difference. Much works against this fragile, distinctive domain, but if its terms and terrain are completely eradicated, all that remains are different institutional iterations of the "right" of the strongest. In such instances, while their functioning may be less immediately corporeal, institutions and the laws they enshrine merely increase the force and will of some. These will be referred to as "political" because they possess the outer trappings associated with its unique aspirations, but may as well be the exchange of blows, of each seizing that from which they can fend off others. Rousseau is right to emphasize that most people will resist participating in *this* kind of "politics." Its colloquial connotations—"it's just political," "dirty politics"—admit a sense of betrayal linked fundamentally to an acknowledgment of misuse.

Rousseau knew well that people did and would gawk at his reflections: *Legitimate government*, they would mock, following David Hume, is nothing more than subjects grown accustomed to those who dominate them. Or, in the spirit of Weber, it is leaders who can expect that their commands will in fact be obeyed, whether or not they should be. Or in Marxist tones, what is ever framed as "general" beyond ideas that secure the position of the ruling class? It is only one more skillful use of cultural capital to frame as progress and emancipation the transformation of the lives of dominated people into further, maldistributed surplus accumulation. Rousseau would reply that to treat these as the only possibilities is to have been deceived by looking only at states badly constituted; to confuse profound challenges for that which cannot be surmounted. Knowing scandalous knaves and credulous urbanites does not eliminate what Rousseau says with certainty: that the people of Berne would have sentenced Cromwell to hard labor. In this instance, while the examples are European, one hears echoes of the individual acts of refusal that I explored in Chapter 1.

As I have discussed, Rousseau clearly argues that the general will is more audible in healthier societies in which public life is real and primary, with coherent and demonstrable meaning for its members. As living projects, however, even these polities begin to die at the moment of their birth. One can prolong their coherence, but its vibrancy remains delicate and easily undercut. Once the social bond, organizing core, and generality is "broken in all hearts" and "the basest interest brazenly adopts the sacred name of the public good" (Rousseau 1994, 198), it can be mended neither by reform nor by revolution.[27] Finally, writes Rousseau, "when the state, on the verge of ruin, subsists only in an illusory and vain form . . . then the general will becomes mute. Everyone guided by secret motives, no more express their opinions as citizens than if the state had never existed; and iniquitous decrees having as their sole purpose the private interest are falsely passed under the name of laws" (1987, 204).

Nothing is more stable and constant than our weakness. And so Rousseau places the beginning of our hopes there: "It does not automatically lead to happiness; and, when it does, this happiness promises neither absolute certainty nor definitive rest. It consists of practicing a healthy form of sociability: it is not much, perhaps, but it is all that is open to us. As Rousseau remarks, we draw the remedy from the very nature of our disease, and do so in a way that most closely conforms to our human condition" (Todorov 2001, 65–66). We travel with Rousseau from moments of inspiration and profound hope to others of dashing disappointment.[28] And we are reminded, again and again, that the verdict on the possible lies only with living people already enmeshed in societies of varied degrees of illegitimacy.[29]

Jason Neidleman (2001) has argued that Rousseau is often charged with contradictions that are features of the projects of self-governance that are his focus. He does combine commitments that democratic notions of legitimacy must also always hold in tension: One is transcendental—it is what is necessary and universal for something to be; in this case, for a political society to have an ongoing shared life requires a discernable general will. The other is general and therefore particular in relation to the universal: an indispensable commitment to the consent of a given people that will interpret and articulate the general will in light of their own, specific predicament.

STILL EMERGING GENERAL WILLS

While societies with eroded general wills could not be mended, there were also general wills that were still in the making. Rousseau considered this to be the case with the island of Corsica for which he was asked to play the role of legislator. Christopher Kelly (2005) argues that what interested Rousseau in this task was precisely the island's reputation as a European backwater, as the opposite of French and English models of eighteenth-century strong states. Kelly writes, "Rather than seeing Corsica as merely the uncivilized abode of bandits in need of colonial rule by a continental power, he regarded it as the one place in Europe still capable of receiving a sound legislation" (xiv).

Formerly colonized by the Moors and then the Genoans, the framing question of Rousseau's work was how the island could aim to become a genuinely postcolonial state: how to move it out of conditions of economic dependence and poverty. He surmised that this would require figuring out how to transform its primarily agricultural economy into an asset, most ambitiously how to translate its produce into international capital. Rousseau insisted, as Fanon would later, that the newly independent Corsicans should not aim to emulate the culture of their former colonizers, but to lead a concerted national effort to identify and cultivate its indigenous resources, most centrally *its people*. This would require Corsicans treating Corsica as its own economic and political center, rather than as an outpost or appendage to another mother country. One indispensable resource for this project was that Corsicans were not decadent; they did not display the individual and collective vices of their supposedly more civilized Western counterparts. This, for Rousseau, meant that they remained spirited. Still, this strength could easily collapse into widespread banditry, especially if people grew impatient with the project of building a legitimate democratically governed state. Rousseau argued that they did not need to become different from how they were but to preserve this in the absence of a shared enemy that united them across differences. They could do this by directing these forces toward maintaining their independence.

Rousseau insisted that the characterization of Corsica as a *lumpenproletarian* island of people more inclined to be thieves than hard-working citizens obscured the origins of these predilections in the culture of colonialism itself. He wrote:

> Who would not be seized with horror against a barbarous Government that, in order to see these unfortunate people cutting each other's throats, did not spare any effort for inciting them to do so? Murder was not punished; what am I saying, it was rewarded. . . . [I]t had as its goal making more onerous these same taxes which it did not dare to increase, always holding the Corsicans in abasement by attaching them so to speak to their soil, by turning them away from commerce, the arts, from all the lucrative professions, by keeping them from rising up, from being educated, from becoming rich. Its goal was to get all produce dirt-cheap from the monopolies of its officials. It took every measure for draining the Island of money in order to make it necessary there, and in order always to keep it from returning to it. Tyranny could not apply a more refined maneuver, while appearing to favor cultivation, it succeeded in crushing the nation; it wanted to reduce it to a heap of base peasants living in the most deplorable misery. (*CW* II, 137)

In other words, Corsicans had come to deplore labor not only as a pure loss to them, but also as a seemingly permanent and destructive sentence. It was from this condition that Rousseau now hoped the Corsicans could emerge. Recommending a temporary isolationism that would force the island to increase the interdependence of its regions, it would turn to agriculture as sustaining predispositions necessary to freedom. Unlike town dwellers, rural people had more children and were more attached to their soil, satisfied by a simple and rustic life that inspired no longing for change. Rousseau contrasted them with those involved in commerce that produced wealth and dependence, rebelliousness and softness.

Having already underscored the appropriateness of specific governmental forms to different environments, Rousseau argued that this rustic place was best fit for a democracy. Ironically, the counties and jurisdictions that the colonists had introduced and the destruction of the local nobility that they had overseen could facilitate a transformation in this direction. This was an instance of the kind of admission that the project of creolization allows: a strategy that had been devised to subdue the Corsicans could be reemployed to enlarge their equity and freedom. In securing Corsican independence, it was key to avoid certain errors frequently made, however. Rousseau warned "not to allow a fixed capital, to make the seat of government move from one town to another, and to assemble the estates of the country in each of them in their turn" and to "populate the territory uniformly, spread[ing] abundance and life all over" (2005, 196). In the case of Corsica, Rousseau insisted that political creativity would be necessary to assure that the administrative capital did not thrive as everywhere else fell into economic stagnation. This meant avoiding creating a small group of cities that drew aspiring bourgeoisies that produced nothing. A government surely did require a center, but this would be a purely administrative one that public men occupied only temporarily before returning to the other dimensions of their lives. Rousseau hoped this might forestall the drawing of cultivators away from the countryside that would be and would have to be affirmed as Corsica's real source of strength (132).

Rousseau therefore sought to link political privileges not to amassed wealth but to productive labor. Wanting to avoid what he considered the debasing introduction of money, he advanced instead the use of a strict system of exchange. Explaining that money was useful only as a sign of inequality, particularly for foreigners, one could make exchanges of goods themselves without mediating values, creating storehouses in certain essential places. Ultimately, he reminded his readers that political independence, their ultimate aim, required that all lived well without becoming rich. He insisted repeatedly that the ease and health of polities were two fundamentally different concerns and that the latter should be their focus. Efficiency, in other words, though a modern ideal, could also be a deeply antipolitical one. In the absence of money and taxation, citizens could be asked instead to contribute in kind. If roads needed to be built, the citizenry would do so through their labor.

Rousseau concluded with reflections about the qualities of human beings: Here echoing Hobbes, he wrote that it is fear and hope that most govern men. Parting company there he qualified that while fear only leads people to recoil lest they face punishment, hope emboldens men and women to act. The task then was to awaken the nation's activity by providing ground for great hopes. Nothing, he wrote, is more "really beautiful than independence and power." What could sustain the character of a newly articulated nation was paying close attention to the emerging nature of civil power, to assure that it would take the form of legitimate authority rather than abusive wealth. With the latter, Rousseau emphasized, power and authority would diverge—to obtain wealth and authority would become two separate tasks with the implication that apparent power was with elected officials while real power remained with the rich who could purchase their authority. Such practices could only lead to disappointment that would spread languor throughout the Island.

The greatest asset of the Corsicans was that unlike most of their modern European counterparts, they remained capable of freedom rather than mere obedience. But the cultivation of a viable political economy would determine whether this could be mobilized in pursuit of a general will or whether a will of some would illegitimately prevail, claiming best to embody the legacy of the fight for the island's hoped for postcolonial condition.

CRITICISMS OF ROUSSEAU'S GENERAL WILL

Rousseau's concept of the general will, the centerpiece of his effort to overcome limitations in earlier theories of consensual government, has been widely dismissed as utopian, authoritarian, repressive, or otherwise flawed. Some of its shortcomings can be amended through the rearticulation I offer here through Fanon. Others are difficulties that are at the core of the project of democratic self-governance itself, difficulties that, because perennial, we have no choice but to engage. It is frequently assumed that one of the most insurmountable of these problems and one that Rousseau is least helpful in adequately addressing is that posed by social difference. Many commentators have argued that the success of the general will in fact turns on the final eradication of human diversity in political life—a goal that is neither desirable nor possible. Here I have contended that the general will can do far more than tolerate and accommodate the most politically relevant of differences. Indeed, if we take seriously one of Rousseau's coexistensive definitions of the term, as "what the differences have in common," it suggests a need for unity that is produced as we grapple with points of divergence seeking in their combination the most viable articulation of a shared good. But, even then, he does offer two cautions: we can articulate a general will within an otherwise healthy polity when two extremities are trenchantly avoided.[30] The first is radical economic inequality, specifically situations in which some can afford to buy others who are sufficiently desperate to agree. The second is extreme religious intolerance that would make it impossible for some citizens to see others as anything other than damned. In both such circumstances, interests are so fundamentally opposed that the triumphing of some necessitates the sacrifice of others. In these moments, one no longer has one polity but splintered and multiple smaller ones.[31]

Critics have rejected Rousseau's distinction between the general will and the will of all or between a collective interest and a collection of interests as enabling and necessitating repressive forms of government intervention. For Lester Crocker (1995, 251), Rousseau's insistence that the will of the people and the general will not be the same as they are in liberal societies led him to aim to make a set of moral responses, presumably those compatible with public life, reflexive rather than reflective. A series of skilled puppeteers and men of deceitful tricks, he interjected, would be necessary to convince citizens that a loss of autonomy (here understood as the pursuit of individual interests) was not really a loss, and that renunciations of liberty were not actual abdications. This was all pursued, argues Crocker, so that "the inner space we call privacy [would] shr[i]nk as far as possible in Rousseau's plans for denaturing men and forming them into social units or 'citizens'" (253). Of this, J. L. Talmon wrote: "The extension of the scope of politics to all spheres of human interest and endeavor . . . was the shortest way to totalitarianism" (1986, 47). Rousseau's plans to make citizens of men offered them no rights in the face of unlimited majorities, Talmon concluded. This oversight, according to Leonard Schapiro (1972, 79), was due to Rousseau's enmeshing in the abstraction of his general will which led him to want to scourge all sectional associations, systems of political representation, and forms of religion incompatible with civil religion.

Rousseau may have sought to curtail the power of kings or of small groups of powerful elites, conceded Crocker, but in order to do so he made the people sovereign, rather than individual people themselves. For Rousseau, this amounted to a sovereignty that involved no actual exercise of power (Crocker 1995, 255). Crocker therefore concluded, "Since adherence to the one right will, the collective will purged of all marks of individual wills, is liberty, it resides outside the experienced will, on the assumption that it is what one really wills, unknowingly. . . . The only freedom, then, is the freedom to conform, to participate in a monolithic conformity whose noble aim is to end alienation" (260). Perhaps worst of all, since the general will was no one's, it encouraged the deception of a set of managers whose narrow self-interested pursuits would brook no criticisms, protest, or dissent (254).

Framed somewhat differently, as "the paradox of politics," are Bonnie Honig (2001) and Alan Keenan's (2003) more recent focus on those problems magnified through discussion of the role of the legislator. For Honig, rather than overcoming the problem of law's arbitrariness and illegitimacy, Rousseau avoids it through recourse to the foreign-founder who governs without the people's consent until he concludes that they have reached political maturity and can therefore depart. The foreignness of the figure, in Honig's account, is an expression of an attempt to organize and disown the inevitability, even in avowedly self-authored democratic societies, of continuing experiences of the authority of the law as alien and, more importantly, that the people in this and other cases could and did not will themselves into existence as a people in the first place. Still, if there is no way to avoid episodes of alienation, it would be a mistake to try to read these out of Rousseau and out of political life. Instead the appearance of foreignness marks ongoing gaps in legitimacy that can be understood as moments requiring augmentation and amendment. More dangerous is to domesticate it in ways that would obscure "the haunting opacity of the people to one another and . . . the ambiguity of law that both is and is not the product of the General Will . . . generated by the people but also imposed by the lawgiver" (Honig 2001, 31). For Keenan, this problem is not so generative. It is more fundamental and worrying. For him, if law is to shore up an endangered generality or existence of a people, it encounters the problem of the people needing to exist already fully in their generality. If there is no natural source of commonality to which the law is to refer and no "shared practice of community," how would laws be articulated and how could it be rational to make oneself implicated by laws and the common fate that they attempt to ensure? Rousseau's "solution," states Keenan, "is for the legislator to trick the people into accepting his laws" (2003, 49). Worse still, making reference to Rousseau's mention of the invocations by foreign founders of G-d and immortals, Keenan comments, "The people's predicament is such that they not only require outside intervention to give them the laws that will make them whole but they can only accept the laws under false pretenses and in a way that denies their autonomy" (50).

In a similar spirit, John Charvet has insisted that the consequences of Rousseau's "fixes" is the denial of any valid social life or social interdependence beyond those derived from the will of the political community. "On the one hand," Charvet writes, "we have each individual absolutely for himself, on his own, and on the other hand we have the all-embracing common life" (1974, 144). This is required, Charvet contends, to avoid the combining of particular interests and ends that would foster personal dependence on any but the shared will. The difficulty with this, however, is that the needs that stimulate these cannot be eradicated through sheer will (ibid.). Steven Johnston, who argues that the general will is a code of cruelty, asks, amplifying the concerns of Charvet, "Is the price of sovereignty an undeclared war between those elements engaged in a continual counter-attack in the name of the so-called particular? Apparently" (1999, 131).

The spirit of the arguments of Talmon and Crocker, if an expression of a vitriolic brand of paranoid liberalism that grew out of experiences of and responses to World War II and then the Cold War, also echo the nineteenth-century concerns of Joseph De Maistre and Benjamin Constant, who insisted that Rousseau had confused true freedom with collective obligations that would substantially restrict it.[32] This was due to a fundamental confusion about the public and private domains and the related seeking of freedom through what they considered Rousseau's design for state control. Particularly nefarious because without explicit individual rights or a conception of natural property, discussion of the infinite malleability of human nature seemed only to promise mass indoctrination and the expanding of the potentially limitless powers of a despotic system. What citizens might imagine as autonomous action would be nothing more than the acting out of a set of ideas surreptitiously instilled in them.[33]

Allan Bloom (1990) and Iain Hampsher-Monk (1995), among many others, have contended that Rousseau has been charged as much with arguing for social atomism as for collectivism. Indeed, the response of Hegel and Marx to Rousseau's writing was to fear that his conception of freedom remained narrowly individualist, without an overarching political or social dimension within which liberty could be fulfilled.[34]

Much like the Bible, interpretations of Rousseau's general will tell us as much, if not more, about its readers than about the idea itself.

There is no question that although dubious about excessive unanimity, Rousseau preferred situations in which the content of the general will was self-evident, when it was obvious which principles and governing norms would benefit the whole community because internal differences within it did not amount to fundamentally opposed interests. While the general will cannot itself create rough economic equality, for instance, it can frame movements away from it as that which would undercut generality itself (endangering the future of the general will). Still, if the orientation that enables citizens to think in such ways appears as nurtured through practice and in this sense reflexive, it is the clear benefits of the given fruits that compel us rather than any skilled puppeteers. Seeing the relative merits of these arrangements as opposed to what we would face in their absence is what spurs us on to maintain them. Recall that for Rousseau this is, after all, a portrait of the conditions that make it possible to form and preserve political associations that introduce a logic other than that of mere force by creating a collective within which we determine rules that constitute the conditions of our lives. It is only in this sense, as a description of what is required and limited by the nature of sociality, that one could call the design total. It does involve understanding ourselves and our freedom as necessarily intertwined with that of others who, if different, share a commitment for the kind of pushing back of arbitrariness that political projects seek.

Still, it is true that Rousseau does not outline blueprints of institutions to protect the rights of minorities. This is, of course, because his design is premised on hopes that there will be no form of internal differentiation that would require such assistance, that dissimilarities would not constitute the lines through which aspirations of some are routinely rendered irrelevant. To build such safeguards into the portrait would be to treat its guiding aims as impossibilities. While one might say that this remains naïve or nefarious in a world as varied as our own, it also offers a very important challenge: that it is erroneous and politically lazy to assume that the varieties of symbolic worlds people occupy must be divided by fault lines and fortresses; that the task is to broach afresh when and why these become so.

Additionally, challenges posed by the idea of the sovereign people, by how legitimate power becomes present, are real. One answer to this for Rousseau is his distinction between sovereignty and government: by setting up the people as articulating and directing that which elected officials are to do, with the ongoing power to challenge outcomes as incompatible with the general will as they have defined it. Setting up this power as inalienable and indivisible forces people prone to fracture to embody a scope of identity entirely innovative and artificial, that of generality. It is to counterbalance through its simultaneous breadth and limits shared concerns and values that will curb internal extremes that would destroy it. One might think here of the difference between the earnings of CEOs and average US citizens when the former catered to a circumscribed national market. Not alienating a finite set of buyers was essential to good business practices. Would that such "national" concerns still had such constraining effects on corporate managers whose market is now the globe. Finally, while Rousseau did want members of groups smaller than the polity not to mistake the scope of the former for the latter, his concern was that loyalties of one did not make those of the other impossible. Even then, recall that when speaking of factions, his response to threatening power of a small set was to multiply the overall number so that the votes of the populace remained multiple rather than coalescing to leverage a few profiteering individuals.

In other words, for Rousseau, the preserving of conditions of meaningful freedom required nurturing a situation that all occupied sufficiently similarly to feel a palpable sense of unity. This did not necessitate total power of the state. Recall here the point emphasized by Cladis, that nothing could be demanded of individuals that was not of use to the community and that what was not could be disposed of at will. At the same time, there is no doubt that Rousseau hoped the general will could be *efficacious*, making it impossible to ignore some members of polity with impunity. As Margaret Canovan (2005) has astutely emphasized, Rousseau's discussion is an effort to grapple with how to make an abstract sovereign people present in politics by uniting the individual and collective dimensions of citizenship in the realization of the general will, an account of when an otherwise ordinary collection of people become present as a mobilized majority making claims as to what best realizes the spirit that shaped the moment of their foundation as a people, and of what revivifies the legitimacy of a compact that was made to enlarge the freedom of members by tying them together into a collective, public self.

The logical conclusion of those who would frame the general will as an unviable collectivism is that the best that we can and should do is to aggregate individual interests while developing and aiming to protect individual rights according to a set of rules or procedures. This position, which is often expressed in the fear that Rousseau's designs would necessarily lead to an absolutist state, convey a cynicism in response to plural and seemingly irreconcilable viewpoints that many conclude have left the modern world only with epistemic claims resting on human perspectives that are intensely fallible and necessarily relative. The result is a demand for a feigned universal human perspective in spite of its known limitations or one that is so minimal in its content not to be useful as a basis for any compelling kind of collective life. Both enable wholesale retreats into relativisms of the particular, in which all that remains of politics are strategic face-offs among crystallized narrow interests, identifications of how they might and absolutely cannot opportunistically ally. There is little sense that what collides within the political arena might, if always indexed in terms of a larger shared *telos*, itself be open and alterable.[35] In such a context, Jason Neidleman has argued, the popular will seems to emerge as the only legitimate arbiter of validity claims (2001, 4). The sense that one might seek positions that could be shown to be right for most of the citizenry is framed not as the meaning of politics but as naïve and outmoded.

CONCLUDING COMMENTS

In this chapter, I have explored the concept of the general will as articulated by Rousseau. In his nimble hands, the general will appears with the very question of how legitimacy might emerge in and through political life. It has, in what often infuriates readers, a double nature that mirrors our own identity as neither gods nor beasts, neither of pure thought nor pure instinct. It similarly mimics the unique domain of politics that emerges from this peculiar configuration of what we are not. Seeking to find and sustain general life among sharply divergent interests and identities, to institutionalize reciprocity, freedom, and self-realization in the units through which enmity and war have been and will be fought, politic is also double. Incredibly quotidian, it is the absolute foundation for the possibility of anything more. And so with the general will. Combining features that are at once transcendental—it is what is universally necessary for the very possibility of a political future—it insists too on the indispensability of the specific challenges of distinctive people from whom it must emerge.

Those who have grappled with Rousseau's multifaceted general will are sure to be immediately struck by lines in Fanon's *Les Damnés de la Terre* or *Wretched of the Earth* describing national consciousness: It was to be the "all-embracing crystallization of the innermost hopes of the whole people," "the living expression of the nation" which was "the moving consciousness of the whole of the people," "the coherent, enlightened action of men and women." The "more the people understand, the more watchful they become," the more they would come to realize "that finally . . . their salvation lies in their own cohesion, in the true understanding of their interests." Unlike Rousseau, who periodically paused to insist on the realizability of his most rigorous of conceptual articulations of the nature of political legitimacy, in Fanon, *how* this is to emerge is his explicit focus, shaping the theoretical endeavor. For him, it emerges in and through history, in struggles of groups, framed as a separate species, trying to reinsert themselves into history rather than remaining forcibly outside of its march. It is the contours of this collective struggle that for him prove determining of the fluidity and malleability of lines of difference in its aftermath. If Rousseau distinguished between the general will and the will in general, for Fanon of greatest significance to questions of postcolonial legitimacy was the necessity of moving beyond nationalism essential to ousting occupiers toward what he called national consciousness. Without such a transition, a form of identification that was, in one moment, broad, fruitful, and innovative became empty, zombified, and dangerous.

In the next chapter I will explore how Fanon effectively takes up, reworks, and expands the notion of "the general will" into the idea of "national consciousness" or the creolized sensibilities of an emergent Algerian nation unified in its diversity. Particularly striking in light of their many significant similarities is one fundamental difference: While one can piece together a sense of how Rousseau would have suggested one move from living under norms of illegitimate governance toward political right, in spite of his periodic insistences to the contrary, his explorations were richest in the philosophical and theoretical mode. They articulated a regulative ideal through which we might critically evaluate existing regimes to articulate directions that would make them less imperfect. Fanon's political theory, by contrast, is embedded in and emerges directly out of describing the stages of trying to forge just such a transition. He thereby deepens and radicalizes Rousseau's insights, underscoring their irredeemably political dimensions and offering the possibility of setting up imaginings that do not only reject but also critically engage the best resources of the project of modern Europe precisely so that we might move beyond it.

Crucially for our purposes, while Fanon's insights affirm the centrality of a revised notion of the general will to the project of creating polities that are no longer colonized, his articulation of a public or common good is not a homogenized but a creolized one. In other words, if Rousseau's general will can be interpreted as making a potentially untenable problem of complex and abiding forms of diversity typical of most modern states, Fanon offers the challenge of political legitimacy as facilitating their negotiability, mediation, and possible reconciliation. He does this by suggesting that divergent identities need not enter the polity only on the model of exclusive, mutually hostile special interests that can at best be incompletely accommodated.

In offering a portrait of how we can conceive of a politics that productively engages dissensus and cultural difference to create new political frames of reference and action beyond, for example, multiculturalism, Rousseau's notion of the "general will" and Fanon's "national consciousness" could not be more appropriate and potentially fruitful as each recognizes the indispensability of attempts to reconcile the contentions between individual and group self-interests while continuing unrelentingly to search for a common or general good.

4

Fanonian National Consciousness

If we want to turn Africa into a new Europe and America into a new Europe, then let us leave the destiny of our countries to Europeans. They will know how to do it better than the most gifted among us. But if we want humanity to advance a step further, if we want to bring it up to a different level than that which Europe has shown it, then we must invent and we must make discoveries.

—FRANTZ FANON[1]

Although his early theoretical work on racism and colonialism focused primarily on the question of disalienation in terms requiring an interrogation of the human sciences, especially psychiatry, Fanon found himself in a difficult situation as head of the psychiatric division at Blida-Joinville Hospital at the dawn of the Algerian War. His experience as a soldier twice decorated for valor in World War II, his medical knowledge, and his commitment to struggles for freedom led to his aiding the Front Liberation Nationale (FLN), his eventual resignation from his state-supported position of head psychiatrist, and his formally joining the FLN. The observations and arguments he subsequently made in *Les Damnés de la terre* or *Wretched of the Earth* are thus informed by his on-the-ground experience in addition to his theoretical acumen.

INTRODUCING NATIONAL CONSCIOUSNESS

Fanon suggested that it was only through directly fighting forces of repression that a submerged Algerian nation or its general will, squelched and rendered irrelevant by colonial relations, could spring to life (*WE*, 131). He warned that where fatality permeated people, those who oppressed them were never blamed (54). Instead the diverse people who together constituted the colonized turned to magic, myth, and internal tribal feuds, all of which preexisted colonialism, in forms of avoidance that amounted to "collective auto-destruction" (ibid.). Although occupying the same physical territory, the colonized had little reason to think of themselves as sharing a political identity or as belonging to one nation with a potentially sovereign will. Indeed their divisions were many: There were, after all, those who managed to benefit and those who were excluded from the advantages of colonial exploitation. People living in the countryside saw those living in the towns as having taken on European dress and speech, as having betrayed the national heritage (112). Urban party and trade union organizers who made ventures into rural areas frequently acted arrogantly by ignoring the authority of respected traditional leaders or the longstanding significance of local clan and tribal diversity. They also generally feared the spontaneous violent outbreaks of the peasantry (113). Finally, there were revolutionary political and intellectual minorities from the towns who, breaking with the legalism and reconciliatory approaches of recognized local leaders, were imprisoned, exiled, and radicalized by country people ready through armed insurrection to take their land back. In an opposite movement were the *lumpenproletariat*, who, fleeing the destitution of the country, swelled the urban fringes. Unwilling to be reformed by a colonial society that they could only ever enter with the use of force, they came to direct this otherwise unpredictable and explosive action decisively toward spearheading "the procession of the awakened nation" (130).

It was initially in efforts to cast off a shared enemy, a shared source of alienation, that people placed unequally and disparately within the polity developed a sense of a collective fate, a sense of themselves as an emergent nation. For it and they to enter history required a combination of all engaging in a chain of discrete, local, irrevocable actions from which there was no turning back and the deliberate rooting out of local rivalries that could stall or interrupt an onward march toward sovereignty (*WE*, 132). In a confraternity more typical of a church, or the indivisibility of which Rousseau spoke, yesterday's enemies joined together to widen a national assault on their occupiers.

Even then, however, if a "racial feeling" or determination to reject all who were foreign was enough to enter a revolutionary fight, it was not enough to sustain it (*WE*, 139). Hatred and resentment alone made even some of the most resolute easily manipulated. Some would be blinded by the simplest of humane gestures, becoming convinced that nicer mundane treatment by the colonists (which, in fact, were each extorted concessions), itself constituted a victory. Others would be tempted with slightly more. With promises of abandoning those who continued courageously to fight, they would move into positions once occupied by settlers. Satisfed with much less than a general will—by what we might call a will of some—they had little or no interest in restructuring the roles themselves. They would not, as an actual decolonial project suggested, continue the reconstructive efforts necessary to make the last first.

Doing so would require supplementing, broadening, and reconstructing this initial nationalism with political, economic, cultural, and therapeutic components. Guiding and emerging out of each and all was the normative ideal of *national consciousness*.

Fanon first argued for the indispensability of radically democratic participation. Colonial relations rendered the vast majority of colonized people political children, beneath citizenship, whose aspirations and anger were irrelevant to determining the shape and direction of their polity. In anticolonial struggle, people, through fighting, made themselves subjects of their own history, seizing responsibility for its present and future. They had been told that they were incapable of such agency and only able to understand the language of force. Through collective decision-making, Fanon describes the nurturing of the humanity of the people—their eyes and ears expanding in a landscape befitting their dignity.

But for governmental institutions to become a locus of belonging and identification, they had concretely to demonstrate that they connected one part of the nation to the others through resource and infrastructural provision.

With the ousting of a community of settlers, many would hope that the nation could be an authentic expression of that which was local. This would lead many into an orientation of cultural retrieval, of seeking that which was most traditional to this place. This quickly could devolve into battles over which traditionalism was the purest expression of a people who now in fact faced new and distinct challenges. While recognizing that Algerians did indeed have a cultural past was essential to affirming their humanity as cultural agents, doing so more meaningfully required seeing them as people who could together articulate living culture through which to forge a shared, political world of the today.

But the challenge of fighting for the emergent nation was not without costs. The brutality of a reversed Manicheanism left scars, some of which could not be undone. One did not want those traumatized by the battles now empowered to run the country. One would need to be able to honor them as appropriate and deserved while turning to the next generation to develop new models for collective living that grew indigenously out of their shared situation.

For Fanon, doing justice to the risks taken and lives lost in revolutionary battle required ongoing, dialectical constructive work of cultivating a unique scope of political identity, that of the nation, which could alone mediate among class, regional, tribal, ethnic, and racial differences, by articulating a past and future in which all were mutually implicated. Securing such sensibilities did not only require prioritizing their cultivation but linking legitimate political activity to the project of evenly distributed economic and political development.

Fanon never diminished the difficulty of this challenge: while insisting that economic redistribution on a massive scale was urgent and essential (lest societies be shaken to pieces), he was as unforgiving of the national bourgeoisie for not putting themselves in the service of the people as he was that they failed to become a genuine bourgeoisie: they did not revolutionize production in the local economy in ways that would upset the existing global division of labor. If they had disproportionately to seize the nation's wealth in what amounted to thieving from governmental coffers, they could at least have refuted the role of Europe's intermediaries, developing a distinctive, national model of what it would mean to be a capitalist class.

While Fanon clearly distinguished the possibilities of *national consciousness* from the failures of a narrowed and increasingly cynical nationalism, the former is more an evocative and challenging idea than one that is fully fleshed out. It is clear that national consciousness, as Rousseau's general will, seeks out and expresses what different people have in common; that it moves beyond an antagonism to foreigners which can quickly be redefined in a xenophobic *reductio ad absurdum*. It is what enables and in turn nurtures ongoing mobilization and is therefore hijacked and undercut by policies that rely on the retreat of most of the citizenry into induced passivity. While drawing on the cultural resources that all bring to the table, it seeks to combine and fuse these into distinctive new national forms in an open-ended constructive process that will be radically rejected by those who in power plays for scarce resources claim that one version of traditionalism is the singular and authentic one that should dominate. It can finally only emerge out of ongoing praxis—ever incomplete political, cultural, economic, and explicitly therapeutic efforts to reduce the causes of unfreedom—to make political institutions more responsive, better loci and expressions of a consciousness of what will cultivate national growth. Absent a sense of political work as never done, the most recent period of mobilization will instead be reified into that which embodied "the nation's" aims and identity and will snidely be invoked by those able to frame the will of some as if it were identical with an actual general will.

Rousseau's conception of the general will—while that which tried in the most classically modern terms to insist that sovereignty could only belong to the active citizenry and that governments, to be legitimate, would have to make a task of seeking that which could be shown to maintain rough equality benefiting the citizenry as a whole—gave little account, save turning to a mythic legislator, of how a society with norms of legitimacy could emerge out of contexts of illegitimacy. Instead Rousseau's discussion, but for the examples of Corsica and Poland, focused on legitimacy as an act of *preservation*, of maintaining rare conditions and fragile relations under which it first emerged.

In Fanon, national consciousness emerges only out of deliberate challenges to relations of subordination and alienation. Unlike in most cases with Rousseau, in which the general will is simply there with little attention to or interest in how it is constituted, in Fanon it takes shape through collaborative struggles first to oust those people and interests fundamentally opposed to the emergence of an indigenous citizenry's will and then to move beyond this to, as I have shown in Rousseau's discussion of Corsica, creating institutions that would develop a nation that had been an appendage to another metropolitan center. This was ongoing and dialectical, demanding that each generation take on the next stage of responsibility, prizing the devising of models that in reflecting local needs could enable growing aspirations.

In this way, Fanon's discussion offers much to the current debate in the academic field of political theory over "the paradox of politics" mentioned in Chapter 3. Briefly, this is a dilemma at the core of theories of popular sovereignty. In Bernard Yack's words, if "the people precede the establishment and survive the dissolution of political authority, then they must share something beyond a relationship to this authority" (2001, 524). If the legitimate basis of their commonality must be civic, rather than racial or ethnic, we face the problem: institutions are supposed to refer to a body of citizens who are to be defined through existing institutions. In Rousseauian language, people would before the creation of laws be what laws were to enable them to become. If a democratic people is rarely, if ever, democratically created, and in fact resorts regularly to nondemocratic criteria to define the sovereign people, we might lament this and treat it as an impossibility in the face of which democratic theory can only fail. Or we might see it as an inevitability that can be made into an opportunity for ongoing political creations that while always imperfect may, in the processes of their institution and the triumphs and disappointments they generate, enrich democratic thought and practice (see, for example, Frank 2010; Honig 2007; Näsström 2007).

Fanon's account clearly affirms the second interpretation, offering some distinctive considerations. Only to make use of "legitimate means" or methods within a colonial society would not only fail to challenge its more fundamental coordinates but in so doing would appear to condone or give them the added credibility of appearing democratic. While engaging in armed struggle breaks from any straightforward understanding of the following of democratic principles of constitution, here its central aim is to reveal the ongoing violence structuring the society, challenging its use as an instance of the rightful dispensation of force. Still the struggle that Fanon describes is democratic to the extent that it is leveled against unfreedom, uncovering structural inequalities, seeking to broaden who constitutes the polity so that it better reflects all implicated, even if this will require ridding it of those most committed to maintaining oppressive conditions. The boundaries of the emergent nation, as I have emphasized, are not based on racial, ethnic, or religious membership but on a particular brand of committed, decisive, and divisive action in which anyone could in theory engage. (Indeed, Fanon emphasizes that there are French men and women who join the anticolonial cause while there are Algerians who resist it bitterly.) Fanon stresses that while the emergent once-submerged nation is forged out of and through disparate and connected actions, even then, it is essential constantly to articulate what the differently located members of it have in common, to creolize and generalize the collective will.

It is clear that while one could nurture national consciousness and that it might even, in some instances, blossom, it functioned primarily as a normative ideal through which the larger aim of political legitimacy, of relations that were no longer fundamentally exploitative, might be clarified and understood.

THE RIGHT OF THE STRONGEST NORMALIZED AND CONTESTED

"Man is born free, and everywhere he is in chains. He who believes himself the master of others does not escape being more of a slave than they. How did this change take place? I do not know. What can render it legitimate? I believe I can answer this question" (Rousseau 1987, 141). So opens Rousseau's *On the Social Contract* and his meditations on the ways in which restraints on liberty of individuals can, under particular arrangements, enhance their freedom. The discussion, itself a portrait of the fragile possibility of "legitimate and sure rule of administration in the civil order," turns on two points that I have already considered: that the "right of the strongest" and its correlative "right of conquest" are incoherent and that the possibility of communities in which disagreements are resolved politically require a set of conditions that are difficult to create or sustain. They rely indispensably on an orientation toward differences that, while not aiming to subsume them, assumes that they may be meaningfully negotiated rather than collapsing into sedimented lines of battle.

Fanon's account of forging an unfinished alternative to political illegitimacy is oriented around these same crucial insights. Offering a rigorous conceptual reconciliation of principle and possibility, Rousseau's sober grapplings do not hide their own paradoxes and limitations. Still, the resulting reflections remain primarily formal and addressed to an audience of other Europeans. Fanon, by contrast, does not only argue that legitimate governance must emerge in and through political life and history; he also demonstrates this claim in the very way that it is advanced.[2] Speaking to the world, he insists that it is in waging a dangerous and unpredictable battle against one's exclusion from the realm of political life that a more fully democratic community emerges with a will and national consciousness. Any limitations to full incorporation are not merely theoretical or strategic oversights. They will have lamentable and lasting consequences that pose ongoing obstacles to approximating a fully represented and representative people.

Rousseau (1987, 143) says of force that it is a physical power to which people surrender, not out of duty or an act of will, but as prudent. One can use force to coerce obedience so long as others lack it. As soon as a capacity for its exercise is in their possession, the roles reverse. Force can secure nothing permanent on its own account unless it is used to create a compelling right that moves us of our own will to obey. In the absence of this, one shakes it off as quickly as one can.[3]

Fanon's discussion begins with just such a predicament. Now neither hypothetical nor individualized, it is the description of the very project of maintaining a colonial society, one that aims literally to carve the world in two. Particularly noteworthy is that unlike the European societies that are Rousseau's primary focus, where institutional investments are made in shaping the aesthetic and moral character of those who do not benefit from the arrangement of life opportunities, the chains of the colonized are laid bare. Apart from a tiny fraction that comprises an urban colonized pseudobourgeoisie, no effort is made to manufacture or elicit what Antonio Gramsci (1971) termed "spontaneous consent." Rather than teachers and ministers, those who mediate between the world of the colonizers and the colonized are the police and the army. In an ironic turn comparable with the notion of the "right of the strongest," Fanon writes, "It is obvious here that the agents of government speak the language of pure force" (*WE*, 38). The realm of politics, classically understood, is one dominated by discursive negotiations of disagreement; language and persuasion come to dominate precisely as physical coercion and conflicts recede.[4]

Force extends beyond the mere ubiquity of weapons and bloodshed, however. For Fanon the unqualified brandishing of the use of force—including statues commemorating settlers' heroes as those there by dint of bayonets—betrays a *project* of dehumanization, the only way through which systematized (in)human relations are normalized. The effort to create a neatly Manichean world of noncomplementary compartments or fundamentally opposed spheres that cannot be reconciled in a higher unity does not only decimate former economic and material relations, but social and symbolic forms as well. Writes Fanon, "The settler's work is to make even dreams of liberty impossible for the native . . . The appearance of the settler has meant in the terms of syncretism the death of the aboriginal society, cultural lethargy, and the petrification of individuals" (*WE*, 93).[5] The absence of any effort to deal with the colonized as potential givers of consent illustrates unambiguously: they are outside and beneath the relations of ruler and ruled on which discussions of political legitimacy typically turn. They would be irrelevant to whatever might be presented as a general will, even though, as we have seen in the previous chapter, this belies the very meaning of the term. Any response of the colonized to this situation, save appreciative affirmation, is itself deemed as violent, since all other reactions involve a challenge to a status quo aimed at securing their unfreedom.

The effort to render the discontent of major portions of the ruled irrelevant is not unique to modern colonial situations. After all, Niccolò Machiavelli (2005, 19) famously cautioned would-be princes that their greatest danger was incurring the *hatred* of those they ruled. Fortresses built upon loyal citizens and subjects supplied the surest protections against shifting tides of fortune. At the same time, one could render the desire for violent revenge irrelevant: This was easiest with people who did not yet know how to live as free men. One had simply to destroy the entire bloodline of their royalty. Those with memories of experiences of freedom posed a greater challenge: The surest solution was obliteration. One could try as well to go and live among them by forming colonies, separating and scattering them so that they were too disorganized and poor to forge a collective threat. *Hold on*, Fanon would say. He, unlike Machiavelli, is not describing Southern Europe in the fifteenth century but instead a France, supposedly remade through Revolution, in its relations with the non-European world. Hence his repeated references to the failure to forge a no longer colonial society as leaving the colonized sleeping in the Middle Ages.

This slumbering is indispensable to preserving what could not be viable if its subjects were not disoriented by a mummified system of meaningful references. Consider here a distinction made by Enrique Dussel (2008, 104–6) between what he terms "compulsion" and "violence." The former, he explains, involves the use of force grounded in laws authorized by representatives of the people. It includes sanctioned practices of stopping, detaining, and holding people. Self-appointed individuals, by contrast, exercise the latter, in the absence of collective critical support. Fanon faces a challenge absent in the writing of Rousseau, of convincing readers of the conclusion drawn by those struggling for their liberation, that the ongoing unmasked force of the settlers cannot be considered legitimate, but is instead worthy of the designation "violence." Doing so challenges who and what constitutes "collective critical support," "legitimate representatives," and "the people" through forging an alternative hegemony in which colonial endeavors are challenged as a justifiable mode of economic development. The official narrative of French settlement, after all, is familiar to everyone implicated: The settler makes history, is an absolute beginning and unceasing cause—if he leaves, the country will be lost, dominated by antediluvian plagues and customs.

In the absence of a clearly formulated rejection of such renderings of colonial history, the anger and counterforce of the colonized that should have been directed at an immediate "shaking off" of the once stronger instead targets their own. Part of the immobilization of the agency of colonized people, their structurally induced collective pathology of liberty is that they can only exist as human beings among themselves, but in each other and in elements of their own selves, primarily see sites of illegitimacy. In efforts to act with freedom within forcefully constrained conditions, they do so in ways that challenge but are unlikely to alter any of the fundamental coordinates of their condition: they reenliven feuds that preexisted the arrival of the colonists and ancestral spirits that are far more powerful than any Frenchman. "By throwing himself with all his force into the vendetta," writes Fanon, "the native tries to persuade himself that colonialism does not exist, that everything is going on as before, that history continues" (*WE*, 54).

Redefining their foci of force or ceasing to commit collective suicide requires an outright challenge to the force of settlers *as* violence. Dussel emphasizes, here informed by Fanon, that the line delineating compulsion from violence is contextually specific and fluid, that struggle for new rights "creates a new legitimacy framing prior legitimate compulsion as illegitimate" (*WE*, 104–5). In so doing, the colonized assert themselves as political subjects capable of normative assessments guided by their own trajectory toward greater freedom. Dehumanization turns on a doubled and paradoxical move, of deliberately refusing to see a human being in particular categories of other people.[6] Although Fanon acknowledges that the settlers know that the colonized look on their living conditions with resentment and envy, they remain shocked at the turn to violence on the part of the colonized, even though this is a move made ordinarily by European countries faced by threats to their sovereignty.

Recall that with Rousseau, the proper response to physical coercion is simply to try to break free of it. At first, in Fanon's setting, decolonial violence follows exactly the Manichean logic imposed by the Europeans but with the values inverted. "The native replies to the living lie of the colonial situation by an equal falsehood . . . Truth is that which hurries on the break-up of the colonialist regime; it is that which promotes the emergence of the nation; it is all that protects the natives, and ruins the foreigners. In this colonialist context there is no truthful behavior: and the good is quite simply that which is evil for 'them'" (*WE*, 50).

But this response, only initially adequate, is itself an interruption of an induced immobility: the decision to end the position of Algeria as defined solely by the history of colonization is to bring the nation into being. Fanon emphasizes, here as both a psychiatrist and revolutionary, that what is significant about liberation, renaissance, or an emerging commonwealth is that they are *willed* and *demanded*. A possibility before experienced only crudely is forged deliberately as a program that is "clear to itself... in the exact measure that we can discern the movements which give it historical form and content." Its advance is nothing less than the replacing of a category of native subpeople with agents of a shared and open present. Here Fanon breaks fundamentally with the conservative (in the sense of aimed at conservation) project of nation-building evident in Rousseau, who sought to recuperate qualities that are essentially shared from their corruption through forces of division.

CHALLENGING ILLEGITIMACY FROM THE BOTTOM UP

But how do people, however imperfectly, refuse habituation and create the polities they deserve? Fanon outlines what is involved with no romance. He writes, "National liberation, national renaissance, the restoration of nationhood to the people, commonwealth: whatever may be the headings used or the new formulas introduced, decolonization is always a violent phenomenon. At whatever level we study it . . . decolonization is quite simply the replacing of a certain 'species' of men by another 'species' of men. Without any period of transition, there is a total, complete, and absolute substitution" (*WE*, 35). Rejecting the lines of force that have structured the geography of colonial society builds upon a nascent sense that while the colonized had been overpowered, they had not been tamed. Having ingested the settlers' story of their shared situation, they had not fully digested it. Fanon writes, "In the colonial context the settler only ends his work of breaking the native when the latter admits loudly and intelligibly the supremacy of the white man's values. In the period of decolonization, the colonized masses mock these very values, insult and vomit them up" (43). If success entails the radical transformation of a social structure, this must manifest itself in what can only be a historical process. Neither magic nor nature can substitute for the meeting of two opposed groups whose relations were created and sustained through violent coercion.

The colonized must claim themselves the equal of the settlers. What makes this plausible is not simply the insistence that it is so. Instead, it is in the moment of an actual fight that the colonized realize that they fight human beings like themselves; that the skin, breath, and heart of the colonizers share the fortitude and fragility of their own forms. This highly concrete realization is transformative. Through it, the colonized conceive of themselves as the match for the problems they face, capable of directly addressing them. Grasping the lies at the core of the social rules that have forcibly regulated their life movements, these easily begin to crumble: "For if, in fact, my life is worth as much as the settler's, his glance no longer shrivels me up nor freezes me, and his voice no longer turns me into stone. I am no longer on tenterhooks in his presence; in fact, I don't give a damn for him . . . I am already preparing such efficient ambushes for him that soon there will no way out but that of flight" (*WE*, 45). People weighed down by their "inessentiality" reemerge as "privileged actors, with the grandiose glare of history's floodlights upon them" (ibid.).

The metamorphosis must be collective, however, and the nature of the emergent solidarity forged. Decolonization unites the people by a decision to "remove from it its heterogeneity," to unify on a national, sometimes racial, basis. For native intellectuals who have imbibed and defended the Greco-Latin pedestal as their own, these become lifeless, dead words. They are utterly irrelevant to the conflict in which they are engaged. Languages of individualism therefore are replaced with vocabularies of kin, family, and trusted friends. For, as Fanon comments, "Henceforward, the interests of one will be the interests of all, for in concrete fact everyone will be discovered by the troops, everyone will be massacred—or everyone will be saved. The motto 'look out for yourself,' the atheist's method of salvation, is in this context forbidden" (*WE*, 47). At the start, this is genuinely a situation of clearly designated lines dividing friend from foe, us from them. What has been submerged as only a latent possibility, he writes, "requires that each individual perform an irrevocable action . . . You could be sure of a new recruit when he could no longer go back into the colonial system" (84). In these cases, he or she had broken with the existent order. To stop there would render each a traitor or terrorist. To be more they would have to continue on in the building of a world for which their actions could be prefatory. In pledging to ensure triumph in his or her locality, each colonized man or woman announced, that where he or she was, so was the nation. As new tribes entered, this nation expanded, linking an increasing number of once discrete villages into a larger chain of national and international action. Striking at a shared enemy became the same as entering politics in an onward march of resistance that was the growing of sovereignty.

Rousseau introduced the figure of the lawgiver to enable a blind citizenry habituated to corrupt and arbitrary rule to become the people who could together articulate the general will. This figure must rid them of the problem of emergence—of how they could, before the existence of good law, be the people who could create it—by "transform[ing] each individual (who by himself is a perfect and solitary whole), into a part of a larger whole from which this individual receives, in a sense his life and his being . . . In a word, he must deny man his own forces in order to give him forces that he cannot make use of without the help of others. The more durable are the acquired forces, the more too is the institution solid and perfect" (Rousseau 1987, 163). Bonnie Honig has stressed the significance of the necessary foreignness of this founding figure, that it proved an essential resource for responding to dilemmas at the center of democratic life itself. Being from elsewhere "secures for him the distance and impartiality needed to animate and guarantee a General Will . . . because he is not one of the people, his lawgiving does not disturb the equality of the people before the law . . . [he has no] known genealogy [that] demystified his charismatic authority" and there appears to be some assurance that he will, after birthing the polity, *leave* (Honig 2001, 21, 23).

In Fanon, the equivalent political transformation is also reliant on foreignness. The estrangement, however, is not in the position of a singular founder but is instead multiple. It entails discrete portions of the nation, previously mutually foreign, substantively reencountering one another. After describing the Manicheanism of colonial relations and the initial eradication of heterogeneity through armed struggle, Fanon therefore differentiates among variably positioned members of colonized society. In particular, there is an indispensable role to be played by native intellectuals whose European training, suddenly appearing irrelevant to the shifting terrain, leave urban centers to live among the peasantry who, in staunch contrast, have always been prepared for dangerous action but need help in its "being educated." The marginalization of members of political parties by an organizational politics too ready for reconciliatory promises build from these institutional inadequacies a different relation to the strengths and weaknesses of sectors of the population who have been treated as peripheral to strategizing. In particular, the *lumpenproletariat* who have left the impoverished countryside only to bloat the urban periphery undergo a transvaluation. There is of course also Fanon himself, who connects instances of racialization between

Africa and its diaspora, bringing psychological and philosophical resources to participation in a struggle that enables him to develop a praxis that contends adequately with societal madness with which he had dealt in individual patients. From Tunis and Algeria, he articulates for it and the world the dream of a nation seeking to model the highest aspirations of humanism. In other words, out of the species of "the native," none are left unchanged. All are touched by a *telos* that draws the so-called natives' specific, indispensable experience and resources into a larger, moving unity that creolizes their discrete points of access into a shared emergent will.

But if for Rousseau there are scales of economic disparity and forms of religiosity that make the pursuit and maintenance of an enlightened general will impossible, for Fanon, colonial relations prove an insurmountable obstacle. A general will quite simply cannot emerge where the majority of the population is violently rendered irrelevant to political life. In these circumstances, civil resistance and demands for inclusion are almost entirely moot. Indeed the slogan of nonviolence—an attempt "to settle the colonial problem around a green baize table, before any regrettable act has been performed or irreparable gesture made" (*WE*, 61)—is that of the colonized pseudobourgeoisie who share more with their colonial counterparts than with their mobilized, primarily rural countrymen. Their preference is for a continuation of the prevailing status quo. In sharp contrast, for those outlawed members of the group long perceived to be predatory pariahs, the *lumpenproletariat*, it is their willingness to flout laws increasingly seen as illegitimate and violently to attack shared enemies whose presence is now deemed fundamentally a crime that amounts to their "royal pardon" (86).

Although anticolonial violence is constitutive, binding "groups [that] recognize each other [into a] future nation [that] is already indivisible" (*WE*, 93), throwing them in a shared direction that introduces into the consciousness of each a sense of common cause, destiny, and past, Fanon's discussion of violence is sobering: There is no alternative literally to seizing one's freedom, to fighting in self-defense for dignity that has been so mightily challenged.[7] Still, many of its consequences are unavoidably tragic. Revolutions, even the most legitimate ones, involve monstrous moments and highly imperfect decisions. There is no doubt that the people responsible for fighting for the possibility of a postcolonial condition will themselves be irretrievably scarred. As Lewis Gordon (2008a, 122–23) has argued, they are a generation that might be compared to the figure of Moses, leading others to a promised land (and promised home) that they can and will not enter.

Many among them will subsequently wonder, as did Rousseau, whether they risked all they did for a future that intensifies the very relations they aimed to overthrow. Even then, their political adulthood does turn on rejecting relations that keep them locked in perpetual pupilage, outside of the domain of mature self-rule and history. They cannot but insist that legitimate governance must reflect a general will that makes it impossible to ignore them with impunity.

In addition to repositioning themselves as having points of view through which they can evaluate and judge colonial relations and conditions, anticolonial struggle also relatedly reopens the possibility of the colonized again being sources of signification beyond the imposed ossification of Manichaeism. Centuries of exploitation emaciate indigenous cultures eroding them into "a set of automatic habits, some traditions of dress, a few broken down institutions" (*WE*, 238). There is neither real creativity nor life in these. "The poverty of the people, national oppression, and the inhibition of culture are one and the same thing" (ibid.). In *A Dying Colonialism*, Fanon explores how liberatory struggle creates an alternative to the two options that colonialism imposes—to embracing its impositions as the present and future or resisting through seeking refuge in a traditionalism of an artificially frozen precolonial domain. The process of deliberately challenging coordinates of their freedom's compromising reopens the corridors to new forms of symbolic life. Indeed, writes Fanon, a "nation which is born of the people's concerted action and which embodies the real aspirations of the people while changing the state cannot exist save in the expression of exceptionally rich forms of culture" (246). He illuminates this process through the example of the changing meaning of the veil of Algerian women.

Depending upon the preoccupations of colonizing forces, certain cultural elements take on vital significance, expressing an overall attitude of locals toward foreign occupation. With the veil, the response to the desires of colonialists to tear it off was, on the part of many Algerian women, to cling to it violently, even if they had not before, so as deliberately to create a setback for colonists who in effect demanded complete and unrestrained access to them.

This shifted with the outbreak of armed, anticolonial struggle and the move toward total war. Male revolutionary leaders needed new strategies including those that would put full confidence in their mothers, wives, sisters, and daughters who had previously primarily receded into private domiciles as a last unoccupied terrain. Suddenly out of such confinement, the same women quickly learned to remove the veil and don themselves as women alone in the street. Disarming French guards with their casual sauntering, they in fact only did so in order to transport a weapon or message pivotal to a particular revolutionary mission.

Fanon emphasizes that such women were unable to undergo any period of apprenticeship. They were not playing a role they had read about or witnessed. Instead they were creating the originals, literally the living prototypes. Fanon observed: "There is not that coefficient of play, or imitation, almost always present in this form of action when we are dealing with a Western woman. What we have here is not the bringing to light of a character known and frequented a thousand times in imagination or in stories. It is an authentic birth in a pure state, without preliminary instruction" (Fanon 1967a, 50). Fanon, again here with psychological insight, illuminates the difficulties faced by such women who must deliberately erode the image of the occupier lodged in their minds. More, they must develop an entirely different phenomenology of the body:

> We must come back to that young girl, unveiled only yesterday, who walks with sure steps down the streets of the European city teeming with policemen, parachutists, militiamen. She no longer slinks along the walls as she tended to do before the Revolution. Constantly called upon to efface herself before a member of the dominant society, the Algerian woman avoided the middle of the sidewalk, which in all countries in the world belongs rightfully to those who command. The shoulders of the unveiled Algerian woman are thrust back with easy freedom. She walks with a graceful, measured stride, neither too fast nor too slow. (58)

By contrast, Fanon emphasizes:

> The body of the young Algerian woman, in traditional society, is revealed to her by its coming to maturity and by the veil. The veil covers the body and disciplines it, tempers it, at the very time when it experiences its phase of greatest effervescence. The veil protects, reassures, isolates. One must have heard the confessions of Algerian women to appreciate the importance of the veil for the body of the woman. Without the veil she has an impression of her body being cut up into bits, put adrift: the limbs seem to lengthen indefinitely. (58–59)

When suddenly unveiled, her body appears to disintegrate: "She has an impression of being improperly dressed, even of being naked . . . The absence of the veil distorts the Algerian woman's corporal pattern. She quickly has to invent new dimensions for her body, new means of muscular control. She has to create for herself an attitude . . . relearn her body, reestablish it in a totally revolutionary fashion" (59). In her direct participation in the uncinching of colonial relations, the Algerian woman renders the symbol of the veil fluid. The world within which its meaning had been posited or challenged was itself no longer stable. First removed and then reintroduced as required by strategies of struggle, the veil, rather than a charged individual cultural element, became an instrument malleably employed to meet and address newly emergent problems. The woman who employs it is herself involved in the forging of a living culture tied to efforts to articulate and give substance to a general-will-in-formation.

"It is only in man," Ernst Cassirer writes, "that the problem of possibility arises" (1944, 56). Since human knowledge is by its nature symbolic, it must distinguish between the real and the possible, the actual and the ideal. "A symbol has no actual existence as a part of the physical world," it instead has meaning. While in most contexts, the elaboration of symbolic forms makes "the distinction between actuality and possibility . . . become more and more pronounced" (57), under special conditions, in which the function of symbolic thought is impeded or obscured, Cassirer emphasizes, the "difference between the actual and the possible becomes uncertain" (ibid.).

The maintenance of colonial relations relies on such impeding and obscuring, the rendering uncertain of the difference between what is and might be through suggesting that only one species within the larger category of human being is capable of symbolic thought and practice, while others can, at best, respond to signals, perhaps aping, but in all cases diminishing and corrupting properly symbolic forms. Repositing the relationship between the actual and forging something other than colonial relations therefore necessarily emerge together.

But progress, always imperfect and incomplete with real consequences for the future nation, cannot be sustained by hatred alone. For one, hatred entails an ongoing dependence on one's enemy. It also leaves a recently awoken people vulnerable to being cheaply bought off. Fanon observes, "The native is so starved for anything, anything at all that will turn him into a human being, any bone of humanity flung to him, that his hunger is incoercible, and these poor scraps of charity may, here and there, overwhelm him" (*WE*, 140). However, these scraps of civility, Fanon emphasizes, are not as they might appear. They are not sudden acts of voluntary good will but instead extortions that signal that increasing efficacy of resistance efforts; that the settlers are more and more on the defensive. Suddenly, now on the receiving ends of the arbitrary brutality of violent relations, the colonial elite reaches out to their pseudocounterpart among the colonizers, asking that they *reason* with the rest of their own people. This is not, however, spontaneous recognition of the willing capacities of Algerians.

Still, making sense of this unsettled Manichaeism demands a less rudimentary orientation, a capacity to distinguish, in particular, those among the colonized whose resistance was little more than a Nietzschean will to power, a resentful and reactive attack on those who ruled based in little more than a desire to usurp them. Their project is to pursue particular and private interests that cannot but collide with those of the rest of the nation for ultimately, as Paulo Freire put it, they do not seek a genuine decolonization or ridding the world of relations of oppressor and oppressed. They simply want to switch roles, leaving their structure intact.

Doing so defines one brand of nationalism, that which implies a "minimum of readaptation," a few reforms above and beneath an undifferentiated mass. This relies fundamentally upon the halting of political education emerging from reflective action, the receding of speech and discursive negotiation. This route, as we shall soon see, is most clearly embodied in the local pseudobourgeoisie that Fanon describes as economically and socially bankrupt. Imagining themselves replacing the colonial middle class, they envisage their *historical mission* as playing intermediary between the outside world, particularly its corporations, and the newly independent nation. They can only think to imitate and so repeat, in exaggerated form, the insults of former colonists. With them, the omnipresence of police and army is reintroduced, now in African uniforms.

TRANSCENDING THE BRUTALITY OF REVOLUTIONARY THOUGHT

Although necessary, the initial throwing off of the occupying force was not sufficient for the emergence of an indigenous general will. It required supplementing, broadening, and reconstructing the initial nationalism on which such efforts were based according to the normative ideal of *national consciousness*.

First and foremost, this treated radically democratic participation as indispensable. While taking active part in national liberation shaped a fundamental orientation against pacification, mystification, and a cultish reliance on leaders (*WE*, 95), the transition from "the status of a colonized person to that of a self-governing citizen of an independent nation" was not immediate (138). The consciousness of the freedom fighter had not kept pace with the efficacy of his or her role within the larger organized force. Nurturing understanding and reflection was therefore itself a battle, especially against those within the movement who would win now and educate later, who feared that discussion necessary to the formation of shared public opinion would be divisive. Fanon warns without qualification: "There exists a brutality of thought and a mistrust of subtlety which are typical of revolutions . . . if not immediately combated, [they] invariably lead to the defeat of the movement within a few weeks" (147). For Fanon, it is not sufficient for one group of people wielding the "right of the strongest" or a will of some to supplant the others. Instead an ending of colonialism must imply the creation of a different set of relations, specifically, politically legitimate ones.

These depart radically from understandings of development that uncritically rest upon stagnant majorities of enslaved and colonized people. In this instance, Fanon makes plain, the nation can only develop as its citizenry does. Therefore *efficiency*, if meaning the quick carrying out of business by a slim fraction of skilled employees, would be a value discredited along with the narrow individualism that proved unsustainable during the early stages of violent liberatory struggle. In the project of decolonization, public business must increasingly become the business of the public. Any other approach would quickly undercut its guiding aim: of the formerly colonized "realiz[ing] that finally everything depends on them; that if [they] stagnate it is their responsibility, and that if [they] go forward it is due to them too, that there is no such thing as a demiurge . . . the demiurge is the people themselves and the magic hands are finally only [their] hands" (*WE*, 197).

While there are reasons to challenge interpretations of Rousseau as an advocate of participatory democracy since he so feared the potentially disintegrative effects of factions and described the process of voting for the general will as listening, in silence, to the inner voice of G-d (rather than the potentially manipulative and misleading arguments and counterarguments of others), he also powerfully disparaged any easy declarations of what was politically impossible. Emphasizing that the people's sovereignty rests in legislative power that must remain active through their ongoing periodic assembly, he writes, "The boundaries of what is possible in moral matters are less narrow than we think. It is our weaknesses, our vices and our prejudices that shrink them. Base souls do not believe in great men; vile slaves smile with an air of mockery at the word liberty" (Rousseau 1987, 195). The last census of Rome counted four hundred thousand citizens bearing arms and an empire of four million citizens. Yet people were called together regularly to deal with public business in what Rousseau considered to be meaningfully democratic activity.

For Fanon, nurturing such capacities and orientations, like Rousseau, would require ongoing opportunities for practice and, here unlike Rousseau, a vision of the task of political parties that far exceeded the progressive role played early on in articulating dreams of the emergent nation. Fanon writes: "The citizens should be able to speak, to express themselves, and to put forward new ideas. The branch meeting and the committee meeting are liturgical acts. They are privileged occasions given to a human being to listen and to speak. At each meeting, the brain increases its means of participation and the eye discovers a landscape more and more in keeping with human dignity" (*WE*, 195). Seductive short cuts of every variety would have to be stringently avoided in cultivating fully conscious human beings rather than a slim set of exceptional leaders for whom the meaning of the nation would quickly shrink. Fanon insists that isolated individuals may refuse to grasp a problem, but that, soon before, entire groups and villages had understood difficult challenges with great rapidity. Government leaders ready to surmise that the citizenry were incapable of understanding the complex work of self-governance would do well to recall how capable, in the mist of revolutionary struggle, these same individuals had shown themselves to be. For Fanon states clearly, "the party is not an authority, but an organism through which they as the people exercise their authority and express their will" (185). Therefore those who claimed that they could not explain a given political matter to the people in fact did not *want* to and so would turn to obscuring and technical language as a mask because their actual aims required hiding. Political education would have to replace mere inculcations of inspiring slogans. Its aim, after all, was "not to treat the masses as children but to make adults of them" (181). Since the "more the people understand, the more watchful they become, and the more they come to realize that finally . . . their salvation lies in their own cohesion, in the true understanding of their interests" (191).

In situations like these, Fanon emphasizes, "the important thing is not that three hundred people form a plan and decide upon carrying it out, but that the whole people plan and decide even if it takes them twice or three times as long" (193). For the future is a closed (or manipulated) book if the consciousness of the people is not enlivened. This would not happen immediately, but could not be overlooked since these "weaknesses which are the heritage of the material and spiritual domination of the country by another is a necessity from which no government will be able to escape" (*WE*, 194). In perhaps the most extreme example of what it is to cultivate indigenous agency and skill, Fanon declares that if building a bridge does not enrich the awareness of those who construct it, they can go on swimming across the body of water. He states, "The bridge should not be 'parachuted down' from above; it should not be imposed by a *deus ex machina* upon the social scene; on the contrary, it should come from the muscles and the brains of citizens" (201). There would certainly be times when even foreign engineers and architects might be needed, but local leaders would have to be present as they did their work "so that the new techniques [could] make their way into the cerebral desert of the citizen." Concerns about national prestige could never upstage priorities of "returning dignity to all citizens, fill[ing] their minds and feast[ing] their eyes with human things, and creat[ing] a prospect that is human because conscious and sovereign men dwell therein" (205).

Such humanizing endeavor turned on the deliberate cultivation of a unique scope of political identity, one through which differences of class, region, ethnicity, and race could be mediated in the form and project of the nation. Nurturing the existence and vibrancy of the sensibilities that could make such dialectical work viable would need to be a priority itself facilitated by an ongoing sense of a shared past and future in which every emerging citizen would be mutually implicated.

Fanon comments that during the revolutionary struggle no one could escape scot-free; everyone would be butchered or tortured. Everybody would be compromised in the fight. No one would retain clean hands. There would be no innocents. If there were any onlookers, they were cowards or traitors. The challenge was to replicate this framework in the independent nation, to assure that neither harm nor privilege would be experienced in isolated pockets. Fanon therefore implores his readers to forge their own models, ones that are not simply pale duplications of those of Europe. Mocking the social contract tradition, he states, "No, there is no question of a return to Nature" (*WE*, 314). Instead for everyone's sake, the task is to work out new concepts and try to set afoot a new man (316).

Crucial to these, and here in a very Rousseauian spirit, is to render the totality of the nation a reality for each citizen, making its history part of his or her own. If national, such experience would "cease to be individual, limited, and shrunken" (*WE*, 200). Just as the fortune of the nation was in the hands of each fighter within the armed struggle, "the period of national construction each citizen ought to continue in his real, everyday activity to associate himself with the whole of the nation and to will the triumph of man in his completeness here and now" (200–1). Fanon writes, "The living expression of the nation is the moving consciousness of the whole of the people; it is the coherent, enlightened action of men and women. The collective building up of a destiny is the assumption of responsibility on the historical scale" (204).

But for political identity and governmental institutions to emerge as loci of belonging, they had to demonstrate concretely that they connected one part of the nation to the others not only in speech and aspiration but also through resource and infrastructural provision. Fanon therefore argued that it would be essential that the Algerian people develop a clear sense that they together owned the soil and mineral wealth of the country. At the political economic level this first would require nationalizing the economy through wholesale and resale cooperatives run on a democratic basis, decentralized so as to involve as many people as possible in public affairs. This, Fanon explained, had been abandoned in capitalist countries that governed with law backed only by economic strength and the police. In addition, as Rousseau also had suggested with Corsica, the nation's capital would have to be remade and deconsecrated. Party members would not reside in the capital, which inevitably would lead to the widely observed trend toward overpopulated and overdeveloped centers flooded by people who left poorer regions abandoned. It would be necessary to privilege the interior rural areas politically, to seek out every opportunity for contact with rural masses and to make national policy for them, in an effort to recognize and remain in immediate touch with those who fought for independence.

A future for politics, rather than the reintroduction of relations managed by force that enabled the uninterrupted profiteering for some, required a people who recognized themselves as essential to its operation and health. As soon as they were made dispensable to ruling, normalized violence defending a partial hegemony would reenter. Sustaining a counter vision demanded framing the growth of people as citizens as a guiding *telos* and priority. When politics is understood not as generating uniquely human resources and relations but only as the administration of scarce resources among necessarily antagonistic parties, it cements rather than rendering fluid lines of force that were outcomes of previous battles.

The national government must be for and by the people, and Fanon adds, also for and including the outcasts. No leader can be a substitute for a popular will. "The search for truth in local attitudes is a collective affair . . . for the success of the decision that is adopted depends upon the coordinated, conscious effort of the whole of the people."

HIJACKED POSSIBILITIES

The aftermath of efforts to give concrete form to a formerly colonized general will is disappointment. Rousseau himself had been ambivalent about the question of revolution. Although his writings inspired insurrectionary activity from the French Revolution to that of Fidel Castro, he feared that many efforts at political reform in fact enhanced the chains under which people lived; that whenever change was deliberately sought in the hope of expanding freedom, the few with a practical sense of what would come of the transformations were the ones who had worked out how financially to profit from them. For Fanon, the national bourgeoisie did precisely this. Hijacking the revolution while invoking what had been shared nationalist terms, they became increasingly snared in narrow tribalisms that masked the ultimate failure: their determination that national consciousness remain an empty shell.

Rather than the "all-embracing crystallization of the innermost hopes of the whole people," the national bourgeoisie, argues Fanon, were content, actually adamant, that it stay "a crude and fragile travesty of what it might have been" (*WE*, 148). As a result, once the focus on bringing an end to definite abuses was complete, tragic mishaps emerged. This congenital problem was due largely to the intellectual laziness of the national middle class, in particular "its spiritual penury" and the "profoundly cosmopolitan mold that its mind is set in" (149). Fanon writes:

> Now, precisely, it would seem that the historical vocation of an authentic middle class in an underdeveloped country is to repudiate its own nature in so far it as it is bourgeois, that is to say in so far as it is the tool of capitalism, and to make itself the willing slave of that revolutionary capital which is the people. In an underdeveloped country an authentic national middle class ought to consider as its bounden duty to betray the calling fate has marked out for it, and to put itself to school with the

people: in other words to put at the people's disposal the intellectual and technical capital that it has snatched when going through the colonial universities. (*WE*, 150)

Instead of this heroic and potentially fruitful path, the national bourgeoisie retreated into a cynically pseudobourgeois existence. Completely ignorant of the local economy, they could not speak with specificity about the nation's minerals, soil, or mines. They would instead talk cultishly of small-scale artisanry and about the groundnut harvest, cocoa crop, and olive yield. They were, Fanon lamented, satisfied to continue as Europe's farmers, generating unfinished products in ways that would never shift the global division of labor inaugurated by colonization, on the one hand, and black and brown enslavement, on the other. Lacking the entrepreneurial, pioneering aspects of the early European bourgeoisie, Fanon balks, they were "already senile before [they have] come to know the petulance, the fearlessness, or the will to succeed of youth" (*WE*, 153).

They did not even consider creating factories that could generate wealth for the nation and themselves. Risk averse, they preferred the security of foreign banks in which they could invest their profits from native soil. And yet they would speak constantly of nationalism while transferring the unfair advantages once possessed by colonialists into their own hands.

This is not an "authentic movement of nationalization" (*WE*, 157), Fanon comments. Although invoking the prioritization of that which was local, the national bourgeoisie "prove[d] themselves incapable of triumphantly putting into practice a program with even a minimum humanist content" (163). Bandying about phrases from European treatises on morals, they were a direct obstacle to the emergence of the general will: "The peoples of Africa have only recently come to know themselves. They have decided, in the name of the whole continent, to weigh in strongly against the colonial regime." By contrast, in seeking to make their own narrow fortunes, the national bourgeoisie became direct obstacles to "the path of this 'Utopia.'" They "have decided to bar the way to [the] . . . coordinated effort on the part of two hundred and fifty million men to triumph over stupidity, hunger, and inhumanity at one and the same time" (164).

This is not, however, only a failure in ideas. In the failure to offer an elaborated conception of viable lives within the emergent nation, there is a "falling back toward old tribal attitudes" (*WE*, 158). In such instances, Fanon writes, "the nation is passed over for the race, and the tribe is preferred to the state. These are the cracks in the edifice which show the process of retrogression, that is so harmful and prejudicial to national effort and national unity" (148–49).

Although once expressing concern with the dignity of the country, the national bourgeoisie now inhabited and maintained colonial homes and business offices. They did not remake rural and urban divisions or recast the global map, but simply settled into a world whose terms were still determined from outside. When they spoke of the nation it was as a cynical recourse in order to make claims to that which they feel entitled. As they temporarily demonized the outsiders to whom they in fact remained beholden, local artisans and craftsmen fought with nonnational Africans in what erupted in racial riots. The chauvinistic language of the local elite echoed out of less fortunate mouths in religious rivalries compounded by ethnic ones in what amounted to one more way of arguing in a condition of scarcity for why one uniquely deserved what should be available to all. "From nationalism we have passed to ultra-nationalism, to chauvinism, and finally to racism" (*WE*, 156). Fanon is unequivocal: such directions are "the historical result of the incapacity of the national middle class to rationalize popular action . . . to see into the reasons for that action" (149).

African unity, an idea that brought immense pressure against colonialism, required the cultivation of political economic conditions for its possibility. In the absence of these, it crumbles.

These difficulties are only augmented by political leaders who refuse to challenge the national bourgeoisie. "Far from embodying in concrete form the needs of the people in what touches bread, land, and the restoration of the country to the sacred hands of the people, the leader will reveal his inner purpose: to become the general president of that company of profiteers impatient for their returns which constitutes the national bourgeoisie" (*WE*, 166). Government jobs swell, but only for the sake of employing newly found cousins rather than in bursts of responsive activity.

Literally bringing the people to a halt, sending them back to "their caves," such leaders now, argues Fanon, expel them again from history, attempting to pacify them into sleep, waking them only occasionally ritually to recall the colonial period and distance from there that had supposedly been traveled. The masses in general, however, are treated as a blind force that must be held in check by mystification or fear. Embryonic oppositional parties that might think otherwise are "liquidated by beatings and stonings," by prison sentences that lead them to silence and marginalization. The masses,

Fanon insists, see through the purely symbolic nationalist celebrations. They may now be Africans, but they are hungry ones.

Claiming not to want to endanger national unity, such leaders refuse to draw up a set of objectives. Any such program with detail would be divisive—"the militants [therefore] disappear into the crowd and take the empty title of citizen. Now that they have fulfilled their historical mission of leading the bourgeoisie to power, they are firmly invited to retire so that the bourgeoisie may carry out its mission in peace and quiet" (*WE*, 171). They begin to sulk and "turn away from the nation in which they have been given no place" (168). Much as Rousseau says of assemblies that neither ask about nor in fact discuss the general will, these citizens begin to lose interest in it. Having not been enriched by "consciousness of social and political needs, in other words into humanism" this nationalism "leads up a blind alley" imprisoning national consciousness in "sterile formalism" (204).

The strength of the police force and army become proportionate to the stagnation in which the nation is sunk. As with colonial relations, mediating between great wealth and great poverty are the "pillars of the regime," the army and the police force, still advised by foreign experts. The behavior of the national bourgeoisie of underdeveloped countries, suggests Fanon, is reminiscent of a gang "who after every holdup hide their share in the loot from the other members who are their accomplices and prudently start thinking about their retirement" (*WE*, 174). This leads to expressions of discontent which are arbitrated more and more harshly, through ever more brutal displays of force. The hands of these army men, "cleverly handled by foreign experts" (ibid.), will gain more and more control with the implication that the former mother country now simply practices indirect government.

This exemplifies what Enrique Dussel has called the fetishizing of power, or those instances in which individual representatives exercise power in favor of some and therefore cannot rest on the strength of the people but instead need the help of imperial powers to help produce obedience. Their shortcomings do not only entail the failure to fulfill normative principles, he emphasizes, but also contribute "to the weakening and rotting of power and of actions and institutions through which he or she governs" (*WE*, 57).

In other words, for it to be apparent what "the differences have in common" they must together form a society that shares in prosperity and despair and that is meaningfully bound by a common destiny. Such generality is not simply a function of will but also of active policy that would make such willing reasonable. Rather than addressing the limitations of the liberation movement, those who come to power exacerbate them.

As Dussel (2008, 80) has emphasized, even the noblest commitment to symmetrical, democratic participation and legitimacy will be imperfect and relative. To treat this as a challenge rather than a justificatory excuse turns on the constant reinvention of the institutions through which the power of communities of people is exercised. Settling for mechanisms that fail to fulfill their purpose of responding to demonstrated needs is one of the clearest marks of the usurpation and then abandonment of forging an alternative model of nationalism, one based in a national consciousness. In other words, the resurgence of ethnic, religious, and regional lines as those only of nonnegotiable difference is a direct reflection of the deliberate shutting down of the project of creating a heterogeneous political culture in favor of the sedimentation of relations that enables the enrichment of a small few, the national bourgeoisie, over and against others—a situation in which a will of some is all that will prevail.

This is a clear abandonment of what Rousseau termed "generality" and the national consciousness that Fanon sought to nurture. For both men, it was in their pursuit alone that legitimacy might emerge from politics.

CONCLUDING CONSIDERATIONS

Fanon's formulation of national consciousness sustains all of the features that make the idea of the general will compelling while, if not transcending its limitations, productively reexamining them through a creolized lens: both Rousseau and Fanon challenge the adequacy of mere proceduralism, the sense that to tally votes itself constitutes a democratic outcome, but in Fanon the general will is not discovered but authored with an emphasis on assuring that the highest of collective aspirations are thoroughly understood by everyone implicated. In Fanon's account the aim is not to try to emulate the work of G-d here but instead to forge models of a shared future realizing that we alone can create the conditions of our own political adulthood or insist on our own ongoing relevance to public decision-making. The general will for Fanon is not articulated by each citizen in isolation rekindling a prepolitical unity, away from the influence of manipulative, dogmatic voices, but emerges out of the deliberate seizing of power, the direct challenging of unfreedom, with risks that make it impossible to turn back. This puts great weight on the deliberative side of Rousseau's general will, a side that introduces its own manifold dilemmas. In the face of these, Fanon makes contemporary Rousseau's discussion of more partial wills that create obstacles for clearly grasping the general will. If for Rousseau smaller, more partial general wills can form within societies and sustain intense loyalties that interfere with identifying interests as large as society itself, for Fanon these kinds of divisions usually run along ethnic and religious lines and are a symptom of political failure, of a retreat into a crude and narrow nationalism that amounts to the abandonment of creating genuinely postcolonial relations that rely upon the maximizing of the possibilities of evening out distributions of resources and political attention.

Grappling with the political stagnation following the independence period in Ghana, Kwame Gyekye (1997) treats the relationship of force to legitimacy as a living question fundamentally intertwined with the creating of viable multinational states. He too affirms that the absence of fluid and dynamic cultures out of which a shared nation might form is an unmistakable consequence of abandoning the state's primary role as contributing through redistributive measures to the forging of a coherent, diverse nation. Continuing the project of setting the material and moral conditions for national consciousness therefore requires prioritizing the formidable challenge posed by ethnic and religious group identity lines, some preexisting, most reified by colonialism.

Gyekye emphasizes that many internal groups are "nations" in the sense of minority cultures that are not coterminous with a state. They share cultural and linguistic homogeneity, life worlds structured around values and mundane feelings of loyalty, solidarity, and belonging. The challenge in multinational states is how to emulate these living senses of community in larger units, transferring thick allegiances of this sort to a larger and seemingly more abstract whole.

In an absence of fairness in the distribution of resources and opportunities, just as Fanon had said, constituent groups are suspicious of a government that appears to be a removed instrument wielded by some over and against others. If, by contrast, it were associated with the provision of roads and schools and medicine that in enfranchising some connected them with others, perhaps what is deemed politically possible would be rather different. In other words, according to Gyekye, the seemingly unshakable understanding of lines of loyalty and allegiance in cultural, ethnic, and religious terms is neither preordained nor primordial. Instead it remains a function of an absence of sustained political will to forge an alternative locus of belonging.

Gyekye stresses that the successful combining of parts into a cohesive whole is not achieved through mere aggregation but through *creolization*: He compares the envisioned metanational state with the construction of a political home, "but the structure, that is, the house, that results from the composition is a unity; but not only that: it is also a new thing, which is neither a stone nor sand nor wood" (1997, 85). It will surely initially be experienced as artificial precisely because, while a human community, it must be purposively built, drawing on cultural and linguistic resources rather than reproducing them uncritically. Still, Gyekye qualifies, all efforts to nurture human growth require care and reflection and although surely entailing struggle, the forging of a viable national infrastructure is a precondition for protecting the dignity of the entire citizenry. This is precisely what politics does aim to achieve: to forge out of distinct and shared needs and aspirations entities that are not natural but general.

Advocates of ethnicism, here like Fanon's narrow nationalists, actively discourage the personal and official recognition of the actual existence of shared cultures that, crossing subgroup boundaries, have emerged out of ongoing practices of living together that would serve as the model for constructing metanational cultures. After all, these are not pluralisms that collect and multiply internal differences without their alteration. Instead they provide an umbrella for them while seeking actively to forge a shared hegemonic culture by identifying underlying affinities of potential value and discouraging those that could only seed nonnegotiable divisions. Much like Dussel's "analogical hegemony," which, through dialogue and translation, builds from criticisms of prevailing national identities articulated by coextensive social movements, seeking to reveal their relations to each other while retaining the distinctiveness of each, the aim is "a world in which all worlds fit," in which distinctiveness sustains rather than eroding unities.

Such a vision turns on at least two stipulations: the first is that in deliberately forging an alternative modernism, one that does not rely on dehumanization, there are elements of cultures and traditions that will be lost. Most of the time, these are ways of acting and thinking that refer to elements of social worlds that no longer exist. But there are, in addition, those that privilege some at cost to most others without liberating cause. In other words, the preservation of a general will cannot tolerate everything. There are customs and practices that it could not sustain lest they shatter its conditions.

While advancing a compelling case for new models and definitions of individual and collective development, Fanon stressed making one's polity its own center without collapsing into a conservative localism that would antagonize non-Algerian Africans or suggest that independence must come from the work of the hands of the formerly colonized alone. To leave the colonized with their own bootstraps, even if the formal demand of decolonization, would represent a failure of the triumph of precisely the alternative hegemony that it sought to sustain. Really to convince the world of the violence of colonization would in addition to requiring a steady retreat of French men and women also necessitate a reinterpretation of the restitution owed. He wrote, "If conditions of work are not modified, centuries will be needed to humanize this world which has been forced down to animal level by imperial power" (*WE*, 100).

Methods used by agents of capitalism to increase their wealth and power included deportation, massacres, forced labor, slavery—in short, the strategies of war criminals. Really to value black and brown lives as one did those of Europeans would entail the kinds of postwar demands made of Nazis for their treatment of other parts of Europe.[8] The moral reparation or symbolic power of national independence could not alone feed the recently liberated. And the "wealth of the imperial countries is [the wealth of Algerians] too . . . [after all] Europe is literally the creation of the Third World. The wealth which smothers her is that which was stolen from the underdeveloped peoples" (*WE*, 102). To continue on as if nothing were due, as if there were not in fact a reversed relation of indebtedness of France to Algeria, was to continue on within an imperial hegemony that would treat the legacies of colonialism borne out in such material discrepancies as a lamentable inevitability, a consequence of compulsions of economic growth.

One can diagnose illegitimacy by active indications of the indispensability of dehumanization to the maintenance of a given order. The degree to which an alternative is legitimate is measured by how extensively people have seized and are then able to set conditions in place to shape, together through action, the contours of their collective lives. This process is necessarily inaugurated by untidy struggles within history against those who would treat a people's will, agency, and even hatred as irrelevant. These mollify former dividing lines as people, facing great potential losses, ally to throw off the structures that violently shape their lives. But anger and resentment cannot alone sustain a difficult battle—this requires a constructive project, the forging of a positive, analogical hegemony, one in which what is right and consented to coheres in what the differences have in common. This requires a dialectical movement between the shared and the different—the formulation of the latter to make the former more rigorous and the refusal for the latter to undercut the grounds of the former. This involves the expansion of the discursive domain in a deliberate effort to curb unnecessary recourses to violence that by definition shut sectors of the population outside of politics. Doing so reminds us of the actual meaning of power and requires that all people can remain awake and occupy a shared time. Within it, no one would remain as the undivided mass, marking time (*WE*, 147).

Rousseau, if in a neutered form, has been canonized within French society—the source of the legitimating language of the very project of the French Republic. Fanon, by contrast, is much studied—by those who occupy or identify with positions of alterity. The response to recent challenges to the inadequacy of the hegemony that sustains the identity of the French nation has largely been discredited as sowing divisions that would destroy a shared political community. In such rhetoric, 1789 is invoked, now conservatively. A more viable and political response would be to call for the creolizing of Rousseau's general will drawing on the ample resources offered by Frantz Fanon. Such an approach would seek out the debates through which difference could move from an abstract principle to lines of disagreement fostered by the unequal reach and provision of the French state.

This would of course also require the historicizing of the political community as one that did not emerge out of a hypothetical state of nature of isolated individuals but instead from political and communal relations that have enlarged the freedom and wealth of some through the dehumanization and rendering irrelevant of others. It is in identifying such limitations and in struggling against them that a diverse, French (meta) national consciousness or the general will is made more rigorous and less imperfect.

There are remarkable similarities between the accounts of legitimate politics in the work of Rousseau and Fanon and the fears in each that these aims might be obscured by prevailing perceptions of authoritative socialscientific methods. Each insists that what renders one acceptable in professional academic circles may well make it impossible to grasp reality in ways that could inform virtuous, political action. For each, the possibility of legitimate political life turns on eradicating cultures of dependence that make seeing and expressing the general will impossible. Both insist that the general will involves identifying what the differences of a polity share while refusing to reify distinctions that have taken form and become tenacious through a lack of political possibility. For both Rousseau and Fanon the alternative to decadent culture is politically-legitimate-culture-in-the-making or, in the case of Fanon, one in which rather than negotiating life as a minefield of controversial elements that one embraces or rejects, one can be the source of meaning and value as one forges a less compromised version of the common good. Such shared well-being for both requires economic conditions that are not so radically unequal that all political argumentation turns on rationalizing such differences as natural and necessary. Challenging unfreedom is work that is never fully or finally accomplished and may indeed lead us into predicaments even more replete with both difficulty and disappointment, but our efforts alone affirm that we are human beings capable of political adulthood.

Rousseau's idea of the general will has been attacked as totalizing, romantic, and repressive and as turning on a capacity for clear and transparent willing that regular citizens do not, in fact, possess. Still, its vision of political legitimacy has moved and captured the imagination of many readers by suggesting the requirements of modern, legitimate, democratic life. Several genealogical lines have been drawn from Rousseau's classic formulation of the general will to figures that both embrace and reject such relations of indebtedness. The most central in contemporary mainstream political theory are John Rawls and Jürgen Habermas. And yet, as I have suggested, it is in conversation with Frantz Fanon that the irredeemably political dimensions of Rousseau's writings are resuscitated.

Rousseau oscillates between radical irreverence and cold feet—for instance, unveiling the illegitimate bases of most modern polities while suggesting that once corrupted, polities cannot be reformed; insisting that all people ultimately seek liberty while insisting that people in some climates were not capable of institutionalizing it. Overemphasizing such passages, however, can obscure the record of Rousseau's challenging the compliance of generations of readers with the compromising of their freedom—whether through urging them not to too readily accept the necessity of political representation or of mistaking scholasticism for thinking. His scathing criticism of modern European life inspired not only Immanuel Kant and G. W. F. Hegel, but also ordinary citizens yearning to create political communities that could mirror unities within social life.

Fanon brought maturity to these analyses, the insight of the psychologist, and a sober sense that nature offered no idyllic refuge. Fanon, after all, would have regretted the failure of Algeria to become no longer colonial even in the aftermath of revolutionary struggle. Still, this, for him, would never have served as a refutation of the need for people to act with agency in history. It would instead affirm that questions of political life could never be settled once and for all. He was willing unambivalently to embrace the full implications of his work and to seize practical possibilities that he inspired his readers to identify. Fanon therefore fruitfully historicizes and reworks Rousseau without ever collapsing into what can be read in the latter as moments of conservative nostalgia. Fanon's political thought instead is a high modernism, a modernism from below, that insists that we alone can be the source of political models under which we live.

In politically living cultures, practical reason dominates and ideas are resources for people who, as sources of signification, interpret what make their worlds meaningful. In a world as diverse as ours, these designs will have to be heavily creolized.

5

Thinking Through Creolization

> The awareness of mixed origins does not mean that individuals can spontaneously retrace the flows that contributed to shaping their current practices and environment. Indeed, the long-term impact of cultural imports is often proportional to the capacity to forget that they were once acquired or imposed. . . . How many Italians today do not see the tomato as an intrinsic part of their cultural heritage? How many Native American leaders would dare to reject the horse as culturally foreign? . . . [W]e could prolong the list interminably in a number of directions: Latin America without Christianity, India without English, Argentina without Germans, Texas without cattle, the Caribbean without blacks or rum, England without tea. . . . Culturally, the world we inherit today is the product of global flows that started in the late fifteenth century and continue to affect human populations today. Yet the history of the world is rarely told in these terms. Indeed, the particularity of the dominant narratives of globalization is a massive silencing of the past on a world scale, the systematic erasure of continuous and deep-felt encounters that have marked human history throughout the globe.
>
> —MICHEL-ROLPH TROUILLOT[1]

Thus far, I have argued that Rousseau's challenging reflections on questions of human inquiry, political illegitimacy and its alternatives remain highly relevant to the present *and* are considerably enriched and extended in the work of Frantz Fanon. In other words, the central ideas produced through Rousseau's efforts to make sense of his shifting world are taken up by Fanon and altered to grapple with the continuous and distinctive predicaments of Martinique and then Algeria. One thereby witnesses a radical critique of the ways in which the project of European modernity implicated everything in its orbit, including what could function as authoritative scholarship, move from an at times desperate longing for that which was gone to deliberate efforts to forge a modernism from below, in which aspirations of popular sovereignty, collective self-determination, or willing for all, even within imperfect and constrained conditions, are embraced in pursuit of living models of what could be a more humane world. While a conversation between Rousseau and Fanon might appear to a particular brand of historian as an undisciplined fusion of disparate genealogies, such a conception of rigor would obscure the vital ways that each might fruitfully illuminate the other, recentering the political concerns that informed both.

Having offered this example of creolization—of the repositing of ideas in Rousseau to think through and make sense of the political situation in the Caribbean and then North Africa in a blend that produces something simultaneously recognizable and wholly new—I now turn to a discussion of creolization more generally as a potentially fruitful approach to theorizing today.

Against a postmodern ethos that has overtaken many communities framing inevitable repression in all efforts to construct collectivities, I aim, in the spirit of Sheldon Wolin (1960), who defined the task of political theory as articulating interests as general as political society itself, to reenvision the conditions for just this task. If unable to fashion genuinely universal theories, creolization can help us to engage in *universalizing* thought or that which facilitates the seeking of concepts and aspirations with what Molefi Asante (1998) has termed *greater transcultural validity*. Moving beyond dialogue of respectful difference, which none of us should denigrate, we instead explore creating ways in which otherwise fragmented accounts of shared political, physical, and geopolitical spaces could and do combine.[2] I will suggest that the impetus and resources to do this emerge out of theoretically engaging modernity's contradictions, or the locations and sites in which widely shared ideals collide with their compromising.

What merits the recentering of the descriptive concept of creolization? Why prioritize a phenomenon that emerged from sites of study long devalued as marginal—"not Western" enough for sociologists, not native enough for anthropologists (Trouillot 1992, 22); insufficiently savage or too hybrid in Munasinghe's (2006) critical assessment—as prototypes for understanding the postmodern human condition (Palmié 2006, 343) or predicaments marked by heterogeneous, stratified convergences of displaced people?[3] Is it an asset or a liability that the idea aimed to illuminate the nature of *illicit blendings* or forms of mixture that were not supposed to occur? Finally, how can I urge you to consider "creolizing political theory" as an approach when instances of creolization explored in what follows in fact emerged not as express aims, not out of a project of celebratory merging of difference for its own sake, but instead when those positioned unequally together found terms through which to coexist or when members of discrete groups sharing political grievances developed mutually intelligible language to describe that which needed to be surpassed?

Indeed when explicitly sought as a political program, creolization is often conservative and much more like multiculturalism than its advocates would ever allow. Instead processes of creolization emerge most in instances like those I considered in Chapter 4, when the coefficients of particular symbolic elements become fluid because the settled coordinates of the world to which they referred are radically interrupted. The emergence of alternative hegemonies then do not come out of deliberate efforts to build them but instead by rejecting the commitments that would render creolization impossible in struggles to seek out political policies that could better approximate something approaching a general will.

CREOLIZATION AS AN ACCURATE PORTRAIT OF THE WORKINGS OF CULTURE

The most influential of political theories root their accounts of desirable models of political life in an account of the human beings who would together constitute them. Indeed, Carl Schmitt once observed that the "problematic or unproblematic conception of man is decisive for the presupposition of every further political consideration, the answer to the question whether man is a dangerous being or not, a risky or harmless creature" (1996, 58).[4] Others have suggested that such orientations are themselves overdetermined, a mirrored reflection of the political fortunes into which each theorist was born. While this assessment is reductionistically causal, it is undeniable that many of the most fruitful disagreements in political theory are not over a respective theorist's method but over the assumptions and commitments with which he or she begins—his or her view of the nature or condition of human being.

A similar set of observations might be made of the treatment of culture. Much recent political theory, especially that which engages questions of difference and recognition, begin with observations about the nature of culture, identity, and identification. While some frame "the culture" of dispossessed or marginal groups as their most treasured resource and its treatment as the ultimate index of the fortunes of the people itself, others see collective designations that describe or prescribe shared habits, customs, and norms as largely repressive and totalizing and aim to reduce their hold on the practical lives of subjects by challenging the adequacy or coherence of their meaning. Such debates are largely oriented around qualifying or critically engaging one of two defining poles that I will suggest creolization has and will effectively mediate.

In what is an all too familiar terrain for many contemporary political theorists, there is, on the one hand, the camp associated with the politics of recognition and multiculturalism of Canadians Charles Taylor (1994) and Will Kymlicka (1995). On the other, there are the poststructuralist challenges as well as those of critical theorists, the latter perhaps most prominently represented in the writings of Seyla Benhabib (2002).

In the former, one envisages culture, much like one would an individual language, as determining the means with which one makes sense of the experiences that determine who we are and what we might become. While cultures are, on this view, internally varied and changing over time, they remain distinct wholes with unique attributes that deserve formal, political efforts to ensure the conditions for their ongoing preservation. Guided by avowed principles of toleration and of recognizing and honoring diversity as consistent with liberal democracy, this approach defends treating separate cultures much like nations that deserve to be (somewhat) self-determining. For them to preserve their authenticity, they require degrees of isolation that sustain their ability each separately to enrich the larger national community. Each is therefore to be left to define its guiding purposes or ultimate aims, so long as none collide with the liberal political framework that organizes and sustains this arranged order.

Although reminiscent of nineteenth century conceptions of the relationship of culture to nation, race, and language, the multicultural movement emerged within the Anglophone political world of the 1980s and 1990s, taking on some of the strategies and tactics mobilized in the civil rights movement, while avoiding more oppositional forms of direct collective action (Song 2007, 67). Undertaken in a less inclusive age, marked by disinvestment from welfare state models and the charting out of what flowered into neoliberalism and neoconservatism, culture, in these models, is treated much like other forms of property—with clearly demarcated boundaries and measurable value that can be trespassed upon or unjustly seized rather than a set of interrelated and mutually constituted responses to a shared, if unequal, set of life conditions.

Many have criticized what is often termed this "strong multiculturalism," for framing culture as a self-acting agent that expresses itself and its internal laws and logic while its members act passively, determined more or less by it. Far from a transparent and univocal system of meaning that claims the spontaneous allegiance of its members, according to their critics, customs, practices, and ideas reflect the balance of power among their different adherents (Parekh 2000, 79).

These concerns inform the second prevailing view of culture, evident, in the main, in poststructural brands of feminist and postcolonial studies. In these accounts, cultures are marked by ongoing, internal contestation, and rather than monolithic, they are polyvocal, fluid, permeable, and constantly renegotiated, exemplifying as much internal diversity as is evident between what are differentiated as distinct traditions. Central to such formulations is the focus on *hybridity* and on *bordercrossers* in the work of Homi Bhabha (1994) and Gloria Anzaldúa (1987). Both focus on particular groups and individuals who, in their individual persons, combine, blur, and remain in between what are often treated as firm and decisive boundaries with corresponding importantly transgressive epistemological insight.

When challenging poststructuralism's extremes, Nikolas Kompridis (2005) suggests that what has emerged from it is an antiessentialist orthodoxy or essentialist antiessentialism that exaggerates the permeability of culture to the point that it would be impossible to recognize anything as a shared set of customs or traditions or to explain why people might wish to choose to pass on any of their particular features. If the accounts of Taylor were unable to explain how cultures change, in other words, critical theorists following Benhabib cannot explain their continuity or why anything but a radically individualistic relationship to all systems of meaning is reasonable. Both such accounts are excessive, if in opposite directions, failing adequately to capture the combined nature of that which they describe, which Ernst Cassirer (1944) accurately defined as the both conservative and transformational, if to different degrees in discrete domains and moments, dimensions of symbolic life.

When offering an example of an alternative view, one that I would call *creolization*, Kompridis offered the example of Bela Bartok's ethnomusicological findings. These exemplified the ways in which culture, more generally, is both identical and nonidentical with itself: When Bartok sought to archive what he feared was disappearing authentic Hungarian folk music, he instead found that it was very much alive. However, the indigenous musical form had survived through being altered—remaining what it was by becoming something new. In it, he discovered "the crossing and recrossing of cultural styles, genres, and materials, which, with each crossing and recrossing, were newly and individually inflected" (Kompridis 2005, 338) in ways that Bartok knew would infuriate those seeking essential purities as the basis of nationalist identification. Blended were discrete elements, those audibly Hungarian and sufficiently sedimented to sound distinctive and "the highly melismatic 'long song' of Persia, Iraq, "Middle-Algeria, Old Rumania, and the Ukraine." It was very unlikely that these had each developed independently of the other, but who was to adjudicate the singular, "true" source? What surprised Bartok was that each of the contributing elements (Arabic-Persian, Eastern-European Hungarian, and Central European) belonged to a distinguishable genealogy that could be detected in its new and transformed combination that was "incontestably Hungarian" (ibid.).

We might add as additional examples of what I am calling *creolization* when James Tully (1995; 2008a; 2008b) refuses to frame the governing challenge as asking again and again what it is that established, hegemonic political societies can and cannot accommodate of the practices of more marginal groups, instead insisting that already complex and contested mainstream political cultures should be equally transformed in such confrontations. Beyond monological struggles for recognition, we must move beyond the abstract evaluation of the compatibility of minority claims with liberal commitments to recognizing that none transcend the field of struggle in which norms of intersubjective relations are crafted. In his brand of democratic constitutionalism therefore one cannot, as is the norm in much Habermasian critical theory, allow certain foundational principles to remain outside of the bounds of negotiation. In suggesting that the norms that define the intersubjective relations that constitute collective life should reflect ongoing deliberations of all implicated parties, he is describing the deliberate and active creolization of political life. In it, any abstract rule, however noble, must be made locally meaningful or indigenous in ways that reflect the changing makeup of the polity. This demands, of course, that interests and needs connected to antagonistic political locations in fact find points of sustained commonality and mutual comprehension. In such an alternative, one would not in moments of adjudication turn only to the intellectual resources of John Locke or John Rawls to ask what ideas that emerged in seventeenth-century England or twentieth-century United States dictate as the necessary response. One would as readily consider the potential usefulness and insights of concepts, ideas, and resources of challenging parties.

It is in precisely this spirit that Drucilla Cornell has lamented that as progressive as the new South African Constitution has been, it remained within the framework that Tully criticizes, one in which *integration* presumes that those outside of the minority-majority culture assimilate into it with, at best, some domains for minority rights, or particular problems and dilemmas that can be resolved under separate "customary" auspices. Cornell commented that the better alternative, especially if the aim was genuinely to constitute a postapartheid state, would have been to draw on the full range of local traditions, forming a distinctive new combination that would bring together the culminations of legal reflection expressive of different, often hostile, locations within a shared polity.[5] This is also what could be meant if one were to say that evident in Western Europe is a desire to resist the creolization of their polities in ways that would reflect their changed demographics, or the impressive presence within them of people from a range of their former colonies.

It is easier to resist the logic of creolization when nation-states think of themselves as only semipermeable, capable of monitoring (even if imperfectly) who it is that could enter and exit. It is far more difficult when boundaries appear thoroughly porous and sovereignty necessarily relational, sub- and transnational. If creolization emerged to describe radically new forms of life that emerged out of the shrinking of the globe in the age of revolutions, as Africa, Europe and the Americas convened in the waters, ports, and territories of each, we face a similar situation now in which little can or will remain in near isolation. None can avoid being resituated in a global age, especially if its unfolding contours are not entirely clear.

In such circumstances, many seek to impute to culture a barrier or line of defense against a homogenizing global market that, even while turning them into market niches, threatens to endanger the internal significance of local peculiarities. As I have shown in Fanon's discussion of the turn to traditionalism, many wish to retreat into the narrow refuges within which they can continue to govern the conditions of their lives. If consistently blocked from doing so outwardly in the public sphere, these efforts are implosive; as the domains shrink they become fortresses to be ever more desperately protected. In such circumstances, creolization, rather than the process through which political worlds better reflect the many people who comprise and make them meaningful, appears as dilution, as one more loss. Perhaps sadly, even then, its avoidance is not completely possible: one cannot but negotiate what it is that one will reject and how. If rootlessness has been said to describe New World conditions in which prototypical examples of creolization flourished, we must consider the range of processes that produce such untethering: In addition to literal transplantation, there is of course the uprooting and unrooting created when the earth itself trembles.

In this closing discussion, I contend that this combination of closure and openness, of sedimentation and fluidity, and of particular forms of identification gaining coherence through their recontextualization is precisely what "creolization" in its descriptive modes has successfully captured. In offering a better account of the nature of the reality in which political life proceeds and our theory is oriented, we would do better systematically to reflect on it and to have it inform our work and method because the framework for understanding culture advanced by theorists like Taylor continues to fashion how it is that we conceive of the meaning of disciplines themselves.

Even so, it is worth emphasizing again from the outset that in many of its prescriptive uses (here barring the recent work of a philosopher like Michael Monahan [2011]), creolization has stood for that which Kompridis challenges, for an ideal that might crudely be useful as a regulative ideal in the domain of artistic and literary creation, but that is incoherent and easily manipulated with destructive consequences when we speak of societies more generally. Rather than making such a prescriptive move, I instead suggest more modestly that using creolization as a lens will prove highly fruitful.

DESCRIPTIVE CREOLIZATIONS IN ITS SOCIAL SCIENTIFIC MODE

Recall that although the first written use of the word *creole*[6] dates back to the 1500s to name people of mixed blood (Chaudenson 2001, 8),[7] *creolization* emerged in its descriptive mode in the nineteenth century to explain what were seen as unique and aberrational human symbolic forms borne of plantation societies primarily in the New World, but also within comparable situations on the coasts of Africa and Asia where trading outposts similarly brought enslaved Africans in contact with Europeans in lands either absent indigenous populations or nearly cleared of them through genocide. In all such instances, previously unconnected people—a colonial class, slaves, dwindling indigenous populations, and subsequent waves of laborers—

whose mutual recognition was unprecedented, were thrown together in violently unequal relations, threatening any and all existing orders of collective meaning. Out of these sudden ruptures, new perspectives, based largely in reinvention, resituating, and mistranslation began to take shape (Buck-Morss 2009). What distinguished creolization from other more familiar and ongoing forms of cultural mixture were the radical and intensified nature of the interchange of symbols and practices that constituted the encounters among displaced groups of individuals who were neither rooted in their new location nor able meaningfully to identify with great civilizations elsewhere (Eriksen 2007, 155).[8] And yet they were there together to stay. Rather than a spread of coexisting parallel direct transplants, though these did also remain, new combinations of once disparate meanings took on degrees of stability and standardization charting a distinctive genealogy, newly indigenous to the place.

Against the grain of once conventional scholarly wisdom, the cultural forms and meanings were neither evidence of Africans stripped of their culture and singularly acculturated into European ways of acting, as some previous accounts had suggested, nor of Africans enveloped in ossified, if pure, remnants and retentions from the mother continent. Instead, in the midst of extreme brutality, those who unequally occupied such societies did not remain sealed off from each other but lived within relations marked by mundane dependency and antagonism, by intimate and complex interpenetration (Gilroy 1993, 48–49) that belied the project to create more Manichean worlds explored in Chapter 4. In these relations of proximity, older habits, customs, and forms of meaning-making were not only retained or rejected they were resignified in an "embattled creativity" (Mintz 1998, 119) that, in the language of Stuart Hall, enables us to envision how "the colonized [also produced] the colonizer" (1999, 6).

The invaluable mirror that laboratories of creolization offered for understanding how it is that shared symbolic forms emerge out of internally differentiated and unequal communities formed through sudden migration and displacement was not lost on linguists. Although there were many for whom such mixtures represented exceptionally lamentable cases of dilution and corruption, for others they offered a rare opportunity for studying more universal processes. Beginning at the end of the nineteenth century, some European linguists turned to creolized languages to resolve debates over how Latin had developed into multiple, distinct European tongues (Chaudenson 2001, 14; Meijer and Muysken 1977, 27). Aiming to determine how substratum languages contributed to the specific ways in which target languages were spoken, even in mastery—one could think here, for instance, of the English spoken in Scotland, on the one hand, and Puerto Rico, on the other—Lucien Adam suggested that just as creole languages were non-European languages with European lexical items, Romance languages had combined a Latin lexifier with the variety of substratal vernaculars spoken throughout Europe. Similarly, Hugo Schuchardt (1842–1927), who first studied Basque and then the Mediterranean *lingua franca* spoken in North Africa until eradicated by French, challenged the system of mapping the descent of languages into family trees as practiced by the neo-grammarian school of Leipzig. Turning to pidgins and creoles as his prototypical examples, he insisted that these discredited the adequacy of prevailing classificatory schemes that restricted each language to one unique genetic originating point. Creole languages and, he implied, perhaps most others, could combine multiple lexifiers and substrates in relations that needed to be illuminated rather than obscured when delineating such genealogies.[9]

Following in this tradition, but now in refuting the designation of creolized languages as windows into the nature of early humanity or as indispensable examples of otherwise inaccessible models of protohuman development,[10] are the French and Congolese sociolinguists Robert Chaudenson (2001) and Solikoko Mufwene (1998) who instead argue that creoles pose and illuminate the hardest of linguistic questions, those that should be the concern to all students of language since they push to their logical conclusion evolutionary tendencies observable in all tongues (Chaudenson 1989).[11] In other words, the processes at work in the development of creole and noncreole languages are not structurally different. Instead regular processes of both, in the case of creole languages, are radically quickened due to "greater ecology-prompted restructuring than in less heterogeneous and more focused settings of language transmission" (Mufwene 1998, 7).[12]

This sociohistorical approach therefore traces the emergence of Francophone creoles to a specific series of conditions or periods of contact that prompted the transmission of restructured elements of language. The first of these was a period that, following initial sporadic intracommunal contact, brought together relatively homogenous, rural, primarily poor French working for companies and landlords who spoke nonstandard varieties of French with mainly very young slaves who were integrated into such homes in a deliberate project of deculturation. This quickly produced a mulatto population that largely spoke French or approximations of it (which combined a nonstandard French lexifier with their own substratal tongues). With the extension of agricultural industry and intensified reliance on slave labor, newly arrived Africans came to form a majority. They were largely segregated as field laborers with limited direct exposure to Europeans and the languages they spoke (here called *acrolects*), and their contact was mediated by mulattos, who were both local and seasoned slaves, and their language (called a *mesolect*). Within slave communities the mulatto approximations of the French of their masters (often also family members) were approximated in a process called *basilectalization* through which core features of their *mesolect* combined with additional substratal languages that were themselves mixed.[13] As creole slaves were radically outnumbered, the language was further reconstructed creating a more complex linguistic continuum between the standard nonstandard French lexifier and various creole forms. Linguists of this camp, especially Chaudenson and Mufwene, insist against prevailing orthodoxies, that while *basilectical* forms are assumed to be the oldest, the opposite is true: creoles are initially closer to their lexifiers; distance in fact grows with social conditions of greater separation or isolation marked by and associated with autonomized elaboration.[14]

Chaudenson and Mufwene emphasize a few additional points key for refining analogies that we will draw between the creolizing of languages and of disciplinary forms: First is that while creole language situations offered exceptionally good conditions for observation and study (as relatively closed settings undergoing recent change with dates, demographic, economic, and social dimensions that can be determined) the models they suggest can be used to explore other symbolic domains by similarly emphasizing their particular sociohistorical features. In none of these does one see a simple or harmonious mix of elements of coexisting prior systems. But in more than any other, the domain of language in colonial societies is defined by a centripetal force of the dominating group. Although, even in this account, language development is multidirectional—creole languages are not only the result of approximations of approximations based on early contact, mediated contact, and then resituation, they are restructured in ways that more substantially reflect the mediation and negotiation of the variety of substratal tongues of speakers for whom, in the face of ongoing infusions of linguistic diversity, the creole emerged as a *lingua franca*—it is less so than with music and dance, the production of food and homes, religion, or medicine.[15] The particularly unequal relations of influence in the linguistic domain should, however, be born in mind when we consider the historical absence of creolized philosophical and theoretical work in terrains where the vast majority of other aspects of symbolic life are so clearly marked by these processes.

Still, on the question of language, what is frequently overlooked when creoles are described as the fruit of abnormal processes of transmission is that no native or fluent speaker entirely possesses or acquires a language.[16] Outside of scholastic systems, it is relevant communicative needs and one's social environment that determine the aspects of a language that one learns. One is not introduced to the system of language but to vocabulary and partial rules through which one infers and through trial and error develops some competence. One's aim is rarely either to create or master a language but instead to use it either to enable or perhaps obfuscate processes of communication (Mufwene 1998, 5).[17] In addition, it is misleading although frequent when studying linguistic development to focus on converging communities when in fact contact, negotiation, and innovation usually took place in individual encounters that collectively produced language (not entirely unlike the ways in which individual acts of reproduction affect the larger species) (6). Finally, degrees of restructuring, including repetition and codification of imperfect replications, or simply errors, are a feature of all spontaneous language transmission, even within communities of native speakers.[18] What distinguishes creole languages is more frequent imperfect feature replication (due primarily to limited contact with speakers of the superstrate language) and more rapid and extensive restructuring than in communities that are monolingual.

Perhaps most significantly, what sociohistorical studies of creole languages demonstrate is how language is "fundamentally implicated in relations of domination," that control over representations of reality is both a source of social power and a site conflict and struggle (Gal 1989, 348). In other words, in linguistic interactions—including those of approximation, imperfect replication, and restructuring—one does not merely witness the reflection but the constitution of social organizations; the enacting of social stratification and identity by the mediating of microinteractions and macrosociocutural formations (Irvine and Gal 2000, 36). Susan Gal (1989, 349) emphasizes that scholars of language have suggested that resistance to dominant representations occurs through the ongoing use of denigrated linguistic strategies and genres that propose and/or embody alternative models of the social world. I would contend that most creolized speech did precisely this: what went under the name of imperfect replication (of already imperfectly replicated, nonstandard versions of European languages) was the ongoing influence of substratal languages of subordinated groups. This put plantation owners and their European patrons in a bizarre situation: if seeking to use indigenous forms of expression, they were those that defied arguments about the incapacity of slaves to be independent sources of signification, to make human meaning of hostile circumstances.[19]

My claim is not that creolized people or languages or food are themselves intrinsically progressive nor that against claims that slaves were completely determined by their enslaved condition, these offer unambiguous evidence of an elusive and suddenly humanizing "agency." Instead, these forms reveal a set of complex and refracted processes that more generally characterize the nature of symbolic life, illuminating in a fresh way the more familiar Marxist maxim that human beings make their own history, but not exactly as they please; they do not make it under circumstances chosen by themselves but under those directly encountered, given, and transmitted. Where the specifically creolizing discussion departs, however, is with the place where Marx's passage ends: "The tradition of all the dead generations weighs like a nightmare on the brain of the living." This is precisely, for better and for worse, what is absent in these circumstances. Even for those who might wish for and prefer such dead weight, its reinsertion required a deliberate project of reinterpolation. Even then it was resituated within an ongoing project of people with differential degrees of access selecting elements of a shared past drawn upon for their relevance to a current situation. In the resulting products one witnesses that while conditioned powerfully by their circumstances, those who endured were not reducible to them. The terms of their situation, while decisive, could be transcended, but, even then, were necessarily made intelligible through symbolic forms that simultaneously assumed continuities and the birthing of shared language for forging alliances through which these might be overturned (Johnson 2003).

In all of these instances and in most other descriptive social scientific work, creolization is used retrospectively to capture a *fait accompli*. Indeed, as the opening epigraph suggests, "the long-term impact of cultural imports is often proportional to the capacity to forget that they were once acquired or imposed" (Trouillot 2003, 34). So creolization names the uniqueness of Jamaican Patois or Haitian Creole; the music one hears throughout the Caribbean or the Cajun food now local to Louisiana. In each are evident the full range of contributing sources which, given prior political histories would not have been expected to converge, that in their combination represent both continuity and something radically new. Among their noteworthy features are:

1. Elements that are brought together are not translated back into the language or symbolic framework of the one who does the borrowing. They are instead *incorporated*. One tries in vain, for example, to find an English equivalent for the Jamaican word *ratid*; one simply learns how to use it. Such acts of incorporation, however, are not necessarily without the transculturation that Michaelle Browers (2008) and Pratt (1992) correctly have suggested we need not lament. Evident here, in other words, is an immediate break with those strands of comparative political theory for which mistranslation is of particular concern. In instances of creolization, rather, an idea, linguistic form, or ingredient with one origin is often willfully resituated with meaningful implications. This is why Raquel Romberg, for instance, has urged theorists of creolization to rethink the neat distinction between creativity and imitation, suggesting that at the core of creolized Caribbean practices is "the strategic unauthorized appropriation of symbols of power . . . against their initial purpose" (2002, 1) or, as Michel de Certeau has suggested, employing hegemonic forms of culture for ends foreign or antagonistic to them (1984, xiii).

2. One can, even within what has emerged as a new form in its own right, trace the contributory origins (themselves often highly syncretized) of elements that now converge. This is precisely why many listeners find Haitian Creole so remarkable: audible are not only sounds they associate with France but those of the Niger-Congo region; they hear each of these discretely enough to name them separately *and* the distinctness that is their combination. The conditions of the creolized product will eventually be forgotten, as Trouillot has emphasized, but within environments characterized by valuing or making creolization central to their self-identities, one witnesses a greater awareness of the permeable and forged nature of all symbolic forms.[20] Patterns of mixture are therefore valuable mirrors into relations that structure a given society and its availability or lack of access to social, economic, and political upward mobility: A particular group that is still relatively marginal to the national political community may significantly mark another domain, say, that of food or music.[21] While one does not want to diminish the significance of either—indeed turning to them is thoroughly consistent with the prescription that we not assume in advance to know the domains within which the philosophical insights of specific

communities were most richly developed—a legacy of the colonial world is the relative comfort of many whites with black and brown contributions in these domains as opposed to more explicitly discursive, political, and intellectual ones. In this sense, a group may have significantly contributed to the symbolic life of a given community without possessing the equivalent power to define its guiding ultimate aims.[22] Or, as with Victor Turner's category of *the liminal* (1995), one may inform the defining of contours of hegemonic self-understandings without being able to direct how they are mobilized.[23]

3. As should be evident from the prior point, framing instances as those of creolization requires a particular approach to the study of the past. Frequently *creolization* describes forms that have become relatively stable, even ossified, especially in those circumstances in which their marketability is linked to their branding and commodification *as* creole. The larger point, however, is that the expectations with which we approach prior historical moments are significantly shaped by how we conceive of symbolic life and its relationship to patterns of human movement. Particularly creolized forms can therefore themselves, if we are willing to grapple with them, belie ways of narrating the past that impose on them a *de post facto* purity. The history of radical antislavery organizations and of the Haitian Revolution offer a good example: Both were thoroughly transnational, with half of the slaves who fought in Haiti born in Africa; leaders and replenishing waves of new slaves coming in from other Caribbean islands; abolitionists of various allegiances entering from various elsewheres, including from the United States and Europe. In a context in which most who fought and led were illiterate, their *lingua franca* was Creole (Fischer 2006, 371–73).[24]

4. Creolization does suggest an intensity of interaction, a much more than casual cohabitation of social and political worlds, opportunities for which are typically furnished by fresh bouts of voluntary or coerced migration. However, situations that render creolization likely may also be due to changes that do not involve crossing dramatic geographic distances but that are also described in spatial terms, for example, the movement of cultural or religious outsiders up or down the class ladder may lead to individuals among them more consistently or intensely interacting with members of communities with whom their previous relations had been at best distant. Their sudden proximity then raises anew very old questions of what in the lives of others to incorporate, mimic, or reject. The flipside of this is also important: often what are considered the most authentic forms of a creolized language are those that have sedimented precisely because the encounters of

people that initially produced them have significantly dwindled due to more extensive racial segregation or isolation (as evident in our previous discussion of Chaudenson and Mufwene) as a result of changed social norms or economic mandates or through the abandonment of efforts to assure that benefits distributed by local, national, or regional governments are equitably dispersed.

But perhaps most significantly, unlike the multitude of other forms of cultural mixture and syncretism, *creolization* has referred very explicitly to *illicit blendings* (Bernabé, Chamoiseau, Confiant 1990) or to those that contradicted and betrayed the project of forging a Manichean racial order in the heavily mixed, transnational movements that shaped the plantation societies of the New Worlds on both sides of the Atlantic. In particular, differently from cultural mixture, in which it is assumed that members of distinct groups will take an idea derived from abroad and make it local in an ongoing process of give and take, what is unique about what is now termed creolization is that it refers to instances of such symbolic creativity among communities that included those thought incapable of it. Racialized logics forged in European modernity suggested a necessary relationship between one's blood as evident in one's phenotype and one's relative ability to be the source and custodian of a culture, civilization, and language. *Cultural mixing* described the interactions of those on comparable rungs. By contrast, what came later to be called creolization described what at the time of their development were seen less as new syntheses than as a unilateral corruption or erosion of cultural life that necessarily originated elsewhere.

One example can illustrate this point succinctly: Guus Meijer and Pieter Muysken (1977) explain that European languages were thought to contain morphological distinctions and syntactic categories that supposedly simple black and brown people were unable to emulate. If, as nineteenth-century linguistic hybridology claimed, different races belonged to varied evolutionary stages, with contact, their linguistic templates cross-fertilized at the lowest common denominator of structural complexity with the more primitive grammar of lower race speakers imposing an upper bound or limit (DeGraff 2003, 395). It was, wrote Pierre Larousse in the *Grand Dictionnaire* of 1869, this stripping of linguistic sophistication that created creoles (cited in Meijer and Muysken 1977, 22). He offered this definition: "The creole language, in our colonies, in Louisiana and Haiti, is a corrupted French in which several Spanish and gallanicized words are mixed. The language, often unintelligible in the mouth of an old African, is extremely sweet in the mouth of white creole speakers" (ibid.). Pieter A. M. Seuren more recently argues that Creole grammars lacked the "more sophisticated features of languages backed by a rich and extended cultural past and a large, well-organized literate society" (1998, 292–93). Others still described Haitian Creole simply as "nothing but French back in infancy" (DeGraff 2003, 392).

One might argue that this more racialized dimension of historical discussions of creolization is no longer evident in or relevant to efforts to make the concept contemporary; that we live in a period in which race and nation are not treated as synonymous and that the expectation that both could be easily aligned to a particular and singular culture and language has long eroded. One might continue that what was remarkable about transplanted people forging monstrous or marvelous shared forms from disparate parts of the globe is no longer so in a world where mixture is the norm and the relation of here and there is increasingly impossible coherently to disentangle. Indeed in the academy, even though "culture" is often used in the place vacated by nineteenth-century conceptions of race, it is often more acceptable to avoid any and all generalizations about identity than it is to advance a politics of racial purity.

There are at least two answers to this objection.

First, it is almost axiomatic that the longing for what many poststructuralist academics insist is discredited intensifies particularly where it is endangered. One witnesses this on both the political Right and Left in the exponential blossoming of as many fundamentalisms in their religious and secular permutations as more explicitly postmodern assemblages of disparate, fragmented political hopes and dreams. Many seek out pockets of the globe that promise to remain premodern, continuing on with precolonial ways of life that in their radical otherness represent the healthier alternatives through which to set one's back against the impending logic or seemingly inexorable rhythm of our times. Shoring up such boundaries inevitably borrows from the language of corruption and dilution, suggesting, in some cases, that the mutually implicated nature of social life is its evil, in others, more modestly, that all engagements with hegemonic developments (whether linguistic or technological) are concessions, undermining a brand of freedom modeled on the supposedly singular sovereignty of states or on the view that one should be capable of absolutely determining that which comes within one's fold.[25]

Second, to reiterate the argument with which we began, many different outcomes for symbolic life emerge when members of previously separated groups collide. One possibility is creolization. In the processes that it describes are revealed the variegated workings of culture itself. However, it is precisely because creolized products were ones that surprised and bothered people—in conjoining distinct genealogies that were not supposed to converge in one—that these other more widespread and universal mechanisms were effectively illuminated. It is for this reason that a concept that derived out of the geographically small Caribbean, the often disavowed birthplace of global modernity, is of such broad usefulness. In other words, if what so perturbed countless linguists was to hear such an African sounding French, one that undeniably gestured toward a new Francophone trajectory, the examples of creolization that will be most striking today might be of another form. But it will be the consternation that they provoke that singles them out more than the larger process of continuity and rupture, conservatism and transformation that are at the very core of the efforts of human beings to carve out distinct domains within an otherwise indifferent world.

PRESCRIBING CREOLIZATION

In addition to the descriptive social scientific accounts of creolization outlined in this book's introduction, there are normative ones that, in some instances, are clearly and unapologetically prescriptive. Their most compelling spokesmen have also been some of the most significant recent Caribbean writers, including Martinican Édouard Glissant, Guyanese Wilson Harris, and Martinican collaborators, Jean Bernabé, Patrick Chamoiseau, and Raphaël Confiant.

Bernabé, Chamoiseau, and Confiant suggest in their manifesto, *Éloge de Créolité*, that at the heart of Creoleness is a set of rules that specify a particular orientation: "no culture is ever a finished product, but rather the constant dynamic search for original questions, new possibilities, more interested in relating than dominating, in exchanging rather than looting" (1990, 903). In a defiant, permanent openness, Créolité advances an account of converging customs and traditions in which, through their rejection of the strong multiculturalist or purist models, they can and will be mutually enriching rather than conflictually colliding, in forms, in Glissant's account, that become durable but not sedimented.[26]

If the conditions that produced Créolité were neither voluntary nor at first reflectively chosen, they did, in Wilson Harris's account, richly "alter conventional linearity and conventional frameworks" (1998, 23). For Édouard

Glissant, the Caribbean Sea after 1492 became "a place of passage, of transience rather than exclusion," here invoking the work of Gilles Deleuze and Felix Guattari, "an archipelago-like reality, which does not imply the intense entrenchment of a self-sufficient thinking of identity, often sectarian, but of relativity, the fabric of a great expanse, the relational complicity that does not tend toward the One, but opens out onto diversity" (2008, 81). The sheer degree of movement and economic displacement, in this (heavily romanticized) portrait, nurtured a sensibility premised upon ongoing and intense permeability, a view of uprooting as something other than a loss and diversification as different from dilution (82).

Here Glissant emphasizes a point that we have already considered, that creolization is "not a mechanical combination of components, characterized by value percentages . . . [it] does not produce direct synthesis, but *resultants* . . . something else, another way" (2008, 83). Alexis Nouss (2009) illuminates this theme when he argues that we need a distinctively social arithmetic that rejects the commonplace practice of people trying to make their relevant components add up to a sum of 100 percent, when talking about themselves in racial, ethnic, and religious terms. Instead, he suggests, when it comes to human beings, what is important and interesting about mixture is precisely that we are 100 percent each of the groups to which we belong.

Finally, Glissant suggests that forging and manifesting creolized mixtures or "the obligation to remake oneself every time" requires a unique capacity, one of repeated and situational forgetting (2008, 86). Ulrich Fleischmann has similarly contended that those "socialized in a creole way" of necessity develop a range of psychological "strategies for presenting different 'selves'" that is emphatic, differentiated, and capable of tolerating stress "without collapsing into conflicting patterns of behaviour" (2003, xvii). In the recent past, understandings of mixture as embodying in one corporeal entity the tugging, competing demands of hostile communities—one can think here of images of the tragic *mulatta*—were assumed to produce anomie and mental disorder, frequently culminating in suicide. For members of the creole literary movement, however, within the Caribbean are models of quintessentially postmodern qualities indispensable for skillfully navigating rather than being made desperate by a shared future in which transnational movement is the norm.

Once denigrated, they allege, regional norms and practices predated and embodied ideals after which French poststructuralism and its Anglo-American varieties groped. Out of failures to confine antagonistic populations into neat and separated cultural, racial, and linguistic niches emerged an insistently creative mode of personhood to be celebrated and exported. Fleischmann writes, "Seen from the angle of globalization, the capacity to construct and reconstruct ethnic and kinship ties that is one of the legacies of slavery and labour migration becomes a highly modern asset. The same switch turns the victims of colonization into forerunners of a new age" (2003, xxxii). In this move, Caribbean "laboratories of disorder" (Glissant 2008, 89) positively anticipated both the character of global cities now and the world of the future. If plantations have vanished, Glissant argues, creolization marks Mexico City, Miami, Los Angeles, Caracas, Sao Paulo, New Orleans, all megapolises "where the inferno of cement slums is merely an extension of the inferno of the sugarcane or cotton fields" (86–87).

Much such writing, in other words, moves between painting a highly evocative normative ideal after which we might strive and suggesting that it has in fact already been rigorously realized in the Caribbean past, in models that should be adopted and are already surfacing around the globe.

For some critics, however, this slippage has made these creative writers mouthpieces of problematic efforts to operationalize the creolizing spirit, particularly in the political projects of the Caribbean independence-era. For example, one might consider the Jamaican effort to forge "one out of many," or deliberately to craft a national identity that required emphasizing the multiple origins of the common cultures that would guide and be embodied in processes of nation-building (Bolland 2006, 2). In assuming that there was no singular primordial nation to which the emergent state could refer, they concluded that there was no original purity that would be endangered by the public recognition of the pluralistic culture that had already grown up there.

Particularly among anthropologists and sociologists, the record of the forgings of national creole identities and cultures is wrought with severe shortcomings. It has been suggested these projects imitated without inverting aspects of colonial societies that they promised to displace and surpass (Misir 2006). What became militant brands of cultural nationalism were seen in fact to enshrine only one, particular form of hybridity, that of nationalist leaders at the forefront of efforts to oust white foreigners. Rather than nurturing the social and political conditions for ongoing processes of creolization, in other words, one ossified instantiation was privileged to the exclusion of others in ways that cultivated xenophobia toward people who failed to exemplify such mixture, seeming to justify the continued unequal distribution of societal rewards (Misir 2006, xxix). Hintzen argues that the shift in racial discourse to the distinction between creole and noncreole "serve[d] to hide commonalities in social practice that [could] form the basis of counter-discursive challenges to power" (Hintzen 2006, 29). The newer lines of division, which were obscured by calls to identify with the language of being creole, remained color inflected, not radically different from earlier periods in which to be "creole" was to be both distinct from nonlocal whites and less mixed Africans (Alleyne 2003a, 41). Alleyne concludes that although perhaps the whole world *will* eventually be creole, and that this may well be desirable, in the meantime, in Jamaica and elsewhere, it is an expression of a desire of both whites and blacks to be "Brown" (2003b, 471). One might consider here Susan Buck-Morss's (2009) challenge that while it is in moments of negation that subterranean universalizing identities emerge, for instance, within anticolonial struggles in Haiti, as soon as one uses them to construct and to build, they fail to be as broad as the societies to which they should refer, reinscribing lines that produce cyclical conflicts between victim and abuser.

Such criticisms of the exclusive nature of creole forms are heavily associated with East Indian Caribbean writers and those indigenous to the region. The former, arriving after the foundational period of Caribbean plantation societies, have insisted that they are outside of a fundamental African-European spectrum within which processes of creolization transpire. Aisha Khan (2006), for example, has argued that the concept of creolization reenforces precisely what it claims to dismantle, while Shalini Puri (2004) insists that its radical potential has been exhausted because of its complicity with the exclusion of East Indians from nationalist projects. This is a particular failing, observes Indo-Trinidadian writer Ramibai Espinet, since East Indians comprise 20 percent of the region. Daniel Segal (1993) has suggested that this is a product of particular perceptions of East Indians—if Africans were framed as lacking culture and therefore raised up through mixture, East Indians were seen as unmixable and Eastern, bearers or assimilators of culture but not its creators, much like the role for many Asian-Americans described by Ronald Takaki (1998) as "the permanent foreigner." By contrast, if East Indians pose the question of whether one can enter too late into processes of creolization, others suggest the opposite problem of having been around too early on. Indeed, Vincente Diaz (2006) has emphasized that part of the formulation of the identity creole is to mark what emerges, *newly* indigenous, from the Caribbean New World, inserting other subjugated people in the place of indigenous or aboriginal ones usually through the claim that such populations were either eliminated or survived in numbers too small to be mobilized.[27]

One could suggest in response that what is here being challenged or rejected is not the *process of creolization* as much as the way in which its discourses and practices were effectively monopolized and hijacked by a creole elite that set themselves up as idealized hybrid exemplifications and gatekeepers in order to interrupt the ongoing living processes of creolization that would better reflect the full range of the relevant societies. In so doing, the focus of these criticisms are not unlike the national bourgeoisie that, as I discussed in Chapter 4, remained locked in a xenophobic nationalism rather than setting conditions to express and nurture a national consciousness that would have had to be more radically redistributive. In these instances, creolization is not completely unlike the heavily prescriptive ideal of "color-blindness" which makes a normative project of not seeing the very lines of difference crucial to diagnosing the historical and ongoing unequal allocation of life opportunities. There is no doubt that in these circumstances, the language of creolization is used to pursue highly conservative ends, with the implication that there is nothing inherently progressive in forms of mixture that emerge out of creolized processes.

With the aim of distinguishing among the implications of disparate forms of creolization, Romberg and Vijay Prasad (2002) (under the name of "polyculturalism") have turned their gaze to instances of active resistance or unwelcome efforts to render more inclusive such clear efforts at hegemony consolidation. For Romberg, as mentioned earlier, in creolization one sees a particular brand of strategic imitation in which objects of great symbolic power of more dominating groups are recontextualized without permission by the relatively disenfranchised against their initial purposes. In these cases, antagonistic parties share a mutually comprehensible set of references for such resistance to be intelligible as such. Still there is enough symbolic disparity and ambiguity for particular elements to speak in multiple, opposed valences and not to be understood entirely in the senses intended by those authoring the resignification.

Prasad similarly insists that polyculturalism, sharply contrasted with multiculturalism, emerges precisely when separate marginalized groups fight together against the terms of their unfreedom. Such efforts, though it is not their aim or purpose, produce practices, symbols, and language that bring together those previously thought to belong to discrete groups and traditions in ways that foster and sustain alliances that those hostile to their potential fruits sought very deliberately to block. In other words, mutually comprehensible forms are created that build on and rework previous meanings to articulate and give expression to what is newly underway. It is in this sense that we described Fanon's national consciousness as a methodically creolized general will with implications that all contemporary efforts to articulate that which is consented to and right for all would have, of necessity, also to be creolized. The vitality of the emergent symbolic forms are striking—rather than funneling intellectual, creative, political, and moral energies into preserving existing identities and what they dictate for behavior and aspirations, polycultural processes pursue a world more befitting the range of people that occupy it, assuming that there are no complete, readymade existing blueprints of how this must look. What materializes is unlikely perfectly to mirror all of the various groups that might seek less constrained social and political conditions, but efforts in this direction introduce new repertoires and examples that might in turn be reworked and recast. Crucially, the creolizing of practices, languages, and ideas is not the object, in such examples, but is the inevitable consequence of together diagnosing a shared world for the sake of generating more legitimate alternatives.

In this sense, in defense of nationalist creolizing projects in Jamaica, we might emphasize that while conservative in relation to the more profound ideals of defining independence as bringing a substantive end to colonial forms of life, what has emerged in their stead is certainly no better. Indeed, the ascendant logic of neoliberalism, which encourages a branding of difference framed as cultural as carefully protected sites of exclusion, leverage, and potential enrichment in an increasingly scarce terrain, has not proven any more effective at addressing racialized forms of radical inequality (Thomas 2004).

In other words, all efforts at forming new hegemonies, even those immediately linked to polycultural forms of struggle, will of course be faulty. In these instances, however, what still singles out creolization for comment and exploration is its disposition toward the nature of symbolic life: As a concept, it is associated with creating that which is local. What is more, as O. Nigel Bolland (2006) has emphasized, while creolization refers to national *cultures*, what it suggests converge, in addition to key elements of language and cosmology, are meanings linked to structural locations, to racial and class identities—black, brown, and white or bourgeois and proletariat—that are incoherent if isolated or delinked from their role in defining a spectrum of opportunities or their denial. In other words, creolization insists on the politicized nature of what is described in more euphemistic terms of "diversity." In so doing, creolization offers a useful antidote to the dangers of exaggerating cultural distinctiveness to the point of mutual untranslatability, a trend described and criticized by Kwasi Wiredu (1996) and Michelle Moody-Adams (1997) who insist that while contexts of meaning are fundamentally shaped by historical contingencies, within these, one sees struggles over power, authority, direction, and purpose in every human community.

The responses of Romberg and Prasad—that one finds living processes of creolization among those who assume that the political future must be constructed rather than simply continued or maintained—are essential to considerations of how one might further creolize creolization or embrace an ethos that does not set up some, specific hybrid identities to be championed over a process that, like the work of politics, is never done.

This is not, however, to leave prescriptive brands of creolization without necessary qualification. To argue that every dimension of life must remain rigorously open, unsedimented, and unfinished may be a valuable ethos in particular kinds of creative work—but they can only appear as such by contrast with and in fact are reliant upon that which is not that way.[28] How, after all, might one gauge progress without any fixed or prior referent? Seeking novelty for its own sake is empty. It can, after all, be as much an index of escapism as a palpable result of unique human forms of creativity.

While there is no doubt that the expectation that one maintain shared customs and habits can feel imprisoning if they are turned to as purities whose protection from corruption alone sustains a community—one might think here of displaced communities who do try to make a territory or a transplanted physical terrain out of prior forms of life—collectivities cannot emerge without shared meanings that in addition to being forged constantly and made anew must be old enough to become familiar and available, at key moments, to invoke. Thus, if particular versions of "creole" identity are to be criticized, it is not so much for their imperfection, which is inevitable, but for attaching to an identity a name for an approach that has been interrupted by those claiming and valorizing the newly achieved label. The response is not to attack the inevitability of sedimentation but to urge for renewed efforts at better crystallizations, more universalizing ones. Even these will be measured, positively or negatively, in comparison with previous shortcomings. In this sense, what is useful about Prasad's formulation of polyculturalism is that it emphasizes that practices and words more generally are signs whose meanings are fixed by convention but also porous and changeable; even when relatively stable, they are open to various interpretations and saturated by contentious relations of power. In this sense, while material conditions of people's lives, as Fanon so powerfully indicated, constrain systems of signification, they can only *appear* to do so absolutely.

Much more common at present than the valorization of creolization are projects of decreolization or those through which efforts are made to purify cultures of what are seen as external and contaminating prior or current influences. Earlier examples of this phenomenon are efforts to stave off the Anglicizing of the French language or, in the Caribbean setting, Brinda Mehta's explorations of how, within Indo-Caribbean communities, creolization as mixture with blackness produced an ambiguous tension: while seen as excluding Hindu experiences from efforts to create indigenous local culture, thereby marginalizing Indians as a group, embracing creolization offered to Indo-Caribbean women an enabling alternative to patriarchal gender roles defended and imposed in the name of cultural integrity. She cites Patricia Mohammed (1988), who argues that when speaking of Indian women in Trinidad, creolization was an insulting way to describe Indian women who consorted with African men (Mehta 2004, 121).[29] In both such instances, one witnesses clear, if negative, admissions that mixture is underway and efforts to rewind and stave off further such developments.

There are certainly moments in which creolization is avoided because it seems only to amount to embracing assimilation into a colonizing culture. This is precisely what we considered in the example of the previous chapter of occupied Algeria and it is a position advanced by several leading US Afrocentrists: for them, to be creolized in this country is to be polluted by Eurocentrism. The difficulty with this position, however, is that new world African cultures, even in their most strongly black nationalist varieties, are already inescapably creolized—frequently communicated in English or Portuguese or Dutch or French and of necessity already in conversation with the full range of modern thinkers, not only those of African descent. One might retort accurately that we are all of African descent. At that point, however, it is no longer clear what Eurocentrism would mean. There are similar decreolizing pressures placed on most Native American communities: asked to exemplify an unadulterated purity; to be a window into a lost and uncorrupted world; to offer a refuge or "otherwise" from the imperial logics of the present. At the same time, indigenous communities in settler societies of the Atlantic and the Pacific are the most racially mixed of any living communities.

One might pause here in light of these arguments to consider the very different reactions of the French government to the Négritude writings of Leopold Senghor and Aimé Césaire, on the one hand, and Fanon's *A Dying Colonialism*, on the other. Négritude, in many ways, is much more compatible with a multicultural than a creolizing model. In it, each community's "culture" is a territory with fortressed boundaries, in the case of the colonized, a sanctuary into which one retreats, even if in petrified and zombified form, having conceded at least temporarily that the public terrain of politics is that of the settler. By contrast, Fanon captures how disturbed were those who suddenly heard *their* French, the language that the colonized supposedly could not learn, being used by North Africans to converse animatedly to one another about the progress of their anticolonial efforts. Suddenly a creolized *lingua franca* (that combined the French lexifier with the full range of North African substrates), a framework introduced to colonize was used to interrupt and throw off its forms. And indeed, in terms of the fate of books advancing these respective visions: it was Fanon's that was banned six months after it came to print.

Before proceeding, we must reiterate two key ironies at the core of a meaningful formulation of the concept of creolization: The first is that processes of creolization while first developed to explore Caribbean peculiarities are underway beyond it. At the same time, these approaches to difference have historically been noticed most precisely when inspiring dread or bemusement for combining previously distinctive genealogies. In these instances of mergings provoking misgivings, those who understood themselves through terms of distance and separation encountered evidence of their mutual constitution near impossible to ignore. It is this disturbing aspect that in fact drew attention to phenomena that while widespread, perhaps even universal, could otherwise go unnoticed. In appearing where they were not supposed to, creolized forms exemplified and thereby pointed to key features of how human worlds are often forged.

Second, the most vital instances of creolization emerge when they are not the aim; when instead groups located differently together try to forge more viable collectivities that necessitate contesting existing symbols in ways that produce newer ones. In other words, creolization is progressive not when we are deliberately rejecting being straightjacketed by any and all existing practices or when we seek novelty as proof of our capacity to create, but when we are not constrained by the misleading commitments that would frame a resulting creolized form as a problematic betrayal or that would make us prematurely foreclose that in which we could or would partake so that we would be unable meaningfully to bridge former divides.

Finally, we do not in *creolizing political theory* want to seek out in the theorists we engage a smattering of worldly cultural difference in a patronizing politics of inclusion. We *do* want to capture what is unfolding around us to offer models of more legitimate, irretrievably global, political futures. The results, if rigorously pursued, will inevitably be creolized.

FURTHER CREOLIZING CREOLIZATION

Several anthropologists have expressed reservations about the adequacy of generalizing the concept of creolization, of borrowing a term born of specific historical geopolitical predicaments to describe the erosion of discretely distributed cultural difference in a wide range of domains. For Mimi Sheller (2003), for instance, this can only mean to gut and overextend the idea in an act she likens to piracy. For others, such as Ulf Hannerz, tensions between links to particular regions and generalized notions remain with all theorizing, no less evident with terms like *mafia* and *apartheid* or, we could add, *democratization* and *legitimization*, than with creolization. We can, Hannerz urges, think internationally and constructively while remaining aware of subtleties of context that may be lost in translation (2006, 585). Carl Schmitt observed this point some time ago, that when we engage in theoretical reflection we take specific ideas rooted in a particular position in a distinct, contentious struggle and use them to make sense of other situations both similar and different, mobilizing and extending while altering their symbolic content. This seems yet more permissible in this case. After all, creolization did aim to describe the process of making forms of life local through their critical resituation. Khan therefore reminds would-be critics of the expansion of the concept that the foundational moments out of which it emerged are themselves highly stylized, even in the hands of the most rigorous of historians. Seeking to "encompass as many contingencies and particularities as possible . . . its purported empiricism is in theory only" (588). Finally, if creolization described a set of processes tied fundamentally to the emergence and spread of mercantile capitalism, it should be reengaged to illuminate the reconfiguration of relational spheres of the global and local, the national and diasporic in the most contemporary instantiations of global capitalism (Crichlow and Northover 2009, 181 and 213; Cohen and Toninato 2010, 7).

While there are dangers of making the meaning of creolization too loose to be useful—if describing everything, it uniquely magnifies nothing—there is an odd irony in aiming to "purify" and fix its meaning in a sequestered particularity. More useful is to distinguish it from alternatives including, as Eriksen has suggested, from the cultural pluralism of multiculturalism and from hybridity, which consists in the mediating role contractually created for exceptional people and groups who help to reassert the logic of pure, distinct groups by serving as their go-between.[30] This is urgent when we turn explicitly to questions of method because, without explicit self-reflection, the ways in which we conceptualize the meaning of culture and symbolic life *decisively overdetermine* how we envisage the disciplines from and within which we think. What do I mean?

A common response, for instance, to the significant challenges posed by heterogeneity to earlier aspirations to formulate universal theories has been to call for interdisciplinary or mixed-method research. These, at the level of method, mimic the politics and mode of multiculturalism: distinct disciplinary approaches, each with unique genealogies of commitment are aggregated in the hope that together the discrete pieces amount to a complete picture that, if not comprehensive, is at least less partial. Each party to such endeavors is understood to contribute most if they authentically represent each of their respective traditions. As I have said of forms of cultural mixture later described as instances of creolization, those skeptical about interdisciplinary initiatives frequently see ensuing intellectual mixtures only in terms of dilution or corruption. They appear illicit. Preferable in times framed as those of scarcity such as our own is to develop the most specialized of masteries, shoring up the necessity of this particular area of study and the indispensability of these specific practitioners.[31]

Creolization, by contrast, would assume, following the accounts that I have considered, that disciplines are the culmination of particular genealogies taken up to make sense of particular problems and current circumstances. These will render specific elements of these fairly sedimented practices especially relevant as others clearly become less so. One is likely to find, as well, that dimensions of other disciplinary formations, those not typically employed, offer categories, foundational analogies, forms of argument, evidence, and ideas that are highly illuminating. However, one will not turn to these for the sake of being ecumenical or exemplifying tolerance or inclusivity but instead because they offer magnifying routes into and through a dilemma that one otherwise would lack. In enlisting them, one can move forward. In such acts of appropriation and incorporation, the purposes to which these disciplinary approaches were originally put might be obscured or, as they are recontextualized, might be brought into focus through a now distinctive use. One does not simply aggregate or add up these respective methods—with the implication that one might say that the work is 10 percent economic and 65 percent sociological, and so on.

Some of the most significant examples of previous creolized methodological endeavors are political economy and genetics, both of which could only materialize if their relevant practitioners abandoned primary concerns with authentically enacting what it already meant to be a member of their given field. In seeking to unlock particular puzzles, they instead came upon what Buck-Morss has described as the edges and gaps among all disciplinary formations, using their own creative abilities to negotiate among distinctive modes of reasoning and argumentation.

In this sense, we might recall Mufwene's earlier observation that creole tongues are not radical exceptions, but instead prototypes that magnify in rapidity and radicality processes at work in all language development. In particular, remember that he observed: outside of scholastic systems, one's aim is neither to create nor master a complete language but instead to use it to meet communicative needs. Even then, it is less the needs of converging communities that drive change than the collective outcomes of the negotiation and innovation of individual encounters. Restructuring is often the result of the codification of imperfect replications or of errors. Still, if creole languages are distinguished by higher rates of this last feature, this is a difference of degree from what goes on within monolingual communities.

One might say the same of disciplines and transdisciplinary work more generally. Their developmental processes are not radically different; the former simply reifies aims that are secondary in the latter. Disciplines themselves, in other words, are significantly altered and refashioned over time. Still, there is much commitment among most practitioners in ensuring their continuity and survival. With transdisciplinary work, by contrast, the world we are trying to understand is centrally assumed to exceed the incomplete grasp of any and each discrete field. While their varied approaches are surely useful, none is framed as capable of being complete in an abstract or absolute sense. Therefore rather than prioritizing trying to master the whole of any singular discipline, transdisciplinary endeavors treat such a goal as unachievable and emphasize that what is considered worthy of such an authoritative grasp is always highly contextual. What leads to scholarly innovation is not disciplines acting in relationship to one another but individual intellectuals encountering one another in constructive debate. What leads to such acts of restructuring is both imperfect replication—the altering of existing arguments through mistakes or alterations and through their combination with ideas from elsewhere.

Within political theory, the writings of W. E. B. Du Bois (for instance, 1938, 1962, 1969, 1996, 1999, 2000a) and Frantz Fanon offer groundbreaking examples of creolizing work. Seamlessly drawing from history, philosophy, sociology, psychology, political economy, and literature to diagnose the centrality of racialization to projects of European modernity. Rather than seeking to authenticate themselves through the mastery of hyper-specialization, to emulate the fields in which they were credentialed, they sought syntheses that deliberately avoided replicating the particular areas of illumination and blindness of each respective disciplinary approach. Guided by the larger aim of disalienating the people whom they studied, they improvised how it was that vantages disclosed by one approach would relate to and be transformed in conversation with others. Ironically, in such creolized work, one sees again the uniqueness of sociological approaches and psychoanalytical ones, the specificity of literary insights and those of political economy. Through resisting their respective isolation, the distinctiveness of each comes newly into view.

Put simply, in interdisciplinary work that conceives of disciplines as advocates of multiculturalism view culture, the guiding ethos is one of tolerance and of honoring diversity. Cultures and fields are approached as if they were somewhat self-determining nations requiring separation to preserve their authenticity. This is crucial since it is through their distinctiveness secured by distance that they can enrich the larger community. In processes of creolization, by contrast, a given aim or project supervenes over principles that would in advance restrict what constitute available resources and reactions by fixing a prior rules of engagement. In seeking to create viable forms out of what is locally available, with creolization one assumes that each, while retaining some of its original character, will, in being resituated, also be transformed as it combines to become something continuous and distinctive. Unlike multiculturalism, the advocates of which typically assume that a more accommodating political liberalism is the singular adequate model for the political present and future, creolization emerged where shared, existing terms for social cooperation were absent. These circumstances therefore threw into sharp relief the politically determined, relational, and malleable nature of the worlds of meaning to which *culture* refers.

In arguing for the usefulness of its generalization, I am not aiming radically to separate creolization from its origins. Indeed, part of what makes creolization particularly useful is its historical and continued connection to the Caribbean and through it to the Global South. This is for at least two primary reasons.

First, the legacy of epistemic colonization is ongoing. Through it an international division of labor constitutes relations between center and periphery, affirming that ideas, directions, and purposes concerning the organizing of political life and the highest forms of theoretical reflection emerge from the metropole and are at best imperfectly applied in the now independent former colonies. The implications are that while those in Euro-America can be considered literate professionals without following the most recent intellectual developments in other parts of the globe, the same is not true in reverse. Intellectual agenda setting continues to take place in a small set of institutions that cannot be ignored with impunity if one hopes to be able to teach and publish in reputable institutions. Still, while for some this means the simple adoption and aping of work from there, for many thinkers outside of these centers (even if physically located within them), it is in the contradictions laid bare in confrontations with such double standards that constructive thought emerges. We might recall here Fanon's critical engagements with Adler or with Freud, with Hegel or with Sartre.[32]

In other words, the project of creolizing theory or of engaging resources that are local and from elsewhere to grapple with domestic challenges of collective life without doubt that such efforts constitute contributions to the world of thought is underway among communities in the Global South. This is perhaps most evident in those who address the challenge stated clearly in Paget Henry's pathbreaking *Caliban's Reason*, of aiming in the domain of philosophy and reflection to emulate the creolization that characterizes Caribbean music, food, literature, and language, rather than allowing for the presumed authority of Europe to continue. At times, this has involved, as Henry demonstrates (and Gerald Larson [1988] and Leigh Jenco [2007] have argued in the context of northeast Asia), looking at spheres of life that contingent historical developments made primary sites of past philosophical reflection (rather than assuming that we know in advance where these should be located) and at others abandoning the quintessentially imperial view that all that is ultimately worth knowing will emanate out of the bellies of empires. In other words, those in the Global North would do well to emulate their Southern counterparts who do not assume that all that they should critically consider will eventually arrive at their door in their deliberate efforts to assure that their scholarship can accurately be called "worldly."[33]

Second, one of the clearest indexes of power is the ability to set the terms of inclusion and exclusion. In radically unequal societies in which benefits are highly concentrated in small communities, the terms of exclusivity are likely to be many. In other words, one might fail to exemplify many different required attributes for membership. In direct proportion and opposite to this are communities of more limited means that become the highly variegated domain of the vast majority who are excluded. In such a predicament, it is overdetermined that creolization is more likely to emerge where the terms of entry, while inevitably exercising a cetrifugal force (as with French lexifiers in the production of Francophone creoles), are less easily controlled. As my discussion of Fanon's *Black Skin, White Masks* revealed, absent efforts to forge an alternative, what goes on among the marginalized is often a monstrous mirroring of the powerful. In this sense, while it is not intrinsically so, there does seem to be a very likely relationship between creolization and projects aimed at addressing the nature of such exclusions.

But if creolization has been used primarily retrospectively and adjectivally, to look backward, even in stylized ways, at various life worlds, can one properly use it, not as a measure of gatekeeping, but as a verb and methodological orientation toward the political future?[34] As the proceeding discussion no doubt suggests, my answer is an adamant and enthusiastic "yes."

The present is described over and over as a globalized or globalizing moment or one in which relations between the here and the there, the local and the worldly are being reconfigured in ways we are still trying both to fathom and direct. While our predicament is more diffuse than the individual encounters that brought Europe, Africa, and the Americas together in the Caribbean of the fifteenth century—making it very difficult for them to understand themselves outside of their entangled interrelations—we too cannot avoid reinterpreting ourselves through worlds previously foreign.

In such a context, there will inevitably be a variety of responses. In addition to the interdisciplinary one against which I am advancing creolization, it is also possible for fields to be absorbed into one another, to be eradicated, or to be decreolized. This third possibility currently abounds. It is one through which scholars once conversant in an overlapping and shared disciplinary language move away from the conditions of cross-fertilization and mutual constitution in increasingly isolated subfield niches that nurture separate trajectories that in one version of "autonomy" or "independence" in fact become less and less intelligible to one another.

The difficulty with this, of course, is that an intellectual division of labor is given its coherence if it ultimately serves a higher unity in which each respective community magnifies pieces of the larger puzzle of reality. In political science, for instance, the questions and problems illuminated by theorists, after all, are supposed to work in tandem with phenomena clarified by qualitative and quantitative work undertaken in American, Comparative, or International politics so that students working among these distinct areas come away with a grasp of how they might navigate a much larger whole.

However, if rigor and sophistication in each subfield are premised on a narrowing purity through which good work is that which is understood by an ever smaller academic community in which one can only meaningfully participate through devoting oneself entirely to mastering its discrete *basolect* language, the larger synthetic work that focused scholarship is ultimately to serve is obscured. In such circumstances, rather than offering unique concepts generated by grappling with enduring particular problems to facilitate broader comprehension, specialized academic tongues function primarily as gatekeeping devices, means of artificially narrowing the pool of who might enter a domain increasingly defined by extraintellectual, frequently economic dictates. As Terrence Ball has argued, communities, including those of inquiry, only exist so long as their members continue to converse in civilized ways—not through an attitude of "live and let live" but through talking and listening that require prioritizing translating among idioms in ways that invite critical exchange over point-scoring that instead breeds niche isolationism and protectionism (1987, 4).

After all, a discipline like political science has historically been very creolized: one might think here of classic works in the field, including those by Theda Skocpol, Robert Dahl, and Hannah Arendt. In each case, one would be accurate to call the given writings works in history or theory or politics—ones from which many audiences beyond those of card-carrying professional political scientists might learn.

It should come as no surprise that in circumstances like our own there is less and less conversation and movement between the scholarly field of political science and the world of politics[35] and that but for the small set of students seeking preparation for graduate school, fewer who want simply to equip themselves to be engaged citizens find resources in the way that the field is presented in undergraduate courses. Often students instead leave the major with feelings of greater alienation and impotence—with a sense that the distance between the world and their grasp of it has only grown.

Should we not be disturbed by such decreolizing trajectories, ones that move in a *reductio ad absurdum* toward a situation in which we cannot be understood by any but ourselves? Is it not the aim, after all, of scholarly work to enlarge the world of human beings through expanding our capacity to communicate that which we do comprehend? Surely, it is not a real strength or actual sign of autonomy if political theorists can speak only to one another—making references to a small set of incredibly rich texts in ever more impenetrable and arcane language. What is more, decreolization does not only involve moving our disciplines further and further away from adequately describing the reality we are to illuminate, it is also costly in ways that are unsustainable. We no longer occupy (indeed few ever did) political and economic conditions in which disciplines can proceed on a model in which one works away in one's narrow corner oblivious to the others.

Here again, the contrast with the Caribbean is striking. There and in its various diaspora, the Renaissance man and woman is the norm: literature professors write novels and read physics, often at a very high level of sophistication in each case. They assume that they will have to fill multiple roles, that there are not resources to emulate the Anglo-American university and therefore that more hinges on individual and collective creativity, on articulating the relation among the parts. One might say that the US academy is graced by this eased relationship to individual breadth—that we can each do less better—however, in so doing, it is not clear that we do not lose sight of the meaning of the unique resources that we, as intellectuals and scholars, are to use and expand.

At present, the response to the neoliberal university clearly must be to reject the model of disciplines as offering discrete bundles of specialized knowledge—instead rearticulating the world to which the separate pieces refer, how they comprise a meaningful whole that can embolden generations of young people to participate in forging the shape of that which they are entering. We would do better, if this is our concern, not to see our work as stronger because it can only be understood by a tiny handful of similarly trained professionals also fluent in our respective *basolects*, but if it can take what is most valuable in this information and use it to illuminate shared dilemmas in ways that enable us to reenliven *mesolects* through which we might articulate how to proceed.

Creolization offers a model of how it is that people have constructed collective worlds out of necessity. It is not through tiny unassociated parts coexisting in mutual hostility but by recognizing, exploring, and enunciating complex interdependencies in ways that transcode and incorporate so that each is understood in and through the terms of each other—so that the conditions of mutual intelligibility and sociality can emerge. In this sense, a creolized method for political theory is one that aims in its guiding assumption to treat symbolic worlds, "culture," as Sigmund Freud (1961) argued in *Civilization and Its Discontents*, as the efforts of human beings to forge domains within an otherwise indifferent or inhospitable natural world. In carving out such spheres we seek reflections of our values and of ourselves.[36]

One could similarly say that politics and theory devoted to reflection about it are centuries-long endeavors to fashion a province guided by a set of rules and shared practices distinctive from those of the market and of war that set conditions in and through which individuals together, through participation, can potentially seek conditions for their collective thriving. In the audacious imagination of Rousseau, through such endeavor, we become something other than what we are when merely duplicated and multiplied as discrete individuals, an indivisible part of the qualitatively different category of political generality, citizenry, or sovereign people. As with creolization, in this formulation, our distinctiveness as individuals becomes apparent precisely in and through our combination with others into something continuous and new. Rather than lost in a totality, generalities alone magnify the distinctiveness of their component parts.[37]

Anne Norton (2004a) has described the fetishism of method that is overtaking the study of the politics in the United States as an expression of a desire of scholars to transcend our own fallibility, to find, once and for all, "a tool that does not turn in the hand" (135). Likening the promises of method to those of liturgy and sacrament, it is, in her words, "ritual for a secular priesthood—if you adhere to the ritual . . . grace will come" (134). Still, she warns, no ritual always works and sacraments only bring grace to those already graced. The implication of course is that the hope "for a method that cannot be used irresponsibly is illusory" (135). Far more likely to prove illuminating would be to recall the ways in which efforts to divest concepts of their ambiguity distances them from practice, that hunting for variables that are treated with abstract, conceptual integrity and autonomy occludes the multidirectional reciprocities and imbrications of variables with one another (7). There is a greater chance that we will reduce the kinds of fallibility linked to an absence of self-awareness if we take seriously, as Fanon warned, that all methods are allied with particular regimes of truth and the rationalities in which they consist (82), integral to larger deeply political projects about the nature of desirable futures.

The desperation to transcend the recurring appearances of our own inevitable responsibilities, we might add, were considered by Karl Jaspers among others to be a defining feature of intellectual life in the modern age. Aware, he wrote, "that the image of a whole can be nothing more than one aspect contemplated as an object, and cannot be a knowledge of the real whole . . . the dangers and hazards of genuine activity in the world should be accepted" (1957, 165–66).[38] The curtain over reality, he announced, had been lifted. Writers and scholars considered and attempted to comprehend the world, but every effort was overshadowed by doubts of the validity of every determination. Behind every interpretation of the unity of life there loomed the distinction between the world and the world as we know it.

Creolization is borne of just this doubled moment: of loss and melancholy and simultaneously of possibilities, even necessities for self-creation, of fashioning what is supposed to have been effective because primordial. There is a desire to posit disciplines as if they too are of timeless ancestry, as if they have always existed rather than being the ambiguous and open-ended products of human endeavor.

Creolizing political theory therefore does mean avoiding treating worlds of meaning as if they are already completely constituted, finished, and closed and instead writing as if we too are part of their construction and therefore broaden or foreclose, empower or silence many diverse and unequal coparticipants living and dead. It means being as committed to the projects with which political theory has been associated as realizing that a vibrant future may require cross-breeding and intermixture that is not bastardization but the charting of a new moment in its genealogy, one in which its terms might be reenlivened particularly because they are not jettisoned but resituated so they are continuous and made new.

CONCLUDING IMPLICATIONS

To creolize political theory then is to grapple with heterogeneity and mixture not as discrete pockets of a fractured world but as coconstituting and cosituating each other in ways that we are obligated to try to understand and reflect in writing that is, after all, aimed to illuminate precisely this sphere.[39] In so doing, one not only pushes against the genre of political theory writing in ways for which Anne Norton and George Shulman (2008), within political theory, have long argued. One also cannot but grapple with how to think among such registers, fostering conversations that do not all partake of the same argumentative modes and conventions. Finally, we aim to make our epistemological limitations, which are unavoidable, sites of openness to unknown horizons so that we can restore human beings as value-giving subjects with meaning-making capacities that are never just those of reproduction, which in turn requires engagement with the plurality of intellectual heritages that constitute the symbolic world (Cornell and Panfilio 2010). This is crucially also to reject being overtaken by poststructural suspicions of any collective aspirations as necessarily totalizing and repressive.

The social scientific literatures concerning creolization that I have discussed thus far document this process under much more constrained conditions than those faced by the scholar or intellectual. Scholars and intellectuals do not, in other words, write on the plantation with the project of developing a functional, mutually intelligible language.[40] When faced with a pressing problem, we may make use of whatever we may obtain with limitations that are primarily our own.[41]

In this sense, the creolized methods I am arguing for do have much in common with what have been called "problem-driven theory" in the writings of Ian Shapiro (2007). Where I depart from Shapiro, however, is his assumption that such an approach is necessarily synonymous with pragmatism, a highly culturally specific, in some cases US-nationalist, way into such work. Doing so assumes in advance that one particular constellation of disciplinary commitments and orientations is sufficient and exhaustive rather than making a question of what, in this particular instance, promises to be most illuminating.[42] For instance, if one were, as I am, concerned with the exponential growth of enslavement worldwide, why would pragmatism be the most obvious resource? The only sense in which this might be true would be if we agreed to define any approach in which one suspends prior methodological commitments so that the problem at hand determines that toward which one would turn only as pragmatism, rather than as the many other approaches, including, say phenomenology, that have also defined themselves through this foundational orientation.

It is with this in mind that I suggested in the introduction that the creolization of theory might be compared with Rousseau's general will rather than, as is the case with multidisciplinary work, to a will of all. When culture is described in the Geertzian or strong multicultural mold, it suggests a world of worlds, each distinct and not overlapping, rather than worlds that necessarily already make sense of themselves in relation to one another. For all of their many dimensions and divergent temporalities, their relations are marked by staunch divisions, inequalities, and contention. But to frame these on the model of divergent private interests promises to erode the very possibility of discussion of what it is that can sustain a global human community. Recall that Rousseau's general will aims to unite what is popular and right in a way that secures and extends the conditions for a polity to have a sense of itself as a social unit rather than a mere aggregate of separated individuals. As such the "we" that it articulates and expresses rather than siphoning off distinct groups makes sense of each in relation to the other.

I have been asked why one would bother to argue for an approach to political theory that so breaks with many established academic norms? Why not simply undertake such work beyond the confines of the academy, where one does not face disciplining disciplines?

However troubled the contemporary academy may be, it remains the set of institutions that represent and offer to every generation what is supposed to be the most rigorous grasp of reality developed by those who have made this their vocation. Even if some of the most vital intellectual endeavors have been and will always be undertaken outside of these frameworks, within them we teach and write with what Lewis Gordon and I have called a "pedagogical imperative" (2006) or, in what will pain postmodern readers, with a concern to honor the trust that students place in us to portray the most accurate account of truths available. If occupying the world as a scholar is to be aware of the enormity of what one does not know, in professional terms it is to try to stay apace with developments and debates at the center of one's chosen fields not only as defined by a small set of others but by a larger, contradictory, and refracted world.

In closing, as I suggested earlier, I do not want to imply that creolization as a method is without limitations. The first of these, as the previous discussion should have made clear, is that processes of creolization are borne of and expressions of loss, of contexts defined by significant interruptions in which long continuities are broken and people work with what remains to fashion a viable alternative. The focus on a creolizing method, therefore, turns our attention away from a focus on developing the greatest possible mastery of particular existing disciplinary formations to selecting what of them is most of use. Even then, not everything combines in a lasting way. In other words, if one's approach to culture and to fields of study is to try as comprehensively as possible to keep elements that one encountered in one's first introduction to them intact through as close to perfect duplication as possible, creolization will not be desirable. Of course, such an effort encounters the challenge posed to all forms of conservatism: to keep anything meaningfully the same requires that it be transformed as it is resituated again and again for each new circumstance.

Still, many might have reservations regarding the radically present- and future-oriented constructive ethos of creolization—that it might lack the self-reflexivity and humility necessary to avoid a crude instrumentalism, that even as we encounter other symbolic forms we might be so overdetermined by familiar frameworks that we will fail to be challenged by that within them which is distinctive. This can be a genuine danger and is not one that is easily addressed. I would suggest, however, that when particular symbolic forms are constantly and deliberately juxtaposed with historically contingent alternatives, their specificity is most apparent. If able to parade in the singular, one particular configuration of forms can become enveloping, appearing to have no outside.

Finally, processes of creolization cannot themselves determine the conditions within which they take place—the particular ingredients that will be available and whether their incorporation or rejection will appear as political accommodation or its opposite. Instead, as the epigraph from Mary Shelley in the next chapter suggests, "Invention, it must be humbly admitted, does not consist in creating out of a void, but out of chaos; the materials must, in the first place, be afforded . . . Invention consists in the capacity of seizing on the capacities of a subject and in the power of molding and fashioning ideas suggested to it."

Creolizing political theory, in conclusion then, involves, in the language of Lewis Gordon (2006, 14), an act of teleological suspension through which we recall a larger *telos*, in this instance, a galvanizing concern with understanding and protecting a distinct domain called political life. Rather than treating our discipline as if it were never born and can never die by ontologizing it (or treating it as isomorphic with Being itself), we must recenter difficult questions over the methods that would determine in advance what can and cannot be asked and assume that we will devise viable models, however in need of subsequent alteration they will be, that put our capacities for reason in the service of the unfinished work of liberation. In so doing, ironically, we emulate those who have served through time as some of our greatest guides, none of whom devoted their lives exclusively to the academy nor addressed their works solely to a small community of other scholars. Their language and ideas necessarily drew on whichever resources lay at hand, some of which, without doubt, in their mistranslation, were wonderfully innovative.

In the political terrain, few are surprised by reminders that what come to feel like the most natural of alliances are contingent and forged, contingent and forged again—made to frame as shared, concerns that are disparate and at times even fundamentally conflicting. However, if the aim of political life is to seek goods as broad as societies themselves, not to make a priori exclusions of who can be ignored with impunity, it will require recentering precisely those on the margins that have been treated as dispensable. There cannot, in other words, be anything remotely approximating a public good that is not creolized through and through.

Conclusion

> Everything must have a beginning . . . and that beginning must be linked to something that went before. The Hindus give the world an elephant to support it, but they make the elephant stand upon a tortoise. Invention, it must be humbly admitted, does not consist in creating out of a void, but out of chaos; the materials must, in the first place, be afforded: it can give form to dark, shapeless substances but cannot bring into being the substance itself . . . Invention consists in the capacity of seizing on the capacities of a subject and in the power of molding and fashioning ideas suggested to it.
>
> —MARY WOLLSTONECRAFT SHELLEY[1]

I have offered readings of Rousseau and Fanon in the preceding pages in the hope of demonstrating the productivity of bringing ideas together in a *creolized* rather than *comparative* way.

Readers may well then wonder what they are to make of the relationship of the creolizing that I am arguing for to the now blossoming subfield of comparative political theory. After all, one striking feature of the work that I call "creolizing" is its bringing into constructive conversation figures whose universal significance is undisputed with those that, at least historically in North America and Western Europe, have been considered only salient within narrowed parameters, or worse, not properly theoretical.

One could conclude with some accuracy that within the US academy no new development has created more disciplinary space for the project of creolizing political theory than comparative political theorizing. Informed fundamentally by heremeneutics and postcolonial thought, comparative political theory, from the outset, has aimed to expand what is designated thought to ensure that "'political theory' is about human and not merely Western dilemmas ... [making] room for the possibility that there is humanly significant knowledge outside the confines of the Western canon" (Euben 1999, 9–10). For Fred Dallmayr (2004), echoing the challenge of Leo Strauss some decades before, especially in the aftermath of September 11, political theorists fiddled as Rome burned. In the face of grand and pressing problems requiring bold imagination, we theorists had, in sizeable numbers, retreated into rehearsing canons—seeking to be enveloped in the worlds of classical texts rather than using them to respond to our own. Dallmayr therefore beckoned to theorists to retrieve a more coherently distinctive role for ourselves at the forefront of developing languages and idioms for an increasingly global civil society. Regularizing such confrontations with difference, he contended, promised to unsettle and repoliticize the creedal quality of core ideas in Western political theory canon.

What is more, from its very beginning, comparative political theory has been marked by an unusual degree of methodological self-reflexivity rooted in an awareness of the instructive and prohibitive lessons of both theoretical and empirical forays into comparisons with non-Western worlds. Dallmayr, for example, warned first against "imperialist modes of theorizing," in which one portion of the globe would monopolize the production of shared meanings and practices that should "only arise from lateral interaction, negotiation, and contestation among different, historically grown cultural frameworks" (2004, 29). In addition, he advanced, worldly theory would emerge out of a middle course between the methods of abstract generalists and of narrow specialists, neither through seeking "indiscriminate 'assimilation'" nor radically untranslatable otherness (1999, 3). With Euben, comparative endeavors constituted a "reclamation" of the foundations of political theory. After all, at the time of Herodotus, she observes, a theorist was "a public emissary dispatched by his city to attend the religious festivals of other Greek cities" (1999, 10–11). (One might reconsider here the opening lines of *The Republic*, when Plato explains that he is en route to a festival being held in Piraeus for the first time. This encounter prefaces the entire work of alternative political imagining that follows.) Additionally, as evident in the instances of Aristotle, Machiavelli, Baron de Montesquieu, Charles-Louis de Secondat, and Alexis de Tocqueville, theory transpires out of journeying to alien political worlds that stir a critical sense of the peculiarity of one's own institutions, challenging their seeming inevitability by nurturing self-understanding that grounds an enlivened sense of possibility.

In addition, Euben stresses that comparative political theory cannot rely upon and should endeavor to challenge any perception of cultures as radically distinct or hermetically sealed. Countering a dangerous tendency also emphasized by Gerald Larson (1988) and Michaelle Browers (2008)—that comparing Western with non-Western philosophical writing fosters the misperception that these traditions developed in parallel, independently of one another—Euben focuses on ambivalent treatments of Western modernity in Arab thought, illuminating internal fissures in both that belie their presumed opposition. If historical designations of this sort (West, non-West, Islam, etc.) cannot simply be dispensed with, since they are forms of representation embedded in mythologies that anchor our understanding (Zerilli, cited in Euben 1999, 12), and, however imperfectly, remain short-hand for constellations of sources, issues, and methods of argumentation that while constructed through *post facto* agendas produce family resemblances and recognizable attributes (Godrej 2009), they still obscure messy and interpenetrating histories. After all, argues Euben, the possibility of engaging in comparative discussions is a function not of radical difference but mutual indebtedness of worlds now juxtaposed as discrete. In the case of "the West" and "Islam," both are fundamentally shaped by Semitic traditions, texts considered classical within Europe were reintroduced to its readers through preserved Arabic translations, and the Golden Age of Islamic thought was defined by efforts to forge syncretic fusions of Greek and Islamic resources.

And one can easily find elements of prescriptive accounts of the project of comparative political theory that resemble that for which I have been advocating. Consider, first, Hwa Yol Jung's suggestion, drawing on Maurice Merleau-Ponty, that comparative political theory offers an approach to a more genuine universalism, one of "lateral" rather than "faceless" claims and aspirations (Jung 1999, 2002, 2007; Merleau-Ponty 1964). Second, is Euben's suggestion that comparative work "makes possible many unimagined . . . conversations . . . that raise the distinct possibility that non-Western perspectives may provide new . . . answers to [the West's] old questions . . . [ones] that actually transform the . . . questions themselves" (1999, 11).

The difficulty, however, is that the conceptual apparatus of "comparative thinking," for all of its necessary and skillful qualification, especially by Euben, Godrej, and Browers, while garnering professional permission to undertake various intellectual projects, is in some cases misleading and in others, as Andrew March (2009) has suggested, even a misnomer. After all, much of the work going on within this rubric is not comparative at all, but instead sustained and sophisticated studies of rich domains of thought beyond Western Europe and Anglo-America of what were once called area specialists (see, for instance, Jenco 2007). For work that is premised on grappling with converging difference, there are other concerns. For March, for instance, if a driving impetus to comparative endeavors is to redress detrimental exclusions of important voices that have left the canon highly partial, this is not merely a comparative consideration but instead an effort to produce better political theory more generally. It is in that spirit, that I have undertaken to read Rousseau through Fanon or that Godrej (2006) reads John Rawls with and against Mohandas Karamchand Gandhi. The value and implications of Fanon and Gandhi are not limited to their particular contexts but more broadly illuminating to the world of thought. For March, by contrast, a bold and generative comparative approach would require the very distinctness of units of analysis that we have thus far been blurring. It is for this reason that he contends that the best candidates for comparative theoretical explorations are in elucidating normative conflicts over the terms of social cooperation from within discrete religious and moral traditions of the implicated adherents. For it is in these cases that the boundaries to be negotiated remain clear (March 2009, 563–65).

For Leigh Jenco, the problems are rather different: First, if one wants to avoid uncritically reproducing the ethnocentric categories that comparative political theory seeks to transcend, one must attend as much to the method of inquiry in culturally situated traditions of scholarship as to their substantive ideas. These approaches to how one undertakes one's scholarship are intended to make distinct traditions accessible to committed and hardworking outsiders. This mode of difference is overridden in the reification of dialogue, however. Even if Jung and Dallmayr do at times suggest protracted fusions of horizons in lateral universals, the prevailing skeptical and hermeneutic emphasis is on mutually illuminating potentially transformative, tolerant conversation. This poses troubles often also put to Habermasian discourse models. In sum, such approaches frequently fail to grapple with the non-neutrality of language and the inadequacy of framing speech as inherently discrete from the logic of force and violence. The egalitarianism assumed for dialogic purposes may not be a feature of the cultures brought together and efforts to move beyond the limits of dialogue produces a horrible circle: either one makes decisions concerning rules and protocol in advance with the implication that the dialogue itself becomes the covert enforcer of those norms or the method requires an endless dialogue about dialogue within which conversation of other subject matter can never begin (Jenco 2007, 744).

It is striking that Dallmayr's (1996) classificatory scheme of modes of cross-cultural encounter includes conquest, conversion, assimilation/acculturation, partial assimilation/cultural borrowing, liberalism/minimal engagement, conflict/class struggle, and dialogical engagement. The first three, for him, are hegemonic and hierarchical models which comparative political theory should eschew as destructive. Partial assimilation, in his account, takes place on an unequal basis and can easily follow a melting pot model, one of ambivalent syncretism, or of genuine mutual transformation. While liberal models tend toward isolation, the alternatives of struggle are too contentious and unstable. For Dallmayr, it is therefore dialogue that exemplifies respect for otherness beyond assimilation and radical untranslatability.

Ideally, argues Michaelle Browers (2008), comparative political theory would involve each participant viewing him or herself as subject and object. More frequent, I would suggest, is the difficulty of double consciousness as articulated by W. E. B. DuBois, that both the dominant and less powerful counterparts see themselves through the eyes of the former. Still, Browers emphasizes, most instances of conceptual change, for all of their inequality, more closely resemble partial assimilation and cultural borrowing in what amounts to instances of transculturation or a process through which more marginal groups often on the political defensive, if unable to determine the content of what is relevant to their reflection on political life, select and invent among ideological elements from more metropolitan cultures, determining how they will be used. Conceptual innovation, in such circumstances emerges precisely from what a more Skinnerian approach would consider *mistranslation*: Rather than trying, as specialists and scholars would, to assure that we demonstrate due respect for otherness by understanding the ideas' meaning in their original context of emergence, we simply put them to work in our own life worlds (Browers 2008, 16). Examples of fruitful mistranslation are multiple. In artistic domains we might consider Vincent Van Gogh's efforts to develop a Dutch style of painting through emulating the bright, sharp line and color of Japanese prints circulating in his day, or the unique sound of British singer Sting's early efforts to sing Caribbean reggae. In politics, observe Danny Postel's recent reflections on the vibrancy of engagements with classical liberalism in the context of contemporary Iran. For Browers, in sum, political creativity and agency are more evident not in the model of dialogue through which one tries to assure that one has gotten Gramsc's or de Tocqueville's conceptions of civil society right but in instances of transculturation. In the latter, Gramsci is a resource on whose partial assimilation one might build, not an imperative whose authentic replication demands duplicating original predicaments that may well prove irrelevant.

I would add an additional fear to the criticism of the preference for tolerant dialogue over the empirically informed considerations of how political conceptual innovation more likely transpires. The scholarly work that has emerged in response to Dallmayr's still very recent clarion call and deliberate creation of professional space both at meetings and through publishing venues, has been a tremendous resource for those who remain primarily interested in the history of ideas and its approximation as the canon as well as those concerned with more contentious contemporary debates.[2] It has revealed as lacking in rigor the vast majority of defenses of the adequacy of the straight march repeated in course after course and reprinted afresh each year in countless new textbooks from Plato and Aristotle to Augustine and Aquinas to Machiaveilli, Hobbes, Locke, Rousseau, Marx, and Nietzsche. Although works eminently worthy of careful and repeated study, the tenacity of this line-up would have many conclude that nothing less than this historical surge of reason, at least in the political realm, leapt from fifth century Athens to the Roman Empire to the warring city-states that became Italy to Western Europe. One cannot simply amend by assimilation figures from Confucius and Mencius to Alfarabi and Averroes to Gandhi and Sayyid Qutb since, at the very least, they reveal the current absence of a viable singular framework for conceptualizing the moments that comprise a world history of political ideas. What has for centuries been referred to as the "Dark Ages" was, after all, a classical period within Islamic civilizations (Robinson 2001). And there was no substantive counterpart to the "Middle Ages" in Chinese history. Additionally, in terms of more contemporary debates, comparative political theory has aimed explicitly to counter Samuel Huntington's (1993, 1996) framing of the post–Cold War moment as a "clash of civilizations" seeking out self-illuminating dialogues with precisely those deemed "enemies."

Still, although avowedly framing and contributing to a global dialogue that would incorporate the Americas, Africa, Europe, Australia, and the full diversity of the expanse called Asia, it is unmistakable that, but for a few very important exceptions, comparative political theory of the last decade has revolved almost exclusively around discussion between Euro-America and the East Asian, East Indian, and Muslim worlds. This is particularly worrying when several recent titles suggest that comparative political theory has in many cases been reformulated as "inter-civilizational dialogue" (Dallmayr and Manoochehri 2007; Gebhardt 2008; Bowden 2008).

One might attribute this pattern of inclusion and exclusion to a contingent matter of the biographies, skills, and professional commitments of the subfield's pioneers *and* to its still early stages. It is after all both unrealistic and unfair to expect what remains a small community of people to do *everything*. And every emergent scholarly area will be an expression of the projects of those that inaugurate them. One could emphasize as well the sustained study and engagement required to redress the genuine dearth of scholarly work focused on Arab and Chinese and Indian thought.

Still, these patterns seem too consistent and unremarked upon to express only these indiosyncracies. They mirror after all something all too familiar: the ethnographic paradigms of the age of exploration and colonialism through which the West typically viewed its non-Western counterparts. East and West Asia have been the object of derisive European and US "orientalizing" that amounts to egregious forms of misrecognition. At the same time, there has seldom been doubt—one could go so far as to say that orientalizing was a perverse expression of precisely the acknowledgment—that ideas, complex civilizations, and genuine political challenges can and would continue to emerge from these regions. As Frederick G. Whelan (2009) recently illustrated, although it became a commonplace in European thought, if at times disputed, to disparage eastern civilizations as despotic and fundamentally lacking in individual dynamism, these regions were those of "sultans" as opposed to those, in the eighteenth-century Scottish Enlightenment parlance, of "savages."

Perhaps one could suggest that these occlusions are not that but instead a function of a particular academic division of labor in which some regions are the purview of postcolonial thought (even though it too increasingly mirrors similar patterns of monopoly and exclusion with East, South, and West Asian writers eclipsing their African and Latin American counterparts in attention and citation), and of African America, Latin American, and Ethnic Studies, and others of comparative political theorizing. The difficulty here is, as already noted, all of the civilizations brought into dialogue have some historical experience with conquest and colonization and writers studying all of them draw, in varying degrees, on relevant postcolonial insights.

One could contend as well that although always porous, some civilizational groups remain more distinctive, more intact, more possible to bring in as the discrete units that many comparativists, with the exception of March, aim to problematize. In other words, for all of the emphasis to the contrary, when it comes to who studies which regions, comparative political theory still needs geopolitico-spatial designators of the "near" and the "far," the "here" and the "there," with thought from the African and Latin diaspora seemingly appearing either too near or too far, neither quite here nor there, both insufficiently the same and inadequately different.

Some comparative political theorists draw on writing from the African and Latin worlds in the same way as they might engage Habermas or Foucault or Gadamer, emphasizing that such writers are within and a substantial part of the inheritance of the "West" they are putting into conversation with thinkers propagandistically portrayed as foreign and dangerous. After all, Dallmayr's typology of cross-cultural encounters is framed around reflections concerning the year 1492 and when describing the coconstitution of metropoles and colonies, he draws on the writing of Emmanuel Eze, Charles Mills, and Paulin Hountondji. Moving beyond the circumscribed role of informants to that of cotheorists is after all one aim of what I am calling the creolizing of political theory. Still, it would be overly sanguine to take these examples as a depiction of the field overall. In it, when it comes to Africa, the Caribbean, and Latin America, in fact, what is evident is the opposite of the fallacy feared, a failure to see that while not radically alien, these regions do pose distinctive questions that should inform more global debates.

One could finally suggest that the periods of primary interest in Africa were those marked by crises and precipitous declines so that, save Muslim North Africa, the study of its political thought would necessarily be work better conducted by archaeologists and historians. On the one hand, most comparativists do not define political theory narrowly and, in the areas to which they are committed, utilize the full range of scholarly approaches. More pertinent, however, is that much of this work is focused on modern thought in which there is ample written political reflection in the Africana diaspora, Caribbean, and Latin America, most of it composed in English, French, and Spanish.

In the absence of commentary on the overrepresentation of some regions of interlocutors over others therefore it would be easy to surmise that the constellation of thinkers and writers is an expression of the ongoing expectation that thought that might be historic and potentially universal does not emerge from Africa, Latin America, and the Caribbean, or that if it does, it is unlikely to be sufficiently distinctive to be framed as a genuinely comparative rather than relative term.

Although I am certain that this is not its aim, what is particularly disturbing is that taken together the work that currently comprises comparative political theory, while framed against the explosive recent writings of Samuel Huntington, appears to affirm his (and G. W. F. Hegel's) geographical estimations of political value and distinctive impact in the realm of historic thought. Recall that in both his infamous essay and book, Huntington mentions African civilization as possibly having some significance for the future and Latin America as a target for incorporation into Western civilization to help counter dangers of Confucian and Islamic configurations. And most controversially, in the longer of his two accounts, Huntington dismisses Haiti out of hand: "While Haiti's elite has traditionally relished its cultural ties to France, Haiti's Creole language, Voodoo religion, revolutionary slave orgins, and brutal history combine to make it a lone country . . . 'the neighbor nobody wants,' a truly kinless country" (1996, 136–37).

I will respond to this final point in a moment, but would like to state clearly in advance that creolizing, with all its attendant difficulties, suggests that the engagement of scholars frequently ignored would improve the overall quality of political theorizing itself, particularly as it seeks to inform challenges that are ever more global.

If comparative political theory has been forged out of an effort to intervene in debates over the meaning and possibilities of cultural and civilizational difference, the work that I am designating that of grappling with "disavowal" begins with a distinct but related challenge: Stated most pointedly, Susan Buck-Morss (2009) insists that in a moment like our own, comparable in significant ways to that of the Age of Revolution, we need a *universalizing* history. This is an endeavor that cannot emerge from readily designated units of analysis or, in the case of comparative political theory, the civilizations and cultures most easily recognized as such. For it is, she provocatively suggests, at the edges of cultures, in the moments when they betray and are betrayed, that more subterranean forms of political identification, those that better approximate universal aims, emerge.

Work on disavowal then critically explores the intellectual and political work required to create, normalize, and reproduce spatial divides and designations that foist particular projects of order on practices and people that resisted them. Studiously avoiding the replication of such uncritical mappings, in Buck-Morss and Sybille Fischer's case, the marginalization of the study of Haiti in historiography devoted to the advent of New World and European modernity that Huntington echoes, is at the core of freeing historical imagination. More specifically then, if comparative political theory addresses major lacunae in political theory through serious theoretical engagement with "threatening" members of the non-West, work exploring "disavowal" has also magnified and complicated the project of the West but by exploring its coconstituting relations with its own "darker sides" (Mignolo 2003). Informed by Black and Caribbean Studies, "disavowal" therefore treats figures and regions that have more typically been sites of internal projection and denial as the focus of substantive engagement and as resources for political thinking.

Against efforts to explain the ongoing, systematic marginalization of the centrality of histories of colonialism and enslavement to the development of the modern West through the concepts of silence or unthinkability, Fischer (2006) advances *disavowal*. Disavowals, she explains, involve the embracing of two contradictory beliefs that in psychoanalytic theory is considered a response to traumatic events, or to theories and occurrences that are too threatening openly to entertain. Attempts to suppress or to repudiate memory do not create silence, as has often been suggested by historians and historiographers; instead, emphasizes Fischer, they create strange *traces* of evasion. In particular, these residual marks are left by efforts to limit the appearance of less desirable subjects, to keep them beneath the terrain of politics, from participation in discursive practices in their own right.

For Fischer, Hegel's engagement with Haiti demonstrates precisely this process.

At the center of Hegel's philosophy of freedom, which is also his philosophy of history, reason, and modernity, is his dialectic between the lord and his bondsman or the master and his slave. Countless Hegel scholars have looked for the origins of this idea, tending, in the main, to ascribe it to other philosophers that Hegel studied, in particular to Aristotle. The assumption, in other words, was that the metaphor was not to be read historically and that if Hegel was considering concrete instances of servitude, they were likely those of fifth-century Athens. This should strike scholars as odd and anachronistic, emphasizes Buck-Morss, since Hegel was such an avowed modernist: When he wrote about economic life, he drew on the writings of Adam Smith. When he argued about the historical realization of freedom, he grappled with the meaning of the events of the French Revolution. Why would it, she asks, never enter the mind of generations of interpreters that Hegel's frequent references to slaves in the *Philosophy of Right* and insistence upon slaves needing to free themselves through direct confrontations and struggle not have reflected his effort to make theoretical sense of his daily reading material in the unfolding coverage in *Minera* and other news sources that documented the events transpiring in eighteenth-century Saint Domingue?

The failure to name Haiti, in Fischer's words, "indicates that his is a knowledge that cannot be recognized as such, a knowledge caught . . . outside the temporality of error and correction, invoked, but not integrated in the great narrative" (2006, 369). Crucial is that he falls silent at the end of the master-slave dialectic, "at the very moment when revolutionary slaves might have appeared" (ibid.). When the *Phenomenology* resumes, writes Fischer, the masters and slaves have vanished, and the locus of the text is again safely and indisputably within Europe. His is a discussion that, for all its insight, is wrought with ambivalence, fascination, fear, and an inability to name its content. If comparative political theory confronts and rejects efforts to frame the challenge posed by people designated as enemies as "cultural" or "religious" rather than political, what of those people and moments past and present that remain disavowed? This is crucial for Buck-Morss since Hegel's reflections on the actual revolution of Caribbean slaves is a universalizing moment, one "when the dialectical logic of recognition becomes visible as the thematics of world history . . . [when theory] and reality converged . . . [and] philosophy burst out of the confines of academic theory and became a commentary on the history of the world" (2009, 59–60).

In fact, the early Haitian Constitutions as the culminations of and efforts to continue the Revolution represented a significant refiguring, or what I would call creolization, of Enlightenment ideas. Taking the French Constitution of 1791 and the Jacobin Constitution of 1793 as their models, they reworked them to include an unequivocal ban on slavery and racial subordination and open asylum to those escaping from enslavement and colonial genocide. In addition, in the Dessalines Constitution of 1805, all Haitians, including naturalized German and Polish women, were to be designated "black," here eliminating the previous designations that encompassed over a hundred different degrees of black mixture (Fischer 2006). "Black" therefore became, as it would in the Black Consciousness movement in South Africa in the mid-1960s, a political rather than racial identity (Biko 2002; Mngxitama, Alexander, and Gibson 2008; L. Gordon 2008b). Fischer argues that these were clear examples of seizing the language of the colonizer and "submitting it to radical resignification" (2006, 371), the very way that we have seen Raquel Romberg redefine the imitation that marks creolization.

In addition, these early constitutions challenged nation-state models of narrowly defined citizenship. The antislavery movement had been thoroughly transnational. Built out of collaborations conducted and maintained in Creole, it brought together slaves born in Africa, Caribbean leaders, and abolitionists from throughout the hemisphere. Fischer explains that in early constitutions, little is said about citizenship, while allowances for taking up residency are expansive. Fischer argues that direct revolutionary action was replaced by a series of immigration schemes, those for instance, that welcomed white men who married black women (anywhere in the world) and offered money for each slave brought to Haiti rather than to slaveholding territories (2006, 373). At the same time, in both instances, universal racial equality and transnationalism ran up against the project of developing economic and political independence in a world in which enslavement was widespread and colonialism expanding into Africa and Asia. Nonetheless, these efforts represented the taking of ideas that had been posed as universal but had in fact only applied to French citizens and trying to expand their reach to anyone who could land on Haitian soil.

Buck-Morss states conclusively:

> The definition of universal history that begins to emerge is this: rather than giving multiple, distinct cultures equal due, whereby people are recognized as part of humanity indirectly through the mediation of collective cultural identities . . . [it] is in the discontinuities of history that people whose culture has been strained to the breaking point give expression to a humanity that goes beyond cultural limits. And it is in our empathic identification with this raw, free, and vulnerable state, that we have a chance of understanding what they say. Common humanity exists in spite of culture and its differences. (2009, 133)

She elaborates, here sounding much more like Benhabib than like Taylor or Kymlicka, that it is in nonidentification with established collectivities that "subterranean solidarities" can emerge with "a chance of appealing to universal, moral sentiment." Against the grain of comparative political theory, she writes, "It is not through culture, but through the idea of culture's betrayal that consciousness of a common humanity comes to be" (ibid.).

She offers by way of example the moment when slaves recognize their enslavement as a betrayal of the project of civilization or when Napolean's soldiers refused to do as they were summoned, seeing the drowning of Africans struggling for their freedom as a contradiction of the stated ideals of the country for which they fought. Such instances, she insists, suggest the inadequacy of the language of "multiple modernities" and politics of "diversality" or "multiversality," moves that would relativize evident inhumanities that are repeated again and again across separate cultural contexts.

Kwasi Wiredu (1996) and Michelle Moody-Adams (1997), as mentioned in Chapter 5, have skillfully made precisely this challenge to efforts to frame moral life as divided by untranslatable, radical cultural difference. They contend that the scale of cultural impermeability has been exaggerated by much anthropological work and its popularization by spokespeople of particular given cultures. In Wiredu's account, to be human is to participate in the world of culture which necessarily includes universal capacities for language, communication, and methods of transmitting knowledge, the particular forms of which are historically contingent. If one aims to specify principles of conduct the presence of which makes human communal survival tolerable, these prove remarkably consistent: They arise from an effort to address the fact that not everybody is inclined to be concerned about others all or most of the time. Efforts to counter this through arguments for sympathetic impartiality again prove strikingly consistent across cultures: Although the particular contexts of meaning suggest different ways of enacting truthfulness, chastity, or courage, their estimation as valuable remains. Serious cross-cultural moral disagreement, after all, argues Moody-Adams, requires a backdrop of basic forms of agreement on a number of moral beliefs. She therefore rejects the commonplace within political liberalism that rationally irresolvable moral disagreement is inevitable, arguing instead that what is evident is a lack of will and commitment to confronting and actually trying to negotiate points of contention. It is not that there are no methods for such adjudication; what is absent is a desire to use them. Both suggest that treating cultures as if they were themselves of special moral value, key kernels of the essential or authentic identities of their adherents, mischaracterizes the nature of culture itself in an effort to place beyond reach critical inquiry into its internal differentiation and broader consequences. Much like Buck-Morss, they reject the view that the fact of diversity amounts to plural discrete truths.

It is dangerous, however, concludes Buck-Morss (2009, 144), to salvage the study of the Haitian Revolution simply as a story of victory, of singular triumph of right over wrong, since doing so requires an antithetical other or collective enemy, inevitably reintroducing an entrenched barrier and a cycle of victim and avenger. We must instead, more modestly, understand such ruptures as fleeting moments of clarity and radical antislavery of this kind as belonging to no particular collective but to everyone (147–48). Seeking such universalizing moments, states Buck-Morss, requires valuing precisely the unhistorical histories dismissed by Hegel and anomalies, including those of collective action, that break with prevalent conceptions of coherent narratives of progress and cultural continuity.

It is no coincidence, in other words, that those people, groups, and nations that are absent from comparative intercivilizational conversation are precisely those that occupy what Enrique Dussel has called "modernity's underside" and, in turn, that the readiest interlocutors are those writing and thinking within empires, both those that are emergent and consolidating and those in periods of decay. One of many clear legacies of colonialism and enslavement, of the construction of categories of people as "savage," is that they are either incorporated within the West all the while being disavowed or assumed to lack sufficiently distinctive cultural traditions, accumulated learning that represents a unique perspective.

They remain largely, as Anne Norton argues, drawing on British anthropologist Victor Turner's *The Ritual Process: Structure and Anti-Structure*, a liminal category, those only partially or ambivalently included in social and political structures. She explains that "[because] they stand on the boundaries of identity, they are often central to debates over those boundaries" (2004a, 41). Others make metaphorical use of literal features of their lives to make sense of their own, identifying with their exclusion or unjust treatment or suggesting that their predicament should be extended to still others. Norton writes, "The primary importance of the liminal [is], however, semiotic. They serve as signs, even when they [act] as agents, and their defining traits [are] often stripped from them and assumed by others" (42). Examples of this process abound: think, for example, of American Revolutionaries, many of whom were directly or indirectly involved with the US slave trade, who charged the British with enslaving them through "taxation without representation" or of the centrality of the language of homelessness for describing what it is to live diasporically or to experience forms of alienation fundamental to the modern world or of the many young men and women who don elements of US or Caribbean blackness, at times suggesting that they are in fact better embodiments of it than black people themselves. In a quintessential example of what it is to be liminal, in such instances, black people are told that they are not only bad at being white people but also bad at being themselves (Gordon and Gordon 2009). As groups of people pivotal to the construction of political identity but disavowed as political agents, neither clearly inside nor out, the condition of the liminal must be a central focus of work aimed at creolization.

Creolization, then, aims to draw on the space for a more rigorous approach to the world of political theory opened by comparative work, while problematizing the ways in which "comparativism" may either problematize itself to the point of incoherence or prove the wrong name. It also builds on the work of disavowal, but while remaining cautious of the dangers outlined by Buck-Morss, rejects both a reluctance toward constructing new collectivities and the assumption that all cultures must collapse into being substantively similar to historical, national ones. As I have already explored, one does not step outside of culture (it is instead disclosed through a variety of forms of symbolic life). When its inadequacies are revealed it is precisely in light of something else. Out of disappointments, one might, in ways that were not so before, be more open to resources and identifications through which to carve homes in the world. These will be highly imperfect, but avoiding them is not possible.

What is more, in such instances, it is not true that all choices amount to more of the flawed same—that articulating a culture through blackness is nothing more than trading one particular exclusive identity for another. "Blackness" as intended here is not an uninterpreted phenotypical identification, but instead the range of political connotations attributed to it. This spectrum includes enslavement and its radical challenging to being forced outside of political membership and aiming through rejecting such exclusion to rearticulate the terms of belonging. In other words, blackness betokens what comes of these contradictions. As the liminal exception and *the* outside, through its engagement we develop a more complete picture of the idealized world for which we strive and the compromises on which it has been premised.

Finally, it would be misleading to suggest that the call for a more responsive study and engagement of political life has been limited to comparative theorists and those of disavowal. Indeed, in addition to an at least three-decade-long project of returning political theory to "the real" (see, for example, Shapiro 2007; Geuss 2008; Schwartz 2008; Isaac 1998; Tully 2008a, 2008b; Tronto 2004), there has been much discussion of *problem-* as opposed to *method*-driven research (Shapiro, Smith, Masoud 2004). The former suggests, in a kindred spirit to the discussion of the preceding pages, that scholarly work on politics should begin with a substantive question "thrown up by" the world itself and only then turn to selecting the most appropriate methods through which it might be illuminated (Shapiro 2004).

Criticisms of this view come in four main varieties. The first advances that such an approach would blur the lines between academic political science and the best writing of journalists and historians; that to maintain a clear and coherent role, the primary imperative of the former is to become more rigorously scientific through prioritizing subjects of study that enable methodological innovation. A second charge suggests that having problems determine the selection of approaches will lead to disciplinary chaos admitting of no standards of adjudication or comparison among multiple, competing theories. In a third, which builds on the second, problem-driven approaches do not surmount the messy terrain of interpretation and orienting commitments. After all, how we choose and conceptualize a problem is already fundamentally informed by our existing theoretical and methodological leanings. Finally, scholars historically aiming to try to solve social, political, and economic problems through scholarly endeavors often end up inadvertently serving state and corporate interests, forgetting that they cannot determine or control the implications of or what will be done with their findings (Norton 2004b). These may well be selectively pruned to provide little more than "scientific justification" to already existing partisan positions (Piven 2004).

To the first, the view that more rigorously scientific approaches will offer a distinctively valuable view into political life has not been persuasively demonstrated. Indeed, a *science* that would properly avail itself to all of the complexly multidirectional relations of dependence and coconstitution that define the field of politics would be "science" in such a unique sense that it would unsettle and multiply the term itself, undercutting the eradication of the sloppiness of pluralism that is sought through it. What is more, the changing nature of the generation, availability, and circulation of information has radically altered not only the internal life of the academy and field of journalism, but the relationship between them. Rather than differences in focus and method, what increasingly differentiates the two are temporal demands of publication and those of audience. Indeed, with some of the most pressing transnational questions, whether of the pronounced vulnerability of labor or shifting ways that wars are fought, journalists have often proven better poised to outline what scholars might then be in positions to explore in greater depth.

The second and third objections are perennial ones that only retreat when the contours of intellectual conversation become sufficiently sedimented to occlude them. Ultimately, facing the challenge of adjudication in a relatively anarchic field is precisely what being rooted in a scholarly world is to enable one to do. However, one sees precisely the opposite—in the face of the sheer volume of people and publications, there is less and less willingness to engage in original, if well-reasoned and informed, acts of judgment and instead an intensified deference to what already established principles of evaluation demand. In other words, problem-driven inquiries recenter the anxiety of responsibility that is at the core of all of our endeavors thus by implication reemphasizing the value of scholarship on creolization that illuminates situations of adjudication where standing rules are either not available or no longer applicable.

There is no doubt that it is dangerous if more and more research is commissioned and if intellectual agenda setting is dominated by think tanks. In these cases, the questions that are to be explored are prematurely narrowed to interests driven by priorities and occupations that may well be antiintellectual. What is more, findings generated are only sought or heeded to the extent that they buttress a priori positions that will not be challenged or rearticulated by contradictory outcomes. And there is no doubt that what is done with any fruit of scholarly or creative labor is idiosyncratic, unpredictable, and, in large part, out of the author's hands.

At the same time, it is a mistake to frame all problem-driven work as necessarily answering and serviceable to corporate imperatives. After all, what of the work of Frantz Fanon or W. E. B. Du Bois? The former, as I have argued, stated from the outset that his aim was to explore in order to dismantle multiple forms of alienated human relations produced by projects of negrification. He proceeded seamlessly to draw on works in psychoanalysis and literature and later in political economy and history in a heavily creolized methodology. With Du Bois, his framing of African Americans as a unique social scientific opportunity—to study the emergence of a race born of forced displacement, coerced intermixing, slavery and then emancipation—led not only through his monumental thousand-page, *The Philadelphia Negro*, to the development of the field of urban ethnography (including the generation of previously nonexistent census data) but to a uniquely New World form of sociology. Ironically, his efforts to disclose and illuminate the workings of modern racialization enabled him to produce a creolized study of complex societies that added to classical European concerns of class, secularization, rationalization, and bureaucracy, particularities of the plantation and its complex aftermath. Unlike his contemporaries who tried in making their sociology rigorous to make it un-American, his writings continue to be available in print and read in classrooms (Henry 2009).

Even if driven by problems, scholars will with good reasons adopt distinct approaches to their study. However, if some only reluctantly accept the resulting methodological pluralism as the inability to explore particular themes through randomized field experiments, it can also illuminate the distinctiveness of different approaches through demonstrating the particular kinds of question each might magnify or occlude (Wedeen 2004). Indeed Rudra Sil (2004) suggests that breakthroughs in understanding phenomena in the political world occur when eclectic scholars draw upon discrete insights, practices, and empirics of otherwise separate research communities, indicating new lines of inquiry. This is underscored by Robert Dahl's (2004) estimation of political science as concerned with relations among human beings, groups, contingency, and agency that, as almost infinite, should make it clearly untenable that it emulate a field like physics.

The tendency of once and necessarily creolized and creolizing disciplines like political science to purify themselves through decreolization is most likely a sign of both an effort to hide from demands of complex adjudication and of decay: it is at great political and intellectual expense that ever narrower conversations continue, avoiding these vexing and ultimately indispensable problems of evaluation and judgment.

It is true that creolization is not very popular at the moment, and that the response to crises in sovereignty borne of ever more porous borders of all kinds is to fix those boundaries we seem able to control like fortresses. The difficulty is not only the Machiavellian insight that fortresses easily become petrified prisons, but that in making these the homes from which we think, we retreat from a shared role in forging a shared political world.

Political life, after all, operates precisely within the messy and unpredictable options opened up by symbolic life—by the ability to forge generalities that can be as manipulated and exploited as they can be used to mobilize cross-cutting and unique scopes of identification and obligation. If our studies of this specific domain are to contribute to disclosing its fragile value they too should possess these same irreducibly human qualities.

Notes

INTRODUCTION

1. This is no. 62 from *If not, Winter: Fragments of Sappho*, Carson (2003).
2. This phrase appeared in one of Paula Wilson's (2010) woodblock prints titled "First Story."
3. The project first began as an exploration of the debates surrounding Rousseau's general will that culminated in a discussion of Fanonian reflections concerning violence when I realized that although most scholars of Fanon focus on his other immediate, named influences (Hegel, Marx, and Sartre, in particular), that many of his most central concerns and significant contributions revisited and reworked central dimensions of Rousseau's political writings. I began to wonder why this would be considered an unconventional conclusion and whether the disciplinary norms that pointed in that direction might in fact be obstacles to constructive contemporary thought. This led me in a more systematic way to conclude that what I was doing was an instance of creolization with broader implications.
4. For further discussion of the politics of survival, see V. F. Cordova (2007). She writes, "The value of survival is being able to recognize yourself after you've managed to survive" (45).
5. For discussion of the concept of *decreolization* in the context of linguistics, see Mufwene (1994).
6. Susan Buck-Morss (2000; 2009) has argued that the ease with which scholars have marginalized the study of Haiti in accounts of modern history is also a function of ways of conceiving of political geographies that have less to do with space and time than commitments that require nearing and distancing. She challenges scholars not to naturalize these creative political feats, but instead to make problematizing them the focus of our scholarship.

7. One might consider here the overrepresentation of many North African Muslim practices in the heavily homosocial worlds of Italian organized crime. Insightful commentary on this phenomenon was outlined in Celeste Morello's introductory comments to the screening of *The Godfather II* in the Politics in Film Series at Temple University in April 2006. For her definitive study of Philadelphia's Mafia and La Cosa Nostra, see *Before Bruno*, Books 1 and 2.

8. Similarly, when one reads the disparaging view that Marx and Engels had of utopian and nostalgic brands of French socialism, one rarely thinks of proto-socialist movements to which they refer as centrally involving the theological writings of thirteenth-century nuns, such as the Poor Clares, Catherine of Siena, and Douceline of Digne, lay mystics including Mary of Oignies, Ida of Nivelles, and Margaret Porete, and heretics (Robinson 2001, 50–51).

9. For examples of the former see Tommy Curry (2009) and Paget Henry (2009a). For an example of the latter, see Jane Anna Gordon and Lewis R. Gordon (2009).

10. There is some disagreement over how best to characterize Rousseau's contributions to such debates. More positive views are well represented by John Oyatunde Isola Bewaji (2003) and Bernard Boxill (2005). The former emphasizes Rousseau's unusual willingness to recognize Egyptian civilization as a precursor to that of Greece and Rome, as one of the litany of places that through imperial enrichment developed arts and sciences at the price of their moral ruin. The latter insists that while Caribs and Native North Americans were unquestionably framed by Rousseau as occupying an earlier, less corrupted stage of collective development than European man, he made equally clear that the innate abilities of human beings are the same the world over with the implication that palpable differences were nothing more than the outcomes of contingent historical events. Furthermore, in Rousseau's early accounts, to be more developed was also to have fallen further away from collective virtue. Louis Sala-Molins (2006) is less forgiving: while Rousseau did not actively endorse theories that buttressed the colonial policies of his day, his failure to be one of a small set of critical voices given his tremendous capacity to speak and think against the conforming grain was, in Sala-Molin's view, worthy of condemnation. For a lengthier account of these discussions, see Jane Anna Gordon and Neil Roberts (2009, 6–8).

1. DELEGITIMATING DECADENT INQUIRY

1. This can be found in Rousseau (1992e, 189).

2. Critics of Rousseau will no doubt accord great significance, proof even, to the (devilish) number of years that he lived.

3. For a complete photographic account of the many regions and towns that Rousseau visited, see "Chronologie de Jean-Jacques Rousseau: présentation en

photos de tous les lieux qu'il a habités et visités," by Takuya Kobayashi, www .rousseau-chronologie.com/.

4. See Robert Darnton (1984, 242). According to Darnton, publishers could not print quickly enough to keep up with demand and began to rent copies of the book by the hour and the day. Readers, profoundly moved by the text, wrote to Rousseau in droves, creating, in Darnton's account, the first celebrity author (243–44).

5. Rousseau managed to offend Catholics and Protestants in equal measure by challenging (through the words of the Catholic vicar in *Emile*) the notions of both original sin and divine Revelation. He thought, in addition, that he was defending the ongoing indispensability of religion when he claimed that all faiths could equally lead men and women to virtue. The position was taken as "religious indifferentism" and his books were banned in France and Geneva, condemned from pulpits, and publicly burned. Warrants were made for his arrest. Even when he found sanctuary in Môtiers in Neuchâtel, a canton of the Swiss Confederation and protectorate of the Prussian crown under the protection of Lord Keith, his house was stoned. In response he took refuge in Great Britain through the machinations of David Hume. Rousseau remained barred from reentering France until 1770 though he returned earlier, in 1768, under the pseudonym, Jean-Joseph Renou.

6. For the authoritative critical discussion of the notion of Jean-Jacques Rousseau's "authorship" of the French Revolution, see James Swenson (2000). While Rousseau was initially buried at Ermenonville, he was interred sixteen years after his death and placed, as a national hero, in the Panthéon in Paris. Rousseau's embrace as a celebrated native son in Geneva was longer in coming. In 1834 a statue was erected on the Île Rousseau in Lake Geneva. In 2002, Espace Rousseau, a museum located in his first home, was opened to the public.

7. There are some very important exceptions to this general rule. Strikingly, they are, for the most part, female and, in many instances, also Jewish. Consider, for example, the organizational work of Fanon's daughter, Mireille Fanon-Mendes France and of Sonia Dayan-Herzbrun (both of Eastern European Jewish descent) that culminated in the 2007 UNESCO conference on Frantz Fanon and the subsequent issue of *Tumultes* (Number 31, 2008), edited by Herzbrun-Dayan.

8. Rousseau was unable to learn English while staying in Britain and made few friends during his stay.

9. He was apprenticed as an engraver while still in Geneva and after leaving briefly attended a seminary with the vague idea of becoming a priest.

10. Indeed using Genevan identification as the basis through which to attack powerful nations, he painted it in terms that it could never in fact match. Starobinski writes, "Hence he was doubly a rebel: the myth of Geneva with

which he attacked France became reason for dissatisfaction with Genevan reality. Rousseau's rebellion quickly cut off all retreat, leaving only the inner resources of feeling and language, only literature to fall back on" (1988, 337).

11. Damrosch notes that when Rousseau visited Geneva for the last four months he would spend there, in addition to being entertained by aristocrats (indeed spending too much time with them, in the eyes of some) and enjoying the scenery, he visited his old neighborhood and nurse. The people who crowded around him in the "rue basses" were proud to see "that he was one of them, and even prouder perhaps that despite his long absence and his eloquence, he had kept their accent" (Rousseau 2005, 249).

12. Fanon was born into a petit-bourgeois family that sent him to the most prestigious lycée on the island. There he encountered his mentor Aimé Césaire, for whom he would campaign (for the position of parliamentary delegate from Martinique to the First National Assembly of the Fourth Republic) when returning home after being wounded and receiving the *Croix de Guerre* in World War II.

13. See Alice Cherki's (2006) description of the much-cited interview with Frantz Fanon's brother, Joby. While many Martinicans considered World War II as one for, by, and of Europeans, Fanon insisted, citing the inspiring words of a former lycée professor that "each time that liberty is affected, be we whites, blacks, yellows, or kakos . . . I swear to you today that no matter where it may be, each time that Freedom is threatened, I'll be there." Fanon was, however, soon disappointed. In a letter to his parents dated April 12, 1945, one year after he had left Fort-de-France, he wrote that he was defending an "obsolete ideal" and implored them never to say that he had "died for a good cause." No, he stated, "I was wrong! Nothing can justify my defending the interests of white farmers while he does not care himself" (Djemaï 2001). The phenomenon of liberal idealists radicalized by the double standards with which they were treated as they risked their lives in dangerous military efforts itself deserves a careful study. A recent poignant example from China is Wai-keung Lau's 2010 film, "Legend of the Fist: The Return of Chen Zhen," starring Donnie Yen.

14. He wrote, "The Antilles Negro is more 'civilized' than the African, that is, he is closer to the white man; and this difference prevails not only in back streets and on boulevards but also in public service and the army. . . . Antilleans who have done military service in Senegalese infantry regiments have Europeans (whether from one's own country or France) on one hand and Senegalese on the other. . . . And yet many Antilles Negroes see nothing to upset them in such European identification; on the contrary, they find it altogether normal. That would be all we need, to be taken for niggers! The Europeans despise the Senegalese, and the Antilles Negro rules the black roost as its unchallenged

master." Fanon goes on to describe a story of Gaudaloupans trying to pass as Martinicans only to be quickly found out (*BSWM* 26).

15. In addition to Fanon's published writings, he also wrote three plays and a dissertation while studying in Lyon.

16. Fanon writes, "I wanted to confine myself to the Antilles. But I was compelled to see that the Antillean is first of all a Negro . . . there are Negroes whose nationality is Belgian, French, English; there are also Negro republics. . . . The truth is that the Negro race has been scattered, that it can no longer claim unity. Against all the arguments I have just cited, I come back to one fact: Wherever he goes, the Negro remains a Negro. . . . There is a quest for the Negro, the Negro is in demand . . . he is needed, but only if he is made palatable in a certain way" (*BSWM*, 172–73, 176).

17. The Republic of Geneva was of course sovereign. The language zones in the region antedated the borders of modern nation-states with the implication that the French spoken in Switzerland was not imposed through conquest or expansion. French writers are indeed not read as foreign in Geneva or Lausanne and within both places local writers resent being relegated to the category of the Francophone, as I am doing here, along with peoples to whom French was introduced through colonialism. Still, comments Starobinski, "they are no happier to be simply subsumed in the French phenomenon. . . . They want their right to first-class citizenship recognized while insisting that there is an essential difference between Swiss literature and the literature of this or that region of France" (1988, 334).

18. Sartre writes in *The Words* of his grandfather's aspirations for him: "In most of the lycées, the teachers of German were Alsatians who had chosen France who had been given their posts in reward for their patriotism. Caught between two nations, between two languages, their studies had been somewhat irregular, and there were gaps in their culture. That made them suffer. They also complained that they were left out of things in the academic community because of their colleagues' hostility. I would be their avenger; I would avenge my grandfather. Grandson of an Alsatian, I was at the same time a Frenchman of France. Karl would help me acquire universal knowledge. I would take the royal road: in my person, martyred Alsace would enter the École Normale Supérieure, would pass the teaching examination with flying colors, and would become that prince, a teacher of letters" (1964, 155–56).

19. We could add to the list all of the born Frenchmen and women whose thought was significantly influenced by time spent in or the sustained study of events unfolding in what was then called "French North Africa." Françoise Lionnet and Shu-mei Shih (2011, 12–21) recently argued that almost all of the radical left social thought of the 1960s in France was informed by direct experi-

ences of writers with wars in Algeria. US readers of these French writers have, they suggest, divorced the works from this creolizing context in ways that obscure their actual inspiration. Lionnet and Shih contend that Vietnam exercised a comparable effect on left US political writing of the same period.

20. A similar point might be made about quintessentially US writers, that most were immigrants who in their project of embodying Americanness in fact played a role in inventing it through their compelling articulations.

21. Then a French colony, Martinique has since become an overseas department of France. In the racialized hierarchical schemes that Fanon encountered in North Africa, the most significant dividing line was between Europeans and "natives" (or native Africans), while Antillians, who were called "blacks from the old colonies," were in between (Ehlen 2001, 53–60). Felix Germain (2011) argues that French policies from the mid-nineteenth century onward elevated West Indian subjects over their African counterparts, as the West Indies receded in all but geopolitical and symbolic importance. "Indeed, as the French colonized sub-Saharan Africa," he writes, "they began to use the French West Indies to showcase the success of French colonial policies" (Germain 2011, 102). Many West Indians worked in the French colonial service in Africa, becoming "walking billboard[s] for the empire . . . advertis[ing] that France rewarded its colonial subjects" and that "colonized people appreciated receiving the gift of French civilization" (103). What became known as the *vieilles colonies* included Guadeloupe and Martinique, Saint-Domingue, French Guiana, Louisiana, Île Bourbon (now Réunion) and Isle de France (now Mauritius). These produced sugar, tobacco, coffee, cocoa, cotton, indigo, roucou, cochineal, vanilla, spices, woods, and decorative materials including pearl and tortoise shell (Dobie 2010, 2–3).

22. For a rich discussion of the particularity of eighteenth-century philosophical engagements with newly foreign lands see Frederick Whelan (2009) and Sankar Muthu (2003). The latter writes, "the prevailing attitude toward non-Western countries had not yet hardened into one of imperious (and imperial) contempt, as was to happen in the nineteenth century" (6–7). This account of the very different character of the eighteenth- and nineteenth-century attitudes toward the non-European world is affirmed by Catherine A. Reinhardt (2006).

23. Voltaire observed, "these countries, which one can scarcely perceive on a globe, produce in France an annual circulation of sixty million in merchandise." This passage, from *Essai sur les moeurs*, was, Madeleine Dobie writes (2010), added in the 1770s. This is Dobie's translation.

24. It is no accident that the trope of the state of nature, while developed two centuries earlier, was the centerpiece of early modern European and especially

liberal thought—that outlining the ideal requirements of legitimate governance began with a detour to states of individuals living outside of recognizable political societies. Although all three of its most canonical articulators—Thomas Hobbes, John Locke, and Rousseau—insisted that it was a situation that had never existed in history, all, as readily, in moments of potential argumentative despair, pointed as evidence to the New World. See, for example, chapter 13 of *Leviathan* and chapter 5, "Of Property," in *Second Treatise of Government*; for discussion, see Muthu (2003, 7, 22–23, 200) and Srinivas Aravamudan (2009). Vividly impressing especially political thinkers, images of it still required imaginative interpretation and elaboration. See, for instance, Frederick Whelan's exploration of the impact of encounters with the non-Western world on the thinking of David Hume (2009, chap. 1). Both outside and in, the Americas' distance due to expansionary voyages, suddenly came within Europe's temporal and spatial orbit. Indeed, its peoples were typically framed as having remained in a permanent state of Europe's and, by extension, man's prehistory. However, if for Hobbes and Locke that meant that these were places that signified wild and undomesticated, primitive beginnings or aberrational states of exception against which the order of organized political life was measured, for Rousseau, they inspired *longing*. Indeed the figure of the Carib, who rejected the encroaching allures of French civilization, embodied the naturally free and good origins of all of humankind and the standard through which alternatives to Western European modernity might be thought.

25. In the mid-eighteenth century France was the world's leading producer of sugar; by the 1780s, what is now Haiti produced close to one half of the sugar consumed in Europe and the Americas (Dobie 2010, 3–4). This was because of the greater efficacy of French planters who extracted 25 percent more sugar per acre than their British counterparts in Jamaica.

26. The British and French sugar islands (especially Jamaica and Saint Domingue) of the seventeenth and eighteenth centuries imported a lion's share of African captives into, in Trouillot's words, "what were not simply societies that had slaves [but] *slave societies* . . . The northern equivalent would be for the whole continental United States to look like Alabama at the peak of its cotton career" (1997, 18). US figures do not include the colony.

27. Trouillot (1997) investigates how, given the respective numbers of people involved, the symbolic relevance of slavery to sociohistorical explanations of the subsequent societies is so much more pronounced in the United States than in Brazil or the Caribbean.

28. Interestingly, unlike most of his contemporaries who when speaking of "savages" wrote of the Huron or Iroquois, studiously avoiding the more problematic features of slavery and miscegenation associated with the Caribbean,

Rousseau's references were to individuals from the Caribbean and Spanish Americas.

29. The only published mention of black people on French soil by Rousseau appears in a rather strange anecdote about him retold in Mercier's *Le Tableau de Paris*: "One day, I was accompanying Jean-Jacques Rousseau along the waterfront; he saw a black man who was carrying a sack of coal [on his head]; he began to laugh and said to me, 'That man is well-suited to his place. He will not have to bother to clean the coal from his face; he is in his place. Would that the others were as well-placed as he.' And I saw him laugh again and follow the black coalman with his eyes" (translation mine). I thank Favcal Falaky for making me aware of this passage. Madeleine Dobie (2010), who also emphasizes the absence of mention of Africans transported in real chains (rather than metaphorical ones at the core of classical republican theory) to the Americas, suggests that Rousseau was more interested in the contrast between indigenous and European people. She points to the only mention of colonial slavery in *Julie or the New Heloise* where the protagonist, St. Preux witnesses the crimes committed against his fellow man on the coasts of Africa and Brazil. The character wrote: "I turned aside my eyes in contempt, horror, and pity, at seeing the fourth part of my fellow man turned into beasts for the servitude of others, I bemoaned being a man." Dobie, here in a very similar spirit to Louis Sala-Molins (2006), still thinks that it is surprising given Rousseau's scathing criticisms of most existing forms of political authority, strong anthropological orientation, and familiarity with travel literature, that he did not say more concerning these themes.

30. This discussion draws on Catherine A. Reinhardt (2006). For further detail of this period in French history and the complicity of many Enlightenment writers, see her first chapter, especially pages 27–35.

31. For further discussion of the politics of race and culture in the Ancien Régime, see Peabody (1996).

32. For a discussion of the production of the distance between France and its West Indian colonies, see Veronique Helenon (2011), "'Tis distance lends enchantment to the view'—Distance as a Mode of Domination: Legal Elements of the Slave and Colonial Periods."

33. Dobie (2010) observes that in the 1760s those who did not oppose the practice made the most transparent references to slavery available in French writing. By contrast, more directly critical discussions did not emerge until the 1770s through 1780s and then as part of abolitionist arguments.

34. Consider on this point chapter 9 of Book I of *On the Social Contract* and Rousseau's 1741 tragedy, "The Discovery of the New World." This is reprinted in Rousseau (2004).

35. Rousseau's first publication was not a work in political theory but a song, also published in *Mercure de France* in 1737. For the first treatment devoted solely to the *First Discourse* see Jeff J. S. Black (2009).

36. Rousseau's descriptions of this event can be found in his January 1762 letter to Malsherbes and in Book VIII of his *Confessions*. Many commentators have noted the similarity with Saint Augustine's description of the experiences (beneath a tree with a Bible) that culminated in his soul-searching autobiographical writings.

37. Subsequent historical research has shown, on the basis of the publication of the announcement of the essay contest and the dates of Denis Diderot's imprisonment, that Rousseau must have encountered the announcement while visiting Diderot on a day in October that was not particularly warm.

38. This was, in large part, due to fortunate and contingent circumstances: the Dijon committee had connections at the *Mercure de France*, and its newly appointed editor, the former Jesuit priest, Guillaume Raynal, was a friend of Rousseau's. He published an elogium and extracts of the *First Discourse*, along with a series of criticisms and Rousseau's replies. Diderot also helped to secure the publication of the work as a pamphlet by a Paris bookseller, Noël-Jacques Pissot.

39. Some anti-Rousseauian contemporaries of both men later suggested that Diderot had implied in conversation that it was he who had initially suggested that Rousseau answer the Academy's question in the negative rather than taking the affirmative position that Rousseau had been considering when first arriving at Vincennes. This seems highly unlikely. As Damrosch (2005, 214) has suggested, Rousseau's position translated a lifetime of disappointment and alienation into one that framed marginality as uniquely providing access to truths unavailable to the well-adjusted. Additionally, the contrary position, if advanced as anything but ironic, collided with all that the *Encyclopédie* represented. Starobinski (1988, 6), a highly creative and sympathetic reader of Rousseau, argues that we witness in Rousseau the proceeding from particular observations inductively toward establishing reasons that in a tone of abstract learning conceal personal disappointments and failures. He is able to give his own nostalgia, for the period in his childhood prior to his first experience of being wrongly accused, an objective history the certitude of which is fortified by his feeling of remembering.

40. Rousseau's assessments of his own work could be scathing. When approached about the possibility of publishing an essay that he had begun and abandoned writing (in response to the Academy of Corsica's 1751 essay contest considering the virtues of a hero) he is said to have replied: "A *torche-cul* [asswipe] like that is not worth the trouble" (quoted in Damrosch 2005, 235).

41. This phrase comes from the "Preface to a Second Letter to Bordes," a response to Charles Bordes's August 1753 "Second Discourse on the Benefits of the Sciences and Arts." Rousseau neither finished the letter nor published it. In the same draft, Rousseau concluded that the question of the *First Discourse* was only a corollary of this larger System (*CW* 2:184).

42. He wrote in the closing paragraph of his Letter to Raynal, "I know in advance the great words that will be used to attack me: enlightenment, knowledge, laws, morality, reason, propriety, consideration, gentleness, amenity, politeness, education, etc. To all that I will reply only with two other words, which ring even more loudly in my ear. Virtue, truth, I will write for myself constantly; Truth, virtue! If anyone perceived only words in this, I have nothing more to say to him" (*CW* 2:27).

43. This observation is not unlike one made by Hannah Arendt (2005) about those who are law-abiding for the sake of being law-abiding rather than in pursuit of the values that law tries to secure. She suggested that such people could as easily be made to follow officially sanctioned rules for robbery and murder as those that aimed to secure civil liberties.

44. Rousseau later described it as a "dangerous frankness" rooted in a courage "caused by his independence" (*CW* 2:182).

45. The citations to the *First Discourse* here refer to Gay (1987) (and to Donald A. Cress's translation). Damrosch cites Trousson's observation, "It would take a book to list the books read by this man [Rousseau] who despised books" (2005, 242).

46. Although a staunch egalitarian in his aspirations and designs for political, social, and economic life, Rousseau thought people were radically unequal when it came to questions of talents and natural abilities. On a separate note, being without formal education and living largely unrewarded were both indexes that Rousseau, at this point in his life, shared with these men he singled out. Although he famously recounted his early sentimental education on the workbench alongside his dad, and briefly with a formal tutor, most of his education was self-education, but for brief spells of intense mentorship and intellectual exchange with highly educated men and women. For an account of this, see Cranston (1982).

47. In his Letter to D'Alembert he wrote, "This is an error which could easily be corrected if it were remembered that most of the literary men who shine in Paris and most of the useful discoveries and new inventions come from these despised provinces. Stay some time in a little town where you had at first believed you would find only automatons; not only will you soon see there men a great deal more sensible than your big-city monkeys, but you will rarely fail to discover in obscurity there some ingenious man who will surprise you by his talents and his works, who you will surprise even more in admiring them, and

who, in showing you prodigies of work, patience, and industry, will think he is showing you only what is ordinary at Paris. Such is the simplicity of true genius. It is neither scheming nor busybodyish; it knows not the path of honors and fortune nor dreams of seeking it; it compares itself to no one . . . indifferent to insult and hardly conscious of praise" (Rousseau 1960, 60). He goes on to say that one finds more original spirits in little towns than in capital cities because people are less imitative; with fewer models, they draw more from themselves, undeterred by the weight of the opinions of others.

48. For further discussion of this point, see Kenneth Knies (2006).

49. If Friedrich Nietzsche had had access to complete editions of Rousseau's writings rather than summaries of them in encyclopedias, phrases like these might have counteracted the disdain he otherwise felt for his predecessor's romantic sentimentalism. Rousseau's depiction of decadent societies as those in which men skillfully slander rather than brusquely confronting their adversaries, his central use of pre-Christian examples of political life, and his description of how language and music decay might also have been seen to invite and foreshadow Nietzsche's own genealogy, distinction between aristocratic and slave moralities, and *Birth of Tragedy*.

50. In his "Final Reply" Rousseau acknowledged a succinct formulation offered by one of his critics as an accurate characterization of his position: "The progress of letters is always proportional to the greatness of Empires" (*CW* 2:116), however, he distinguished "morals and virtues" from "success and greatness."

51. These less hubristic nations had their counterparts in unique individuals living within more corrupt places, among them Socrates and Cato the Elder, who resisted the vicious allures of their contemporaries. Socrates, unlike the many artists of his day who mistook a particular specialized knowledge for wisdom, knew the limits of his own understanding. Rousseau suggests that if reborn in eighteenth-century France, Socrates would hold most men of arts and sciences in contempt and would not "aid in the enlargement of the mass of books that inundates us from every quarter. Instead he would leave only the example and memory of his virtue" (1987, 10). (Rousseau suggests that Socrates speaks in praise of ignorance. It would be more accurate to say that he treats being aware of the limits of what one knows as a necessary starting point for learning, understanding, or truthful rediscovery. One might also add that it is a real question whether we would have "memories" of Socrates's noble actions if his student and disciple, Plato, had not so skillfully committed them to writing. Damrosch notes that both Rousseau and Diderot envisaged themselves in the role of a Socrates, as martyrs for the cause of truth.) If spared the hemlock, he would have been given a cup far more bitter: one of ridicule and scorn "a hundred times worse than death" (ibid.).

52. Cranston (1982) suggests that Diderot and D'Alembert were able to overlook the anti-Enlightenment position of the *First Discourse* because of its other dimensions, in particular its paganism and silence on questions of Christianity. This quotation is the primary example of the former.

53. Rousseau frequently used the metaphor of the veil which was also a central trope in the writing of W. E. B. Du Bois, who associated veiled life with the consciousness of black people in an antiblack society, and was a more literal concern of Fanon in his writings on the hostile interactions between colonial officers and veiled Algerian women. John Rawls also chose the veil as the centerpiece of his twentieth century updating of the social contract device.

54. Rousseau emphasizes: "I am very far from thinking that this ascendancy of women is itself an evil. It is a gift bestowed on them by nature for the happiness of mankind. Better directed, it could produce as much good as it today does harm. We are not sufficiently aware of the advantages that would come to pass in society if a better education were given to that half of mankind which governs the other. Men will always be what is pleasing to women. Thus if you want men to become great and virtuous, teach women what greatness of soul and virtue are" (1987, 13n28). This passage is remarkably similar to several in Mary Wollstonecraft's *A Vindication of the Rights of Women*, especially the conclusion of "On National Education."

55. Polish King Stanislaus asked whether Rousseau was not praising as valor and courage what was in fact ferocity and cruelty, audacious men with violent passions followed by troops of slaves who left only ruin in their wake? Rousseau did later withdraw his praise of military qualities, stating that he only admired battles undertaken in defense of liberty not those of conquest and conceded that soldiers were less praiseworthy than hunters, shepherds, and laborers, even if he did still admire the citizen-soldiers in the writing of Machiavelli. While being a soldier should not be made into a profession, he suggested, "to die in the service of one's fatherland is too noble a task to be confined to mercenaries" (*CW* 2:118).

56. In such times, it is preferred that one distinguishes oneself through "babble" than by knowing how to act or think (*CW* 2:192). Rousseau suggests that far better is to resemble a sheep than a fallen angel (*CW* 2:115).

57. The kernel of this thesis, developed in the *Second Discourse*, can be found in Rousseau's "Final Reply" where he wrote: "Before those dreadful words *thine* and *mine* were invented, before there were any of that cruel and brutal species of man called masters and of that other species of roguish and lying men called slaves; before there were men abominable enough to dare have superfluities while other men die of hunger; before mutual dependence forced them all to become imposters, jealous, and traitors; I very much wish someone would ex-

plain to me what those vices, those crimes could have been with which they are reproached so emphatically" (*CW* 2:117; italics in the original).

58. Simply because of their scale, empires do tend to standardize education systems and intellectual rewards—the primary example Rousseau offers is of the China of his day—with the consequence that the vast majority of students seek not only to be successful, but also able to describe themselves as brilliant or clever.

59. He too, in the tradition of the reluctant prophet who speaks with illuminating honesty precisely because an exile, told of a danger in the hope of forestalling its most disastrous consequences but also suggested that perhaps the damage was in fact already done.

60. Much like Hobbes, Rousseau says that to study men, he closed his books, listened to what they said and then watched how they acted. Rousseau suggested that his critics came to very different conclusions because they had remained in their studies, between book covers.

61. The epigraph comes from Ovid's *Tristia*, Book V, x. 37.

62. After Rousseau's *Emile* and *Social Contract* were condemned in Geneva, he deleted "citizen of Geneva" from new works and new editions of older writings. Before that, however, he had been reinstated in the religion of his fathers and regained his legal status when traveling back to Geneva with his friend Gauffecourt. At that time, he was spared the more public, humiliating, and punitive dimensions of the process of reconversion, having only to be interrogated by a council delighted to have won such a celebrated figure for the Reformation.

63. This is a repeated theme in Rousseau's work, much like the passage in the *Emile* when a rich man replies to the question of where he lives, "I am one of the rich." The implication is that his home is anywhere his money will carry him, his country any with room for his strong box.

64. One might consider C. L. R. James' (1989) depiction of Jean-Jacques Dessalines versus Toussaint L'Ouverture on this point. He suggested that the former had little to lose and was generally less friendly to white people while the latter saw a bit less precisely because he was more "enlightened."

65. This is from Rousseau's "Final Reply," which was published in *Mercure* in April 1752. It did not prove to be his final word in the debate over his *First Discourse*.

66. In response to Gautier's claim that Rousseau's arguments lacked historical evidence—that it was not true that more primitive men had been more virtuous or that there had been a golden age in historical time—Rousseau suggested he had been misunderstood. He was, in fact, offering "a genealogy," a philosophical and speculative anthropology or philosophy of history (*CW*

2:190). This was a theoretical rather than practical exploration, a general thesis rather than a tracing of a particular set of events (*OC* 3:31–32). It was one in which the golden age functioned as a philosophical abstraction, indispensable to clarifying the meaning of human well-being. In his "Final Reply" he stated: "I am assured that people have long since been disabused of the chimera of the Golden Age. Why not add that people have long since been disabused of the chimera of virtue?" (*CW* 2:117).

67. In an earlier exchange, Rousseau had challenged the assumption of his critics that the mere fact of Europeans being unable to "penetrate" Africa and thereby know what happened there was proof that it was full of vice. He suggested that vices would have been there precisely if Europeans had found a way to enter, that they would have introduced them along with themselves (*CW* 2:124–25). He writes, "If I were the leader of one of the peoples of Niger, I declare that I would hang without pardon the first European who would dare enter it, and the first Citizen who would try to leave" (*CW* 2:125).

68. Later in a note in his "Preface to Narcissus," he wrote, "When I said that our morals were corrupted, by that I did not claim to say that those of our ancestors were good, but only that ours were even worse" (*CW* 2:190n).

69. Rousseau here says about arts and sciences what sounds much like what his critics had said about the role and function of politeness in complex societies.

70. When asked why he would rail against the value of arts and sciences, of eloquence, rhetoric, and the written word while so clearly engaged with them (in both the *Discourse* and previous musical and theatrical works), he offered three replies: First, he too had once been taken in by the allure of the prejudices of the century (*CW* 2:188). Admiring such endeavors, he sought to see what he too might achieve, having no idea of their dangers. Once having grasped their vacuity, however, he looked at his own prior works as the "amusements of [his] youth . . . [as] illegitimate children whom one still caresses with pleasure while blushing to be their father" (*CW* 2:189). At this point, his weakness was of another kind, one characteristic of so many other men: of being led astray by passions from one's principles. But finally, even then, in an already fallen world, one could do creative work if one maintained the proper attitude toward it. Rousseau suggested: "Thus I advise those who are so eager to seek reproaches to make to me, to study my principles better and to observe my conduct better before they accuse me of inconsistency in them. If they ever perceive that I am beginning to court the favor of the public, or that I become vain from having written pretty songs, or that I blush at having written bad Plays, or that I seek to damage the glory of my rivals, or that I pretend to speak ill of the great men of my century in order to try to raise myself to their level by lowering them to

mine, or that I aspire to a position in an Academy, or that I go to pay court to the women who set the tone, or that I flatter the stupidity of the Great, or that ceasing to wish to live from the labor of my hands, I hold in ignominy the trade that I have chosen and take steps toward wealth, in a word if they notice that the love of reputation makes me forget that of virtue, I beg them to warn me about it, and even publicly, and I promise them instantly to throw my Writings and my Nooks into the fire, and to concede all the errors with which they will be pleased to reproach me" (*CW* 2:197).

71. This is from Book VIII of *The Confessions*. The passage can be found in the 1959 *Oeuvres complètes* on page 388.

72. Rousseau compared domesticated men and animals, pointing both to the relative health of "savages" versus "modern men" documented by travelers and suggesting that "nature" closely resembled the treatment in Sparta of the children of citizens—it strengthened the already robust, he claimed, and left others to perish.

73. This argument again foreshadows Nietzsche.

74. Rousseau here anticipated Sigmund Freud's observation: "The liberty of the individual is no gift of civilization. It was greatest before there was any civilization."

75. Rousseau observed that in situations in which the aim is to get ahead at all costs and where doing so is zero-sum, there "is perhaps no rich man whose death is not secretly desired by his greedy heirs, often indeed by his own children; there is no shop at sea of which the sinking would not be good news for some merchant; not a business house that a dishonorable debtor would not happily see burned down with all the papers in it; no community that does not relish the disasters of its neighbors" (*OC* 3:202).

76. Rousseau comments later in the text, "Since the poor had nothing to lose but their liberty, it would have been utter folly for them to have voluntarily surrendered the only good remaining to them, gaining nothing in return. On the contrary, since the rich men were, so to speak, sensitive in all parts of their goods, it was much easier to do them harm, and consequently they had to take greater precautions to protect themselves" (1987, 71).

77. Wokler (2001) writes that Friedrich Engels described Rousseau's *Second Discourse* as a dialectical interpretation of history that foreshadowed that of Marx. Marx, who read Rousseau through Hegel, instead saw him as a theorist of abstract natural rights realized in the triumph of the bourgeoisie in the French Revolution. Wokler thinks he would have had to conclude otherwise if he had read the second part of the *Second Discourse* more closely, "Never again," comments Wokler, "was Rousseau so Marxist in his interpretation of society" (2001, 68).

78. For a more elaborated discussion of theorizing culture and the impact of doing so on understanding the concept of the human being, see Clifford Geertz (1973), Parts I and II. Geertz does not engage Rousseau explicitly there, though he does in "The Cerebral Savage: On the Work of Claude Lévi-Strauss" in the same volume. For a discussion of the limitations of the ways in which political scientists have used the work of Geertz, see Lisa Wedeen (2002).

79. Or as Anne Norton puts it, "Is nothing outside culture? The answer . . . is: no, there is nothing outside of culture for us. Nothing we study is outside culture. The enterprise of studying it would bring it within culture, if it were not already there" (2004a, 5).

80. This was another instance in which Voltaire and Rousseau took rather different stances: In Voltaire's *The Ingenu* (1767), the prized insights of the Native American character are ultimately traceable back to European influence. Dobie comments, "By domesticating his savage protagonist, by depicting him as more Frenchman than Huron, Voltaire implies that the encounter with cultural alterity was not a necessary preliminary to the formulation of cultural critique. This move makes it possible to view the critique of laws and conventions from the standpoint of nature as a homegrown, European tradition rather than as a phenomenon born of the encounter between peoples" (2010, 182).

81. No other work was more cited in the *Second Discourse* than Buffon's. Wokler (2001, 58) explains that Rousseau's text was conceived as a set of conjectures in terms of human and civil history similar to those Buffon offered for the origins of the earth and the birth, growth, and decay of animals.

82. Euben emphasizes that the circulation of big ideas of extraordinary thinkers "rarely brings alive . . . those theoretical moments that erupt erratically in ordinary lives, those less than grand encounters with what is strange and estranging . . . in which quite ordinary people willingly and unwillingly run up against the disorienting friction between what they think they know and what they do not yet know, and the openings and closures this sometimes explosive tension produces" (2008, 12). She emphasizes that such journeys—which could involve crossing the street or an actual encounter with the past—do not formulaically produce enlightenment. Whether or not they do is an unpredictable consequence of a set of personal, historical, political, and institutional factors that together shape an attitude or disposition.

83. Against Aristotle, Rousseau asserted that if there are slaves by nature it is "because there have been slaves contrary to nature" (1994, 133). In other words, although Rousseau acknowledged that many people's ability to resist was compromised by their experiences of enslavement, he insisted with what Frederick Douglass later explored more fully, that to make human beings slaves requires ongoing, brutal reinforcement, precisely because such relations are not a reflection of the unequal natures of masters or their slaves.

84. Sankar Muthu (2003) and Madeleine Dobie (2010, 170) have also made this point.

85. Unlike public festivals, in which members of a community could equitably gather as both active participants and spectators, the theater was a sequestered space that made corruption interesting and goodness banal. Here Rousseau considered a concern that Simone Weil explored two centuries later (in "Morality and Literature" published in the 1985 reader with her name): the achievement of goodness does not make for the interesting storytelling that wickedness does. Additionally of concern to Rousseau, theaters were costly to build and maintain and required that one retain a class of actors who, as Socrates had feared, spent their lives simulating the characters of anyone or anything that was necessary. In so doing, they familiarized themselves with the internal lives that made antipolitical and anticivic behavior thinkable. But perhaps most significantly again, actors would form their own discrete class and class interests, sustained by the profits of idle and divisive luxury.

86. Rousseau wrote, "The taste for philosophy loosens in us all the bonds of esteem and benevolence that attach men to society, and this is perhaps the most dangerous of ills engendered by it. The charm of study soon renders any other attachment insipid. Further, by dint of reflecting on humanity, by dint of observing men, the Philosopher learns to appreciate them according to their worth, and it is difficult to have very much affection for what one holds in contempt. Soon he concentrates into his person all the interest that virtuous men share with their fellows: his contempt for others turns to the profit of his pride: his *amour-propre* increases in the same proportion as his indifference to the rest of the universe. For him, family, fatherland, become words void of meaning; he is neither parent, nor citizen, nor man; he is philosopher" (*CW* 2:192).

87. Rousseau yearns for simpler times when it was the beauty of the natural world that was arresting and we lived before it and its gods in humble, largely undifferentiated equality. We move from this to wishing not to be observed and answerable to forces greater than ourselves and in acts of self-deification, we nurture differences that emphasize not what will sustain a healthy community, but that which makes us individually distinct in ways that are necessarily zero-sum.

88. For further exploration of how groups were made into anthropology's objects through temporal displacement or through constructing them as remaining in and occupying a time different from the contemporary one of their observers, see Johannes Fabian (1983).

89. This was an answer to another of the Academy of Dijon's essay contest questions, in this case, one announced in the autumn of 1753. It might be said that losing was largely Rousseau's own fault: in submitting a hundred-page-long

text, he completely ignored the length limit for submissions to the Academy of Dijon. At the same time, the content of the winning essay, one that argued that original sin was the cause of inequalities among men, suggests a mood among judges that was unlikely to be amenable to Rousseau's arguments. In truth, already famous and infamous, Rousseau did not need the Academy's imprimatur this time round. He received permission to publish the work in France by its censors and it was prepared by a lead publisher of French books in Europe, a fellow Genevan, named Marc-Michel Rey. Trained in Lausanne and then settling in Amsterdam, Rey had a network through whom to smuggle books that French authorities did not like. He became a close and tolerant friend of Rousseau's, putting up with his meticulous fussing over every stage of the publication process and eventually making Rousseau his child's godfather. For further discussion, see Damrosch (2005, 250–51).

90. As Cranston has noted, this was not a discourse that could appeal to conservatives since it was "as merciless to tradition as to modern culture" (1991, 306). Several critics charged Rousseau as writing primarily with envy and resentment, with Voltaire famously sending Rousseau a sarcastic note of thanks "for his new book against the human race" (*CW* 3:102). In a pamphlet Voltaire ridiculed Rousseau more extensively, putting the following words in his imagined mouth: "It is dreadful to live in cities where one can carry a golden means of measuring time in one's pocket, where silkworms are brought from China to cover one with their own down, and where one can hear a hundred instruments in harmony that enchant ears and soothe the soul in sweet repose. All of this is horrible, and it is clear that the Iroquois are the only good people; but they had better stay far away from Quebec, where I suspect the damnable sciences of Europe have been introduced" (Damrosch 2005, 241). Dobie observes that Voltaire wrongly assumed that Rousseau, when speaking of "savages" spoke of the Huron and Iroqouis, who were the focus of most of his French contemporaries. Focusing on New France, she argues, made it easier to avoid problematic features of slavery and miscegenation that emerged in the Caribbean after about the 1720s. Instead, Rousseau focused exactly here, on the Caribbean and Spanish Americas (Dobie 2010, 171). Voltaire was one of the few writers living in Paris who had managed to amass great wealth and he did not much like Rousseau's depiction of the rich as having an unquenchable taste for dominating others (Damrosch 2005, 241) Voltaire wrote in the margins of his copy of Rousseau's *Second Discourse*, "Voila the philosophy of a beggar who would like to see the rich robbed by the poor." This was a radical overstatement. While it was true that Rousseau had been an apprentice and a lackey and had seen his father exiled from Geneva through quarreling with a patrician, and that he often spoke and wrote in highly critical terms

about the character of people who could deliberately acquire wealth and of the hidden injustices of those of rank and power, he did not advocate forcibly redistributing wealth in pursuit of absolute economic equality. What is more, he was quite at home with the old nobility of Paris who despised the alliance of riches and royal absolutism that dominated the kingdom. In fact the titles of this aristocracy were empty privileges without power; they were superior in social rank while inferior in political importance, dreaming of a dead France of chivalry and noble feudal lords protecting their people. For further discussion, see Cranston (1991, 308–9).

91. In addition, in late colonial Saint Domingue where opera was very popular, performances of Rousseau's "Le Devin du village" were advertised thirteen times between 1764 and 1790. This continued into independence with the music for Emperor Dessalines's coronation being drawn from the opera. An annotated and illustrated edition of the eighteenth-century Creole version of the opera, *Jeannot et Thérèse*, is currently being prepared by Laurent Dubois, Deborah Jenson, musicologist Bernard Camier, and artist Edouard Duval-Carrié. See Sasha Frere-Jones (2009) and Laurent Du Bois and Bernard Camier (2007).

92. For Rousseau scholars, the parallels between his relationship to his children and to the social scientific areas (and Revolution) to which he is ascribed the role of progenitor are no doubt striking: Much has been made of the supposed hypocrisy of the man who wrote in such sentimental terms about ideal practices of child-raising taking his own five offspring to the foundling home. At the same time, as Wokler has emphasized, even then his advocacy of the practice of prolonged breast-feeding is thought to have saved the lives of a considerable number of children.

2. DECOLONIZING DISCIPLINARY METHODS

1. Fanon (1967b, 137).

2. Fanon does not cite Rousseau here or elsewhere. My argument is not that Fanon made a deliberate project of taking up and reworking the insights of Rousseau. Instead, the claim is that the problems of interest to both thinkers necessitated engaging a particular range of themes and questions and that it is fruitful to see how Fanon's formulations expand Rousseau's earlier related endeavors.

3. Patrick Ehlen notes that Fanon in general did not have an easy time feeling welcome, especially since even when people acted solicitously toward him, it tended to be for the wrong reasons. "In every encounter," Ehlen writes, "he found himself 'tucked away' by others, reduced to some pocketable description" (2001, 88) which Fanon experienced as an amputation, excision, or hemorrhage (*BSWM*, 112–13).

4. He writes, "If there can be no discussion on a philosophical level . . . I am willing to work on the psychoanalytical level—in other words, the level of the 'failures,' in the sense in which one speaks of engine failures" (*BSWM*, 23).

5. Even then, as Lewis Gordon has explored in chapter 2 in *Existentia Africana*, there is much greater willingness to see black writers and speakers as sources of experience than of ideas or thought.

6. Fanon might have been more easily located had he allied with the "culturalists," including the Négritude writers linked to *Présence Africaine*, however, unlike them he saw cultures as points of reference and conduits that could radically alter one another rather than as distinct cultural spirits or mentalities.

7. In so doing, Rousseau muddied his own claims to hypothetical and explanatory rather than historical reasoning, to the state of nature as a regulative ideal that may never have been and was certainly gone.

8. Ehlen wrote of Fanon's decision to leave Paris for Lyon, that he might have made an easier choice, that he could have moved easily into an existing category, however distorted, "in exchange for a false air of belonging. But perhaps, for Fanon, it was exactly this false acceptance that would be the most unbearable" (2001, 87).

9. Those who speak pidgin to a man of color see nothing wrong in what they do because, Fanon writes, they have never been made to stop and think. If, however, a man were to respond, "I am in no sense your boy . . . it is something new under the sun" (*BSWM*, 33–34).

10. Fanon quotes from George Mounin who said of himself that "he gained the possibility of always being natural with a Negro—and [of] never, in his presence, [falling] stupidly and imperceptibly into that attitude of the ethnographic investigator that is still too often our unbearable manner *of putting them in their place*" (*BSWM*, 199).

11. An example to which Fanon frequently returned was the grinning black man, "showing all his teeth in a smile made for us always means a gift, service with a smile, every time" (*BSWM*, 49n7).

12. In popular depictions of black people, it is always "yassuh-boss" and physical displays that are "all *nigger*, walking backwards [and] shaking at the slightest sign of irritation on the part of a petty officer" and ultimately being killed (*BSWM*, 34). Fanon asks why in a democratic France with sixty million citizens of color and with the need to dub US films, these North American stupidities are replicated without alteration. The response he says, "It is because the Negro has to be shown in a certain way" (ibid.).

13. This erasure of the colonized person as an independent, human point of view is captured in the Creole saying, "*Zié békés brilé zié nèg*" ("the eyes of the beke burned the eyes of the negro").

14. Fanon remarked that in the colonial context, while the slave sought to be like the master, the master did not seek recognition but work from the slave.

Edward Said writes, "Despite its bitterness and violence, the whole point of Fanon's work is to force the European metropole to think its history together with the history of the colonies awakening from the cruel stupor and abased immobility of imperial domination" (1989, 223–25).

15. Fanon cites G. Legman who wrote that, with rare exceptions, every American child who was six years old in 1938 had seen at the very least eighteen thousand scenes of ferocious violence. He commented, "Except the Boers, the Americans are the only modern nation that within living memory has completely driven the autochthonous population off the soil that it occupied." Fanon adds that the Caribs (to whom Rousseau referred) experienced the same fate at the hands of French and Spanish explorers (*BSWM*, 146–47).

16. Fanon adds that he would like nothing more than the creation of children's magazines, songs, and history texts written especially for black children.

17. Fanon describes Senegalese who learn Creole in the hope of passing for an Antillean. His assessment? "I call this alienation" (*BSWM*, 38), a larger phenomenon magnified through the study of language.

18. Fanon emphasizes that a similar phenomenon goes on in the internal periphery of France, that those from Lyons first visiting Paris boast constantly of their home and of "all that fascinates people who have nothing to do." When returning home, however, the same people cannot stop talking about Paris. It is to "know Paris and die" (*BSWM*, 19). Within Martinique, the same is true of smaller places in relationship to Fort-de-France and then of Martinique and the world beyond. Imprisoned on the island without outlets, stranded, Europe is "breathed in like pure air" (*BSWM*, 21–22).

19. In Antilles, as Fanon emphasizes in Brittany (*BSWM*, 28), there is a dialect and then there is the French language. The difference, Fanon emphasizes, is that Bretons do not see themselves as inferior to or as having been civilized by the white man.

20. Fanon describes such women as describing it as *illogical* for a mulatto woman to accept a Negro husband since "it is a question of saving the race" (*BSWM*, 54–55; a remarkably illogical statement since "saving the race" means trying to dilute it to the point of its no longer being visibly distinct or recognizable as such) and expecting apologies from (and in some instances making formal charges against) black men who dared to offer their love to a whiter soul. Sadly, all of the efforts of such women are directed at what they will never attain: to be the bride of a white man from Europe. Fanon recounts the similar desire of Jean Veneuse, the black abandonment neurotic, to be acknowledged and loved as a white man through the love of a white woman. The framing of the road to total realization as one of "marrying white culture, beauty, white whiteness" (63), was observed by Louis-T. Achille who, in a report to the Interracial Conference of 1949, stated that people marry in another race what would

be beneath them within their own because these other considerations are overridden by access to that illustrious race and its wiping out in himself in his own mind of the color prejudice from which he has suffered for so long (71–72).

21. Fanon wrote, "The patriarchal European family with its flaws, failures, and vices is closely linked to a society we know and produces about 30% neurotics—the problem is to create with the help of psychoanalytical, sociological, political lessons, a new family environment capable of reducing, if not eliminating, the proportion of waste, in the asocial sense of the word" (*BSWM*, 48–49).

22. On this point, consider Lewis R. Gordon's (2008c) *An Introduction to Africana Philosophy*, which considers questions of philosophical anthropology ("in reality, who [and what] am I?") as one of three defining tropes of this tradition of thought.

23. The ongoing expectation is that while the Negro is savage, the student is civilized. While there may be others within the university who do not think in such ways, "beyond its walls," writes Fanon, "is an army of fools," who are "the product of a psychological-economic system" (*BSWM*, 35).

24. Simone de Beauvoir describes a remarkably similar phenomenon in *The Second Sex*'s discussion of professional women. See chapter 25, especially page 701.

25. Like Rousseau, Fanon, when returning home, would not stay long or ultimately return. He found it more difficult to relate to local people's concerns and his own manner was less like the island's bourgeoisie than that of the French intellectuals of his day (Ehlen 2001).

26. This is to be, as Lewis Gordon has described it, an experience without experience or a human being supposedly without inner life (2000, chap. 2).

27. Given the constant suggestions that the Negro has no culture or civilization or long historical past, it makes sense that many Negroes seek "to prove the existence of a black civilization to the white world at all costs" (*BSWM*, 34). Still, the view of any essential monopoly on particular forms of culture was highly mistaken. Fanon wrote, "To ask a Negro of the Upper Niger to wear shoes, to say of him that he will never be a Schubert, is no less ridiculous than to be surprised that a worker in the Berliet truck factory does not spend his evenings studying lyricism in Hindu literature or to say that he will never be an Einstein. Actually, in an absolute sense, nothing stands in the way of such things. Nothing—except that the people in question lack the opportunities" (95–96).

28. It is worth emphasizing that Fanon's *A Dying Colonialism* (originally *Year Five of the Algerian Revolution*) explicitly explored the relationship of cultural change to revolutionary action and was banned in France six months after its publication. By contrast, none of the work of the Négritude movement met with such a fate (Macey 2002, 180). Fanon stated in *BSWM*, "In no way must I

derive my original vocation from the past of peoples of color. In no way must I devote myself to resurrecting a negro civilization that has been unfairly misrecognized . . . I do not want to sing the past at the expense of my present and my future. My black skin is not the repository of specific values" (184). This is not, however, to suggest that he did not recognize the need, however ultimately insufficient, of Négritude in struggles toward black subjective emancipation.

29. Fanon (*BSWM*, 172–73) wrote, "Analysis of the real is always difficult. An investigator can choose between two attitudes toward his subject. First, he can be satisfied only to describe, in the manner of those anatomists who are all surprised when, in the midst of a description of the tibia, they are asked how many fibular depressions they have. That is because in their research there is never a question of themselves but of others. In the beginning of my medical studies, after several nauseating sessions in the dissecting room, I asked an older hand how I could prevent such reactions. 'My friend, pretend you're dissecting a cat, and everything will be alright.' . . . Second, once he has described reality, the investigator can make up his mind to change it. In principle, however, the decision to describe seems naturally to imply a critical approach and therefore a need to go farther toward some solution. Both authoritative and anecdotal literature have created too many stories about Negroes to be suppressed. But putting them all together does not help us in our real task, which is to disclose their mechanics. What matters for us is not to collect facts and behavior, but to find their meaning. . . . The question that arises is this: Can the white man behave healthily toward the black man and can the black man behave healthily toward the white man?"

30. This approach was as evident within Europe as in its periphery: varicose veins evident on legs that stood too long were not blamed on their working conditions but on a prior, if latent, genetic weaknesses.

31. The structure of this argument parallels that of another: "One cannot be in favor of the maintenance of French domination in Algeria and opposed to the means that this requires. Torture in Algeria is not an accident, or an error, or a fault. Colonialism cannot be understood without the possibility of torturing, of violating, or of massacring. Torture is an expression and a means of the occupant-occupied relationship" (1967c, 66). In other words, the police agent who tortures does not break the law, he acts within the framework of colonial institutions, indeed manifesting "an exemplary loyalty to the system" (71).

32. It is in contrast that Fanon describes what he has tried to do: "In this work I have made it a point to convey the misery of the black man. Physically and affectively. I have not wished to be objective. Besides, that would be dishonest. It is not possible for me to be objective" (*BSWM*, 86).

33. Fanon continues, "When a bachelor in philosophy from the Antilles refuses to apply for certification as a teacher on the ground of his color, I say that

philosophy has never saved anyone; when someone tries to prove that black men are as intelligent as white men, intelligence has never saved anyone. . . . If philosophy and intelligence are invoked to proclaim the equality of men, they have also been employed to justify the extermination of men" (*BSWM*, 28–29). There is nothing intrinsic to their valence or direction, they are not above the political fray, even when used in the most well intentioned of ways.

34. Fanon's brother, Joby, suggested that this was too modest a title.

35. Macey (2002, 155) comments that the book's psychiatric and psychoanalytic content made it unacceptable to more literary publishers like Gallimard while its politics would have made it anathema to any house close to the Parti Communiste Français. Academic medical publishers would have objected to the juxtaposition of clinical data, literary allusions, and personal reflections. It is most likely, Macey suggests, that he did not approach *Présence Africaine* because he did not share the culturalist approach of many of the works it oversaw and he did not want to be pigeonholed as a black writer.

36. The thesis that Fanon ultimately wrote also advanced an individualized, cultural approach to psychotherapy that emphasized the importance of a patient's worldview above any isolated mental process (Cherki 2006, 99). "The task of the psychiatrist, then, becomes not simply to interview the patient and then thumb through a book to uncover the diagnosis and solution, but to make an effort to 'reach' the patient through the patient's own symbols and belief systems. Rather than focusing on symptoms, the approach focuses on the patient, or even beyond the patient" (99–100).

37. Although Macey reiterates that this characterization is not meant to be insulting or diminishing, it is replete with just such language—from the "plundering of libraries" at institutions in which Fanon was a student to going on to describing him as crafting work to explore and analyze his own situation "even though he had no real academic training as a philosopher and no extensive knowledge of psychoanalysis."

38. Fanon wrote, "Besides phylogeny and ontogeny stands sociogeny. . . . But society, unlike biochemical processes, cannot escape human influences. Man is what brings society into being" (*BSWM*, 11).

39. Fanon writes that all forms of racism show the same collapse, the same bankruptcy of man (*BSWM*, 86). He describes this as having been made clear to him by his philosophy professor who was a native of the Antilles. He had said, "Whenever you hear anyone abuse the Jews, pay attention, because he is talking about you." Fanon clarifies, "He meant, quite simply, an anti-Semite is inevitably anti-Negro" (122). It is not sufficient to frame European civilization and its best representatives as free of responsibility for colonial racism since it was the adventurers and politicians who were responsible. Quoting from Jean-

son, Fanon states, "If you succeed in keeping yourselves unsullied, it is because others dirty themselves in your place. You hire thugs, and, balancing the accounts, it is you who are the real criminals: for without you, without your blind indifference, such men could never carry out deeds that damn you as much as they shame those men" (from *Esprit*, April 1950; Fanon *BSWM*, 92). Rejecting Mannoni's claim that France was the least racialist-minded country in the world, Fanon writes, "France is a racist country, for the myth of the bad nigger is part of the collective unconscious" (*BSWM*, 92).

40. It is interesting that the third figure most would add to this list would be Plato, whose writing aimed explicitly to capture the spirit of the dialogue. All three men, at the level of the form of the text, embodied a particular orientation to how others should be engaged when one seeks to advance the space of reason.

41. He wrote, "Walking is something that drives and fuels my thoughts: I can hardly think when I stay in place, it is necessary that my body is in motion . . . the removal of everything that makes me feel my dependence, all that reminds me of my situation . . . gives me more courage to think" (*OC* 1:162).

42. Cherki writes, with the exception perhaps of "Racism and Culture," all of Fanon's writings, even if later revised, "began as spoken words, words that were communicated to an interlocutor, preferably a close and trusted one" (2006, 27).

43. Simone de Beauvoir described Fanon "with a razor sharp intelligence, intensely alive, endowed with a grim sense of humor, he explained things, made jokes, questioned us, gave imitations, told stories; everything he talked about seemed alive again before our eyes" (quoted in Bulhan 1985, 31).

44. Both Sartre and Father Celeste commented that Fanon did not like partners in conversation who were reticent; he wanted them to share what they thought and why (Djemaï 2001).

45. This challenge, at times, appears momentous. Consider Fanon's discussion of the Negro with the agonizing conviction that he would never gain recognition from his white physician colleagues or patients who therefore enlists in the army as a medical officer refusing to serve in the colonies or in a colonial unit because he wants to have white men under his command, fearing and respecting him. Fanon writes, "That was just what he wanted, what he strove for: to make white men adopt a Negro attitude toward him. In this way he was obtaining revenge for the *imago* that had always obsessed him: the frightened, trembling Negro, abased before the white overlord" (*BSWM*, 61).

46. Fanon writes that he decided to accept his identification by others with enslaved and lynched ancestors. "It was on the universal level of the intellect that I understood this inner kinship—I was the grandson of slaves in exactly

the same way in which President Lebrun was the grandson of tax-paying, hard-working peasants" (*BSWM*, 113).

47. He argued that one had to investigate the extent to which the conclusions of Freud or Adler could be applied to understand the man of color's view of the world (*BSWM*, 141).

48. He continued, "I owe it to myself to affirm that the Arab, permanently an alien in his own country, lives in a state of absolute depersonalization."

49. Suspicion of this kind makes a good deal of sense if one considers the ubiquity of abuses: from experiments done on patients to estimate pain thresholds of distinct races; to selling water pills as penicillin and B12 tablets to fight cancer; accepting money for what were said to be x-rays when behind the sheet, no radiological equipment was present; and reporting on nationalists rather than honoring codes of confidentiality that pertained to them. For further discussion, see Bulhan (1985).

50. Bulhan (1985) explains that Algeria was a prized colony, not only for economic and strategic reasons, but also because of the large and powerful settler community there. Considered an integral part of France, expropriation of labor and land followed soon after conquest. Countless Algerians were displaced and forced into temporary tenancy—by 1890, four million acres of the best land were in European hands while by 1940, about one-third of the profitably cultivatable land was owned by 2 percent of the population, mainly by European settlers. Not all of these were French, many were Southern Europeans of varied nationalities. Bulhan writes, "Algeria became a new frontier where land was grabbed without question and native labor exploited with impunity" (1985, 235). Much land was used for vineyards and to make Algeria an export enclave for wine, which most Algerians did not drink. A small Algerian elite, opposed by most European settlers, was manipulated with promises of reform and assimilation that were largely dashed.

51. Fanon argued that such patients could not be happier in Europe than at home but that repatriation was not the answer so long as social and economic inequalities remained. A total social reconstruction was needed, "houses to be built, schools to be opened, roads to be laid out, slums torn down, cities to spring from the earth, men, women and children to be adorned with smiles."

52. When Fanon returned to Martinique after defending his medical thesis in 1951 he found that the source of the majority of problems he encountered were political and economic, that most patients suffered from nutritional needs, lack of sanitation and health services on an island under colonial rule and "in no mood for independence." For the many who identified strongly with France, Fanon was a traitor (Bulhan 1985, 207). Bulhan describes Fanon's search for an appropriate context as a search for himself, for what to live and die for. Psychia-

try, Bulhan writes, promised a means for making a living and tool for correcting what was amiss.

53. Fanon writes, "Whenever I have read a psychoanalytic work, discussed problems with my professors or talked with European patients, I have been struck by the disparity between the corresponding schemas and the reality that the Negro presents" (*BSWM*, 150) He offers by way of example that the black person's inferiority or superiority complex or feelings of equality are conscious and present; he is without the affective amnesia typical of the average white neurotic. In a separate discussion he also writes, "I believe it is necessary to become a child again in order to grasp certain psychic realities. This is where Jung was an innovator: He wanted to go back to the childhood of the world, but he made a remarkable mistake: He went back only to the childhood of Europe" (*BSWM*, 190).

54. Tosquelles was a pioneer in milieu therapy and the first rigorously to apply in a hospital environment the ideas of therapeutic communities developed in England and the United States in the 1930s and 1940s.

55. Fanon undertook this research and writing with Lacaton who, as the intensity of the Algerian war increased, was arrested on suspicion of collaboration. When standard interrogation procedures led nowhere, Lacaton was pushed and punched around, submerged in a bathtub and subjected to enemas of soapy water and electric shock to the genitals. He was eventually released in a manner reserved for ambiguous personalities: while half-conscious, he was taken to a European farm and dumped in a pigsty. He managed to escape only to depart for France (Geismar 1971, 77; Bulhan 1985, 238). Fanon, for his part, was initially protected somewhat by being a foreigner, by being neither Algerian nor European and linked into an international community. When his body was brought to Tunis, "in the middle of the war the Algerians paused to honor one of their own in a national funeral" (from Simone de Beauvoir). He was considered to be a citizen of the new Algerian nation. The Swiss journalist and novelist François Bondy wrote in his 1966 "The Black Rousseau" *New York Review of Books* article, "Fanon belonged to the cosmopolitan fringe—like ardent foreigners who fought in Russian and Spanish revolutions—eager to give wide international meaning to a specific struggle, always shaken off at some later stage. The men who rule Algeria today would have little use for Fanon's ceaseless exhortations; and the Algerian 'masses' would make a Martinican Negro feel foreign in ways he would never have experienced in Paris. The prophet of Algeria's national revolution would have found himself an exile from his chosen homeland, in search of another revolutionary war with which to identify himself. Che Guevara could have been at home practically anywhere in Hispanic America, but Frantz Fanon would remain a stranger, even in Black Africa" (3).

Bondy bases the supposed likeness of Rousseau and Fanon in his claim that Fanon cares less for economic development than for brotherhood, democracy, and new nationalism which Bondy suggests was also the doctrine of Rousseau who advised Poles not to catch up to the West but become more distinctly Polish. If the aim was for Africa to become a new Europe, it would be better to leave its destiny to Europeans who could achieve this aim better than the most gifted of Africans. See Bondy (1966).

3. ROUSSEAU'S GENERAL WILL

1. Rousseau (1928, 630–31).

2. My claim does not extend to ancient polities that included a vast array of legitimating practices from the problematics of the Greek city-state to Egyptian and Mesopotamian cities to Chinese dynasties. To attempt to account for all of these would certainly be beyond the scope of this discussion.

3. It was Aristotle's claim that it is only gods and beasts that can live outside of a *polis*. For the rest of us, the "we" to which I here refer, there is and must be politics (Aristotle 2000, 61).

4. Rousseau is arguing here explicitly against Sir Robert Filmer's (1680) *Patriarcha; or the Natural Power of Kings*, which Rousseau felt had already received more attention than it was due, particularly given that Aristotle had anticipated and rejected its central arguments centuries before. Rousseau is not, however, suggesting that political leadership is unnatural because it is uncaring.

5. Rousseau cautioned that comparisons of political with physical bodies were inaccurate in many respects. Still they were useful to emphasize an alternative to the model for which Filmer urged. In the *Discourse on Political Economy*, Rousseau elaborated: "The sovereign power represents the head; the laws and customs are the brain, source of the nerves and seat of the understanding, the will and the senses, of which the judges and magistrates are the organs; the commerce, industry and agriculture are the mouth and the stomach which prepare the common subsistence; the public finances are the blood that is discharged by a wise *economy*, performing the functions of the heart, in order to distribute nourishment and life throughout the body; the citizens are the body and members that make the machine move, live, and work, and that cannot be harmed in any part without a painful impression immediately being transmitted to the brain, if the animal is in a state of good health" (1987, 114). Citizens each are not then independent parts of the whole. I cannot be the arm, with my own tasks to do and strains to feel, separated from you who may be the ear or a strand of hair. We are, instead, all both body and members, healthy when of a piece. Rousseau notes that in politics, as with the body, there must be a common self that simultaneously makes the parts one and living. Without this, both perish. To be a moral being, the body politic requires a will. This is the general will.

6. Robert Wokler notes that Rousseau never refers to the sovereign people as a democracy. Many writers quote Rousseau's caution that democracy would be appropriate for a people of gods . . . "but that so perfect a form of government is not suited to men" (1987, 180). Wokler adds that Rousseau understood democracy as a system of direct government rather than one of direct sovereignty and feared that it would require that the majority of people execute public policy. This did not only seem a logistical nightmare and an impossibility, it would make corruption and civil war inevitable. See Robert Wokler (2001, 82).

7. In Tzvetan Todorov's words Rousseau discovered and invented our modernity, "'Discovered,' because this modern society existed before he did, but it had not yet found such a penetrating interpreter. But also 'invented,' because he has passed down to posterity the concepts and themes that, for two hundred years, we have not ceased to examine" (2001, 2).

8. It may be objected that in marriage one makes precisely this commitment, a commitment to someone from whom one can demand everything. Surely, however, there are certain kinds of demands that would compromise the very meaning of what is involved in marriage.

9. This is an insight in Jean-Paul Sartre's *Critique of Dialectical Reason*, a work arguably heavily guided by the concept of the general will. Sartre distinguishes between "seriality" and a "group-in-fusion." The former is a mere collection of people, as, for instance, in the case of random passengers on a bus; the latter is what happens when they become aware of themselves as a unity, as, for instance, in the case of a hijacker taking over the bus and thereby threatening the lives of each of them, making all aware of their shared endangered reality. For a discussion of these Sartrean concepts, see William L. McBride (1991) and Iris M. Young (1994).

10. Pufendorf had suggested that in the creation of the state, each person promised to submit his particular will to the will of one person or an assembly of people so that his decisions would be deemed the positive will of everyone in general and in particular. Burlamaqui argued that a union of will created civil society which in turn required a "supreme power to intimidate" anyone who dared act against the common utility. The resolutions of the intimidators were considered "the positive will of all in general, and of each in particular." See Rosenblatt (1997, 188).

11. There is therefore, for a particular brand of Rousseauian, a strange irony at the core of antipolitical nostalgia for or idealization of the state of nature: To reflect in this way is to make use of capacities that only emerge out of shared life, out of a curtailing of the right to everything that one is tempted to try to acquire in a way that is only limited by one's force and that of others. Intelligent life, in which we are capable of collective willing, emerges with reflection and an ability to think retrospectively. These are all fruits of a social world, a world

through which we do not move isolated and alone, but with other human beings who we must consider and who consider us. Their lives and our own intertwine. Tzvetan Todorov puts it this way: "Even from an egoistic point of view, the 'other' is indispensable. Society, then, is not a lesser evil, a supplement; it is the source of qualities that do not exist without it" (2001, 58).

12. Graeme Garrard (2003) has argued that Rousseau, against the *philosophes*, insisted that "sentiments of sociability" needed to be artificially produced and sustained through institutions and social norms. He saw both social cohesion and the strength of communities as fragile. They in turn saw his insistence on the sacrifices required to sustain a precarious social life as unnecessarily austere. Diderot, for instance, argued in his *Encyclopédie* entry on "natural right" that human beings formed natural societies with their own general wills before the formation of political societies. These were evident to anyone who made use of their reason. Those who could not were unnatural beings undeserving of their rights as men.

13. This is suggested in passages that state that while the general will is always right, a particular iteration of it might not be enlightened; that all that is just comes from G-d (Rousseau 1987, 160); or that the voice of the sovereign people is, in effect, the voice of G-d (115).

14. John Noone writes, "The distinction between a person's actual will and his real will can be traced back at least to Plato. What an individual does or intends is for the most part an index of his actual will. But if the unforeseen consequences of an act are or would be disastrous, it is claimed that the actual will was not the real will. It is on the basis of this distinction that forcible frustration of an actual will is sometimes justified: the man who is prevented from crossing a bridge known to be unsafe, the thirst of a child whose mother snatches a bottle of poison from him, the drunk who is not allowed to drive, and so on. It would save a lot of analytical headaches if one could simply identify a person's general will as his real will. Unfortunately, this will not do, because the distinction between actual and real cuts across both particular and general wills" (1980, 74).

15. Brian Barry has outlined a set of conditions in which it is likely that the majority would be right and in which one may be glad that one's minority opinion did not prevail. These include: if there is a uniquely right answer that is in conformity with the general will; if everyone has an equal opportunity to discern the right answer; if everyone wants right to prevail. In such instances the majority will is not the general will but is in conformity with it, with the implication that this is not majoritarianism, the imposing of one limited preference and opinion on and over all others. This interpretation seeks to escape such a relativism by framing our efforts as a collective process to ascertain what

is correct. See Brian Barry (1967, 119–26). This is also the way through which Rousseau's general will has been read as Codorcetian. See Bernard Grofman and Scott L. Feld (1988, 567–76).

16. John Charvet (1974, 44) has insisted that Rousseau does indeed seek the elimination of individual differences and that this is clearest in his disdain for factions. Charvet argues that the desire to break these up is unrealistic: we are unable to eradicate the interests that make them coalesce. It is also undesirable, for it requires individuals who relate to each other only as mirrors to themselves. He depicts Rousseau's political society as one in which there can only be the individual, absolutely alone, and the all-embracing common life.

17. The legitimacy brought to law by the general will could also be compared with H. L. A. Hart's (1961) idea of the "rule of recognition" delineated in *The Concept of Law*. He contends that every legal system has a set of second-order understandings, arrangements, institutions, and rules through which legally authoritative particular laws and authors of law can be recognized as such and thereby come into being. This idea is a reformulation of the nineteenth-century English legal philosopher John Austin's theory of positive law through which he insisted that law is a matter of historical decisions made by people who possess political power and occupy the role of sovereign. Hart sought to frame law as more than the formalization of command. His success is a matter of debate. For a brief discussion of this, see Ronald Dworkin (1986, 33–35).

18. For a fascinating exploration of the relationship between illegitimacy and living as an imitation, see Gary Schwartz (1997, 111–28). Schwartz contends, here in the spirit of the discussion in Chapter 2, that in US society, black girls are told that to be beautiful is to be white. They thus face a predicament in which attempting to be desirable requires trying to be what they are not.

19. Indeed, gone from this discussion are Rousseau's earlier obsessions with the destructive consequences of seeking public attention and acclaim.

20. See McCormick (2007; 2011).

21. Former Secretary-General of the United Nations Kofi Annan was recently asked why Africa was such a brutal place, why it was that the people of its decolonized nations seemed better at butchering than governing each other. His answer was poignant: He pointed out that the planes that hit the World Trade Center on September 11, 2001, left many US citizens volunteering to give up the institutions that could protect the civil rights that they once pointed to as uniquely defining their nation. He asked the man with whom he was speaking to imagine what hundreds of years of ongoing but magnified September 11 attacks would do for the challenge of governing. He might have added that Europe is no stranger to human butchery, that it has quite a rich history, at home and abroad, on this score.

22. Rousseau (1987, 155) insists, even then, that this is not the sign of a corrupted people but of one that has been fooled into wishing for something that could make the "they" of which they are a part disintegrate. Their deliberate deception, it would seem, is normally the work of opportunistic individuals who weigh on the naïve, innocent, and vulnerable within smaller, partial societies. Knowing the currency of generality, they might mask their narrow ambitions under its banner. Or they might speak to the wrong parts of us that are always partial to what will further eat away at a public spirit already always under duress. In both cases, the people mistake a narrower general will as comparable to, indeed perhaps even preferable to, the more comprehensive one of the polity as a whole with the outcome of either an unenlightened general will, one that does not embody a skilled reconciliation of what is right with what is popularly willed, or the will of all. Worth noting is that the idea of a less enlightened general will suggests another implicit standard, another general will that functions as a regulative ideal, that which could in principle be discernible to informed members of the citizenry as a more perfect realization of the justice sought. Laurence Cooper has argued that Rousseau endorses and condemns ways of life based on a psychological standard: does it lack or promote psychic integrity? There are several implications, one of which is a concern with psychology over behavior or with what one is or intends rather than with what one does. One sees countless examples of this in the *Confessions*, including when Rousseau accepts Madame's indulgences but does not consider himself a rogue since he would have preferred to have acted differently. Cooper argues that no moral code is invulnerable to bad faith but that Rousseau's may create even more space with which to evade moral accountability. See Cooper (1999, 194, 206–7).

23. Rousseau does not here entertain a dilemma outlined by Richard Dagger, drawing on Henrik Ibsen's *An Enemy of the People*, in which a city finds its economic fortunes tied to the fate of a single industry that produces pollution hazardous to its residents. Which concern, he asked, the loss of money and jobs or increasing rates of severe birth deformities, should be the focus of the citizen? See Dagger (1997, 96–97).

24. John T. Scott, following Jean Starobinski's suggestion, argues that the idea of unity ties together Rousseau's aesthetic and political concerns with his interest in communication, emphasizing the instrumental and metaphoric role of music and language in the development of a harmonious community capable of the affect necessary to act together. See Scott (1997, 803–29) and Starobinski (1977, 195–210).

25. One might compare this with speech acts or those instances when, as J. L. Austin observed, circumstances permit speaking and doing to become identical. In such cases, one speaks in a way that is neither description nor reporting,

saying words that are neither true nor false. One names a child, agrees to marry, makes a bet, announces a shared beginning. If in appropriate circumstances, usually those that meet conditions of an existing and accepted convention and with the feelings and intentions required by sincerity, the act will be a speech act, rather than a "misfire." See Austin (1979, 235).

26. These were comments made following a summary of Abizadeh's paper, "Word versus the Public Thing: Verbal Threats to the Rousseauian Republic," American Political Science Association meeting held in Chicago, September 2–5, 2004.

27. Judith Shklar and more recently Steven Johnston have argued that Rousseau's work is tragic. For Johnston, Rousseau's political theory is "tucked within the confines of a munificent ontology the critical feature of which is a presumption of resolution: political projects can be conceived and executed according to a plan, thus lacking any significant unwanted features. The nature of things, including the nature of human being, allows for it," (1999, 13). With much of the rest of the Western tradition of thought, Johnston suggests, alienation and discord remain simply as a function of untruth of one kind or another. These are irredeemable, providential, ontological assumptions in Johnston's view, that fail to wrestle with the "lack of transcendental warrant for social and political practices and values" (16). He claims boldly, "To bring [these] out, then, is to force Rousseau to be free" (ibid.). Shklar sees Rousseau seeking "a mechanical evasion" of people's limitations. She writes, "[No] one knew better than Rousseau that moral self-injury cannot simply be undone. Moral and social errors are irreversible" (1969, 192). No one takes a different position, closer to if not identical with the one advanced here: Conceptual success may have required disembodying the spirit of politics. He reflects, "In one sense a purely conceptual analysis of Rousseau's approach to the problem of legitimacy is complete. If you view his complicated argument from a high level of abstraction where all assumptions can be granted, I think you will find that he has indeed *conceptually* solved his problem. But this is hardly satisfactory. What we have is a disembodied spirit; what we need to supply is some corporeal substance" (Johnston 1999, 87).

28. One of the many ingenious qualities of Rousseau's writing is the way in which it replicated in form what it is trying to convey in substance. In this instance, the tumultuous read reenacts a fundamental feature of the political. In Ellen Kennedy's words, it "is the gateway into the substantive concerns that constitute the seriousness of human life and are at times its affliction and at others the source of its grandeur." She continues in a discussion of Carl Schmitt in a way that is highly relevant here, "Whether the engagement [in the public] is meaningful or the source of darkest nihilism will depend on precisely those elements of the political beyond the system of needs. That in Carl Schmitt's

time this venture ended in horror does not negate its necessity if we are to lead human lives" (2004, 183).

29. One might object that Rousseau describes obeying the general will as giving each citizen to his homeland, guaranteeing him against all personal dependence "a condition that produces the skill and performance of the *political machine*, and which alone bestows legitimacy upon civil commitments," (Rousseau 1987, 150; italics added). Yet this is a metaphor Rousseau used sparingly and even here the machine emerges out of virtuous action that limits dependence. In other words, even in talking about a political machine, Rousseau emphasizes that it is human agency and freedom that will bring this into being. Freedom for him, particularly as manifested in virtuous action could counteract the idiosyncratic dependence on men which he wrote in *Emile* (1979) is "without order."

30. Both of these extremities are evident in the United States right now.

31. One might think here of the arguments of US black nationalists who have suggested that rather than a unified polity, the United States is a collection of smaller unequal nations with an insufficient number of overlapping priorities and interests.

32. See, in particular, De Maistre's *Considerations on France* and *Study on Sovereignty*. Both appear in *The Works of Joseph De Maistre*,(1971). Benjamin Constant's "The Liberty of the Ancients Compared with that of the Moderns" is included in *The Libertarian Reader: Classic and Contemporary Readings from Lao-tzu to Milton Friedman* (1997, 65–70). For excellent retrospective discussions of Rousseau as a proto-totalitarian, see Iain Hampsher-Monk (1995) and Wokler (1995).

33. This distilled list of charges against Rousseau is outlined in Robert Wokler (1995, 189–91).

34. G. W. F. Hegel (1991). Hegel explicitly mentions Rousseau in Part Three, passages 153 and 258. His discussion of the upbringing of children in passage 174 also engages Rousseau's *Emile* and the characterization in it of the kind of teaching advocated by John Locke. See also Marx (1984) and (1978, 66–125).

35. Patrick Riley is not among Rousseau's critics. Still his formulation in *Will and Political Legitimacy* (1982, 112–13) is useful for understanding this point. Riley argues that will is a concept of individuality and particularity. It can only be spoken of as general metaphorically.

4. FANONIAN NATIONAL CONSCIOUSNESS

1. Fanon (1963, 315). Hereafter, all references to *Wretched of the Earth* are cited as *WE*.

2. For a related discussion from which I have learned a great deal, see Paget Henry (2009a). He advances the view that Rousseau's "general will," an effort

to honor and realize the values and aspirations of the public self of the nation, is rearticulated by C. L. R. James in a proletarian or postbourgeois form as the "creative self-movements" of the majority classes of workers and farmers in Trinidad and England.

3. Rousseau's discussions of violence do not describe collectivities facing one another. Instead they focus primarily on encounters of individuals, as in the case when he says that the enslaved are entitled violently to rebel so long as it was likely to be effective. He does, in addition, describe instances when disenfranchised majorities face singular tyrants. Evident in the closing pages of his *Second Discourse*, while discussing the final stage of inequality, in which all private individuals return again to equality because they are all nothing beneath a tyrant for whom the only laws are his own idiosyncratic and ephemeral whims. For Rousseau, this constitutes a return to "the law of the strongest" and a new state of nature. Only the master because strongest, Rousseau says he can be ousted since "he has no cause to protest against violence. The uprising that ends in the strangulation or the dethronement of a sultan is as lawful an act as those by which he disposed of the lives and goods of his subjects the day before" (1987, 79).

4. Both models usually coexist within societies, with some, who fully belong, primarily occupying spheres that law is seen to constitute and protect while others experience these same government mechanisms as primarily punitive and violent. The consistency of this coexistence is one of the many dimensions of political life obscured in Giorgio Agamben's (1998) depiction of a trajectory through which the polis on the model of the classical city-state is displaced by that of the camp. Iterations of both are as old as theorizing about politics much of which in turn involves efforts of those outside political relations to expand their realm in ways that clarify foundational political concepts from freedom to personhood.

5. This is akin to Rousseau's discussion of benighted Europeans who must eliminate internal barriers of *amour propre* and structural institutions of inequality really to experience liberty.

6. *Amour propre* has a similar, if distinct, effect on Europeans to the extent to it causes them to see one another only in instrumental terms.

7. For a highly illuminating discussion of this point, see Bernard Boxill (1992) on the nature of "self-respect."

8. Fanon writes, "for all the speeches about the equality of human beings—these cannot hide the commonplace fact that seven Frenchmen killed or wounded kindles indignation of civilized consciousness while massacre of whole populations is treated as unimportant (*WE*, 89). He notes as well that after seven years of crime in Algeria, not a single Frenchman had been indicted in a French court of justice for the murder of an Algerian (92).

5. THINKING THROUGH CREOLIZATION

1. Trouillot (2003, 34).

2. Political speech can aim to be more and less inclusive. The range of forms of American English spoken when politicians campaign for the presidency is striking. In those instances, one index of the diversity of the US citizenry becomes evident. One could ask whether this diversity is a strength or a sign of ongoing segregaion of various communities from each other since autonomous and distinctive accents often betoken economic and social isolation of both the privileged and their opposites.

3. Stephen Palmié (2006, 236) argues that this is a function of much of the rest of the globe becoming more Caribbean as locations where previously separate worlds collide multiply.

4. By evil or problematic, Schmitt offered as specific examples being corrupt, weak, cowardly, stupid, brutal, sensual, vital, or irrational; by unproblematic or "good," Schmitt meant reasonable, perfectible, capable of being manipulated or taught, or peaceful.

5. Cornell made these comments in a discussion at the University of Cape Town in February 2009 following a presentation of an earlier essay version of what became this chapter.

6. There is disagreement about the word's etymology, though it is always linked either to Portuguese or to Spanish, with Kamau Brathwaite provocatively suggesting that it combines the Spanish word *criar* (to create, imagine, establish, and found) with *colon* (a colonist, founder, settler) into *criollo*, one identified with the area of settlement, localized through blending, though not ancestrally indigenous to it (1974, 10).

7. Chaudenson observes that creole people "preceded by many years the languages that are identified by the same name." For discussion of the many different ways that creole people were defined throughout the French colonies, from designating locally born whites, mulattos, or blacks to identifying specifically those who were not Franco-Mauritian, Indo-Mauritian, or Sino-Mauritian, to a way of referring to those whose primary or only language was Creole as opposed to an immigrant or more official tongue, see Chaudenson (2001, chap. 1).

8. Eriksen (2007) explains that there are a variety of ways that groups can relate to each other in such circumstances. One group can be culturally absorbed into another; groups can merge to form another entity; a hierarchical complementary or competitive relationship can follow; one group can exterminate another, and so on.

9. Schuchardt insisted that universal linguistic structures were key to understanding Creole genesis and the processes of their emergence were therefore crucial to understanding language change everywhere.

10. The first such approach is perhaps most evident in one of the two camps that continues to dominate contemporary creole linguistic scholarship, in the extensively cited writing of Derek Bickerton and John McWhorter. Insisting on defining creole languages according to criteria inherent to the languages themselves (rather than by the sociohistorical conditions for their emergence), they insist that these are languages that grew out of rudimentary tongues developed in the absence of any first language resources and that they thereby offer the closest approximation of protohuman language. As such, they supposedly provide insights into the workings of our genetic capacity for speech in their crudest, unelaborated form. They are universal, in this view, to the extent that they are shorn of particular varieties of cultural elaboration. John McWhorter writes, for example, "Because as a rule any language spoken on earth traces back to unbroken development from a former full language (or languages), when we see pidgins transformed into creoles we come closest to witnessing the birth of a human language" (2001, 138). His position is indebted to Derek Bickerton who distinguishes among a range of situations between the normal child in a normal language community who masters his or her ancestral language through the linguistic input of elders and the feral or traumatized child in isolation with no mastery of any language (1977, 63). He writes, "One situation that stands between these poles is surely that of the child of speakers of an unstable pidgin in a displaced community where ancestral languages are of very limited utility. . . . The pidgin that is presented as a model is, in comparison with its competitors, too impoverished and unstable a medium to serve all the communicative needs of an individual. This matters not at all to the pidgin speaker, who will usually have fellow-speakers of his own language to consort with. But the child creole speaker will be driven to 'expand' the pidgin through a 'process [that] must consist of internalizing linguistic rules for which there is no evidence in terms of linguistic outputs. If such rules are not induced from primary data, they must be derived directly from the human *faculté de langage*'" (64). Michel DeGraff (2003) characterizes the depiction of creole languages as the fruit of abnormal breaks in transmission with an exceptional genealogy as a manifestation of the search for primitive language or for living linguistic fossils not far removed from depictions of the Caribbean as an early Eden in the writings of Rousseau. There was, emphasizes Alleyne, significant diversity within the Caribbean, including instances like Jamaica where populations of adult male slaves came largely from the same places of origin and shared languages. More frequent were cases in which no single African language was numerically dominant, which would have led to rapid linguistic deculturation and replacement by a shared medium that would have been the primary shared language of bi- and multilingual adults and the first language of their children. This would be rather different from pidgins that were used in instances of trade by communities in sporadic contact

who, from the store of their own languages and exposure to *lingua franca*, made guesses about words and phrases that could be understood in instances of cross-cultural communication (174).

11. This debate over defining creole languages according to their intrinsic structural features or by the sociohistorical conditions of their emergence has largely eclipsed earlier debates over the genesis of creole languages as mono- or polygenetic. The former position suggested that all subsequent creole languages derived from one Afro-Portuguese protopidgin *lingua franca* spread through the Portuguese sea empire while polygenetic advocates argued for separate ancestry. Also much contested was whether creole languages were simplified, restructured varieties of European lexifiers or derived from non-European languages and re-lexified through contact languages. These are respectively called the super- and substratist positions.

12. Mufwene writes, "[Creoles] are socially disfranchised dialects of their lexifiers, especially since dialects of the same language need not be mutually intelligible" (1998, 7). DeGraff (2003) continues, that what emerges with Haitian Creole (HC) is not substantively different from what follows in other instances of language change through contact—core aspects of its grammar (sound patterns, verb and object placement, inflectional morphology) fall within developmental patterns in instances of "regular" language change. Indeed, he suggests, it could be argued that French and HC and English and Jamaican Creole are closer to each other than French and Latin or English and proto-Germanic.

13. One might compare the role of lexifying and substrate languages to that of theology and religion in Edward Blyden's (1994) classic observation that "you may change the theology of a people, but you cannot change their Religion." This is a key point about creolization—although focused on the emergence of new forms out of once separated and perhaps antagonistic genealogies—people do not construct from nothing. They forge out of the materials at hand, from particular, even if ruptured, ways of understanding relations that structure and animate life worlds. To continue to be meaningful, however, these had to be refashioned in light of new circumstances so that the results were both continuous and distinctive.

14. This question becomes one of great contestation when it comes to projects of standardizing creole languages so that they can be written. For some, the basis should be the more autonomous, conservative basilect forms spoken in rural areas that have changed far more slowly because of their ongoing economic and social isolation. Others argue that the mesolect urban varieties are better windows into larger processes of creolization, creativity, and innovation. For their critics, these are the tongues of relative elites that are coming to resemble too closely the European languages that supply much of their vocabulary (see

Romaine 1994). Such matters are not narrowly academic and indeed are informed by an effort to balance recognition of the international cultural capital of European languages along with the local significance of basilect creole languages. While Prime Minister Michael Thomas Somare of Papua New Guinea argued that English skills be nurtured to foster international trade relations in ways that simultaneously would avoid its saturating Tok Pisin, which, he argued, should remain the home and affective language that could bridge growing urban and rural divides (Romaine 1994, 37–38), others insisted that prioritizing teaching creole in order to enfranchise alienated Caribbean students effectively create a two-tiered education system that would intensify the perceived illiteracy of most of the citizenry in the eyes of its elite and the world beyond them (123, 128). DeGraff insists that this has only emerged as a dilemma because of the ongoing prizing of European language by local Caribbean elites seeking to affirm their unique cultural capital through insisting on the indispensability of a language that separates them from most of the rest of the polity.

15. In some of these instances one sees the survival of larger pieces of distinct traditions that continued to be practiced by separate communities and, from a greater distance, to influence one another. With agriculture and cuisine, the construction of homes, and prescription of herbal medicines, the pre-enslavement practices of African people (who came from intertropical regions comparable to those in which they now found themselves) were more relevant or easily adaptable than many of the life ways of their previously European counterparts.

16. Mufwene explains that the main difference between child language acquisition and second language is that in the latter, learners can draw on features in previously spoken languages and therefore have a pool of competing features that child learners lack.

17. I would like to thank Hilary Dick for insisting that I take seriously that language is not always used to facilitate clear communication.

18. One could think here of the many instances of such words and phrases generated by academic speech and prose. The use of the word *disconnect* or *human* as nouns come immediately to mind.

19. A puzzling feature of even Chaudenson's (with Mufwene) (2001) often masterful work is their resistance to efforts to explore similarities among creole languages with different European lexifiers that combine with the same or related substrates. Part of this appears to be a response to the criticism of what Dillard (1970) called "the cafeteria principle," or the over-eager and not sufficiently sophisticated linking of creole to any African language that appeared to share words or morphemes. However, given that subsequent rigorous exploration has disentangled words that do appear to be shared across many African languages and much of the Caribbean from more specific linguistic tributaries

(see especially Parkvall 2000), I suspect that the ongoing aversion is twofold: it is (rightly or wrongly) assumed to be a function of a romantic approach to race and racial identification and a reflection of a very real concern with the ways in which radical inequalities appeared to mark language development more significantly than symbolic forms expressed through music, dance, cooking, and healing and religious practices.

20. One might think here of the delight at a Jewish *seder* of representing the fully global nature of "Jewish food." This might draw in recipes from India and China, from Singapore and Nigeria, as well as from Poland, Spain, Argentina, and Morocco. In some cases, the enthusiasm would be little more than a reflection of a trendy cosmopolitan ethos hungry for ever-new hedonistic pleasures. In others, it is an effort to grapple with what it means to share in a community that is both so diverse and one that has historically thought of itself as bound by shared blood and ancestry. Creolization helps to understand the meaning of food in diasporic communities more generally or how it is, in particular, that the range of foods called "Jewish" in China, India, Nigeria, Russia, and New Jersey, for all their distinctness also are marked by sufficient continuities to remain under one compelling category. This is often, as Claudia Roden (1998) has suggested, the consequence of efforts to comply with specifically Jewish dietary laws, the holidays around which much food preparation and eating revolved and revolves, and the specific, often more cosmopolitan networks (because of merchants and peddlers, traveling rabbis, teachers and beggars, as well as the more widespread propensity for migration and exile) of Jews within their varied locations. It is often those who do not retain connections to particular physical territory who cling most tenaciously to the continuity of these practices. The same, of course, could be said of Chinese and Indian cuisines that reflect both what is available and local culinary tastes at the same time as particular prohibitions, dishes and dates of unique significance, and distinctive communal networks that bridge the domestic and foreign. In all such examples, one recognizes what creolization describes: elements that are continuous and shared with those that are new and different. Their combination emphasizes the contingent ways that commitments to or identification with particular practices and customs will be made and remade in light of the mandates of new circumstances. As such, one particular form is precisely that, one of many instantiations of an effort to keep a form living, refashioning it afresh in new environments. I emphasize the Jewish example because it reintroduces another key dimension of creolization: that of surprising genealogical developments. For many Ashkenazic Jews, the suggestion by other Jews that their food is *so* Eastern European is a surprise and an insult, an example of the ways in which they are but one instantiation of Jewishness (rather than the only and universal standard) and are

of course implicated by societies in which they were marginal and from which most ultimately had to flee.

21. One could think here of the centrality of newly arrived immigrant groups to the eating economies in any major city.

22. One could here consider the tendency among Jamaican candidates for political office, observed by Reisman (1970, 140), of trying to indicate authenticity by using patois or the borrowing in the U.S. of black idioms by the full range of races of speakers when trying audibly to be soulful or even moral.

23. Reflect here on the omnipresence of the phenomenon of "the black best friend" (who is a plot device rather than a character) in historical and contemporary US fiction, film, and television. His or her sole purpose is to enable and drive on the protagonist's quest to realize his or her aspirations.

24. Ernest Pépin and Raphaël Confiant (1998, 98) and Wilson Harris (1998, 23) have also argued that créolité is not only an approach to the present and future but also a particular orientation toward the past. They suggest, more specifically, that créolité involves rediscovering another history of the world, one that makes visible its multiplicity; that what we in an undifferentiated way call Egyptian, Greek, Chinese, and East Indian were all past créolités. This view of creolization is precisely what I hope could infect the textual study of political theory, especially if we want the exploration of our canon better to illuminate contemporary and unfolding politics. This would also suggest that the instances of imperial decadence that Rousseau so scathingly criticized as undercutting the possibility of productive human inquiry were also some of the most heavily creolized.

25. For a discussion of Hannah Arendt's rejection of modeling notions of sovereignty on a monotheistic G-d, see Jane Anna Gordon (2009).

26. Although the literature of creole creative writers is oriented primarily by a committed refusal to become or endorse the historical role of cultural gatekeepers, there are quite different pressures within creole linguistics. In this context, one treats a language as more than a derivative dialect through giving it official, standardized form. As I have argued, this poses questions of choosing one over other versions of a linguistic continuum and, within it, the orthographic system that is most appropriate. Creole linguists have stressed that these dilemmas differ in *diglossic* contexts, such as Jamaica (and much of the Anglophone Caribbean), in which the "creole continuum" refers to the linguistic variation between the standard, official language, and acrolect and the creole basilect (Winford 1994, 43). In such circumstances the standard European language, for instance, English on the British model, is considered with prestige and treated unqualifiedly as the preferred language of public communication, literacy, and education. The primary language of only a very small elite, for the rest who

face few educational and occupational opportunities or motivation to use it, it is an index of status (Alleyne 1994, 12). Donald Winford affirms that negative evaluations of creole languages as inferior derivatives are particularly strong where they are associated with poverty, ignorance, and lack of moral character (paraphrase of DeCamp cited in Winford 1994, 54). Still, with Reisman, Winford affirms that creole also carries positive symbolic meanings: where Standard English dominates, creole is "intrinsically felt to be the code of the genuine" (Reisman 1970, 140), a badge of friendship, intimacy, and solidarity. It is creole languages that do not compete with European languages *to which they are lexically related* that are uncritically treated as separate languages and that have most steadily proceeded to the status of national languages (Alleyne 1994, 10). They may still not be the equals of dominant European languages, but certainly are not disdained. This is reflected in the fact that they are called by their own distinct names (Sranan, Sramaccan, Ndjuka in Suriname, for instance), rather than simply as *patois* (Romaine).

27. For discussion of the relation of indigineity to creolism in the context of Australia, see Robbie Shilliam (2011, 2012).

28. Ulf Hannerz (1992) makes a similar claim when he observes that cosmopolitanism to make sense requires a comparatively rooted referent.

29. Eriksen (2007, 163) notes that in Mauritius, the identity, Creole, increasingly incorporates those traditionally considered Creole—dark-skinned, working class people of African/Malagasy descent—and "postmodern Creoles," who, for various reasons, primarily intermarriage, do not fit anywhere (they do not belong to one of the distinct Asian or European communities) and speak Kreol as their first language. Having once specifically referred to people of (mixed) African/Malagasy descent, to claim this identity in this new, broader way is not to try actively to assert a distance from African/Malagasy people. He notes that Creoles are considered to be more tolerant of intermarriage than other groups and most significantly, that "one can become a Creole within one's own lifetime—while one cannot conceivably become a Hindu, a Sino-Mauritian, or a Franco-Mauritian." Eriksen emphasizes that within Indian communities, although Kreol is spoken, the language of reference is an Indian language and there is a self-identity premised on notions of purity, continuity, and boundaries. Creoles, by contrast, do not have fixed criteria of membership and are associated with impurity and individualism. Kreol is still seen as a primarily oral idiom that lacks history and literature and as superficial compared to languages of great civilizations.

30. For further discussion of this argument, see the discussion of the hybrid monster as exemplified by Barack Obama and Nelson Mandela in Jane Anna Gordon and Lewis R. Gordon (2009, chap. 4).

31. Lewis Gordon recently observed that when asked to present ideas among colleagues and interested lay people, philosophers and political theorists increasingly present "job talks," or papers that demonstrate their skill as readers of canonical texts, techniques for which they might be (and usually are already) employed. This is, Gordon laments, one of many manifestations of the increasing colonization of the academy by the market, one of many instances of scholars taking the cues for the substantive focus and approach of their work from what has been shown to lead to professional awards and opportunities. See, for instance, Lewis Gordon (2010b).

32. None of this is to underestimate the decimation of universities taking place in many parts of the world (while others are experiencing unparalleled moments of growth). Consider, for example, Tunde Bewaji's exploration of the destruction of Nigerian universities in "Epistemicide, Epistemic Deficit, Sterile Leadership and the Vicious Cycle of African Underdevelopment," presented at the Caribbean Philosophical Association meeting, October 2011, Rutgers University at New Brunswick.

33. One might consider here the difference between the cosmopolitan who travels the world, able always to set the terms with which difference is encountered and the stateless migrant who has constantly to negotiate and navigate existing rules whether of immigration restrictions or prevailing linguistic norms. Creolized outcomes are more likely to emerge from the latter example.

34. I would like to thank my colleague Heath Fogg Davis for pushing me to consider this question.

35. On this point, consider a recent essay by David Adamany, "Are Political Scientists Ready for Politics," presented at the annual State Politics and Policy Conference, Springfield, Illinois, June 2010.

36. Such realms, clearly for us, are those that can coherently be conceived as ones that might have originated from the mind and hands of G-d and that, in so doing, make the very notion of G-d conceivable.

37. As Cristina Beltrán (2010) has demonstrated, we need to produce the terms of commonality through which we might individuate ourselves through acting with others in ways that forge webs of meaningful human relations in what alone can secure particular dimensions of self-realization.

38. Jaspers here was writing about Max Weber, suggesting that he had grappled with a situation in which we were all enmeshed.

39. It may also, suggests Adom Getachew, involve pushing for a more fragmentary historiography that does not silence the voices of the vanquished or the unexpected, the contingent moments when things could have been otherwise, when in refusing to follow sedimented roles, new collectivities might emerge. See her "Reconceptualizing the Universal in the Haitian Revolution," a paper

presented at the Caribbean Philosophical Association meeting, October 2011 at Rutgers University New Brunswick.

40. Though there are writers who have persuasively likened US academic institutions to the plantation. For an example, see Houston Baker (2006).

41. Still, this is not to say that aspects of them are not elusive. It is for this reason that Norton (2004b) cautions against the self-congratulatory spirit she perceived to saturate many problem-solving approaches to the study of politics. In other words, while creolization does break from an approach to culture and to disciplines as sealed off little units modeled on semisovereign territories that are wholly discrete, internally coherent and logical, it does not therefore suggest that we are not always already enmeshed in symbolic worlds or universes of meaning. We do not and cannot step into and outside of culture, as much multicultural writing suggests, or into a domain completely outside of representational life. Indeed, even, perhaps especially, "the wilderness" is wrought with symbolic meaning.

42. It is for this reason that a creolized positivism is most likely impossible.

CONCLUSION

1. This passage comes from Mary Wollstonecraft Shelley (1831, 8). Describing the process of trying to think of a story, she tried to imagine a tale that "would speak to mysterious fears of our nature and awaken thrilling horror—one to make the reader dread to look around, to curdle the blood, and quicken the beatings of their heart."

2. Consider as examples the single-authored and edited volumes in the Global Encounters book series, Dallmayr's 2010 comparative political theory textbook, and the writings of Jenco, Ackerly (2005), Godrej, and March.

References

Ackerly, Brooke A. 2005. "Is Liberalism the Only Way Toward Democracy?: Confucianism and Democracy." *Political Theory* 33 (4): 547–76.

Adamany, David. 2010. "Are Political Scientists Ready for Politics?" Paper presented at the annual State Politics and Policy Conference, Springfield, Illinois, June.

Agamben, Giorgio. 1998. *Homo Sacer: Sovereign Power and Bare Life*. Translated by Daniel Heller-Roazen. Stanford, CA: Stanford University Press.

Alleyne, Mervyn C. 1994. "Problems of Standardization of Creole Languages." In *Language and the Social Construction of Identity in Creole Situations*, edited by Marcyliena Morgan, 7–18. Los Angeles: Center for Afro-American Studies Publications.

———. 2003a. "The Role of Africa in the Construction of Identities in the Caribbean." In *A Pepper-Pot of Cultures: Aspects of Creolization in the Caribbean*, edited by Gordon Collier and Ulrich Fleischmann, 29–42. Amsterdam: Rodopi B. V.

———. 2003b. "Closing Discussion." In *A Pepper-Pot of Cultures*, 459–77.

Althusser, Louis. 1972. *Politics and History: Montesquieu, Rousseau, Hegel, and Marx*. Translated by B. Brewster. London: New Left Books.

Anzaldúa, Gloria. 1987. *Borderlands/La Frontera: The New Mestiza*. San Franciso: Aunt Lute Books.

Aravamudan, Srinivas. "Hobbes and America." In *Postcolonial Enlightenment*, edited by Daniel Carey and Lynn Festa, 37–70. New York: Oxford University Press.

Arendt, Hannah. 1958. *The Human Condition*. Chicago: University of Chicago Press.

———. 1978. *The Jew as Pariah: Jewish Identity and Politics in the Modern Age*. New York: Grove Press.

———. [1979] 1951. *The Origins of Totalitarianism*. San Diego, CA: Harcourt Brace Jovanovich.

———. 2005. "Personal Responsibility Under Dictatorship." In *Responsibility and Judgment*, edited with an introduction by Jerome Kohn, 17–48. New York: Schocken Books.

Aristotle. 2000. *Politics*. Translated by Benjamin Jowett, with an introduction by H. W. C. Davis. Mineola, NY: Dover Publications.

Asante, Molefi. 1998. *The Afrocentric Idea*. Philadelphia, PA: Temple University Press.

Aurenche, Louis. 1921. "Un dernier ami de Jean-Jacques Rousseau. Le chevalier de Flamanville." *Revue catholique de Normandie*, 13–37.

Austin, J. L. 1962. *How To Do Things With Words*. Edited by J. O. Urmson and Marina Sbisà. Cambridge, MA: Harvard University Press.

———. 1979. *Philosophical Papers*. Oxford: Oxford University Press.

Baker, Houston. 2006. "On My First Acquaintance with Black Studies: A Yale Story." In *A Companion to African-American Studies*, edited by Lewis R. Gordon and Jane Anna Gordon, 3–19. Malden, MA: Blackwell Publishing.

Ball, Terence. 1987. Introduction to *Idioms of Inquiry: Critique and Renewal in Political Science*, edited by Terence Ball, 1–9. Albany: State University of New York Press.

Barry, Brian. 1967. "The Public Interest." In *Political Philosophy*, edited by Anthony Quinton, 119–26. Oxford: Oxford University Press.

Beltrán, Cristina. 2010. *The Trouble with Unity: Latino Politics and the Creation of Identity*. New York: Oxford University Press.

Benhabib, Seyla. 2002. *The Claims of Culture: Equality and Diversity in the Global Era*. Princeton, NJ: Princeton University Press.

Bernabé, Jean, Patrick Chamoiseau, and Raphaël Confiant. 1990. "In Praise of Creoleness," *Callaloo* 13 (4): 886–909.

Bernard, Shane K. 1996. *Swamp Pop: Cajun and Creole Rhythm and Blues*. Jackson: University Press of Mississippi.

Bewaji, J. A. I. 2003. *Beauty and Culture: Perspectives in Black Aesthetics*. Ibadan, Nigeria: Spectrum Books Limited.

———. 2011. "Epistemicide, Epistemic Deficit, Sterile Leadership and the Vicious Cycle of African Underdevelopment." Paper presented at the Caribbean Philosophical Association meeting, October 2011, Rutgers University at New Brunswick.

Bhabha, Homi K. 1994. *Location of Culture*. London and New York: Routledge.

Bickerton, Derek. 1977. "Pidginization and Creolization: Language acquisition and language universals." In *Pidgin and Creole Linguistics*, edited by Albert Valdman, 49–69. Bloomington: Indiana University Press.

Biko, Steve. 2002. *I Write What I Like: Selected Writings*. Edited by Aelred Stubbs C. R., preface by Archbishop Desmond Tutu, introduction by Malusi and Thoko Mpumlwana, and new foreword by Lewis R. Gordon. Chicago: University of Chicago Press.

Black, Jeff J. S. 2009. *Rousseau's Critique of Science: A Commentary on the Discourse on the Sciences and the Arts*. Lanham, MD: Lexington Books.

Bloom, Allan. 1990. *Giants and Dwarfs: Essays, 1960–1990*. New York: Simon and Schuster.

Blyden, Edward Wilmot. 1994. *African Life and Customs*. Baltimore, MD: Black Classics Press.

Bolland, O. Nigel. 2006. "Reconsidering Creolization and Creole Societies." *Shibboleths: Journal of Comparative Theory* 1 (1): 1–14.

Bondy, François. 1966. "The Black Rousseau." *New York Review of Books* 6 (March 31). www.nybooks.com/articles/archive/1966/mar/31/the-black-rousseau/.

Boulle, Pierre H. 2007. *Race et esclavage dans La France de l'Ancien Régime*. Paris: Perrin.

Bowden, Brett. 2008. "The Ebb and Flow of Peoples, Ideas, and Innovations in the River of Inter-civilizational Relations: Toward a Global History of Political Thought." In *Western Political Thought In Dialogue With Asia*, edited by Takashi Shogimen and Cary J. Nederman, 87–108. Lanham, MD: Lexington Books.

Boxill, Bernard R. 1992. *Blacks and Social Justice*. Revised Edition. Lanham, MD: Rowman and Littlefield.

———. 2005. "Rousseau, Natural Man, and Race." In *Race and Racism in Modern Philosophy*, edited by Andrew Valls, 150–68. Ithaca, NY: Cornell University Press.

Braidwood, Stephen J. 1994. *Black Poor and White Philanthropists: London's Blacks and the Sierra Leone Settlement*. Liverpool: University of Liverpool Press.

Brathwaite, Edward Kamau. 1971. *The Development of Creole Society in Jamaica: 1770–1820*. Oxford: Clarendon Press.

———. 1974. *Contraditory Omens: Cultural Diversity and Integration in the Caribbean*. Mona, Jamaica: Savacou Publications.

Browers, Michaelle. 2008. "The Reconciliation of Political Theory and Comparative Politics." In *New Approaches to Comparative Politics: Insights from Political Theory*, edited by Jennifer S. Holmes, 7–22. Lanham, MD: Lexington Books.

Buck-Morss, Susan. 2000. "Hegel and Haiti." *Critical Inquiry* 27 (4): 821–65.

———. 2009. *Hegel, Haiti, and Universal History*. Pittsburgh, PA: University of Pittsburgh Press.

Bulhan, Hussein Abdilahi. 1985. *Frantz Fanon and the Psychology of Oppression*. New York: Plenum Press.
Canovan, Margaret. 2005. *The People*. Cambridge, UK: Polity.
Carson, Anne, translator. 2003. *If not, Winter: Fragments of Sappho*. New York: Knopf.
Cassirer, Ernst. 1944. *An Essay on Man: An Introduction to a Philosophy of Human Culture*. New Haven, CT: Yale University Press.
Caws, Peter. 1992. "Sartrean Structuralism?" In *The Cambridge Companion to Sartre*, edited by Christina Howells, 293–317. Cambridge: Cambridge University Press.
Charvet, John. 1974. *The Social Problem in the Philosophy of Rousseau*. London: Cambridge University Press.
Chaudenson, Robert. 1989. *Créoles et enseignement du français*. Paris: L'Harmattan.
———. 2001. *Creolization of Language and Culture*. Revised in collaboration with Salikoko S. Mufwene and translated by Sheri Pargman, Salikoko S. Mufwene, Sabrina Billings, and Michelle AuCoin. London: Routledge.
Cherki, Alice. 2006. *Frantz Fanon: A Portrait*. Translated by Nadia Benabid. Ithaca, NY: Cornell University Press.
Cladis, Mark 2003. *Public Vision, Private Lives: Rousseau, Religion, and 21st-Century Democracy*. New York: Oxford University Press.
Cohen, Robin, and Paola Toninato. 2010. "The Creolization Debate: Analysing Mixed Identities and Cultures." In *The Creolization Reader: Studies in Mixed Identities and Cultures*, edited by Robin Cohen and Paola Toninato, 1–22. London: Routledge.
Confiant, Raphaël. 2009. "Le Creole, Cette Langue Orpheline" (2è partie et fin). *Chronique du temps present* (Novembre). www.montraykreyol.org/spip.php?article3168.
Constant, Benjamin. 1997. "The Liberty of the Ancients Compared with that of the Moderns." In *The Libertarian Reader: Classic and Contemporary Readings from Lao-tzu to Milton Friedman*, 65–70. New York: The Free Press.
Cooper, Laurence. 1999. *Rousseau, Nature, and the Problem of the Good Life*. University Park, PA: Pennsylvania State University Press.
Cordova, V. F. 2007. *How It Is: The Native American Philosophy of V. F. Cordova*. Edited by Kathleen Dean Moore, Kurt Peters, Ted Jojola, and Amber Lacy, with a foreword by Linda Hogan. Tucson: University of Arizona Press.
Cornell, Drucilla, and Kenneth Michael Panfilio. 2010. *Symbolic Forms for a New Humanity: Cultural and Racial Reconfigurations of Critical Theory*. New York: Fordham University Press.

Cranston, Maurice. 1982. *Jean-Jacques: The Early Life and Works of Jean-Jacques Rousseau, 1712–1754*. Chicago: University of Chicago Press.

———. 1991. *The Noble Savage: Jean-Jacques Rousseau, 1754–1762*. Chicago: University of Chicago Press.

Crichlow, Michaeline A., with Patrician Northover. 2009. *Globalization and the Post-Creole Imagination: Notes on Fleeing the Plantation*. Durhan, NC: Duke University Press.

Crocker, Lester. 1995. "Rousseau's *soi-disant* liberty." In *Rousseau and Liberty*, edited by Robert Wokler, 244–66. Manchester: Manchester University Press.

Curry, Tommy. 2009. "From Rousseau's Theory of Natural Equality to Firmin's Resistance to the Historical Inequality of Races." *C. L. R. James Journal: A Review of Caribbean Ideas* 15 (1): 135–63.

Curtin, Phillip D. 1969. *The Atlantic Slave Trade: A Census*. Madison: University of Wisconsin Press.

Dagger, Richard. 1997. *Civic Virtues: Rights, Citizenship, and Republican Liberalism*. New York: Oxford University Press.

Dahl, Robert. 2004. "What Have We Learned." In *Problems and Methods in the Study of Politics*, edited by Ian Shapiro, Rogers M. Smith, and Tarek E. Masoud, 377–94. Cambridge: Cambridge University Press.

Dallmayr, Fred. 1996. *Beyond Orientalism: Essays on Cross-Cultural Encounter*. Albany: State University of New York Press.

———, ed. 1999. *Border Crossings: Toward a Comparative Political Theory*. Lanham, MD: Lexington Books.

———. 2004. "Beyond Monologue: For a Comparative Political Theory" *Perspectives on Politics* 2 (2): 249–57.

———, ed. 2010. *Comparative Political Theory: An Introduction*. New York: Palgrave Macmillan.

Dallmayr, Fred, and Abbas Manoochehri, eds. 2007. *Civilizational Dialogue and Political Thought: Tehran Papers*. Lanham, MD: Lexington Books.

Damrosch, Leo. 2005. *Jean-Jacques Rousseau: Restless Genius*. Boston and New York: Houghton Mifflin.

Darnton, Robert. 1984. *The Great Cat Massacre and Other Episodes in French Cultural History*. New York: Viking.

Dayan-Herzbrun, Sonia. 2008. "Présentation." *Tumultes: "Vers une pensée politique postcoloniale à partir de Frantz Fanon,"* 31 (Octobre): 5–10.

De Beer, Sir Gavin. 1972. *Jean-Jacques Rousseau and His World*. New York: G. P. Putnam's Sons.

de Certeau, Michel. 1984. *The Practice of Everyday Life*. Berkeley: University of California Press.

DeGraff, Michel. 2003. "Against Creole Exceptionalism." *Language* 79 (2): 391–410.

de las Casas, Bartolomé. 1992. *In Defense of the Indians*. Translated by Stafford Poole, foreword by Martin E. Marty. DeKalb: Northern Illinois University Press.

de Maistre, Joseph. 1971. *The Works of Joseph De Maistre*. Translated by Jack Lively, foreword by Robert Nisbet. New York: Schocken Books.

Diaz, Vincente. 2006. "Creolization and indigeneity." *American Ethnologist* 33 (4): 576–78.

Dillard, J. L. 1970. "Principles in the history of American English: Paradox, Virginity, and Cafeteria." *Florida Foreign Language Reporter* 8: 32–33.

Djemaï, Cheikh, 2001. *Frantz Fanon: His Life, His Struggle, His Work*. New York: ArtMattan Productions.

Dobie, Madeleine. 2010. *Trading Places: Colonization and Slavery in Eighteenth-Century French Culture*. Ithaca, NY: Cornell University Press.

Du Bois, Laurent, and Bernard Camier. 2007. "Voltaire, Zaïre, Dessalines: Le Théâtre des Lumières dans L'Atlantique français," *Revue d'histoire moderne et Contemporaine* 54, no. 4 (December): 39–69.

Du Bois, W. E. B. 1938. *Black Reconstruction in America, 1860–1880*. New York: Harcourt, Brace.

———. 1962. *John Brown*. New York: International Publishers.

———. 1968. *The Autobiography of W. E. B. Du Bois: A Soliloquy on Viewing My Life from the Last Decade of Its First Century*. New York: International Publishers.

———. [1903] 1969. *The Souls of Black Folk*. New York: Signet Classics.

———. [1939] 1975. *Black Folk: Then And Now; An Essay In The History And Sociology Of The Negro Race*. Millwood, NY: Kraus-Thomson Organization.

———. [1928] 1995. *Dark Princess: A Romance*. Introduction by Claudia Tate. Jackson: University Press of Mississippi.

———. [1897] 1996. *The Philadelphia Negro*. Introduction by Elijah Anderson. Philadelphia: University of Pennsylvania Press.

———. [1940] 1997. *Dusk of Dawn: An Essay Toward an Autobiography of a Race Concept*. New Brunswick, NJ: Transaction Publishers.

———. [1921] 1999. *Darkwater: Voices from within the Veil*. Introduction by Manning Marable. Mineola, MI: Dover Publications.

———. 2000a. "The Study of the Negro Problems." *The Annals of the American Academy of Political and Social Science* 56: 13–27. [Originally published in the same journal in 1898.]

———. 2000b. "Sociology Hesitant." *boundary 2* 27 (3): 37–44.

Duchet, Michèle. 1971. *Anthropologie et histoire au siècle des lumières: Buffon, Voltaire, Rousseau, Helvétius, Diderot*. Paris: Librairie François Maspero.

During, Simon. 1994. "Rousseau's patrimony: primitivism, romance, and becoming other." In *Colonial Discourse/Postcolonial Theory*, edited by Francis Barker, Peter Hulme, and Margaret Iversion, 47–71. Manchester, UK: Manchester University Press.

Durkheim, Emile. 1960. *Montesquieu and Rousseau: Forerunners of Sociology*. Foreword by Henri Peyre. Ann Arbor: University of Michigan Press.

Dussel, Enrique. 2008. *Twenty Theses on Politics*. Translated by George Ciccariello-Maher. Durham, NC: Duke University Press.

Dworkin, Ronald. 1986. *Law's Empire*. Cambridge, MA: Harvard University Press.

Ehlen, Patrick. 2000. *Frantz Fanon: A Spiritual Biography*. New York: The Crossroad Publishing Company.

Eriksen, Thomas Hylland. 2007. "Creolization in Anthropological Theory and in Mauritius." In *Creolization: History, Ethnography, Theory*, edited by Charles Stewart, 153–77. Walnut Creek, CA: Left Coast Press.

Euben, Roxanne L. 1999. *Enemy in the Mirror: Islamic Fundamentalism and the Limits of Modern Rationalism: A Work of Comparative Political Theory*. Princeton, NJ: Princeton University Press.

———. 2008. *Journeys to the Other Shore: Muslim and Western Travelers in Search of Knowledge*. Princeton, NJ: Princeton University Press.

Fabian, Johannes. 1983. *Time and the Other: How Anthropology Makes Its Object*. New York: Columbia University Press.

Fanon, Frantz. 1952. *Peau noire, masques blancs*. Paris: Éditions du Seuil.

———. 1963. *The Wretched of the Earth*. Translated by Constance Farrington, introduction by Jean-Paul Sartre. New York: Grove Press.

———. 1967a. *A Dying Colonialism*. Translated by Haakon Chevalier, introduction by Adolfo Gilly. New York: Grove Weidenfeld.

———. 1967b. *Black Skin, White Masks*. Translated by Charles Lamm Markman. New York: Grove Press.

———. 1967c. *Toward the African Revolution*. Translated by Haakon Chevalier. New York: Grove Press.

———. 1967d. "The North African Syndrome." In *Toward the African Revolution*, translated by Haakon Chevalier, 3–16. New York: Grove Press.

———. 1967e. "Racism and Culture." In *Toward the African Revolution*, translated by Haakon Chevalier, 29–44. New York: Grove Press.

Filmer, Sir Robert. 1680. *Patriarcha; or the Natural Power of Kings*. London: Walter Davis.

Fischer, Sibylle. 2006. "Unthinkable History? The Haitian Revolution, Historiography, and Modernity on the Periphery." In *A Companion to African-American Studies*, edited by Lewis R. and Jane Anna Gordon, 360–76. Malden, MA: Blackwell.

Fleischmann, Ulrich. 2003. "The Sociocultural and Linguistic Profile of a Concept." In *A Pepper-Pot of Cultures: Aspects of Creolization in the Caribbean*, edited by Gordon Collier and Ulrich Fleishmann, xv–xxxvi. Amsterdam: Rodopi B.V.

Frank, Jason. 2010. *Constituent Moments: Enacting the People in Postrevolutionary America*. Durham and London: Duke University Press.

Freire, Paulo. 2005. *Pedagogy of the Oppressed*. 30th Anniversary Edition. Translated by Myra Bergman Ramos, introduction by Donaldo Macedo. New York: Continuum.

Frere-Jones, Sasha. 2009. "Roundtable: Haitian Music, Part 2: 'What Does Revolution Sound Like?'" *The New Yorker* (July 13). www.newyorker.com/online/blogs/sashafrerejones/2009/07/haitian-music-part-2-what-does-revolution-sound-like.html.

Freud, Sigmund. 1961. *Civilization and Its Discontents*. Translated and edited by James Strachey. New York: W. W. Norton & Co.

Gal, S. 1989. "Language and Political Economy." *Annual Review of Anthropology* 18: 345–67.

Garrard, Graeme. 2003. *Rousseau's Counter-Enlightenment: A Republican Critique of the Philosophes*. Albany: State University of New York Press.

Gates, Henry Louis Jr. 2010. *Tradition and the Black Atlantic: Critical Theory in the African Diaspora*. New York: Basic Books.

Gay, Peter. 1987. Introduction to *Jean-Jacques Rousseau: The Basic Political Writings*, translated by Donald A. Cress, vii–xvii. Indianapolis, IN: Hackett Publishing Company.

Gebhardt, Jürgen. 2008. "Political Thought in an Intercivilizational Pespective: A Critical Reflection." *The Review of Politics* 70: 5–22.

Geertz, Clifford. 1973. *The Interpretation of Cultures*. New York: Basic Books.

Geismar, Peter. 1971. *Fanon*. New York: Dial Press.

Germain, Felix. 2011. "In Search of Full Citizenship: The French West Indian Case (1848–2009)." *Journal of Contemporary Thought* (Winter): 99–112.

Getachew, Adom. 2011. "Reconceptualizing the Universal in the Haitian Revolution." Paper presented at the Caribbean Philosophical Association meeting, Rutgers University, New Brunswick.

Geuss, Raymond. 2008. *Philosophy and Real Politics*. Princeton, NJ: Princeton University Press.

Gibson, Nigel. 2011. "Introduction: Living Fanon?" In *Living Fanon: Global Perspectives*, edited by Nigel Gibson, 1–10. New York: Palgrave Macmillan.

Gilroy, Paul. 1993. *The Black Atlantic: Modernity and Double Consciousness*. Cambridge, MA: Harvard University Press.

Glissant, Edouard. 2008. "Creolization and the Making of the Americas." *Caribbean Quarterly* 54 (1–2): 81–89.

Godrej, Farah. 2006. "Nonviolence and Gandhi's Truth: A Method for Moral and Political Arbitration." *The Review of Politics* 68 (2): 287–317.

———. 2009. "Towards a Cosmopolitan Political Thought: The Hermeneutics of Interpreting the Other." *Polity* 41 (2): 135–65.

Gordon, Jane Anna. 2006. "Challenges Posed to Social-Scientific Method by the Study of Race." In *A Companion to African-American Studies*, edited by Lewis R. Gordon and Jane Anna Gordon, 279–304. Malden, MA: Blackwell.

———. 2009. "Hannah Arendt's Political Theology of Democratic Life." *Journal of Political Theology* 10 (1): 327–42.

Gordon, Jane Anna, and Lewis R Gordon. 2006. "On Working through a Most Difficult Terrain: Introducing *A Companion to African-American Studies*." In *A Companion to African-American Studies*, edited with an introduction by Lewis R. Gordon and Jane Anna Gordon, xx–xxxv. Malden, MA: Blackwell Publishers.

———. 2009. *Of Divine Warning: Reading Disaster in the Modern Age*. Boulder, CO: Paradigm Publishers.

Gordon, Jane Anna, and Neil Roberts. 2009. "Introduction: The Project of Creolizing Rousseau." *The C. L. R. James Journal: A Review of Caribbean Ideas* 15 (1): 1–16.

Gordon, Lewis R. 2000. *Existentia Africana: Understanding Existential Thought*. New York: Routledge.

———. 2006. *Disciplinary Decadence: Living Thought in Trying Times*. Boulder, CO: Paradigm Publishers.

———. 2008a. "Décoloniser le savoir à la suite de Frantz Fanon." *Tumultes* 31: 103–23.

———. 2008b. "Phenomenology of Biko's Black Consciousness." In *Biko Lives!: Contestations and Conversations*, edited by Amanda Alexander, Nigel Gibson, and Andile Mngxitama, 83–93. New York: Palgrave.

———. 2008c. *An Introduction to Africana Philosophy*. Cambridge: Cambridge University Press.

———. 2010a. "Fanon on Decolonizing Knowledge." In *Fanon and the Decolonization of Philosophy*, edited by Elizabeth A. Hope and Tracey Nicholls, with a foreword by Mireille Fanon-Mendès-France, 3–18. Landham, MD: Lexington Books.

———. 2010b. "The Market Colonization of Intellectuals," *truthout* (April 6). www.truthout.org/the-market-colonization-intellectuals58310.

Gould, Stephen Jay. 1996. *The Mismeasure of Man*. Revised and Expanded. New York: W. W. Norton.

Gramsci, Antonio. 1971. *Selections from the Prison Notebooks*. Translated and edited by Quintin Hoare and Geoffrey Nowell Smith. New York: International Publishers.

Grofman, Bernard, and Scott L. Feld. 1988. "Rousseau's General Will: A Condorcetian Perspective." *American Political Science Review* 83 (June): 567–76.

Gyekye, Kwame. 1997. *Tradition and Modernity: Philosophical Reflections on the African Experience.* Oxford: Oxford University Press.

Hall, Stuart. 1999. "Thinking the Diaspora: Home-Thoughts from Abroad," *Small Axe* 6 (September): 1–18.

Hampsher-Monk, Iain. 1995. "Rousseau and totalitarianism: with hindsight?" In *Rousseau and Liberty*, edited by Robert Wokler, 267–88. Manchester: University of Manchester Press.

Hannerz, Ulf. 1992. *Cultural Complexity: Studies in the Social Organization of Meaning.* New York: Columbia University Press.

———. 2006. "Theorizing the New World? Not Really." *American Ethnologist* 33 (4): 563–65.

Harris, Wilson. 1998. "Creoleness: The Crossroads of a Civilization?" In *Caribbean Creolization: Reflections on the Cultural Dynamics of Language, Literature, and Identity*, edited by Kathleen M. Balutansky and Marie-Agnès Sourieau, 23–35. Gainesville: University Press of Florida/Mona, Jamaica: The Press University of the West Indies.

Hart, H. L. A. 1961. *The Concept of Law.* Oxford: Clarendon Press.

Hegel, G. W. F. 1991. *Elements of the Philosophy of Right.* Translated by H. B. Nisbet and edited by A. Wood. Cambridge: Cambridge University Press.

Helenon, Veronique. 2011. "'Tis distance lends enchantment to the view'— Distance as a Mode of Domination: Legal Elements of the Slave and Colonial Periods." *Journal of Contemporary Thought* (Winter): 91–98.

Henry, Paget. 2000. *Caliban's Reason: Introducing Afro-Caribbean Philosophy.* New York: Routledge.

———. 2005. "Africana Phenomenology: A Philosophical Look," *The C. L. R. James Journal: A Review of Caribbean Ideas* 11 (1): 79–112.

———. 2009a "C. L. R. James and the Creolizing of Rousseau and Marx." *The C. L. R. James Journal: A Review of Caribbean Ideas* 15 (1): 178–205.

———. 2009b. "Africana Studies as an Interdisciplinary Discipline." Paper prepared for a departmental session devoted to articulating the aims of the new doctoral program in Africana Studies at Brown University.

Hintzen, Percy. 2006. "The Caribbean: Race and Creole Ethnicity." In *Cultural Identity and Creolization in National Unity: The Multiethnic Caribbean*, edited by Prem Misir, 9–31. Lanham, MD: University Press of America.

Hirschmann, Nancy. 1992. *Rethinking Obligation: A Feminist Method for Political Theory.* Ithaca, NY: Cornell University Press.

Hobbes, Thomas. 2000. *Leviathan.* Edited by Richard Tuck. Cambridge: Cambridge University Press.

Honig, Bonnie. 2001. *Democracy and the Foreigner*. Princeton, NJ: Princeton University Press.
———. 2007. Between Decision and Deliberation: Political Paradox in Democratic Theory. *The American Political Science Review* 101 (1): 1–18.
Huntington, Samuel. 1993. "The Clash of Civilizations?" *Foreign Affairs* (Summer).
———. 1996. *The Clash of Civilizations and the Remaking of World Order*. New York: Touchstone.
Irvine, Judith T., and Susan Gal. 2000. "Language Ideology and Linguistic Differentiation." In *Regimes of Language: Ideologies, Polities, and Identities*, edited by Paul V. Kroskrity, 35–83. Sante Fe, NM: School of American Research Press.
Isaac, Jeffrey C. 1998. *Democracy in Dark Times*. Ithaca, NY: Cornell University Press.
James, C. L. R. 1989. *The Black Jacobins: Toussaint L'Ouverture and the San Domingo Revolution*. Second Revised Edition. New York: Vintage Books.
Jameson, Fredric. 2009. *Valences of the Dialectic*. New York: Verso.
Jaspers, Karl. 1957. *Man in the Modern Age*. New York: Anchor Books.
Jenco, Leigh Kathryn. 2007. "What Does Heaven Ever Say: A Methods-centered Approach to Cross-cultural Engagement," *American Political Science Review* 101 (4): 741–55.
Johnson, Walter. 2003. "On Agency." *Journal of Social History* 37 (1): 113–24.
Johnston, Steven. 1999. *Encountering Tragedy: Rousseau and the Project of Democratic Order*. Ithaca, NY: Cornell University Press.
Jung, Hwa Yol. 1999. "Postmodernity, Eurocentrism, and the Future of Political Philosophy." In *Border Crossings: Toward a Comparative Political Theory*, 277–96. Lanham, MD: Lexington Books.
———. 2002. *Comparative Political Culture in the Age of Globalization*. Lanham, MD: Lexington Books.
———. 2007. "Merleau-Ponty's Transversal Geophilosophy and Sinic Aesthetics of Nature." In *Merleau-Ponty and Environmental Philosophy: Dwelling on the Landscapes of Thought (SUNY Series in the Philosophy of the Social Sciences)*, edited by Suzanne L. Cataldi and William S. Hamrick, 235–58. Albany: State University of New York Press.
Keenan, Alan. 2003. *Democracy in Question: Democratic Openness in a Time of Political Closure*. Stanford, CA: Stanford University Press.
Kein, Sybil. 2000. "The Use of Louisiana Creole in Southern Literature." In *Creole: The History and Legacy of Louisiana's Free People of Color*, edited by Sybil Kein, 117–56. Baton Rouge: Louisiana State University Press.
Kelly, Christopher. Introduction to *The Plan for Perpetual Peace, On the Government of Poland, and Other Writings on History and Politics*. Vol. 11 of *The*

Collected Writings of Rousseau, translated by Christopher Kelly and Judith Bush and edited by Christopher Kelly, xiii–xxiii. Hanover, NH: Dartmouth College Press.

Kennedy, Ellen. 2004. *Constitutional Failure: Carl Schmitt in Weimar*. Durham, NC: Duke University Press.

Khan, Aisha. 2006. "Feats of engineering: Theory, ethnography, and other problems of model building in the social sciences." *American Ethnologist* 33 (4): 566–70.

Knies, Kenneth Danziger. 2006. "The Idea of Post-European Science: An Essay on Phenomenology and Africana Studies." In *Not Only the Master's Tools: African-American Studies in Theory and Practice*, edited by Lewis R. Gordon and Jane Anna Gordon, 85–106. Boulder, CO: Paradigm Publishers.

Kobayashi, Takuya. n.d. "Chronologie de Jean-Jacques Rousseau: présentation en photos de tous les lieux qu'il a habités et visités." www.rousseau-chronologie.com.

Kompridis, Nikolas. 2005. "Normativizing Hybridity/Neutralizing Culture." *Political Theory* 33, no. 3 (June): 318–43.

———. 2009. "Romanticism." In *The Oxford Handbook of Philosophy and Literature*, edited by Richard Eldridge, 247–70. Oxford: Oxford University Press.

Kymlicka, Will. 1995. *Multicultural Citizenship: A Liberal Theory of Minority Rights*. Oxford: Clarendon Press.

Larson, Gerald James. 1988. "Introduction: The 'Age-Old Distinction Between the Same and the Other.'" In *Interpreting Across Boundaries: News Essays in Comparative Philosophy*, edited by Gerald James Larson and Eliot Deutsch, 3–18. Princeton, NJ: Princeton University Press.

Lau, Wai-keung. 2010. *Legend of the Fist: The Return of Chen Zhen*.

Lévi-Strauss, Claude. 1966. *The Savage Mind*. Chicago: University of Chicago Press.

Lionnet, Françoise, and Shu-mei Shih. 2011. *The Creolization of Theory*. Durham, NC: Duke University Press.

Luxemburg, Rosa. 2004. "This Historical Conditions of Accumulation, from *The Accumulation of Capital*." In *The Rosa Luxemburg Reader*, edited with an introduction by Peter Hudis and Kevin B. Anderson. 32–70. New York: Monthly Review Press.

Lynch, John. 2006. *Simón Bolívar: A Life*. New Haven, CT: Yale University Press.

Macey, David. 2002. *Frantz Fanon: A Biography*. New York: Picador.

Machiavelli, Niccolò. 2005. *The Prince*. Translated by Peter Bondanella, introduction by Maurizio Viroli. Oxford: Oxford World's Classics.

Maldonado Torres, Nelson. 2008. *Against War: Views from the Underside of Modernity.* Durham, NC: Duke University Press.
———. 2009. "Rousseau and Fanon on Inequality and the Human Sciences." *The C. L. R. James Journal: A Review of Caribbean Ideas* 11 (1): 113–34.
March, Andrew. 2009. "What is Comparative Theory?" *The Review of Politics* 71 (4): 531–65.
Marx, Karl. 1976. *Capital: A Critique of Political Economy, Volume 1.* Introduction by Ernest Mandel, translated by Ben Fowkes. London: Penguin Books.
———. 1978. "Economic and Philosophical Manuscripts of 1844." In *The Marx-Engels Reader*, Second Edition, edited by Robert C. Tucker, 66–125. New York: W.W. Norton.
———. 1984. "Critical . . . Notes on . . . Social Reform." In *Legitimacy and the State*, edited by William Connolly, 20–31. New York: New York University Press.
McBride, William. 1980. *Social Theory at a Crossroads.* Pittsburgh, PA: Duquesne University Press.
———. 1991. *Sartre's Political Theory.* Bloomington: Indiana University Press.
McCormick, John. 2007. "Rousseau's Rome and the Repudiation of Republican Populism." *Critical Review of International Social and Political Philosophy (CRISPP)* 10 (1): 3–27.
———. 2011. *Machiavellian Democracy.* New York: Cambridge University Press.
McWhorter, John. 2001. *The Power of Babel: A Natural History of Language.* New York: Times Books.
Mehta, Brinda. 2004. *Diasporic (Dis)locations: Indo-Caribbean Women Writers Negotiate the Kala Pani.* Mona, Jamaica: University of the West Indies Press.
Meijer, Guus, and Pieter Muysken. 1977. "On the Beginnings of Pidgin and Creole Studies: Schuchardt and Hesseling." In *Pidgin and Creole Linguistics*, edited by Albert Valdman, 21–45. Bloomington: Indiana University Press.
Merleau-Ponty, Maurice. 1964. *Signs.* Translated with an introduction by Richard C. McCleary. Chicago: Northwestern University Press.
Mignolo, Walter. 2003. *The Darker Side of the Renaissance: Literacy, Territoriality, & Colonization.* Ann Arbor: University of Michigan Press.
Mintz, Sidney W. 1998. "The Localization of Anthropological Practice: From Area Studies to Transnationalism" *Critique of Anthropology* 18 (2): 117–33.
Misir, Prem. 2006. Introduction to *Cultural Identity and Creolization in National Unity: The Multiethnic Caribbean*, edited by Prem Misir, xxi–xxix. Lanham, MA: University Press of America.
Mngxitama, Andile, Amanda Alexander, and Nigel Gibson, eds. 2008. *Biko Lives!: Contestations and Conversations.* New York: Palgrave.

Monahan, Michael J. 2011. *The Creolizing Subject: Race, Reason, and the Politics of Purity*. New York: Fordham University Press.
Mohammed, Patricia. 1988. "The Creolization of Indian Women in Trinidad." In *Trinidad and Tobago: The Independence Experience 1962–1982*, edited by Selwyn Ryan, 381–413. Saint Augustine, Trinidad and Tobago: Institute of Social and Economic Research, University of the West Indies.
Montaigne, Michel D. 1934. *The Essays of Michel De Montaige, Volume I*. Translated and edited by Jacob Zeitlin. New York: Alfred A. Knopf.
Moody-Adams, Michele M. 1997. *Fieldwork in Familiar Places: Morality, Culture, and Philosophy*. Cambridge, MA: Harvard University Press.
Morello, Celeste A. 1999. *Before Bruno: The History of the Philadelphia Mafia, Book 1, 1880–1931*. N.p. [Library of Congress CIP Data: 00–130483. Printed in the United States.]
———. 2001. *Before Bruno: The History of the Philadelphia Mafia, Book 2, 1931–1946*. Philadelphia, PA: Jefferies & Manz, Inc.
Mufwene, Salikoko S. 1994. "On Decreolization: The Case of Gullah." In *Language and the Social Construction of Identity in Creole Situations*, edited by Marcyliena Morgan, 63–99. Los Angeles: Center for Afro-American Studies Publications.
———. 1998. "Creolization is a Social, Not a Structural, Process." Paper presented at the International Symposium on *Degrees of Restructuring in Creole languages*, Regensburg, June.
Munasinghe, Viranjini. 2006. "Theorizing World Culture Through the New World: East Indians and Creolization." *American Ethnologist* 33 (4): 549–62.
Muthu, Sankar. 2003. *Enlightenment Against Empire*. Princeton, NJ: Princeton University Press.
Näsström, Sofia. 2007. "The Legitimacy of the People." *Political Theory* 35 (5): 624–58.
Neidleman, Jason Andrew. 2001. *The General Will is Citizenship*. Lanham, MD: Rowman and Littlefield Publishers, Inc.
Nettl, Bruno. 1964. *Theory and Method in Ethnomusicology*. New York: The Free Press of Glencoe.
Nissim-Sabat, Marilyn. 2010. "Fanonian Musings: Decolonizing/Philosophy/Psychiatry." In *Fanon and the Decolonization of Philosophy*, edited by Elizabeth A. Hoppe and Tracey Nicholls, 39–56. Lanham, MD: Lexington Books.
Noël, Erick. 2006. *Etre noir en France au dix-huitième siècle*. Paris: Tallandier.
Noone, John B. Jr. 1980. *Rousseau's Social Contract*. Athens: University of Georgia Press.
Norton, Anne. 2004a. *95 Theses on Politics, Culture, and Method*. New Haven, CT: Yale University Press.

———. 2004b. "Political Science as a Vocation." In *Problems and Methods in the Study of Politics*, edited by Ian Shapiro, Rogers M. Smith, and Tarek E. Masoud, 67–82. Cambridge: Cambridge University Press.

Nouss, Alexis. 2009. "From Metiçagem to Cosmopolitanism." *The C. L. R. James Journal: A Review of Caribbean Ideas* 11 (1): 54–67.

Ogrodnick, Margaret. 1999. *Instinct and Intimacy: Political Philosophy and Autobiography in Rousseau*. Toronto: University of Toronto Press.

Ortega y Gasset, José. 1932. *The Revolt of the Masses*. New York: W. W. Norton.

Orwell, George. 2005. "Politics and the English Language." In *Why I Write*. New York: Penguin Books.

Ovid. 1924. *Tristia/Ex Ponto*. Translated by Arthur Leslie Wheeler. London: William Heinemann.

Pagden, Anthony. 1993. *European Encounters with the New World*. New Haven, CT: Yale University Press.

Palmié, Stephan. 2006. "Creolization and Its Discontents." *Annual Review of Anthropology* 35: 433–56.

Parekh, Bhiku. 2000. *Rethinking Multiculturalism: Cultural Diversity and Political Theory*. Cambridge, MA: Harvard University Press.

Parkvall, Mikael. 2000. *Out of Africa: African influences in Atlantic Creoles*. London: Battlebridge.

Peabody, Sue. 1996. *"There are No Slaves in France": The Political Culture of Race and Slavery in the Ancien Régime*. New York: Oxford University Press.

Pépin, Ernest, and Raphaël Confiant. 1998. "The Stakes of Créolité." In *Caribbean Creolization: Reflections on the Cultural Dynamics of Language, Literature, and Identity*, edited by Kathleen M. Balutansky and Marie-Agnès Sourieau, 96–100. Gainesville: University Press of Florida/Mona, Jamaica: The Press University of the West Indies.

Piven, Frances Fox. 2004. "The Politics of Policy Science." In *Problems and Methods in the Study of Politics*, edited by Ian Shapiro, Rogers M. Smith, and Tarek E, 83–105. Masoud. Cambridge: Cambridge University Press.

Prasad, Vijay. 2002. *Everybody was Kung Fu Fighting*. Boston: Beacon Press.

Pratt, Mary Louise. 1992. *Imperial Eyes: Travel Writing and Transculturation*. New York: Routledge.

Puri, Shalini. 2004. *The Caribbean Postcolonial: Social Equality, Post-Nationalism, and Cultural Hybridity*. New York: Palgrave.

Rawls, John. 1971. *A Theory of Justice*. Cambridge, MA: Belknap Press of Harvard University Press.

———. 1993. *Political Liberalism*. New York: Columbia University Press.

———. 1999. *The Law of Peoples*. Cambridge, MA: Harvard University Press.

Rehfeld, Andrew. 2010. "Offensive Political Theory." *Perspectives on Politics* 8 (2): 465–86.
Reinhardt, Catherine A. 2006. *Claims to Memory: Beyond Slavery and Emancipation in the French Caribbean*. New York: Berghahn Books.
Reisman, Karl. 1970. "Cultural and Linguistic Ambiguity in a West Indian Village." In *Afro American Anthropology*, edited by Norman E. Whitten and John F. Szwed, 129–44. New York: The Free Press.
Renault, Matthieu. 2011. "Ruptre and New Beginning in Fanon: Elements for a Genealogy of Postcolonial Critique." In *Living Fanon: Global Perspectives*, edited by Nigel Gibson, 105–16. New York: Macmillan.
Riley, Patrick. 1982. *Will and Political legitimacy: A Critical Exposition of Social Contract Theory in Hobbes, Locke, Rousseau, Kant, and Hegel*. Cambridge, MA: Harvard University Press.
———. 1988. *The General Will Before Rousseau: The Transformation of the Divine into the Civic*. Princeton, NJ: Princeton University Press.
Robinson, Cedric J. 2001. *An Anthropology of Marxism*. Aldershot, UK: Ashgate.
Roden, Claudia. 1998. *The Book of Jewish Food: An Odyssey from Samarkand to New York*. New York: Alfred A. Knopf.
Romaine, Suzanne. 1994. "Language Standardization and Linguistic Fragmentation in Tok Pisin." In *Language and the Social Construction of Identity in Creole Situations*, edited by Marcyliena Morgan, 19–42. Los Angeles: Center for Afro-American Studies Publications.
Romberg, Raquel. 2002. "Revisiting Creolization." www.sas.upenn.edu/folklore/center/ConferenceArchive/voiceover/creolization.html.
Rosenblatt, Helena. 1997. *Rousseau and Geneva: From the First Discourse to the Social Contract, 1749–1762*. New York: Cambridge University Press.
Rousseau, Jean-Jacques. 1928. *The Confessions of Jean-Jacques Rousseau*. Translated by W. Conyngham Mallory. New York: Tudor Publishing Company.
———. 1960. *Politics and the Arts: Letter to M. D'Alembert on the Theatre*. Translated with notes and an introduction by Allan Bloom. Ithaca, NY: Cornell University Press.
———. 1964. *Oeuvres complètes de J.-J. Rousseau, volume 3*. Edited by B. Gagnebin et al. Paris: Bibliothèque de la Pléiade.
———. 1979. *Emile or On Education*. Translated with an introduction and notes by Allan Bloom. New York: Basic Books.
———. 1987. *The Basic Political Writings*. Edited and translated by Donald A. Cress, introduction by Peter Gay. Indianapolis, IN: Hackett Publishers.
———. 1992a. *Discourse on the Sciences and Arts (First Discourse) and Polemics*. Vol. 2 of *The Collected Writings of Rousseau*. Edited by Roger D. Masters

and Christopher Kelly, translated by Judith R. Bush, Roger D. Masters, and Christopher Kelly. Hanover, NH: University Press of New England.

———. 1992b. "Letter to M. the Abbé Raynal." In *Discourse on the Sciences and Arts (First Discourse) and Polemics*. Edited by Roger D. Masters and Christopher Kelly, translated by Judith R. Bush, Roger D. Masters, and Christopher Kelly, 25–27. Hanover, NH: University Press of New England.

———. 1992c. "Letter . . . to Mr. Grimm." In *Discourse on the Sciences and Arts (First Discourse) and Polemics*, 84–92.

———. 1992d. "Final Reply." In *Discourse on the Sciences and Arts (First Discourse) and Polemics*, 110–29.

———. 1992e. "Preface to a Second Letter to Bordes." In *Discourse on the Sciences and Arts (First Discourse) and Polemics*, 182–85.

———. 1992f. "Preface to Narcissus." In *Discourse on the Sciences and Arts (First Discourse) and Polemics*, 186–98.

———. 1992g. *Discourse on the Origins of Inequality (Second Discourse), Polemics, and Political Economy*. Vol. 3 of *The Collected Writings of Rousseau*. Edited by Roger D. Masters and Christopher Kelly, translated by Judith R. Bush, Roger D. Masters, Christopher Kelly, and Terence Marshall. Hanover, NH: University Press of New England.

———. 1994. *Social Contract, Discourse on the Virtue Most Necessary for a Hero, Political Fragments, and Geneva Manuscript*. Vol. 4 of *The Collected Writings of Rousseau*. Edited by Roger D. Masters and Christopher Kelly, translated by Judith R. Bush, Roger D. Masters, and Christopher Kelly. Hanover, NH: University Press of New England.

———. 1995. *The Confessions and Correspondence, Including the Letters to Malesherbes*. Vol. 5 of *The Collected Writings of Rousseau*. Edited by Christopher Kelly, Roger D. Masters, and Peter G. Stillman. Hanover, NH: University Press of New England.

———. 1997. *Julie, or the New Heloise: Letters of Two Lovers Who Live in a Small Town at the Foot of the Alps*. Vol. 6 of *The Collected Writings of Rousseau*. Edited by Christopher Kelly, Roger D. Masters, and Peter F. Stillman, translated by Christopher Kelly. Hanover, NH: University Press of New England.

———. 1998a. *Essay on the Origin of Languages and Writings Related to Music*. Vol. 7 of *The Collected Writings of Rousseau*. Translated and edited by John T. Scott. Hanover, NH: University Press of New England.

———. 1998b. "Dissertation on Modern Music." In *Essay on the Origin of Languages and Writings Related to Music*, translated and edited by John T. Scott, 27–98. Hanover, NH: University Press of New England.

———. 2004. "The Discovery of the New World." Translated and edited by Christopher Kelly. In *Letter to D'Alembert and Writings for Theater*. Vol. 10

of *The Collected Writings of Rousseau*, edited and translated by Allan Bloom, Charles Butterworth, and Christopher Kelly, 12–36. Hanover, NH: University Press of New England.

———. 2005. "Plan for a Constitution for Corsica." In *The Plan for Perpetual Peace, On the Government of Poland, and Other Writings on History and Politics. Vol. 11 of The Collected Writings of Rousseau*, translated by Christopher Kelly and Judith Bush, edited by Christopher Kelly, 123–55. Hanover, NH: University Press of New England.

Said, Edward. 1989. "Representing the Colonized: Anthropology's Interlocutors." *Critical Inquiry* 15 (Winter): 223–25.

Sala-Molins, Louis. 2006. *Dark Side of the Light: Slavery and the French Enlightenment*. Translated with an introduction by John Conteh-Morgan. Minneapolis: University of Minnesota Press.

Sartre, Jean-Paul. 1963. Preface to *The Wretched of the Earth*, 7–31. New York: Grove Press.

Schapiro, Leonard. 1972. *Totalitarianism*. London: Macmillan.

Schmitt, Carl. 1996. *The Concept of the Political*. Translated with an introduction and notes by George Schwab. Chicago: University of Chicago Press.

Schwartz, Gary. 1997. "Toni Morrison at the Movies: Theorizing Race through *Imitation of Life*." In *Existence in Black: An Anthology of Black Existential Philosophy*, edited with an introduction by Lewis R. Gordon, 111–28. New York: Routledge.

Schwartz, Joseph M. 2008. *The Future of Democratic Equality: Rebuilding Social Solidarity in Fragmented America*. New York: Routledge.

Scott, John T. 1997. "Rousseau and the Melodious Language of Freedom." *Journal of Politics* 59 (3): 803–29.

———. 1998. Introduction to *Essay on the Origin of Languages and Writings Related to Music. Vol. 7 of The Collected Writings of Rousseau*, edited and translated by John T. Scott, xiii–xlii. Lebanon, NH: University of New England Press.

Segal, Daniel. 1993. "Race and 'Color' in Pre-Independence Trinidad and Tobago." In *Trinidad Ethnicity*, edited by Kevin Yelvington, 81–115. Knoxville: University of Tennessee Press.

Sekyi-Otu, Ato. 2011. "Fanon and the Possibility of Postcolonial Critical Imagination." In *Living Fanon: Global Perspectives*, edited by Nigel Gibson, 45–60. New York: Macmillan.

Seuren, Pieter A. M. 1998. *Western Linguistics: An Historical Introduction*. Oxford: Wiley-Blackwell.

Shapiro, Ian. 2004. "Problems, Methods, and Theories in the Study of Politics, or: What's Wrong with Political Science and What to do About It." In *Prob-

lems and Methods in the Study of Politics, edited by Ian Shapiro, Rogers M. Smith, and Tarek E. Masoud, 19–41. Cambridge: Cambridge University Press.

———. 2007. *The Flight from Reality in the Human Sciences*. Princeton, NJ: Princeton University Press.

Shapiro, Ian, Rogers M. Smith, and Tarek E. Masoud. 2004. *Problems and Methods in the Study of Politics*. Cambridge: Cambridge University Press.

Sheller, Mimi. 2003. *Consuming the Caribbean: From Arawaks to Zombies*. London: Routledge.

Shelley, Mary Wollstonecraft. 1985. "Introduction." In *Frankenstein or the Modern Prometheus*, Revised Edition, edited with an introduction and notes by Maurice Hindley, 5–10. London: Penguin Books.

Shilliam, Robbie. 2010. "Keskidee Aroha: Translation on the Colonial Stage." *Journal of Historical Sociology* 24 (1): 80–99.

———. 2012. "Civilization and the Poetics of Slavery." *Thesis Eleven: Critical Theory and Historical Sociology* 108 (1): 97–116.

Shklar, Judith N. 1969. *Men and Citizens*. London: Cambridge University Press.

———. 1988. "Jean-Jacques Rousseau and Equality." In *Rousseau's Political Writings*, translated by Julia Conaway Bondanella and edited by Alan Ritter, 260–73. New York: W. W. Norton.

Shulman, George. 2008. *American Prophecy: Race and Redemption in American Political Culture*. Minneapolis: University of Minnesota Press.

Sil, Rudra. 2004. "Problems Chasing Methods or Methods Chasing Problems? Research Communities, Constrained Pluralism, and the Role of Eclecticism." In *Problems and Methods in the Study of Politics*, edited by Ian Shapiro, Rogers M. Smith, and Tarek E. Masoud, 307–31. Cambridge: Cambridge University Press.

Song, Sarah. 2007. *Justice, Gender, and the Politics of Multiculturalism*. New York: Cambridge University Press.

Starobinski, Jean. 1977. "Eloquence and Liberty." *Journal of the History of Ideas* 38: 195–210.

———. 1988. *Jean-Jacques Rousseau: Transparency and Obstruction*. Translated by Arthur Goldhammer with an introduction by Robert J. Morrissey. Chicago: University of Chicago Press.

Swenson, James. 2000. *On Jean-Jacques Rousseau: Considered as One of the First Authors of the Revolution*. Stanford, CA: Stanford University Press.

Takaki, Ronald. 1998. *Strangers from a Different Shore: A History of Asian Americans*. Boston: Back Bay Books.

Talmon, J. L. [1986] 1952. *The Origins of Totalitarian Democracy*. London: Peregrine Books.

Taylor, Charles. 1994. "The Politics of Recognition." In *Multiculturalism: Examining the Politics of Recognition*, edited and introduced by Amy Gutmann, 25–74. Princeton, NJ: Princeton University Press.

Thomas, Deborah A. 2004. *Modern Blackness: Nationalism, Globalization, and the Politics of Culture in Jamaica*. Durham, NC: Duke University Press.

———. 2006. "New Savage Slots, Response to Viranjini Munasinghe's 'Theorizing World Culture Through the New World: East Indians and Creolization.'" *American Ethnologist* 33 (4): 573–75.

Todorov, Tzvetan. 1999. *Conquest of the Americas: The Question of the Other*. Foreword by Anthony Pagden. Norman: University of Oklahoma Press.

———. 2001. *Frail Happiness: An Essay on Rousseau*. Translated by John T. Scott and Robert D. Zaretsky. University Park: Pennsylvania State University Press.

Tronto, Joan. 2004. "Frantz Fanon." *Contemporary Political Theory* 3: 245–52.

Trouillot, Michel-Rolph. 1992. "The Caribbean Region: An Open Frontier in Anthropological Theory." *Annual Review of Anthropology* 21: 19–42.

———. 1997. *Silencing the Past: Power and the Production of History*. Boston: Beacon.

———. 2003. *Global Transformations: Anthropology and the Modern World*. New York: Palgrave.

Tully, James. 2008a. *Public Philosophy in a New Key, Volume 1: Democracy and Civic Freedom*. Cambridge: Cambridge University Press.

———. 2008b. *Public Philosophy in a New Key, Volume 2: Imperialism and Civic Freedom*. Cambridge: Cambridge University Press.

Turner, Victor. 1969. *The Ritual Process: Structure and Anti-Structure*. Hawthorne, NY: Aldine de Gruyter.

Virgil. 1997. *Aeneid*. Translated by John Dryden and edited by Frederick M. Keener. London: Penguin Books.

Viroli, Maurizio. 1988. *Jean-Jacques Rousseau and the "Well-Ordered Society."* New York: Cambridge University Press.

Weber, Max. 1994. "The Nation-State and Economic Policy." In *Political Writings*, edited by Peter Lassman and translated by Ronald Speirs, 1–28. Cambridge: Cambridge University Press.

Wedeen, Lisa. 2002. "Conceptualizing Culture: Possibilities for Political Science." *American Political Science Review* 96 (4): 713–28.

———. 2004. "Concepts and Commitments in the Study of Democracy." In *Problems and Methods in the Study of Politics*, edited by Ian Shapiro, Rogers M. Smith, and Tarek E. Masoud, 274–306. Cambridge: Cambridge University Press.

Weil, Simone. 1985. "Morality and Literature." In *The Simone Weil Reader*, edited by George Panichas, 290–95. Kingston, RI: Moyer Bell.

Whelan, Frederick G. 2009. *Enlightenment Political Thought and Non-Western Societies: Sultans and Savages*. New York: Routledge.
Winford, Donald. 1994. "Sociological Approaches to Language Use in the Anglophone Caribbean." In *Language and the Social Construction of Identity in Creole Situations*, edited by Marcyliena Morgan, 43–62. Los Angeles: Center for Afro-American Studies Publications.
Wiredu, Kwasi. 1996. *Cultural Universals and Particulars: An African Perspective*. Bloomington: University of Indiana Press.
Wokler, Robert. 1995. "Rousseau and his critics on the fanciful liberties we have lost." In *Rousseau and Liberty*, edited by Robert Wokler, 189–212. Manchester: University of Manchester Press.
———. 2001. *Rousseau: A Very Short Introduction*. Oxford: Oxford University Press.
Wolin, Sheldon. 1960. *Politics and Vision: Continuity and Vision in Western Political Thought*. Boston: Little & Brown.
Yack, Bernard. 2001. "Popular Sovereignty and Nationalism." *Political Theory* 29 (4): 517–36.
Young, Iris M. 1994. "Gender as Seriality: Thinking about Women as a Social Collective." *Signs* 19 (3): 713–38.

Index

abnormal, 86, 173, 258
aboriginal(s), 136, 183
Achille, Louis-T., 241n
Adamany, David, 264n
Africa, 52, 129, 168, 169, 193, 214, 234, 249, 253
African(s), 22, 49, 152, 153, 154, 158, 170, 177, 182, 225, 229, 260, 263; civilization, 211; diaspora, 142, 210; framed as lacking culture, 182; languages, 258, 260; sounding French, 179; struggling for freedom, 215; unity, 153
African American(s), 42, 219, 262n
Africana philosophy, 12, 243
Agamben, Giorgio, 256
agency, 65, 73–75, 84, 89, 93, 131, 138, 149, 158, 161, 174, 207, 220, 255; cultural, 57
Alexander, Amanda, 213
Algeria, 19, 20, 21, 25, 70, 75, 85–87, 127, 131, 142, 244n, 255n; men in, 87; occupied, 186; prized French colony, 247; war in, 129–38, 150, 158, 160–61, 162, 227, 248n; women in, 143–46, 233n
Algerian School of Psychiatry, 86
Alleyne, Mervyn C., 182, 258n, 263n
American Political Science Association, xiii, 254n
animals, 45–46, 48, 60, 74, 96, 101, 236n, 249n; anthropomorphizing of, 57; "savages" and, 236n
Anzaldúa, Gloria, 5, 166
Aravamudan, Srinivas, 228n
Arendt, Hannah, 31, 194, 231n, 262n
Aristotle, 40, 96, 102, 114, 203, 207, 211, 237n; on gods and beasts, 249n
Asante, Molefi, 163
Asia, 192, 208, 209, 263; slave trade in, 169, 214; Southeast, 60
Asian(s), 49
Asian-Americans, 182
audience(s), 135, 194, 218

Aurenche, Louis, 61
Austin, J. L., 253n, 254n
Austin, John, 251
Australia, 208, 263n
authority, 12–14, 29, 36, 37, 39, 78, 107, 120, 133, 148, 185, 192, 229n; charismatic, 141; -complex, 77; hereditary conceptions of, 97–98; of the law, 122; of leaders, 130

bad faith, 253n
Baker, Houston, 265n
Ball, Terence, 194
Barry, Brian, 251n, 252n
Barvosa, Edwina, xiii
Belton, Don, vii, xiv
Beltrán, Cristina, 264n
Benhabib, Seyla, 165, 166, 214
Bernabé, Jean, 177, 179
Bewaji, J. A. I., 223, 264n
Bhabha, Homi K., 5, 166
Bickerton, Derek, 258n
Biko, Steve, 213
black(s), 18, 22, 69–74, 80, 158, 162, 176–77, 182–84, 213, 225n, 227n–228n, 244n, 257n; bodies, 73; child(ren), 86, 242n; colonized subjectivity of, 67; enslaved, 23, 152; existentialists, xiv; girls, 252n; insularity of, 68; intellectuals, xiv; men, 241n, 242n, 244n, 255n; nationalists, 186, 255n; New World, 76; person, 66, 248n; poets, 57; problem, 58, 77; racism against, 67, 69, 233n; radical thought, 14, 16; *the*, 21, 80; women, 83, 214; writers, 241n, 245n
black civilization, 243n
black consciousness, 66, 186, 213
blackness, 64–72; Caribbean, 216–17
black studies, 212
Bloom, Allan, 123
Blyden, Edward Wilmot, 258n

287

Bolland, O. Nigel, 76, 181, 184
Bonaparte, Napoleon, 58
Bondy, François, 247n, 249n
Boxill, Bernard R., 222n, 255n
Boulle, Pierre H., 23
bourgeoisie, 20, 119, 152, 154, 243n; colonized, 142; national, 132, 151–55, 183; pseudo-, 136, 146; triumph in the French Revolution, 235n
Bowden, Brett, 208
Braidwood, Stephen J., 23
Brathwaite, Edward Kamau, 257n
Brazil, 20, 228n, 229n
Browers, Michaelle, xiii, 175, 205, 207
Buck-Morss, Susan, 8, 170, 182, 190, 210, 211, 222n; on universal history, 212–16
Buffon, Comte de, 236n
Bulhan, Hussein Abdilahi, 84–86, 89, 93, 246n, 257n, 248n
Burke, Edmund, 58

Canada, 22
Canovan, Margaret, 125
capitalism, 151, 158; global, 189; mercantile, 188
Caribbean, 2, 10–12, 19, 21–22, 42, 50, 60, 162, 163, 175–76, 186–87, 192, 210, 214, 216, 229, 257n, 262n; as birthplace of modernity, 179–82; fifteenth-century, 193; music in, 174, 192, 207; plantation societies of, 182; Renaissance men and women of, 195; slavery in, 213, 228n, 239n, 258n; students, 260
Caribbean Philosophical Association (CPA), xii, 264n
Caribbean studies, 212
Carson, Anne, 222n
Cassirer, Ernst, 48–49, 61, 145, 166
Caws, Peter, 74
Chamoiseau, Patrick, 177, 179
chaos, 200, 203; disciplinary, 218
Charvet, John, 122–23, 252n
Chaudenson, Robert, 169, 170, 171, 172, 177, 256n, 260n
Cherki, Alice, 64, 225n, 245n, 246n
children, 41, 118, 234n, 235n, 247n; arts for, 242n, 258n; black, 67, 69, 72; breast-feeding of, 240; feral, 21; political, 131; treating the masses as, 148; rich man's, 236; Rousseau's relationship with his, 240; underdeveloped, 96; upbringing of, 255n
China, 149, 225n, 234n, 239a, 261n
choice, 53, 68–69 76, 81, 217, 240n; and freedom, 84, 120
Christian missionaries, 50, 57, 67
Christianity, 162, 233n; principles of, 53
Christianized teleology, 25
citizenship, 213; 225n
civilization(s), 8, 23–24, 36, 42, 67, 72, 90, 92, 110–11, 170, 177, 214–15, 236n, 243n; African, 211; "clash of," 209; Egyptian, 223n; Enlightenment and, 55; European, 245n; French, 227n–228n; Islamic, 208; "negro," 244n
Cladis, Mark, 101, 125
Cohen, Robin, 189
Cold War, 123; post-, 208
colonialism, 4, 9, 16, 76–77, 80, 89, 93, 118, 129, 130, 156, 209, 212; coloniality, 78; ending of, 147, 153; epistemic, histories of, 212, 214; legacies of, 158, 216; Négritude writers on, 187; options imposed by, 143; settler, 11; supposed nonexistence of, 138; violence of, 244n
colonies, 21–23, 66–67, 77–78, 85, 92, 137, 168, 177, 192, 210, 227, 242n, 246n, 257n
Comaroff, Jean, xv
Comaroff, John, xiii, xv
communication, 53, 103, 106, 214, 252n, 260n, 262n; cultural, 60, 258n; political, 56; process of, 173
Communist Party (French), 245n
comparative political theory, 2, 5, 17, 175, 203, 205, 207–14, 264n. *See also* political theory
Confiant, Raphaël, 179, 262n
consciousness, 21, 214, 233, 263n; Black, 213; double, 207; of Europeans, 93; national, 17, 126–61, 183–84, 256n; third-person, 66
conservatism, 16, 179; neo-, 165
Constant, Benjamin, 123, 255n
constitution(s), Dessalines', 213; French, 213; Haitian, 213; Jacobin, 213; South African, 168
constitutionalism, 167
consumption, 34
Cooper, Laurence, 253n
Cornell, Drucilla, xv, 168, 198, 257n
Corsica, 117–20, 133, 150, 230n
courage, xiv, 41, 66, 131, 230n, 233n, 246n
Cranston, Maurice, 26, 28, 38, 43, 58, 231n, 233n, 239n, 240n
creature(s), 24, 45, 57, 60, 73, 78, 85; symbolic, 93, 164
Creole(s), 2, 6, 60, 172, 182, 185, 214, 240n, 263n; color inflection of, 182; elite, 16, 183; first written use of, 169, 259n; Haitian, 10, 174–75, 178, 210, 259n; languages, 60, 171–77, 190, 258n–263n; linguistics, 7, 172, 178–79, 190, 195, 258n–263n; national identities of, 181; newly indigenous, 182; origins of, 2, 160, 169–72, 260n; passing for, 242n; postmodern, 263n; slaves, 172, 241n; writers, 262n
créolité, 179, 261n, 262n. *See also* Glissant, Édouard
creolization, *passim, but see especially* xii–xiii, xv, 1–17, 22, 76, 157, 162, 163–201, 213, 219, 222n, 256n, 261n; as accurate portrait of human life, 164–69, 177, 181, 185, 261n–262n; of canonical figures, 1–2, 9; creolizing, 188–200; de-, 7, 12, 186, 220, 222n; of disciplines, 6, 11–16, 217, 264n; distinguished from, 6–7, 170, 175; in literary criticism, 6, 12; as methodology, 4, 7, 16, 55, 199, 217;

Index   289

process of, 7, 9, 179, 181–83, 199–201; as a project, 5, 119; in universalizing thought, 163
Crichlow, Michaeline A., 189
crime(s), 40, 87, 88, 142, 222n, 228n, 233n, 256n
criminal(s), 38, 158, 246n
criticism, 6, 17, 81
Crocker, Lester, 102, 121, 123
crowd(s), 154
Cuba, 20
culture(s), 143, 145, 155, 156, 164–79, 182, 183, 191, 192, 211, 214–17, 225n, 228n, 237n–243n, 245n, 265n; as agent, 166; colonizing, 187, 189; decadent, 160; eradicating, 159; hegemonic, 175; living, 161; minority, 156, 168; national, 184; nature of, 164–65; permeability of, 166; pluralistic, 181; as property, 165; "purifying," 186, 189, 205; shared, 157, 181, 215; as symbolic world, 196, 199–200; translation of, 207
Curry, Tommy, 223n, 252n

Dagger, Richard, 107, 253n
Dahl, Robert, 194, 220
Dallmayr, Fred, 204, 206–10, 265n
Damrosch, Leo, 20, 26, 28, 225n, 230n, 231n, 232n, 239n
Darnton, Robert, 224n
Dayan-Herzbrun, Sonia, 224n
DeCamp, David, 263n
decadence, xii, 9, 17, 34, 36, 42; of eighteenth-century France, 78, 262n
DeGraff, Michel, 177, 178, 258n, 259n, 260n
de las Casas, Bartolomé, 50
de Maistre, Joseph, 123, 255n
democracy, *passim, but see especially* 109, 114, 119, 249n–250n; debate on founding of, 141; liberal, 165; participatory, 147
Diaz, Vincente, 182
Diderot, Denis, 26, 28, 36, 51, 57, 230n, 232n, 233n, 250n; *Encyclopedia* of, 60
Dillard, J. L., 253n
discipline(s), academic, 3, 6, 11–12, 15, 81, 169, 189, 190, 191, 194–95, 197, 265n; of the body, 144; creolizing, 220; disciplining, 199; un-, 163
Djemaï, Cheikh, 20, 225n, 246n
Dobie, Madeleine, 22, 23, 49, 227n–229n, 237n, 239n
Douglass, Frederick, 237
Du Bois, W. E. B., 16, 42, 76, 191, 219, 233n
Du Bois, Laurent, 240n
Duchet, Michèle, 43
Durkheim, Emile, 45
Dussel, Enrique, 137–38, 154–55, 157, 216
Dworkin, Ronald, 252n

economy: Algerian, 150; colonial, 78; France's, 22; local, 132, 152; political, 4, 47, 96, 120, 190, 191, 249n

education, xi, xii, 29, 34, 231n, 230n, 233n, 262n, 263n; enslaving, 83; political, 146, 148 230n; religious, 22; systems in the Caribbean, 260
Ehlen, Patrick, 65, 80, 227n, 240n, 241n, 243n
Einstein, Albert, 242n
Engels, Friedrich, 223n, 236n
equality, 18, 50, 97, 109, 133, 141, 238n, 245n, 248n, 256n; economic, 108, 124, 240n; legitimate, 110; natural, 110; political, 102; racial, 214n; radical, 184
Eriksen, Thomas Hylland, 170, 189, 257n, 263n
ethics, 9
ethnicity, 85
ethnic studies, 5, 208
Euben, Roxanne L., 14, 51, 204–5, 237n
Eurocentrism, 56
Europe, 12–14, 18, 28, 29, 30, 41, 50, 57, 61, 67, 68, 78, 110, 117, 152, 158, 169, 172, 176, 193, 228n, 242n, 244n, 247n, 248n, 249n; authority of, 192; intermediaries of, 132; mimicking, 129, 149, 246n, 248n; provincialization of, 88; sciences of, 239; Southern, 137; violence of, 252n; western, 5, 39, 168, 203, 205, 208, 209
European(s), *passim, but see especially* 12, 14, 18, 23, 50, 54, 67–68, 85–94, 116, 229n, 25n; becoming, 42; central, 167; class concerns of, 219; confrontations with others, 21–22, 52, 120, 135–41, 169, 209, 227n, 237b; Eastern, 167, 261n; globality of, 38; greed of, 52; imperial, 21, 23, 28, 42, 77–78, 235n, 247n; languages, 171, 173, 260n, 262n–263n; linguistics, 170, 359n, 260n; man, 40, 223n; metropole, 242n; mimicking of, 52, 130, 135, 170, 249n; modernity, 59, 72, 129, 162, 177, 191, 211, 227n–228n; myth, 30; political thinkers, 21, 40–41; self-anointed world judges, 51; Southern, 247n; travelogues of, 49; violence of, 158
evolution, 58, 65, 177; de-, 110
extinction, 39

Fabian, Johannes, 238n
Falaky, Fayçal, 229n
Fanon, Frantz, *passim, but see especially* 1–10, 18, 23, 222n–233n, 240n; on Algeria and Algerians, 85–86, 249n; on antiblackness, 57, 69–75, 83–86, 241n, 243n; at Blida-Joinville Psychiatric Hospital, 86–87; canonization of, 20; challenge to white supremacy, 71; on colonial illness, 57; on colonial logic, 75–76, 84, 90; on colonialism versus domination, 77; creolizing and transcending Rousseau, 16–17, 61, 63, 65, 92–94, 120–28; on culture, 86; life of, 19–21, 64; dehumanization, 65; on epistemic colonization, 35, 78, 84; on freedom and unfreedom, 87, 89, 91, 133, 134, 136, 155, 160; on health, 84, 87; humanism

Fanon, Frantz (*continued*)
and the human sciences, 74–79, 87; humanistic psychiatry of, 87; on intellectual work, 78; on interracial intimacy, 80, 83, 242n; on Jean Veneuse/René Maran, 68, 242n; on language, 187; on liberation as first philosophy, 81; on liberatory education, 83; on meaning, 73; on method, 24–25, 63–76, 79–84, 95, 197; on mimicking colonizers, 117; on the national bourgeoisie, 132, 136, 142, 146, 151–55, 183; on national consciousness, 127–61, 183–84, 255n; on *le nègre*, 67, 71; on Négritude, 71–72, 78, 241n; on normality and normalization, 86; on normalization of colonial relations, 63, 66, 73–77, 86; on oppression, 76, 88, 143; on paradoxes of human existence, 24; on petrification, 70–73; on political legitimacy, 10, 127, 134, 136; on racial psychiatry and psychology, 80–81, 84, 89–90, 248n; on racism, 57–86; on radical democratic participation, 131; on "reason," 72; on "speaking well," 70; on slavery, 91; on sociogeny, 245n; on traditionalism, 76, 131–32, 143, 168, 184; on values, 69, 90–91; writings of, 1, 64, 80, 82, 219
Fanon-Mendes-France, Mireille, 224n
Feld, Scott L., 252n
Ferdinand II of Aragon (King), 13
Filmer, Sir Robert, 249n
Firmin, Anténor, 16
Fischer, Sibylle, 8, 176, 211–14
Fleischmann, Ulrich, 180–81
Foucault, Michel, 24, 210
Frank, Jason, 134
freedom, 13, 18, 20, 23, 46, 49, 53, 57, 61, 75, 79, 81, 84, 87, 91, 98, 106, 107, 109, 118, 119–21, 123–26, 129, 135, 137, 138, 142–44, 147, 151, 159, 160, 178, 212, 215, 225n, 255n, 256n; compromising of, 143, 160; to conform, 121; from constraint, 102, 106, 138; individualist, 123; meaningful, 102, 125, 131, 148, 161; moral, 49, 53, 57, 92; political, 61; seizing, 142, 131, 202; unfreedom, 63, 89, 91, 133–34, 136, 155, 160, 183
Freire, Paulo, 146
Freud, Sigmund, 78, 192, 196, 236n, 247n

Gal, Susan, 173
Gandhi, Mohandas, 206, 208
Garel, Yvonne Patricia Solomon, vii, xiii
Garrard, Graeme, 251n
Gates, Henry Louis, Jr., 81
Gay, Peter, 27, 82, 231n
Gebhardt, Jürgen, 209
Geismar, Peter, 248n
general will, the, *passim, but see especially* 1, 3, 17, 61, 90, 95–128, 184, 199, 249n–253n, 255n. *See also* Fanon, Frantz: on national consciousness; Rousseau, Jean-Jacques

genocide, 169, 213n
Germain, Felix, 227n
Getachew, Adom, 264n
Geuss, Raymond, 217n
Gibson, Nigel, 80, 213
Gilroy, Paul, 170
Glissant, Édouard, 179–81
G-d, as self-evident, 26; conceptual capacity of, 264n; fixity of species by, 60; inner voice of, 147; refutation of, 36; monotheistic conception of, 262n; as source of justice, 112, 122; will of, 95
Godrej, Farah, xiii, 205, 206, 265n
Gordon, Elijah, xv
Gordon, Jane Anna, 223n, 262n, 263n
Gordon, Jennifer, xv
Gordon, Lewis R., xii, 74–75, 142, 199, 241n, 243; on experience without experience, 243n; on market colonization of intellectuals, 263n; on questioning, 84; on situationality of flesh and blood, 75; teleological suspension of disciplinarity, 89, 200; theory of perverse anonymity, 65
Gordon, Mathieu, xv
Gordon, Sula, xv
Gould, Stephen Jay, 86
government, 31, 34, 112, 114, 119, 131–33, 136, 150, 151, 153, 177, 250n, 256n; consensual, 120; as distinguished from sovereignty, 124; and governing, 56, 148–49; illegitimate, 100, 118, 121; indirect, 154; legitimate basis of, 95, 102–3, 115, 249n
Gramsci, Antonio, 136, 207
greed, 47, 69, 236n
Greek(s) (ancient), 204, 205, 249n, 262n
Grofman, Bernard, 252n
Guadeloupe, 22, 227n
Gyekye, Kwame, 156–57

Haiti, 22, 211–15, 222n, 228n; Creole, 10, 174–78, 259n
Haitian Revolution, the, 13, 182, 211–15, 264n; enslaved who fought in, 176
Hall, Stuart, 170
Hampsher-Monk, Iain, 123, 255n
Hannerz, Ulf, 188, 263n
Harris, Wilson, 179, 262n
Hart, H. L. A., 252n
Hegel, G. W. F., 13, 222n, 236n; on Africa, 211; Fanon on, 78, 192; on Haiti, 13, 212; on history, 212, 216; on Rousseau, 58, 123, 160, 255n; on slavery, 212–13
hegemony, 8, 137, 150, 158–59, 183; analogical, 157
Helenon, Veronique, 229n
Henry, Paget, 8, 223n; on creolizing Caribbean philosophy, 12, 192; on complex, synthetic methodology, 81; on the knowing subject, 14; on the general will, 255

Hintzen, Percy, 182
Hirschmann, Nancy, xi, 111
Hobbes, Thomas, 36–37, 44, 101, 110, 119, 208, 228n, 234n
humanism, 142. *See also* Fanon, Frantz
Honig, Bonnie, xiii, 122, 134, 141
Huntington, Samuel, 208, 211

Ibsen, Henrik, 253n
illegitimacy, 122, 133, 138, 158, 252n; challenging, 139–51; degrees of, 116; political, 90, 99, 135, 162
immigrants, 227n
India(n), 8, 20, 162, 182, 186, 208, 209, 261n, 262n, 263n
indigenous people(s), 10, 50, 169, 183, 186, 229n; becoming indigenous, 3, 167, 170; creating what will be indigenous, 10, 132, 182, 186, 256n; an indigenous general will, 133, 146; indigenous needs, 89; indigenous nurses, 87; indigenous resources, 117, 149; indigenous systems of reference, 75, 89, 143, 167, 174
injustice, 32, 55, 240n
interdisciplinarity, 5–7, 189, 191, 193
Iran, 8, 20, 207
Iraq, 167
Irvine, Judith T., 173
Isaac, Jeffrey C., 217
Isabella I (Queen), 13

Jamaica, 174–75, 181–82, 184, 228n, 262n; Creole in, 259n, 262n; enslaved population of, 258n
James, C. L. R., xii, 16, 234n, 256n
Jameson, Frederic, 59
Jaspers, Karl, 197, 264n
Jenco, Leigh Kathryn, 192, 206n–207n, 265n
Jews, 13, 245n, 261n
Johnson, Walter, 174
Johnston, Steven, 123, 254n
Jung, Hwa Yol, 205, 206
justice, 47, 88, 96, 98, 104–5, 109, 112, 253n, 256n

Kant, Immanuel, 57, 97, 160
Keenan, Alan, 122
Kein, Sybil, 61
Kelly, Christopher, 117
Kennedy, Ellen, xi, 254n
Khan, Aisha, 182, 188
knowledge, 4, 6, 24, 38, 43, 53, 57, 61, 89, 111, 125, 197–98, 213, 215, 225n, 230n, 264n; colonization of, 192; deceitful, 41; episteme, 92; epistemic conditions of social life, 84, 91; necessarily symbolic, 145; new, 44, 204; origins of, 32; self-, 44, 51; specialized, 195, 231n; transgressive insight, 166
Kobayashi, Takuya, 224n
Kompridis, Nikolas, 166–67, 169
Knies, Kenneth Danziger, 232n
Kymlicka, Will, 165, 214

Lacan, Jacques, 78
Larson, Gerald James, 192, 205
Latin America(n), 162, 209–11
Latin American studies, 208
Lau, Wai-keung, 225n
law(s), 34, 47, 95–96, 101–7, 112, 230n, 237n, 244n, 249n, 252n, 256n; affecting all, 109; amending, 103; applying, 114; authority of, 122, 150; backed by force and wealth, 150; bad, 115–16, 122, 142; colonial, 244; dietary, 261n; divine, 113; effects of historical decisions and political power on, 252n; equality before, 141; equitable, 109–10; first or foundational, 113; formal, 104; generation of, 113–14, 134; good, 141; of justice, 112; legislating, 112–13, 115, 137; -like rules, 24, 74, 166; obedience to, 102, 231n; positive, 252n; purpose of, 134; for transformation from beasts, 101; wise, 47, 141. *See also* illegitimacy; legitimacy
legitimacy, 14, 98, 107, 138, 155, 252n, 254n; of contract, 125–255n; democratic, 1, 114, 117, 155; force's relation to, 156; foreignness marking gaps in, 122; of inequality, 56; norms of, 133; political, 2, 8, 10, 18, 90, 97–99, 108, 127, 127, 134–36, 160, 162; postcolonial, 127; realization of, 109; source(s) of, 102, 107, 126; varied degrees of, 116
Lévi-Strauss, Claude, 58, 81, 237n
liberalism, 207; classical, 207; neo-, 165, 184; paranoid brand of, 123; political, 5, 191, 215. *See also* Rawls, John
liminal, the, 21, 63, 71, 176, 216–17
Lionnet, Françoise, 226n–227n
Locke, John, 44, 101, 167, 208, 228n, 255n
Lucas, Phillipe, 85
lumpenproletariat, 130, 141, 142
Luxemburg, Rosa, 90
Lyceé Schoelcher, 64
Lynch, John, 16

Macey, David, 20, 64, 65, 81, 82, 85, 243n, 245n
Machiavelli, Niccolò, 13, 137, 204, 220, 233n
Maldonado Torres, Nelson, xii, 56, 78, 81
manicheanism, 132, 141
Mannoni, Octavio, 77–78, 246n
Manoochehri, Abbas, 209
Maran, René, 68
March, Andrew, 205–6, 209, 265n
Marx, Karl, 74, 90, 123, 174, 208, 222n, 223n, 236n, 255n; Marxist, 59, 74, 116, 174, 236n
Masoud, Tarek E., 217
McBride, Keally, 250n
McBride, William, 250n
McCormick, John, 109, 252n
McWhorter, John, 258n
Mehta, Brinda, xii, 186
Meijer, Guus, 170, 177
Merleau-Ponty, Maurice, 81, 205

Middle Ages, the, 137, 208
Mignolo, Walter, 212
Mills, Charles, xii, 15, 210
Mintz, Sidney W., 170
Misir, Prem, 181–82
Mngxitama, Andile, 213
modernism, 157, 161, 163
modernity, 14–16, 18, 38, 59, 65, 79, 96, 111, 125, 133, 160, 197, 212–20, 225n, 250n; and colonialism, 137, 181, 210; contradictions of, 163; early, 14, 39, 227n; European, 14, 21, 23, 55, 72, 92, 120, 127, 160, 162, 177, 191, 205, 211–12, 227n, 236n; global, 11, 179; multiple, 215; post-, 163, 178, 180, 199, 263n; pre-, 178; racial, 219; in social science, 58; thinkers of, 186; and traditionalism, 239; underside of, 216
Mohammed, Patricia, 186
Monahan, Michael J., xii, 169
Montaigne, Michel D., 31–32, 57
Moody-Adams, Michele M., 185, 215
morality, 81, 231n
morals, 26, 40, 51, 152, 232n, 235n
Morello, Celeste A., 223n
Moses (Moshe, biblical), 113, 142
Mufwene, Salikoko S., 12, 171–73, 177, 190, 222n, 259n, 260n
mulatto(es), 171–72, 242n, 257n
Munasinghe, Viranjini, 163
music, 10, 12, 19, 167, 172, 174, 175, 192, 232n, 235n, 240n, 253n, 261n; copyist, 20, 60; ethnomusicology, 55, 60, 166; as offering key metaphors for politics, 114
Muslim(s), 13, 88, 208, 210, 223n
Muthu, Sankar, 57, 227n, 228n, 238n
Muysken, Pieter, 170, 177
myth(s), 30, 38, 81, 130, 205, 224n, 246n; mythic, 133; mythologized, 20

Näsström, Sofia, 134
nationalism, 85, 127, 131, 146, 181, 249n; crude nationalism, 132, 152–56, 183; transnationalism, 214
nature, 21, 29, 32, 34, 35, 37, 42, 43, 46, 48, 58, 60, 91, 98, 110, 111, 113, 123, 139, 149, 160, 164, 171, 236n, 237n, 254n; state of, 44, 45, 52, 53, 59, 100, 101, 110, 111, 159, 227n, 241n, 250n, 256n
négritude, 71–72, 78, 80, 81, 93, 187, 241n, 243n–244n
Neidleman, Jason Andrew, xiii, 117
neoconservatism, 165
Nettl, Bruno, 60
Nietzschean, 146
The "nigger(s)," 67, 83, 225n, 241n; bad nigger, 246n; niggerhood, 68
nihilism, 254n
Nissim-Sabat, Marilyn, xii, 67
Noël, Erick, 23

Noone, John B., Jr., 97, 251n, 254n
North Africa, 19, 20, 21, 85, 163, 171, 172
North African(s), 66, 89, 187, 210, 223, 227
Norton, Anne, xi, 196, 198, 216, 218, 237n, 265n
Nouss, Alexis, 180

Obama, President Barack, 263n
Ogrodnick, Margaret, 115
ontogeny, 245n
ontology, 254n
Ortega y Gasset, José, 110–11
Orwell, George, 56
Ovid, 37–38, 234n

Pagden, Anthony, 52–54, 57
Palestine, 20
Palmié, Stephan, 163, 257n
Parekh, Bhiku, 166
Parkvall, Mikael, 260
Patois, 174, 262n, 263n
Peabody, Sue, 229n
Pépin, Ernest, 262n
Piven, Frances Fox, 218
Plato, 31, 204, 208, 232n, 246n, 251n
political science, xi, 11,194, 218; decreolization in, 220; distanced from the world of politics, 194, 264n; as a field of application, 15; as historically creolized, 194; as a human science, 220; methods in, 17; quantitative work in, 194; subfields of, 12
political theory, *passim, but see especially* xi–xii, 1–7, 13–17, 127, 133, 160, 163–64, 175, 188, 191, 196–200, 203–20; Africana, 67, 210, 241n, 243n; comparative, 2, 5, 7–8, 17, 48, 57–58, 65, 92, 175, 203–14, 216–17, 265n; canon of, 1, 13, 17, 20, 26, 82, 228n, 262n, 264n; creolizing, 1, 4, 7, 13–15, 164, 188, 197, 200; decolonial, 79, 131, 138, 147; feminist, 166; postmodern, 178. *See also* conservatism; liberalism
politics, *passim, but see especially* 15, 31, 95, 140, 141, 196; assimilationist, 65; beyond force, 96–98; colonial, 89; and the common self, 249n; creating equality through, 109; diffuse nature of, 105; of "diversality" or "pluriversality," 215n; domain of, 126, 136, 212; engaging dissensus and cultural difference, 128; in film, 223n; future for, 150; and generality, 115, 155, 157; and inclusion, 188; maxims of, 113; of multiculturalism, 165, 189; "paradox" of, 122, 133; and the *polis*, 111, 249n; public terrain of, 187; of racial purity, 178; reason to write about, 98; of recognition, 165; scholarly work on, 218n; scope of, 121; study of, 24, 196, 265n; of survival, 222n; tasks of, 115; and truth, 80. *See also* illegitimacy; legitimacy; political science
poststructuralism, 166, 188
poverty, 47, 117, 143, 154, 262n

power, 99, 100, 117, 120; abuse of, xii, 240n; administrative, 113; balance of, 166; of the bourgeoisie, 154; capitalist rise in, 158; of communities, 155; of despots, 123; empty privileges of, 240n; executive, 107; fetishizing of, 154; human, 44; imperial, 154, 158; indexes of power, 193; institutions of, 2; of kings, 121; legislative, 102–3, 114, 147; legitimate, 124; meaning of, 159; of molding ideas, 200, 203; monstrous mirroring of, 193; physical, 135; political, 13–14, 37, 29, 251n; revolutionary, xiv; seizing of, 155; of settler communities, 247n; social, 173; sovereign, 105, 107, 114, 121, 249n; struggles over, 185–86; supreme, 47, 250; symbolic, 158, 175–76, 183; total, 125; weakening of, 154; will to, 146

Prasad, Vijay, 183–85
Pratt, Mary Louise, 175
Présence Africaine, 245n
proletariat, the, 184
property, 40, 123; private, 34, 46, 49–50, 57, 74, 92, 165
psychoanalysis, 219, 245n
Puri, Shalini, 182
purpose, 4, 35, 73, 98, 116,165, 175, 183, 185, 192, 206, 262; across generations, 113; common purpose, 113; of disciplinary approaches, 190; failing to fulfill one's, 32, 155; of the general will, 100, 111; imposed from without, 58; of the legitimate leader, 153; of social structures, 87, 100

race(s), xi, 16, 70, 72, 74, 84, 85, 165, 177–78, 219, 226n, 246n, 262n; culture of, 229; Interracial Conference of 1949, 241n; intimacy between, 80, 242n–243n; mixed and mixing, 2, 80, 162, 169, 172, 177, 182, 187; romantic approaches to, 261n; saving the, 242n, 243n. *See also* blacks; Du Bois, W. E. B.; Fanon, Frantz; genocide; indigenous; whites
racism, xi, 67, 73, 75, 86, 129, 153, 245n. *See also* Fanon, Frantz
Rawls, John, 9, 97, 160, 167, 206, 233n
Rehfeld, Andrew, 15
Reinhardt, Catherine A., 227n, 229n
Reisman, Karl, 262n–263n
religion, 13, 33, 38, 53, 113,172, 234n; civil, 112, 121; as distinguished from theology, 259; indispensability of, 224n; priests of paganism on, 27; Voodoo, 211. *See also* Christianity
Renault, Matthieu, 88
reparations, 158
revenge, 137, 246n
revolution(s), 30, 41, 137, 139, 142–49, 151, 161, 168; age of, 211; Algerian, 21, 130, 143–46; 247n; of the enslaved, 213; French, 58, 212, 224n, 236n, 240n; Haitian, 13, 176, 213–15; 264n; Russian, 248; Spanish, 248; U.S./American, 216n
revolutionary: action, 214, 243n; humanism, 19; males in Algeria, 143; party, 148; politics, 130; power of committed love, xiv; slaves, 151, 211, 213; struggle, 130–32, 149, 161; the, 65; women in Algeria, 143–46, 233n
Riley, Patrick, 95–96, 255n
Robinson, Cedric J., 208, 223n
Roden, Claudia, 261n
Romaine, Suzanne, 258–59, 263n
Romberg, Raquel, 175, 183–85, 213
Rome, 30, 31, 108, 148, 204, 223n
Rosenblatt, Helena, 95, 250n
Rousseau, Jean-Jacques, *passim, but see especially* 1, 9, 10, 18, 61; accused collectivism and totalitarianism of, 108, 121–23; as analyzed by Ernst Cassirer, 48–49; as caricatured by Voltaire, 239n; on conquest, 41, 54, 135, 233n; as contributing to the overturning of the fixity of species thesis, 60; as a contributor to the field of ethnomusicology, 60; on Corsica, 117–20; on the education of women, 233n; on equality and inequality, 43, 46, 102, 108–10, 119, 121, 124, 238n, 256n; as exemplifying an "anti-European Eurocentrism," 56; on facts, 44; on the general will, 1–3, 17, 25, 56, 61, 90, 95–128, 132–33, 141, 142, 147, 150, 156, 159, 160, 199, 250n, 251n, 252n, 253n, 255n; Haitian Creole version of Rousseau's "Le Devin du Village," 240n; as legislator, 117; on the legislator, 98, 112–14, 122, 133; life of, 19–21, 26, 223n–225n, 230n, 234n; on military prowess, 33, 233n; on moral freedom, 49, 53, 57, 92; as a narrow individualist or social atomist, 123; pinning hopes on the periphery, 18, 54, 117; on the "right" of the strongest, 54, 90, 99, 100, 107, 110; on "savages," 28, 32, 39–40, 42, 52–54, 228n, 236n, 239n; on the social contract, 43, 95, 97, 149, 227n; on sovereignty, 97, 99, 102, 106, 107, 114, 249n; will in general, 97, 127. *See also* general will, the
rule, 96, 98, 99, 117, 135, 136, 141, 225n, 247n; disciplinary rules, 89; of ethnology, 89; by force, 47, 99; law-like, 74; "of recognition," 252; ruled, 97, 137, 146; rules, 88, 113, 124, 125, 167, 173, 179, 206, 219, 231n, 258n; rules of justice, 47; self-rule, 97, 114, 143; social rules, 5, 29–30, 46, 68, 79, 96, 140, 191, 196; when one cannot be treated as a, 75

Said, Edward, 242n
Sala-Molins, Louis, 223n, 229n
Sartre, Jean-Paul, 21, 67, 78, 81, 82, 93, 192, 222n, 226n, 246n, 250n
"savage slot," 14, 59, 86. *See also* Trouillot, Michel-Rolph
Schapiro, Leonard, 121

Schmitt, Carl, 164, 188, 254n, 257n
school(s), 5, 20, 31, 68–69, 156, 247n; the Algiers School, 85–86; neo-grammarian school of Leipzig, 171; "schooling," 28, 37
Schwartz, Gary, 252n
Schwartz, Joseph M., xii, 217
Scott, John T., 60, 253n
Segal, Daniel, 182
Sekyi-Otu, Ato, 71
Senghor, Léopold, 187
September 11, 2001 (9/11), 204, 252n
Seuren, Pieter A. M., 178
Shame, 40, 45, 55, 246n
Shapiro, Ian, 198, 217–18
Sheller, Mimi, 188
Shelley, Mary Wollstonecraft, 16, 200, 203, 265n
Shih, Shu-mei, 226n–227n
Shilliam, Robbie, 263n
Shklar, Judith N., 109, 254n
Shulman, George, 198
Sil, Rudra, 220
Skinner, Quentin, 15; Skinnerian approaches, 207
Skocpol, Theda, 194
slavery, 23, 46, 90–91, 99, 102, 158, 181, 213, 218, 228n, 229n, 239n; antislavery organizations, 176, 214, 216
Smith, Rogers, xi, xiii, 217
sociogeny, 245
sociology, 11, 55, 58, 191, 219
Song, Sarah, 165
Spain, 2, 260
South Africa(n), xiv, 20, 66, 168, 213
Starobinski, Jean, 20, 38, 57, 224n, 226n, 230n, 253n
Swenson, James, 56, 224n
symbol(s), 49, 145, 170, 183, 187, 244n; hollowed symbolism, 49, 76, 110, 154, 158; symbolic form(s), 7, 10, 49, 136, 145, 164, 169–70, 200, 261n, 263n; symbolic life worlds, 11, 14, 16, 48, 55, 61, 77, 86, 124, 143, 166, 169, 172–78, 184, 196, 198, 217, 219, 265n; symbolic power, 183–84, 189, 226n, 228n; symbolic rejection, 65, 92

Takaki, Ronald, 182
Talmon, J. L., 121–23
Taylor, Charles, 165–66, 169, 214
teacher(s), 28, 65, 68, 70, 72, 136, 226n, 244n, 261n
teleological suspensions, 89, 200
theodicy, 58, 70
theology, 259n
Thomas, Deborah A., 184
Tobin, Gary, vii, xiv
Todorov, Tzvetan, 50, 116, 250n–251n
Toninato, Paola, 189
torture, 244n; tortured, 56, 149; torturer, 67

Tosquelles, François, 87, 248n
transdisciplinarity, 6
Tronto, Joan, 217
Trouillot, Michel-Rolph, xiv, 14, 21, 22, 59, 86, 162, 163, 174, 175, 228n, 257n; on non-naïve optimism, 59
truth, 25, 27, 64, 88, 232n; access to, 230n; accounts of, 199; discrete, 215; embodiments of, 65, 226n; enacting, 215; entanglement(s) of, 80; at a glance, 41; historical, 44; Orwell on, 56; political, 80, 138; regimes of, 197; seeking, 35, 39, 151; speaking, 88; un-, 254n
Tully, James, 167–68, 217
Tunisia, 37
Turner, Victor, 176, 216

United States (USA), 5, 14, 20, 72, 101, 168, 176, 196, 228n, 248n, 255n

values, 7, 18, 24, 29, 56, 69, 76, 88, 196, 215, 231n, 244n, 254n, 256n; alternative, 35, 72; colonization as introducing, 90; as consistent across cultures, 215; as the core of "nations," 156; that curb extreme inequalities, 124; inverted, 138–39; objectivity of, 88; as reflected through work of culture, 196; in relation to aims of law, 231n
Vatin, Jean-Claude, 85
victim(s), 88, 89, 181, 182, 216; victimization, 87
Virgil, 109
Viroli, Maurizio, 109
Voltaire, 227n, 237n, 239n

war(s), 32, 47, 67, 196, 218; in Algeria, 129, 248n; citizens recalling themselves as a people in the midst of, 103; civil, 44, 250n; criminals, 158; as a lens for understanding the absence of a legitimate political domain, 110; relation of sophistication of warfare to moral virtue, 41; as shaping the character of theory, 227n; slavery/colonization as protracted state of, 90, 99; total, 143; World War II, 20, 123, 224
Weber, Max, 103, 113, 115, 264n
Wedeen, Lisa, 220, 237n
Weil, Simone, 238n
Whelan, Frederick G., 209, 227n, 228n
white(s), 22, 67, 176, 182, 225n, 257n
Winford, Donald, 262n–263n
Wiredu, Kwasi, 186, 215
Wokler, Robert, 26–27, 59, 236n, 237n, 240n, 250n, 255n
Wolin, Sheldon, 163

xenophobia, 132, 181

Yack, Bernard, 133
Young, Iris M., 15, 250n

just ideas

Roger Berkowitz, *The Gift of Science: Leibniz and the Modern Legal Tradition*

Jean-Luc Nancy, translated by Pascale-Anne Brault and Michael Naas, *The Truth of Democracy*

Drucilla Cornell and Kenneth Michael Panfilio, *Symbolic Forms for a New Humanity: Cultural and Racial Reconfigurations of Critical Theory*

Karl Shoemaker, *Sanctuary and Crime in the Middle Ages, 400–1500*

Michael J. Monahan, *The Creolizing Subject: Race, Reason, and the Politics of Purity*

Drucilla Cornell and Nyoko Muvangua (eds.), *uBuntu and the Law: African Ideals and Postapartheid Jurisprudence*

Drucilla Cornell, Stu Woolman, Sam Fuller, Jason Brickhill, Michael Bishop, and Diana Dunbar (eds.), *The Dignity Jurisprudence of the Constitutional Court of South Africa: Cases and Materials, Volumes I & II*

Nicholas Tampio, *Kantian Courage: Advancing the Enlightenment in Contemporary Political Theory*

Carrol Clarkson, *Drawing the Line: Toward an Aesthetics of Transitional Justice*

Jane Anna Gordon, *Creolizing Political Theory: Reading Rousseau Through Fanon*

www.ingramcontent.com/pod-product-compliance
Lightning Source LLC
Chambersburg PA
CBHW031234290426
44109CB00012B/296